D1498244

This study focusses on the way the Letter to the Hebrews explains the Christian doctrine of salvation by means of sacrificial symbols drawn from the Old Testament. Theories about the nature of sacrifice are taken from the work of social anthropologists to show the underlying meaning of these symbols and how they affect the meaning of this text

In relating New Testament studies to the methods of the social sciences, this book differs from most writings about Hebrews, which are either historical studies of the letter's background or theological studies of the author's ideas. Dr Dunnill assesses Hebrews, not as an argument, but as an act of symbolic communication; he thus aims to identify some of its underlying structures and reveal the source of its power.

SOCIETY FOR NEW TESTAMENT STUDIES

MONOGRAPH SERIES

General Editor: Margaret E. Thrall

75

COVENANT AND SACRIFICE IN
THE LETTER TO THE HEBREWS

Covenant and sacrifice in the Letter to the Hebrews

JOHN DUNNILL

Lecturer in New Testament Studies,
Anglican Institute of Theology, Perth,
Western Australia

CAMBRIDGE
UNIVERSITY PRESS

ATS Library
Nyack. NY 10960

Published by the Press Syndicate of the University of Cambridge
The Pitt Building, Trumpington Street, Cambridge CB2 1RP
40 West 20th Street, New York, NY 10011–4211, USA
10 Stamford Road, Oakleigh, Victoria 3166, Australia

© Cambridge University Press 1992

First published 1992

Printed in Great Britain at the University Press, Cambridge

A catalogue record for this book is available from the British Library

Library of Congress cataloguing in publication data
Dunnill, John.
Covenant and sacrifice in the Letter to the Hebrews / by John Dunnill.
    p.   cm. – (Monograph series / Society for New Testament
Studies: 75)
Revision of thesis (doctoral) – University of Birmingham, 1988.
Includes bibliographical references and index.
ISBN 0 521 43158 1
1. Bible. N.T. Hebrews – Criticism, interpretation, etc.
2. Covenants – Religious aspects. 3. Covenants (Jewish theology)
4. Sacrifice – Christianity. I. Title. II. Series: Monograph
series (Society for New Testament Studies): 75.
BS2775.6.C63D86   1993
227'.8706 – dc20   92–3180   CIP

ISBN 0 521 43158 1 hardback

WG

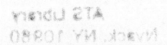

ATS Library
Nyack, NY 10960

CONTENTS

PREFACE

This book is a revised version of a doctoral thesis presented to the University of Birmingham in 1988. The research was conducted under the supervision of David Ford, and the final product owes a great deal to his searching questions, his patience and his endless encouragement. I am also extremely grateful to Frances Young, from whose wise guidance I have benefited at several stages, and to Leslie Houlden, Andrew Chester and the former editor of this series, Graham Stanton, who read the original version and made helpful comments from which I have tried to learn in making this revision.

Like any writing, this owes much to the communities in which its various stages have come into being: especially to the very lively Theology Department of Birmingham University, where the work was begun; to my former colleagues and students at Westminster College, Oxford, where the project broadened and put down some roots; to the Principal, staff and former fellow-students at Ripon College, Cuddesdon, who provided a very amenable atmosphere for theological writing; and finally to John Hall-Matthews and my colleagues and friends in the parish of St Paul's, Tupsley, Hereford, who have encouraged me to do this revision, helped me to think more clearly about its purpose and lightened my load of other work to make it possible.

The appearance of the work in this revised form is a belated tribute to my parents, Anne Dunnill and Leslie Dunnill, and to my aunt Elizabeth Stewart, who, among many other gifts of faith and life, did much to support me in the difficult early stages of research. I wish to record also my thanks to David Ravens, who first directed me towards theological study, and whose comments on early versions of this book stimulated further thought; to Alan Browning and Philip Budd, for their friendship and encouragement of this project at different times; and most of all to my wife Maggie who, inheriting this as 'work in progress', has helped me to believe both that it was worth doing, and that it should be finished.

ABBREVIATIONS

Journals

ASR	*American Sociology Review*
CBQ	*Catholic Biblical Quarterly*
ExpT	*Expository Times*
HTR	*Harvard Theological Review*
HUCA	*Hebrew Union College Annual*
JAAR	*Journal of the American Academy of Religion*
JBL	*Journal of Biblical Literature*
JEH	*Journal of Ecclesiastical History*
JRH	*Journal of Roman History*
JSJ	*Journal for the Study of Judaism*
JSNT	*Journal for the Study of the New Testament*
JSOT	*Journal for the Study of the Old Testament*
JTS	*Journal of Theological Studies*
NovT	*Novum Testamentum*
NTS	*New Testament Studies*
SJT	*Scottish Journal of Theology*
VT	*Vetus Testamentum*
ZAW	*Zeitschrift für die Alttestamentliche Wissenschaft*
ZNW	*Zeitschrift für die Neutestamentliche Wissenschaft*

Books

Douglas, *PD*	M. Douglas, *Purity and Danger*, London, 1966
Friedlander, *PRE*	G. Friedlander, ed. and trans., *Pirke de Rabbi Eliezer*, New York, 1965
Leach, *CC*	E. Leach, *Culture and Communication*, Cambridge, 1976
Lévi-Strauss, *SA*	C. Lévi-Strauss, *Structural Anthropology*, Harmondsworth, 1968
von Rad, *OTT*	G. von Rad, *Old Testament Theology*, London, 1975
de Vaux, *AI*	R. de Vaux, *Ancient Israel. Its Life and Institutions*, 2nd edn, London, 1965

Young, *SI*   F. M. Young, *The Use of Sacrificial Ideas in Greek Christian Writers from the N.T. to John Chrysostom*, Philadelphia, 1979

Texts

Add. Est.	Additions to Esther
B. Pes.	Babylonian Talmud, Tractate Pesahim
B. San.	Babylonian Talmud, Tractate Sanhedrin
Ep. Barn.	Epistle of Barnabas
FT (P or V)	Fragment Targums (Paris (P) or Vatican (V) texts)
Gen. R.	Genesis Rabbah
Lev. R.	Leviticus Rabbah
LXX	Septuagint
MT	Masoretic Text of Hebrew Scriptures
Midr.	Midrash
Mish.	Mishnah
P. Az.	Prayer of Azariah
PRE	Pirke de Rabbi Eliezer
Tg. Ps-J.	Targum Pseudo-Jonathan

A NOTE ON TRANSLATIONS

Translations of Biblical passages are usually taken from the Revised Standard Version, although occasionally the New Revised Standard Version has been preferred. It will be clear in the text when it has been found necessary, especially in detailed discussions of passages from Hebrews, to amend these versions or to translate afresh from the Greek.

INTRODUCTION
HEBREWS AND HISTORICAL CRITICISM

Though perennially popular as devotional reading, the Letter to the Hebrews has always been problematic for interpreters. It is interesting to compare the epithets with which commentators of quite different viewpoints describe it: a 'riddle',[1] an enigma',[2] a 'lonely and impressive phenomenon',[3] 'as solitary and mysterious as Melchizedek upon whom its argument turns';[4] but also 'a little masterpiece of religious thought'[5] which 'rises like a massive column, a soaring grandeur of faith in the edifice of first-century Christianity';[6] 'an unknown text' which yet discloses 'the beating of a Jewish-Christian heart'.[7] Contradictory and unignorable, there is about the book something complete, 'perfect' in its own sense of the word, and therefore enigmatic: standing somewhat apart from the New Testament as a whole and contriving to treat even common New Testament topics in its own terms; combining anonymity with an unquestionable air of authority; seeming always to be concealing more than it discloses. Perhaps that is why, though widely read in the early church, it did not receive clear recognition in the canon till the fourth century.[8]

The aim of this study is to demonstrate that ways into an understanding of this book with all its strangeness may be provided by the social sciences, especially structuralist methods as they have been developed in linguistics, literary theory and, most particularly, anthropology. To this end, the argument of these introductory pages

---

[1] E. F. Scott, *The Epistle to the Hebrews* (Edinburgh, 1922), p. 1.

[2] W. Manson, *The Epistle to the Hebrews* (London, 1951), p. 1.

[3] J. Moffatt, quoted by A. Nairne, *The Epistle of Priesthood* (Edinburgh, 1913), p. 7.

[4] Scott, *Hebrews*, p. 1.

[5] J. Moffatt, *The Epistle to the Hebrews* (Edinburgh, 1924), p. xiii.

[6] Manson, *Hebrews*, p. 3.

[7] E. Schillebeeckx, *Christ: The Christian Experience in the Modern World* (ET London, 1980), p. 238.

[8] Cf. F. F. Bruce, *The Epistle to the Hebrews* (Edinburgh, 1964), pp. xliv–xlvii.

will move freely between the two, identifying some characteristics of Hebrews which call for special treatment and setting them alongside some corresponding features of structuralism and the sociology of religion, to point to their potential usefulness in interpreting Hebrews.

Interpretation is certainly called for. The last two centuries of scientific criticism have done remarkably little to dispel the air of mystery which surrounds the letter. The ancient question of its authorship has been reopened and new candidates proposed (Montefiore lists twelve[9]), without any consensus emerging. On the question of the book's date, scholars are equally divided between those who think an origin before the fall of Jerusalem in AD 70 'impossible'[10] and those who think an origin after AD 70 'inconceivable'.[11] Intriguing speculations about the location and situation of its addressees abound.[12] Even if no single hypothesis can command full support, all these arguments are able to aid interpretation by reminding us that both the author and the readers had a very definite identity (whether or not we know it, or need to know it). Indeed, the writer is plainly a person of such marked individuality as to be problematic for those who attempt to discern trends and parties in New Testament theology: does Hebrews belong to Jewish or Hellenistic Christianity? Does it lean towards Paul or John or Luke? Is it part of 'Deutero-Paulinism' or 'Emergent Catholicism'?[13]

With the failure of these critical questions to achieve any assured results, the commentator is reduced to reading the text. Given that this is the most self-consciously artistic book in the New Testament, it might seem that literary criticism would shed more light, but here too debate has settled fruitlessly in introductory questions which, finding no clear answer, are unable to act as steps to higher matters. Much discussion has taken place on the question of the book's genre: should it be regarded as a letter (as its end, though not its beginning, suggests), or as a sermon, or as some other form?[14] What, in this

[9] H. W. Montefiore, *The Epistle to the Hebrews* (London, 1964), pp. 1–12.

[10] N. Perrin, *The New Testament: An Introduction* (New York, 1974), p. 137.

[11] Montefiore, *Hebrews*, p. 3.

[12] See, for example, Manson, *Hebrews*, pp. 25–45; Montefiore, *Hebrews*, pp. 11–29.

[13] See, for example, the evident discomfort which the book causes to Perrin, whose carefully defined categories break down at this point. He is reduced to discussing Hebrews in his chapter on Deutero-Paulinism 'because it was ascribed to Paul in the early church' (Perrin, *New Testament*, p. 137). The second edition admits that this is done 'for convenience'.

[14] Bruce, *Hebrews*, pp. xlviif; F. V. Filson, *'Yesterday': A Study of Hebrews in the Light of Ch. 13* (London, 1967), pp. 16ff; Manson, *Hebrews*, pp. 3–5; Moffatt, *Hebrews*, pp. xxviiiff; Nairne, *Priesthood*, pp. 9f; Scott, *Hebrews*, pp. 8ff.

respect, is the status of chapter 13? If an appendage, was it added by the same author or by another; and, in either case, was this an attempt to imitate Paul's style and therefore borrow his authority?[15] Moving on from these concerns, it would seem that analysis of the powerful imagery of the book would enable us to enter more deeply into the text, but this has received little consistent attention. Because the imagery is never decorative but always fully integrated with the theological argument, study of the imagery falls swiftly into examination of its sources in the Old Testament, Philo and elsewhere.[16] This is perfectly proper, but it fails to capitalise on the strong impression of the unity of its imaginative world which any reading of Hebrews communicates, and leaves unexplored the question whether the theological sources and imaginative effect can be treated simultaneously. This question is the more pressing since it is generally agreed that Hebrews exhibits also a marked theological coherence: studying the book's theology or its intellectual background in piecemeal fashion – whether general topics like eschatology, or specific themes such as Melchizedek or the high-priestly Christology – the parts so abstracted somehow fail to add up to the observable whole. There is here no suspicion of provisional or *ad hoc* conclusions on even the least central topics; rather the theological viewpoint seems to spring forth, like Athene from the side of Zeus, fully armed.

This brings us back to the perceived 'completeness' referred to at the start, and implies that we shall learn at least as much about Hebrews by reading it in isolation as a unity as by attempting to establish cross-references to other New Testament theological and historical data. This is not to suggest that Hebrews stands in any final sense outside the historical and theological context of the church in the middle of the first century; nor is this a pretext for dismissing the detailed and difficult critical questions, which will be dealt with as appropriate below; it may be thought of rather as a Coleridgean argument that it is the property of a complex unity to alter the very nature of its constituent parts in the process of unifying them.[17]

[15] Bruce, *Hebrews*, p. 386; Filson, *'Yesterday'*, ch. 2 *passim*, pp. 13ff; Montefiore, *Hebrews*, pp. 237f; Moffatt, *Hebrews*, p. xxix. On Heb. 13, see further below, pp. 45f and ch. 1, n. 27.

[16] See, for example, Montefiore, *Hebrews*, pp. 6ff; Moffatt, *Hebrews*, pp. xxxiff; Nairne, *Priesthood*, pp. 98ff; Scott, *Hebrews*, pp. 50ff.

[17] This is to apply to the object the power attributed by Coleridge to 'the poet, described in ideal perfection', who 'diffuses a tone and spirit of unity that blends and (as it were) fuses, each into each, by that synthetic and magical power...of imagination'

Thus Hebrews' Christology and its concept of 'faith', for instance, are both continuous with those found elsewhere; but both are also distinctive and belong, distinctively, to the ambience of Hebrews. The relation of 'faith' as found here to 'faith' in the New Testament in general is through the argument, assumptions and symbolism of Hebrews as a whole; to abstract themes and concepts without taking account of their place in that whole is to run the risk of distorting both the concepts and the arguments we build upon them.

The fact that most of the New Testament literature is openly addressed to particular groups and specific situations, and the past success of scholarship in adding internal to external evidence to build up an increasingly complex picture of Christian life in the first century – and especially of certain elements within that (such as the situation in Corinth, and Christian attitudes to scripture) – cause us to overestimate the interpretative value of such factual knowledge, inclining us to assume that a book is easier to understand if we know a lot about the situation it addresses, and that therefore we need to provide plausible guesses in this direction where too little is known. The traditional view of Hebrews, that it was a letter of warning to Jewish Christians in danger of returning to Judaism, was an attempt to provide the book with a recognisable place within the familiar debates and problems of the New Testament church as currently reconstructed.[18] There is plenty of food for speculation, though little unambiguous evidence; but, whether or not hard facts would be desirable, they are not necessary.[19] Hebrews' addressees are subject to a temptation to 'drift away' (2:1), a temptation which is, in several places, characterised but not identified – for we do not know what they are drifting towards, or why, or what form this 'drifting', as the writer sees it, takes in practice. But the book's theological impact is unharmed by our ignorance, for its positive theological content stands as a sharply delineated shadow of this object, this situation 'out there' which we cannot get into focus.

Thus, to return to the example named above, we can say a good deal about the author's conception of faith: the strongly future-orientated and eschatological flavour it gains by appearing to be

(S. T. Coleridge, *Biographia Literaria* (ed. G. Watson, London, 1956), pp. 137f).

[18] See discussions in Bruce, *Hebrews*, pp. xxiiiff; W. G. Kümmel, *Introduction to the New Testament* (London, 1966), pp. 279ff; Manson, *Hebrews*, pp. 10ff; Moffatt, *Hebrews*, p. xvi; Scott, *Hebrews*, pp. 14ff; B. F. Westcott, *The Epistle to the Hebrews*, 2nd edn (London, 1892), pp. xxxvff. See further chapter 2 below.

[19] Hughes also attempts to deduce the letter's life-situation from the theological thrust, rather than vice versa: see p. 119 below.

inseparable from hope, endurance and inheriting the promises; the communal overtone it acquires from its function in the sketch of Israel's history in chapter 11 and by contrast with the tale of Israel's disobedience in chapter 3; and its objective character as a state of living appropriate to the church, rather than an individual frame of mind or a mental act, as conveyed through its narrative presentation in terms of a public event. What more could new historical information enable us to say about the book's doctrine, or about the only church-situations finally relevant to us as readers, those which the author projects as false and true within the terms of the theology expounded here?

Of course, we make use of whatever information we have, from whatever source. But the advantage of a 'situation' which happens to be wholly or almost wholly internal to the text is the demand it makes on the reader to locate the book's centre within the book, to allow it to set its own questions as well as to draw its own conclusions, rather than assuming we can use the book as solver of questions we frame independently. For this reason, this book begins, in part I, with an approach to such 'introductory' questions, not in the form of an historical investigation of the identity of these readers or the author who addresses them, but in the context of a sociological analysis of the community and the situation presupposed within the text.

The aim of the sociological chapter is to root this work in historicity, but it leaves us still facing the problem of the interpretation of symbolism. The story is told of the shepherd 'who, when asked why he made, from within fairy rings, ritual observances to protect his flocks, replied: "I'd be a damn' fool if I didn't!"'[20] A gulf commonly exists between the power of symbols and symbolic actions and our ability to understand them, and those closest to participation in the symbols seem to be the least well placed to 'explain' what is happening. The main argument begins from this point, and asks whether there is a connection between the unsatisfactory nature of writing about the Letter to the Hebrews and the centrality it gives to the symbolism of bloody sacrifices, as well as to other symbolic figures and events. Just as Leviticus, though preserved as a 'book', makes sense only when treated as rules for sacrificial actions, perhaps the mistake we make with Hebrews is in treating it as a 'book',

---

[20] Dylan Thomas, *Collected Poems* (London, 1953), prefatory note (n.p.).

examining its 'argument', its 'imagery', the 'intention' of its 'author', and providing piecemeal exegesis of its surface meaning.

The preceding pages have illustrated a general failure of modern criticism to come to grips with the text as a whole and the theological vision it presents. It is a failure which arises, in large part, from the separation of religious and non-religious ways of reading Biblical literature, characteristic of the post-Enlightenment period. In their recent contribution to the methodological debate, Morgan and Barton argue for the necessity of a 'theological interpretation' which combines rational and scholarly exegesis with a religiously committed reading. They suggest that, to provide the middle term between critical explanation and religious appropriation, some 'theory of religion and reality' is needed,[21] and this is the strategy which will be adopted here. The substance of the study which follows is an attempt to offer an holistic reading of Hebrews through the medium of its sacrificial symbolism, a reading which draws extensively on the work of scholars outside the field of Biblical studies, in particular, from social anthropology. Recent developments in techniques of structural analysis have contributed fresh insights into the meaning of ritual and myth, and some attempts have been made by Biblical scholars to apply these insights to the study of the Old Testament, especially to the Pentateuch, in both its narrative and its legal portions. We shall see that they can also shed light on the meaning of this material as it is used in, and interpreted by, Hebrews.

Among the many factors which hinder the reading of Hebrews, the greatest, it will be suggested, is the use of sacrificial terminology and symbolism, which strikes the modern reader as both difficult and irrelevant. Sacrificial categories are often deeply obscure and even repulsive for the modern reader – the emphasis on blood, on priestly action, on the element of the numinous with its wonder and its shuddering – yet they are expounded in this text without explanation, laying down as axioms statements that are far from self-evident – for example: 'without the shedding of blood there is no forgiveness of sins' (9:22) – and equally bizarre necessities – the need to offer sacrifice (8:3), the need to purify even the heavenly sanctuary (9:23). Such axioms and necessities seem to spring from a whole world of compulsions we either do not feel at all or, it may be argued, have repressed with a partial success which makes dwelling on such themes psychologically painful and dangerous.

---

[21] R. Morgan with J. Barton, *Biblical Interpretation* (Oxford, 1988), p. 227; cf. pp. 185–9, 269–96.

William Johnsson has described the way nineteenth- and twentieth-century scholarship has recoiled from this so-called 'primitive' aspect of ancient religion as it features in Hebrews.[22] We have to go back to the commentary of Westcott to find a work which takes the anthropological accounts of religion seriously as a contribution to understanding Hebrews. But, as Johnsson points out, Westcott's commentary was published in 1889, the year of Robertson Smith's *Religion of the Semites* which gave persuasive expression to an evolutionary account of religion.[23] After him, expositors of Hebrews either continued to translate sacrificial terms into doctrinal terms along sectarian lines – thus 'blood' has meant the saving death of Christ or the Real Presence in the eucharist – or else such terms were treated Platonically, as material metaphors for spiritual realities, to be swiftly transcended. Always the tendency is to treat sacrificial language as an instance of something else. It will be argued here that this area of sacrifice, with its strange logic and disturbing compulsions has to be understood for its own sake if we are to make sense of the text built around it. The aim will be to show that there is a 'logic of sacrifice' which is the source, not only of the axioms and necessities referred to just now, but also of the book's tendency to generate contradictions: such as the contradictions between its highly in-tellectualised argument and the sense of crisis it is apparently addressing; between a very high and a very low view of Christology; between the drift of its argument (no Christian priesthood) and the encouragement its symbolism gives to priestly ways of thinking about salvation; between the apparent obscurity of its symbolic materials and the immediate power they have possessed and for some still possess. In all this it will be maintained that it is the use it makes of this logic that is the source of the book's permanent theological claims.

This argument will form the substance of parts II and III. Chapter 2 develops the argument for preferring an holistic, hermeneutically based approach over conventional historical criticism, and relates the methodology adopted here to other Biblical criticism inspired by structuralism. In chapter 3 the sacrificial symbolism of the Old Testament will be examined in the light of recent anthropological approaches, and some criticisms will be offered, both of the theology

[22] W. G. Johnsson, 'Defilement and purgation in the Book of Hebrews' (unpublished PhD thesis, Vanderbilt University, 1973), pp. 27–96.

[23] W. Robertson Smith, *The Religion of the Semites* (London, 1889); cf. Johnsson, 'Defilement and Purgation', pp. 46ff, 83ff.

that is mediated by the sacrificial system, and of the limits of the methodology being employed.

Part III takes us to Hebrews itself. In chapter 4 it is argued that Hebrews demands direct participation in its symbolic world, and may be treated as if to read it was to be caught up into a feast in God's presence, a 'Liturgy for the Day of Salvation', an event in which meaning and behaviour are governed by the 'logic of sacrifice'. This idea is then given concreteness, first by showing how, in contemporary Jewish writings, very varied symbols and stories interact in an associative or paradigmatic fashion to form a systematic body of covenant symbolism, and how this text also fuses many ideas around the concept of the covenant and the covenant-renewal rite; and second by showing how the situation of the addressees is given quasi-liturgical characterisation through the categories of 'sacred time' and 'sacred place'.

Chapter 5 goes on to demonstrate the rich interrelation of the Pentateuchal narratives given in the text, including Abel, Rahab and Aaron's Rod, Moses and Joshua, Abraham and Isaac, and the anomalous figure of Melchizedek. It shows how they too circle around covenantal and sacrificial concepts, furnishing the argument, through overt references and subtle allusions, with a complex symbolic substructure. One of these motifs, the Akedah or Binding of Isaac, is considered further in chapter 6, where it is presented as the focal expression of a widespread myth of 'Testing', related to major strands in Old Testament theology as well as to the Christian proclamation of Christ. Through this mythological pattern, the Christology of Hebrews is expounded, looking particularly at the importance of Jesus' 'temptation', at the anthropology implicit in the concept of the 'seed of Abraham', and at the function of Jesus' 'flesh' and death.

In chapters 7 and 8 it is contended that the author's interest in expiatory sacrifice is strictly subordinate to the problem of death and the ambivalence this induces in human perceptions of God; expiatory sacrifice is shown to be subsumed within a rich pattern of symbolism of communion and gift, expressing a new covenant theology of the actual presence of God.

Hebrews is a highly integrated and coherent work, and this study will aim to understand it through that coherence, which is fundamental to its theological vision, by means of a broadly structuralist approach. In accordance with this, the text is regarded as a closed and self-regulating whole, the individual parts having meaning not in themselves, nor in reference to anything outside, but in relation to the whole which they constitute. The historical and exegetical approach (what did the text mean to its author and its first readers?) cannot be separated from the properly interpretative question: what does the text mean now? As Paul Ricoeur argues, the mere fact of being *written* detaches a discourse from its author, its original situation and its first readers, so that they lose their authority as arbiters of meaning: the text then attains a free existence as potential meaning, having to be actualised, given reference, by each new reader in his or her concrete situation, for whom it becomes a 'possible world'.[24]

Where historical data is in any case deficient, as it is with Hebrews, this approach carries a particular aptness. It is emphatically not necessary, however, to fall into the 'ideology of the absolute text'.[25] Structuralism is being adopted here not as a deterministic philosophy but as an heuristic tool, in the hope that it will generate a reading which is itself coherent as well as fruitful. The author of Hebrews can be seen to be a consummate reader of Old Testament texts, and it is in the hope that we may benefit from the method and the content of such reading that this study has been done.

[24] P. Ricoeur, *Hermeneutics and the Human Sciences* (ET Cambridge, 1981), p. 177, and cf. pp. 182–93.
[25] *Ibid.*, p. 148.

PART I

SOCIOLOGY

1

THE NEW COVENANT COMMUNITY

Since the inception of the form-critical movement, twentieth-century scholarship has been insisting that New Testament literature cannot be understood in isolation from the Christian communities in which it took shape, although it is unfortunate that the complexity of the social history of the first-century Roman world, and the obscurity of the church's origins, have largely prevented this claim from being realised. As regards Hebrews, the primacy of this presupposition has contributed greatly to its current neglect and misreading, and on this account, too, the composition of the gospels has sometimes been tied, by way of explanation, to a few stereotyped life-situations so broad ('apologetic'; 'preaching') as to give less specificity, not more, to our picture of the origins of the material. But the social description of first-century Christianity is a field in which genuine advance has been made, and most recently, with the increasing application of sociological procedures to the sparse historical data, reconstructions of the earliest worshipping communities have begun to emerge that are substantial enough, at last, to bear the weight of theological interpretation.

Making use of these procedures, then, this chapter is offered as an essay in sociological interpretation. As such it is complementary to the main argument of the book, with rather different aims and methods, but it shares its synchronic, intratextual perspective. The more overtly historical nature of the material, especially pages 22–9, and the hypothesis advanced there, do not constitute this an 'historical introduction'. The community life here reconstructed is that which appears *within the text*, and though it makes use of sociological and historical techniques it is not a contribution to the history, or the sociology, of the first-century Mediterranean world. Similarly, the term 'author' means here, as throughout, the authorial presence within the text, not some supposed intentions of the work's anonymous writer. The methodology of this chapter is therefore consonant with that of the whole, and many of its results will be found to echo those of the main argument. Its specific function is to complement a symbolic reading by grounding it in that quality of *historicity* which is indispensable to Hebrews itself, and therefore to any true reading of it.

Sociology and New Testament interpretation

The aims of sociological inquiry into the New Testament have been broadly of three kinds.[1] First, it may aim to describe the composition and structure of the Christian communities, the dynamic of their inner life and their relations to surrounding society. Reference will be made later to notable recent contributions to this *social description* or *social history* of early Christianity by E. A. Judge, A. Malherbe and others.[2] Second, there have been attempts to apply to aspects of the material thus provided various sociological models of behaviour, in the hope of supplementing hard data by probable inference, and thus building up a *sociological analysis* of the early church. Thus, R. Scroggs has examined the early church as a sectarian movement, using B. Wilson's typology of sect-development; G. Theissen has analysed in succession Palestinian and Corinthian Christianity by means of categories of social factors; J. Gager has tested Festinger's theory of 'cognitive dissonance' (derived from observation of modern millenarian sects) on the disciples' response to the death of Jesus and the later reaction of the church to the delay of the Parousia.[3]

[1] This threefold division is that used by J. H. Elliott, *A Home for the Homeless* (London, 1982), pp. 1–13. For other analyses of methodology, see for example P. J. Richter, 'Recent sociological approaches to the study of the New Testament', *Religion*, 14 (1984), 77–90; R. Scroggs, 'Sociological interpretation of the New Testament – the present state of research', *NTS*, 26 (1980), 164–79; J. Z. Smith, 'The social description of early Christianity', *Religious Studies Review*, 1 (1975), 19–25; G. Theissen, *The Social Setting of Pauline Christianity* (ET Edinburgh, 1982), pp. 175–200; B. J. Malina, 'The social sciences and biblical interpretation', *Interpretation*, 36 (1982), 229–42.
[2] E. A. Judge, *The Social Pattern of Christian Groups in the First Century* (London, 1960); E. A. Judge, 'The social identity of the first Christians', *JRH*, 11 (1980), 201–17; E. A. Judge, 'The early Christians as a scholastic community', *JRH*, 1 (1960), 4–15, 125–37; A. Malherbe, *Social Aspects of Early Christianity* (2nd edn, Philadelphia, 1983). See also the works by Frend, Filson and S. E. Johnson cited below.
[3] R. Scroggs, 'The earliest Christian communities as a sectarian movement', in J. Neusner (ed.), *Christianity, Judaism and other Greco-Roman Cults* (Leiden, 1975), vol. II, pp. 1–23; G. Theissen, *The First Followers of Jesus* (ET London, 1978); Theissen, *Social Setting*; J. G. Gager, *Kingdom and Community* (Englewood Cliffs, 1975).

Despite the obvious dangers of anachronism which attend the application of twentieth-century models to first-century behaviour, this work has been highly productive, and some of the general conclusions from these studies will be employed below.

However, a third kind of approach is most directly relevant for our purposes: this attempts to relate the 'social world' of a specific community to the theological interests manifested in a specific text, interpreting each by each to discover the social function of theological ideas.[4] With J.H. Elliott, this interest in the 'situation' underlying a text and the author's strategy towards that situation may most conveniently be called *sociological exegesis*.[5] In a less theoretically oriented fashion, of course, this situational approach has long been normal in Pauline studies, and Paul's letters, with their abundant prosopographic and sociographic details and their paraenetic function, remain the most easily accessible field for this work: the recent, sociologically informed, Pauline studies by W.A. Meeks and G. Theissen have vastly extended our sensitivity to the complex interactions of social and theological symbols in these letters and among these urban Christian groups. H.C. Kee,[6] taking his cue from Theissen's reconstruction of Palestinian Christianity as a community of village-based itinerant charismatics, has attempted to show how such a community could plausibly require and produce a document like Mark's gospel.

One way of measuring the success of sociological inference in supplementing deficient historical data is demonstrated in the access it gives to the Christianity of the countryside. Little was recorded by contemporaries about rural life in the Roman world, the transmission of literature being an urban pursuit and Hellenism the civilisation of the πόλις; besides, given the conservatism and slowness of country life, they saw little to record. The pious Jew expressed the same townsman's contempt, though with a characteristic slant: 'the

---

[4] The most important representatives of this approach are Elliott, *Home*; H.C. Kee, *The Community of the New Age* (London, 1977); W.A. Meeks, *The First Urban Christians* (London, 1983) and the works of Theissen already named. Other interesting examples are W.A. Meeks, 'The Man from Heaven in Johannine sectarianism', *JBL*, 91 (1972), 44–72; N.R. Peterson, *Rediscovering Paul* (Philadelphia, 1985) – on Philemon. A good general summary is given in H.C. Kee, *Christian Origins in Sociological Perspective* (London, 1980). P.L. Berger, *The Social Reality of Religion* (London, 1969), is probably the major source of theoretical assumptions underlying these works; see D. Tidball, *Introduction to the Sociology of the New Testament* (Exeter, 1983), pp. 137ff.

[5] Elliott, *Home*, pp. 7ff. For the concept of 'strategy', see pp. 10ff.

[6] Kee, *Community*.

"rustic" was virtually identical with the "godless".'[7] Christianity, allowing its view of its origins to be dominated by St Paul's mission to the great cities, has replicated this cultural pattern.[8] Yet Jesus and his Twelve were men of the Galilean countryside; the Hellenised πόλεις of Galilee and Judaea were the places they very pointedly avoided;[9] it can be argued that, in the early development of Christianity, turning to the cities and losing sight of Jesus' essential vision were simultaneous and inseparable processes.[10] At any rate, one interesting trend in the work of Theissen and Kee is the sketching of a distinctively rural style of Christian life and thought,[11] which has contributed to Elliott's exegesis of 1 Peter and is relevant also, as we shall see, for the study of Hebrews.

In *A Home for the Homeless*, his full-scale study of 1 Peter, Elliott argues that the letter is addressed to a loose federation of rural and small-town Christian communities scattered through the mountain ranges of Asia Minor, and that the letter's 'strategy' corresponds to this concrete situation and the problems that it throws up.[12] Basic to his reconstruction is a literal understanding of the description of the readers as a 'spiritual household' (2:5) and as 'aliens and exiles' (2:11) – that is, as either Jewish or other foreign immigrants, or else native inhabitants lacking citizenship.[13] He has therefore to distance 1 Peter from Hebrews where, in his view, πάροικος ('sojourner' or 'resident alien') is a Platonic metaphor of the soul exiled from its heavenly

[7] M. Weber, *The Sociology of Religion* (London, 1963), p. 83. For a survey of the relations between town and country at this period, see R. MacMullen, *Roman Social Relations* (New Haven, 1974), pp. 32ff.

[8] Whereas the church is ἡ ἐκκλησία, a countryman is *paganus* (Weber, *Sociology of Religion* p. 83). See W. H. C. Frend, 'Town and countryside in early Christianity', in D. Baker (ed.), *The Church in Town and Countryside*, Ecclesiastical History Society Studies in Church History 16 (Oxford, 1979), pp. 27–42; and W. H. C. Frend, 'The winning of the countryside', *JEH*, 18 (1967), 1–14.

[9] See Frend, 'Town and countryside', pp. 30ff; G. E. M. de Ste Croix, 'Early Christian attitudes to property and slavery', in D. Baker (ed.), *Church, Society and Politics*, Ecclesiastical History Society Studies in Church History 12 (Oxford, 1975), pp. 2ff; Judge, *Social Pattern*, pp. 15f; Kee, *Community*, p. 102.

[10] See Theissen, *First Followers*, pp. 111–19; *Social Setting*, pp. 57–9.

[11] W. H. C. Frend, in the two works cited above, and in 'The ecology of the early Christianities', in G. Irvine (ed.), *Christianity in its Social Context* (London, 1967), pp. 15–28, argues for the importance of this rural alternative to city-based Christian developments as the source of Montanism, Donatism and other prophetic minority sects. On Montanism and its Phrygian origins, see J. M. Ford, 'Was Montanism a Jewish-Christian heresy?', *JEH*, 17 (1966), 145–58; and S. E. Johnson, 'Unsolved questions about early Christianity in Anatolia', *Supp. to NovT*, 33 (1972), pp. 181–93.

[12] Elliott, *Home*, pp. 59ff, 101–50.

[13] On 'household' see Elliott, *Home*, pp. 200ff, and pp. 32–8 below; on 'aliens and exiles', see Elliot, *Home*, pp. 37ff and pp. 25–32 below.

home.[14] It will be argued later that, although in the past 1 Peter has certainly been misconstrued in accordance with Platonising interpretations of Hebrews, the contrast is less sharp than he supposes. However, even if Elliott mistakenly rules out a social 'strategy' in Hebrews, he at least recognises that, like 1 Peter, the problem it deals with has an inescapable social dimension. By contrast, in a view more representative of the majority of scholars, we find it described recently as a 'treatise', having 'only the external features of a letter', a piece of sophisticated rhetoric intended to provide arguments 'to engage thoughtful pagans' and 'persuade them of the truth of Christian claims'.[15] The lack of definite information about either the author or the readers (though we should be less conscious of this lack if James, or the Petrine or Johannine letters, were to be taken as the norm, rather than Paul's) has lent great weight to this view of Hebrews as a work of abstract doctrinal reflection. Add the obscurity of its theological interests – Melchizedek; the sacrificial cultus – to the density of its argument, and it can seem the most theoretical of New Testament books, the furthest removed from any conceivable communal life, in either the first or the twentieth centuries. It is, then, all the more urgent to recognise that it is what its author calls it, a 'word of exhortation' (13:22). By punctuating the subtle theological argument with hortatory passages, turning repeatedly from theory to practice with a 'therefore' (2:1; 3:1; 4:1,14; 6:1; 7:26; 9:15; 10:19; 12:1,12; 13:13), the author indicates incontrovertibly that the purpose of the work throughout is practical and, to use Elliott's word, strategic.

Frustrating though it may be to the sociologically inclined critic, the absence of internal information about the social situation of his readers has to be understood as integral to the author's strategy. For, since the aim is to point them away from a lingering interest in their past, and towards God's future, the author wisely spends little time reminding them of what they need to forget. Even the imagery, which elsewhere so often helps us by conveying, as it were by accident, what the author takes for granted, here gives little away: it is almost exclusively Biblical in character, and conformed in its purpose.

That purpose is to confirm the readers' positive sense of identity as *a community of outsiders*, to which end the author employs the

[14] See especially pp.31f, 99f, 129f.
[15] Kee, *Origins*, pp.150f.

concept of the 'stranger and sojourner' and that of the 'household'. In Hebrews, the primary use of these terms is certainly metaphorical rather than literal, but it remains to be seen which of the many senses of these terms the metaphors depend on, and what reality they relate to. Our analysis must therefore move towards these symbols elliptically. It will begin with what Theissen calls a 'comparative procedure',[16] using a modern model of 'sect' to link the letter's evidence of persecution with other features not obviously related, so establishing that the context of this work is sectarian; second, it will attempt a profile of the churches addressed, using a mixture of historical argument and reference to contemporary (that is, first-century) social categories. We shall then be in a position to reflect on the theological function of the leading symbols of exclusion and belonging.

A sectarian perspective

The discussion which follows is based on two variant typologies of sects presented by Bryan Wilson.[17] In 1959, in an essay entitled 'An analysis of sect development', he approached this theme by first setting out some common features of sects, then distinguishing between four types. In 1963 he turned his attention directly to the question of typology, adopting a different criterion and extending his list of types to seven. The criterion he uses in the second essay to differentiate sects is their 'response to the world'; it is important for our purposes that Wilson is here consciously aiming to escape the historically determined character of sociological study of sects from Troeltsch and Weber onwards, which has tended to focus on the doctrinal peculiarities of sects in modern Western culture or (like his own previous essay) on the transformation of sects into 'denominations' and 'churches'. Even so, this work must be used with caution, and more weight will be placed on the common features of sects as they emerge here than on the nature of individual types.

Among these common features, Wilson notes the following emphases:[18] the sect's distinctiveness from its surrounding society;

---

[16] Theissen, *Social Setting*, pp. 192ff.
[17] B. R. Wilson, 'An analysis of sect development', *ASR*, 24 (1959), reprinted in B. R. Wilson (ed.), *Patterns of Sectarianism* (London, 1967), pp. 22–45; B. R. Wilson, 'A typology of sects', in R. Robertson (ed.), *Sociology of Religion* (Harmondsworth, 1969), pp. 361–81.
[18] Wilson, 'Analysis', pp. 25f.

exclusive membership with strict qualifications; a high degree of commitment to the group and its beliefs and aims, involving symbolic or actual isolation from others; a target of perfection; strong internal discipline, though with few organisational or liturgical structures, that is, 'charismatic' leadership combined with a fraternal ethic and plain, often 'enthusiastic', worship.

In line with this, the *isolation* of these 'Hebrews' is strongly attested. Though the nature of their present sufferings is less clear, they have in the past been subjected to public abuse, plundering of property, imprisonment and probably physical attack (10:33f – though we are told the present readers have 'not yet' shed any blood (12:4)). Though imprisonment appears to imply action by the civic authorities, most of the terms used could as well indicate informal and unsystematic persecution by groups or individuals. But whether the harassment is official or private, verbal or physical, it is typical of a sect to emphasise the difference between member and non-member which it implies, and to affirm the necessity of such hostility.[19] Thus, these readers are the 'enlightened ones' (10:32) and their goal is 'perfection' (6:1); persecution is the 'discipline' which proves they are regarded by God as his 'sons', and which he has sent to test and perfect their commitment, their 'faith' (12:5ff); to apostasise in the face of this persecution is to 'fall into the hands of the living God' (10:26ff); the sufferings of Jesus and the patriarchs are introduced as inspiring examples (5:7ff; 12:1–3; 11 *passim*), and the fate of Esau as a dreadful warning (12:16).

The author's view of leadership likewise bears out this sectarian description. No reference is made to authority-structures or offices; both the colourless references to 'leaders' in chapter 13 and the roles of Jesus, Moses and Abraham are of a 'charismatic' type, each individual appointed directly by God (not via a tradition or structure) as his representative (servant, prophet or exemplar).[20] Thus, Moses is servant (3:5) and route-leader (3:16); Abraham is exemplar of faith (11:8); the Christian ἡγούμενοι are exemplars (13:7) and pastors (13:17); and similarly, at a higher level, Jesus is 'pioneer' (12:2, and also 'perfecter of faith'), servant (3:6, though as Son he is God's plenipotentiary) and prophet (1:2, though as Son he is God's *final* spokesman). Institutional roles are explicitly rejected: Abraham's patriarchal authority, though not denied, is notably played down, as

[19] *Ibid.*, pp. 36f.
[20] On prophetic and 'charismatic' styles of leadership, see Weber, *Sociology of Religion*, pp. 45ff.

when he is described as 'living in tents with Isaac and Jacob' (11:9), three generations appearing on terms of equality; Moses refuses his position as an Egyptian prince (11:24); Jesus is High Priest only in a sense which devalues the entire Aaronic tradition.

Along with this goes the fraternal ethic of mutual responsibility and encouragement (10:24f, 33f; 13:1–3) and the paucity of references to liturgical matters. Certainly they practise 'washings' and 'laying on of hands' (6:2),[21] but the omission of eucharistic features is notorious. What occurs when these Christians gather (ἡ ἐπισυναγωγή, 10:25) remains unclear, though many factors – the emphasis on the Christian's 'confession' (3:1; 4:14; 10:23); on God's message (1:2; 2:1ff; 12:25ff) and promise (4:1; 6:12f); on Jesus' fulfilment of the functions of Moses (3:5f) and the prophets (1:2) – give prominence to the teaching function of leadership and (however little is said about the content of belief) a doctrinal definition of Christian identity.

These twin features, the doctrinal self-definition of the group and its leadership, are, among sects, specially typical of Wilson's category of 'Adventist' or 'Revolutionary' sect,[22] and when we ask what is the purpose of the Christian life as presented here we find the author's exhortation to endurance and perfection of faith likewise character-istic of this type and its passive stance. Though urged to 'lift your drooping hands' and so on (12:12), it is not for outward action but for vigorous maintenance of their 'hope' against all discouragement. In this we may distinguish them sharply from the aims and practices of a 'Conversionist' sect (whose practical programme also leads naturally to the need for a more developed authority-structure), though less easily from the 'Pietist' or 'Introversionist' focus on personal holiness and a 'spiritual' concept of salvation.

[21] For the meaning of these terms, see J. C. Adams, 'The exegesis of Hebrews 6.1f', *NTS*, 13 (1966–7), 383f.

[22] Three of Wilson's sect-types will be referred to here, the Adventist, Conversionist and Introversionist (see 'Analysis', pp. 26–8, 'Typology', pp. 364–7). The defining feature of the *Conversionist* type is the conversion-experience as mode of entry to the group, so that it stresses individual piety, God as one's personal saviour, an emotional awareness of being one of the 'elect', together with a moralistic distrust of the 'world'; its central aim is to convert the unconverted majority, understood as 'bringing in the Kingdom'. By contrast, the *Adventist* (or Revolutionist) type tends to be doctrinally based and passive, proving from scriptural exegesis the imminence of the Day when God (conceived as an autocratic ruler) will overturn the world-order, as preordained. (If the number of the elect is predetermined, there will be little incentive to proselytise, though the Jehovah's Witnesses appear to be an exception to this trend.) An *Introversionist* sect puts as much emphasis on separation from the world, but less on evangelism and common worship and common action: salvation is an interior state of personal holiness. This radically dualistic attitude tends to favour an impersonal, disembodied concept of God as Spirit.

This question of whether they stand closest to the Adventist or the Introversionist type (that is, whether salvation is an event they await, God's imminent overturning of the world-order, or an inward, spiritual reality achieved by holiness of life) is related to the question whether Hebrews is as Platonic in its outlook as interpreters have often believed,[23] or whether this inference itself represents a dominant individualist and introversionist tendency in post-apostolic Christian thought. C.K. Barrett has shown convincingly that eschatological elements are central to Hebrews' perspective, and that the 'mystical' stress is only a heightened form (owing its peculiar flavour to the influence of Platonic writings) of Jewish eschatological anticipation:[24] so, for example, in 6:4f, the 'heavenly gift' is not an escape from the world but the surety of a promise to be fulfilled in the 'age to come' to those who with proper eagerness await the Day. Thus, although the book is notably restrained in its use of apocalyptic imagery, and shows no interest in predicting the time of the Parousia, and although (unlike the English Fifth Monarchy men, for example) there is no sign that its readers engage in action to bring it about, it is this Adventist perspective that the author urges through a 'prophetic exegesis' and exhortation to 'vigilance and doctrinal purity'[25] as they await the inevitable outcome.

If the readers are being persecuted by non-Christians, then, it is unlikely to be a response to aggressive proselytism: socially speaking, both author and readers are inward-looking in their concerns. Besides, it appears that this is not the main problem: present 'hostility from sinners' (12:3) is described rather vaguely; by comparison, the very specific reference back to the sufferings of the 'former days' (10:32) looks like an appeal to a previous survived situation which, though similar, was actually more acute. Particular references to current problems have a different character: loss of faith (10:23) and of brotherly concern (10:24), neglecting to meet (10:25), internal strife caused by some 'root of bitterness' (12:15), the slackness of disappointed hope (12:4; 10:25, 39). The temptation to 'sell one's birthright' (12:16f) is leading some towards apostasy, as 6:6 and 10:29 make clear, but the source of the difficulty seems to be, on

[23] See, for example, Moffatt, *Hebrews*, pp. xxxff.
[24] C.K. Barrett, 'The eschatology of the Epistle to the Hebrews', in W.D. Davies and D. Daube (eds.), *The Background of the New Testament and its Eschatology*, Studies in honour of C.H. Dodd (Cambridge, 1956), pp. 363–93. See the discussions below, pp. 32, 46, 137, 227–9, 234–7.
[25] Wilson, 'Typology', p. 366.

the whole, internal rather than external, and the evidence above is consonant with a failure of nerve, or perhaps with a parallel tendency towards a more individualistic and spiritualised concept of salvation, by which the cohesion and purposefulness of the group is sapped. The author points would-be apostates to the wrath of God (6:4ff; 10:26ff; 12:28f), and for those losing hope reaffirms belief in the Parousia (9:28; 10:25, 37f; 12:26ff), and in God's promise as both a future certainty and a present possession (4:14ff; 6:4f, 13ff; 12:18ff). It is at these points that the most vivid imagery is employed, to make of the eschatological hope a reality more imposing than whatever doubts or distresses afflict the present and threaten to dissolve the group. For it is the group, conceived as the elect community of the end-time, which is, as Kee has argued, the primary reference of all apocalyptic literature – in Berger's terms, the 'plausibility structure' of its cosmology, without which it will seem the merest fantasy.[26] It is therefore to the maintenance of this group and its self-understanding as the people of God that the author's words are directed.

The social setting

It is now necessary to sketch a profile of the location of these Christians in space and time. The argument, which will be presented in summary form, is that Hebrews is an encyclical letter addressed to a series of small churches of predominantly Jewish Christians, most probably in Western Asia Minor.

An encyclical letter

It is the particular mix of personal and general that identifies this among the many encyclical letters contained in the New Testament. Thus, it is addressed to a specific problem, as we have seen (and therefore to specific persons), but names none of them and is couched in an impersonal style; despite the urgency of its appeal, it is plainly the fruit of mature reflection and careful craftsmanship. It belongs to the middle ground, between Paul's close relationship with his readers and the notion of a 'general epistle' addressed to no one in particular; and between the often hasty quality of Paul's argument and the rounded theological treatise. This author has definite readers in mind, even if few of them (perhaps not any) are known in person; they are being addressed on a matter of central concern to their

[26] Kee, *Community*, pp. 106f; Berger, *Social Reality*, p. 45.

Christian lives, and therefore it is appropriate that the tone should be that of an authoritative apostolic pronouncement.[27]

To Asia Minor?

Though not incompatible with the slight internal evidence on the matter, the location of the addressees in Asia Minor is a conclusion which follows loosely from the argument above.[28] As a means of communication, the encyclical letter is most appropriate to a group of churches in a relatively restricted area with common concerns, and too small to have their own outstanding leaders or to merit individual treatment. Such conditions would fit the great majority of churches around the Eastern Mediterranean up to the end of the first century, including those in Northern Greece and Macedonia, in Syria, Italy and North Africa, so far as we have any knowledge of them at all; that it certainly applies to the many churches of Western Asia Minor is confirmed by the fact that many of the contemporary encyclicals we possess are addressed to the churches of this region: Ephesians, Colossians (and the 'letter from Laodicea', Col. 4:16), 1 Peter, Revelation 2–3, and probably the Johannine letters. The presence of overlapping themes between these letters and Hebrews (this is especially true of its relationship to 1 Peter and

[27] In this case, Heb. 13 demands some further explanation. (For discussion of the literary problems of this passage, see Moffatt, *Hebrews*, pp. xxviii–xxx; Bruce, *Hebrews*, p. 386, and the literature cited there.) More informal in style and more practical in content, though not obviously written by another hand, it has the appearance of an appended note, attached to one copy and directed to one particular church. Even here, though, the advice is of a fairly general sort – as though the author has heard of their leadership problems, and so on, at second hand. On balance, it seems more likely that this chapter, though written in a different mood – after the delay necessary for producing fair copies of the main section, perhaps – is intended for as wide a readership as the rest. Therefore, although in close contact with the readers, and expecting to see them (again) soon, the author is under no compulsion to say everything that might be said.

[28] The internal evidence is far from profuse or unambiguous. 'Those who come from Italy send you greeting' (13:24) has been used to argue that the author writes from Italy (presumably Rome?), or alternatively *to* Italy; but in view of the amount of travelling accomplished by the early apostles it is equally likely that expatriate Italians should be known to foreign churches – as Prisca and Aquila would have been, for example, after their period of residence in Ephesus (1 Cor. 16:19) – and there are, besides, several examples of warm Christian greetings being extended between individuals and groups who must have been total strangers (Rom. 16:21–3; 1 Cor. 16:19f). That Timothy is known to the readers, and expected to travel through their area (Heb. 13:23) could, on the evidence we possess, indicate anywhere from Italy to Palestine; but perhaps his associations with Lystra and Ephesus (Acts 16:13; 1 Cor. 16:10f; 2 Cor. 1:1; (?) Col. 1:1) may help to support the contention that Asia Minor is the most likely destination.

Revelation 2–3) – though mixed with sufficient diversity to rule out any simple picture of Asian Christianity, and not denying that those themes could as well be manifested elsewhere – adds to the likelihood of this identification.[29] However, no positive conclusions will be derived from this view.

Jewish Christians

There is less reason to dissent from the assertion that the Christians of Hebrews are Jews. More precisely, they are Christians for whom Judaism offers the natural *alternative* identity-base, and who are vulnerable to theoretical and social pressures to turn back, or turn aside, to that alternative. (As well as Jews by birth and conversion, this could include Gentiles, not all of whom would necessarily be regarded by their Jewish neighbours as 'Godfearers', a fairly fluid term.) This conclusion is based on two premises.[30] First, the author's appeal to the Septuagint assumes that it is not only authoritative for the readers but so well known to them that even passing allusions will be familiar and their force acknowledged. If Gentile Christians accepted the Old Testament as scripture, it was because this was an assumption basic to the (predominantly Jewish) churches they joined, but the kind of knowledge of the Septuagint assumed here could only be expected of those with a long-term, preferably a lifetime, knowledge, who were, actually or effectively, Jews. Unless the details, and not merely the gist, of the letter were available to the hearers as a group (that does not mean to every individual), this

[29] Among these overlapping themes we may note the sacrificial imagery of 1 Peter and the similarity of the situations to which Hebrews and Rev. 2–3 seem to be addressed: a Jewish problem (Rev. 2:9; 3:9), poverty and powerlessness (2:9; 3:8), the need for endurance (2:3; 3:10) and reminders of God's judgement (his 'words' associated with 'the sharp two-edged sword', τὴν ῥομφαίαν τὴν δίστομον τὴν ὀξεῖαν, 2:12). The letter to Philadelphia (3:7–13), in particular, offers a surprising range of echoes: in addition to the Jewish issue and the need for endurance already mentioned, these include an 'open door' and Christ the 'key of David' (3:7f: cf. 'a new and living way', Heb. 10:19), the Temple and the New Jerusalem. Some historical features of this city are of interest: situated in the volcanic region known as the Burnt-lands (κατακεκαυμένη, cf. Heb. 6:8?) it was subject to geological disturbance and had, together with Sardis, been destroyed by an earthquake in AD 17; in view of this danger, 'many of the inhabitants preferred to live in the open country round about' (D. Magie, *Roman Rule in Asia Minor* (Princeton, 1950), pp. 124f. 'Here', says our author, 'we have no continuing city' (οὐ ... μένουσαν πόλιν, 13:14), but 'let brotherly love continue' (ἡ φιλαδελφία μενέτω, 13:1).

[30] See C. Spicq, *L'Epître aux Hébreux* (2 vols., Paris, 1952–3), vol. I, pp. 221f, and Bruce, *Hebrews*, pp. xxiii–xxvii. The alternative view is argued by Moffatt, *Hebrews*, pp. xvif; E. Käsemann, *The Wandering People of God* (ET Minneapolis, 1984), pp. 24f; Scott, *Hebrews*, pp. 14ff.

would be a very inefficient way of writing. Second, there is no evidence here of a 'circumcision problem' of the kind that racked St Paul, a fact which, if we rule out (on the argument just advanced) the possibility that they were all Gentiles, implies that, if they were not all Jews, then at least the Jewishness of Gentiles was not (or was no longer) an issue – however it may have been settled.

There is no cause to doubt the broad accuracy of the picture given in Acts of the spread of Christianity in the cities of the Diaspora as a secession of Jews and Godfearers from the synagogue, with the establishment, in effect, of a rival synagogue, in which Jews and Gentiles mixed on somewhat easier terms, and in which Gentiles were able to take part in Christian worship (even among a Jewish majority). But there remained the question whether those Gentiles were full members of the group or not: that is, whether Christians were to be a 'party' within Israel, or an excluded and excluding 'sect'.[31] In Hebrews, the memory of struggle indicates that (whether on the circumcision issue or some other) these Christians have long ago become a 'sect', and are now regretting the extremity of their commitment.

However keenly this separation was felt by those involved, though, to the outside world it was decades before Christians were generally distinguished from Jews,[32] and even then regarded as a dissenting movement, more similar than different. Thus to understand the peculiar ambiguity of Christians in Greek cities we must see how it mirrors, and also differs from, the anomalous status of the Jews.

Diaspora Judaism

By the first century, the communities of dispersed Jews which were ubiquitous throughout the Eastern Mediterranean had achieved, in the eyes of most of the Greek cities, a distinctive identity, but only after a long period of ambiguity and consequent social tension. The structure of the πόλις was well adapted to deal with temporarily resident groups of artisans and traders, and the first Jewish immigrants to a town could be simply assimilated as a household of strangers (ξένοι) distinguishable by their foreign customs with regard to food and worship, and even as it increased in size, like other immigrant groups, the Jewish community tended to retain something

---

[31] On the distinction between 'party' and 'sect', in this connection, see pp. 28f below.

[32] Cf. the uncertainty evident in the famous letter of Pliny the Younger to Trajan, as late as AD 111 to 112 (Ep. X.96).

of the character of an enlarged *household* (οἶχος):[33] racial solidarity, intermarriage, shared dwelling-space, patriarchal authority, common business concerns. But by the time the Jews numbered hundreds or thousands – and the Jewish population of Alexandria at this time has been estimated at 100,000 – other categories seemed to be more appropriate: their tendency to gather together in shared trades (such as textile manufacture and metalworking) gave them the character of a *trade-guild*;[34] their practice of meeting to worship their God – and especially when Greek proselytes came to be included so that the synagogue appeared to the observer as much a voluntary as a national gathering – gave them the character of one among many *cultic associations*;[35] in major cities, where the intellectual elite was being appealed to by Stoics, Cynics, Epicureans and the rest, it was not absurd to regard the synagogue as the *school* of a rival philosophy, and as such it plainly exerted a strong influence on many.[36]

So with this idiosyncratic aspect, overflowing the traditional categories of social organisation, the synagogue was by the first century a thoroughly established institution in most cities and towns of the Mediterranean basin, and many Jewish communities had long passed beyond meeting in houses, even houses converted to permanent public use, and had been given, or permitted to build, specially designed synagogues.[37] At Sardis, in Asia Minor, the publicly donated synagogue was the largest building in the city. The problems of assimilating so large and exclusive a minority had, it seems, been overcome in most places, and antisemitic rioting, once widespread, was now a rare occurrence. Many wealthy Jews were prominent in the affairs of their cities.[38]

Yet, despite these signs that the Jews had been accepted as a normal (though special) part of the life of the πόλις, their legal status remained ambiguous.[39] Jews were not permitted to own land since

[33] For a fuller treatment of the sociological categories referred to here, and the way Jews and Christians related to them, see Meeks, *Urban Christians*, pp. 75–84. On the household, see Judge, *Social Pattern*, pp. 30ff.

[34] See S. Safrai and M. Stern (eds.), *The Jewish People in the First Century* (2 vols., Assen, 1974/6), vol. II, pp. 716f.

[35] See MacMullen, *Roman Social Relations*, p. 83; Safrai and Stern, *Jewish People*, vol. I, p. 464; Judge, *Social Pattern*, pp. 40ff.

[36] On Jewish proselytism, see S. Sandmel, *Judaism and Christian Beginnings* (New York, 1978), pp. 228–36.

[37] Safrai and Stern, *Jewish People*, vol. I, pp. 478ff.

[38] On the social status of Jews, see Safrai and Stern, *Jewish People*, vol. II, pp. 701–27.

[39] Safrai and Stern, *Jewish People*, vol. I, pp. 420–63.

(with a few individual exceptions) they were not citizens (πολῖται) of the cities they lived in; but nor were they simply classified as resident aliens (πάροικοι or μέτοικοι). Strabo, for instance, cites four groups in the population:[40] citizens, metics (μέτοικοι), slaves, Jews. Referring to the Jews in Alexandria, Josephus claimed that they had been granted the privileges of ἰσοπολιτεία and ἰσοτελεία:[41] of these the first is 'honorary citizenship', such as was reciprocally offered to each other's citizens by states linked by treaty, while the second, 'equality of taxation', was an exemption, sometimes offered to favoured foreign residents, from the usual tax-disabilities of aliens. So in the legal sphere, too, we see the accustomed categories being stretched to accommodate the peculiar position of the Jews who, though not part of the citizen body, enjoyed many of the outward features of that status.

The simplest, and therefore the most serviceable, analogy was provided by the Jewish military colonies set up under the Ptolemies in rural areas of Egypt and Asia Minor which had, for practical purposes, been granted self-government as πολιτεύματα.[42] Though the pattern was not yet uniform throughout the Empire, it was increasingly the case that the Jews were regarded as holding a 'parallel citizenship', and constituting a self-governing πολίτευμα within the πόλις.[43] Similarly, on the larger scale, the very rigidity of the Jews' self-definition and entry-requirements compensated for the indeterminacy of their legal position, and made it possible for the Emperors to treat them, in practice, as a special case, as though they were a *nation* granted treaty rights. The synagogue was specifically exempted, for example, from the Julian law abolishing *collegia* (that is, cultic and other 'voluntary associations'),[44] and regular decrees freed individuals from the obligation to observe local and imperial cults.[45] A not inconsiderable factor in the rise of proselytism was the advantage offered by this special status to those who were not citizens, particularly slaves, freedmen and metics; conversely, citizens attracted to Judaism found the exclusiveness of the Jewish rules regarding food and sabbath observance incompatible with normal

---

[40] Safrai and Stern, *Jewish People*, vol. II, p. 445.
[41] Safrai and Stern, *Jewish People*, vol. I, pp. 434ff.
[42] *Ibid.*, pp. 426f.
[43] *Ibid.*, pp. 450–4.
[44] *Ibid.*, p. 459. This is the main confirmation that it was as *collegia* that the synagogues (as opposed to the communities) were legally classified by the Roman authorities.
[45] Safrai and Stern, *Jewish People*, vol. I, pp. 450–9.

life, and were more likely to remain in the uncommitted status of 'Godfearer'.[46]

Sects in Judaism

If our 'Hebrews' are Jews, and Jews in conflict with their neighbours, it is relevant to ask how uniform, in fact, was the Jewish community in the Diaspora once it had, as described, carved out a place for itself in Greek society. To what extent, before the advent of the Christian mission, was it possible for Jews to hold unorthodox opinions and remain within the synagogue? Firm evidence of theological debate within Judaism outside Palestine is lacking for our period, but we must suppose that the currents represented by Pharisaism and Qumran were not confined to Palestine but reproduced in varied fashion in the Diaspora, not necessarily in the formation of distinct groups, but at least in factional arguments.[47]

At this point it will be useful to adopt E. P. Sanders' distinction between 'sect' and 'party' according to degrees of 'soteriological exclusivism'; that is, the difference between those who 'deny salvation to all but the members of the group' (a 'sect') and those who 'simply say that all in the community *should* agree with the party tenets'.[48] Sanders concludes that 'in this sense, the only definitely sectarian literature is the Dead Sea Scrolls',[49] the refusal of the community that produced them to recognise non-members as part of Israel being matched by their physical withdrawal into the desert. But we should notice that the Pharisees, though they did not regard the 'people of the land' as excluded from Israel, refused, for reasons of ritual purity, to associate with them:[50] how would that conceptual distinction, neat enough on paper, be expressed in practice? If there were groups with Essene sympathies in the Diaspora, what level of outward separation, if any, did they seek? Does the existence of synagogues 'of the Hebrews' in Rome and Corinth signify a closed association of Essene or other purists, or is it merely the residual description of

[46] For evidence of the different origins of proselytes and Godfearers, see Theissen, *Social Setting*, pp. 102–4.

[47] See M. Simon, *Jewish Sects at the Time of Jesus* (Philadelphia, 1967), pp. 9ff, 96ff.

[48] E. P. Sanders, *Paul and Palestinian Judaism* (London, 1977), p. 425. This definition of 'sect', which concerns their boundaries, and their membership of wider categories, is of course quite different from that of Wilson quoted earlier, based on a particular 'response to the world' and used to determine the *inner* characteristics of religious groups.

[49] *Ibid.*, p. 425.

[50] *Ibid.*, pp. 152–7, 425.

the first meeting place of Jews there?[51] On the evidence we possess, we can only say that the primary cause of the multiplication of synagogues was the growth in numbers, and that, in the names and other associations of the ten or more synagogues known to have existed in Rome, none apart from the 'Hebrews' carries any theological overtones whatever. If in Palestine the differences were, with the extreme exception of the Qumran sect, those between *parties*, the pressure to remain in communion must have been far more intense in the conditions of the Diaspora where those who were divided by theology were still united by family and commercial ties and by physically sharing the same small space. So far as we can tell, differences remained internal, even in the great cities, under a central organisation.

In principle, then, there was room for Christianity as a party or sect within Israel. Like any new group attracting adherents from among the members of several existing groups, though, its effect would be to unsettle long-standing loyalties and 'set father against son' (Luke 12:53) − a situation reflected in Acts 6 to 7, where not his affirmation of Jesus as the Christ but his radical critique of the Temple cultus causes the death of the 'Hellenist' Stephen by mob violence at the hands of the 'Hebrews'. With Paul, too, it was not his affirmation of Jesus as Messiah but his insistence that, since the crucifixion, 'all who rely on works of the Law are under a curse' (Gal. 3:10), which set him apart from his countrymen. His letters show the difficulty he found in persuading his churches to stick to this line, against the temptation (for any, probably the majority, who were Jews by birth or conversion) to return to worshipping with their friends and families in the synagogue, and thus to end the (often, surely, intolerable) tension of living and working among them as aliens and deniers of God.

Exclusion and belonging

Citizens and exiles

The readers of this letter, then, have found themselves excluded from their community as betrayers of their race, culture and religion, and exposed to the bitter force of the pariah group's suppressed resentment. Nor is there any escape from this exposed position. Too literal

[51] See H. J. Leon, *The Jews of Ancient Rome* (Philadelphia, 1960), pp. 147−9; M. Black, *The Scrolls and Christian Origins* (London, 1961), pp. 78f.

a reading of the imagery of isolation and geographical movement in
Hebrews 11, including an emphasis on its vision of the 'pilgrim
church',[52] can easily miss the point: in a sense, the plight of these
readers would be less severe if they were really wandering, for though
they would face the dangers and distresses of the wilderness their
distinctness would be less in doubt. It is those who remain in the
city, in possession of their (plundered) homes, surrounded by hostile
'sinners' (12:3), who require encouragement by being shown that
Abraham, Isaac and the rest shared their situation, *having and yet
not having* (compare Abraham who 'sojourned in the land of promise
as in a foreign land', 11:9), who likewise sacrificed a definite state
in exchange only for a promise of a new 'city' and 'homeland'. In
comparison with their position, the image of 'hopeful pilgrims'
may be sheer sentimentality. What defines a 'sojourner' is neither
nomadism nor loneliness but *lack of rights*,[53] living on sufferance
and at the mercy of the strong, and having no justice to which he
or she can appeal in distress. Perhaps not in law, but in experience,
this appears to have been the position of many early Christians,
including these readers, strangers in their own street and denied the
friendship and cooperation of their neighbours. But the legal image
may be literally accurate, too. A Jewish πολίτευμα was for the
most part self-governing: to whom could a Jewish Christian appeal
for redress if beaten up or robbed, but to the γερουσία or other
governing body of the Jewish community? Would the city authorities
listen to an appeal on such a charge against their verdict? How much
more likely that the court should view Christians as 'troublemakers'
and turn a blind eye (Acts 18:12–17) or lock them up (Acts 16:19–24;
Heb. 10:34; 13:3).

In these circumstances, they could not help but be bitterly aware
that with their distinctive feast day and style of worship, their closed
meetings in private homes, their vulnerability to verbal, commercial
and physical attack from their neighbours, richer, more numerous
and more secure, they were as Christians recreating among the established Jewish community the story of the early Jewish settlers among
the indigenous pagans, and, having set themselves effectively outside
their πολίτευμα, the battle for citizen's rights must begin all over
again. They might well recall (as the Septuagintal translation of

[52] But see W. G. Johnsson, 'The pilgrimage motif in the Book of Hebrews', *JBL*,
97 (1978), 239–51 for a good phenomenologically based study of the letter from this
point of view.
[53] Hence Torah's insistence on the duty to *protect* the stranger, Lev. 19:37f.

Genesis 14:13 suggests the third-century Diaspora had recalled) that 'Hebrew' means 'outsider'.[54] If so, the author is wise to affirm precisely that aspect of their experience as definitive of Israel's past. Like the patriarchs, they are 'strangers and exiles' (ξένοι καὶ παρεπίδημοι, 11:13) by choice, having responded to God's call, and the place where they sojourn is therefore — as faith (but only faith) reveals — 'the land of promise' (11:9). But accepting their exile is only the beginning of the story. Like the patriarchs they are not shunning the city but seeking a 'city with foundations' (11:10), and unlike the patriarchs they will find it (11:40): under the new covenant, the neighbour and brother who shares their knowledge of God's Law 'written on the heart' will be a *fellow-citizen* (πολίτης, 8:11).[55] Indeed, it is not even future: 'You *have come*', they are told, 'to Mount Zion and the city of the living God.' In what way can that bold assertion be given substance?

Standing at the centre of social organisation, the πόλις acted as the symbolic focus of many values: the source of all things Greek, whether admired or loathed, the source of wealth and tax demands, of enlightened philosophy and pagan idolatry, of civilised manners and immoral corruption.[56] In this matter, rabbinic Judaism occupied a somewhat ambivalent position, between contempt for rustic god-lessness and horror at Hellenistic idolatry: though Jerusalem had many of the advantages of civilised living, attempts to turn it into a πόλις on the Greek plan were strongly resisted, with bitter memories of the Maccabean revolt; the recently built πόλεις like Sebaste and Tiberias were, so the gospels suggest, pointedly avoided by Jesus.[57] This attitude is less in evidence, of course, among the predominantly city-dwelling Jews outside Palestine, but it appears in the mistrust of the city's luxury shown in Hebrews 11:24ff, and more clearly in the signs that the Christians, like the Essenes, were longing for the advent of *God's* city, the New Jerusalem where God could be truly worshipped in a renewed Temple, or without need of any Temple

---

[54] Gen. 14:13 (LXX) translates Abram *the Habiru* as Abram ὁ πηράτης, the foreigner. See Spicq, *Hébreux*, vol. I, pp. 243ff; J. Lewy: 'The origin and significance of the biblical term "Hebrew" ', *HUCA*, 28 (1957), 7f. Is it only coincidence that this rendering occurs in the same chapter of Genesis as Abram's meeting with the outsider, Melchizedek?

[55] Here, unusually, Hebrews follows the B-text of Jer. 38:34 (LXX). The LXX A-text reads πλησίον, neighbour.

[56] See Judge, *Social Pattern*, pp. 1–29; Tidball, *Introduction*, pp. 76–9.

[57] See Ste Croix, 'Early Christian attitudes', pp. 1ff; Theissen, *First Followers*, pp. 47f, 51f.

(Rev. 21,22; cf. John 4:23). Though the vision of a future or heavenly New Jerusalem features in many strands of the New Testament writings, the claim to see God's city as a *present* reality, with which the argument of Hebrews culminates, is understandably unique. However, the city offers through its *citizenship* a wider and less exact form of identity to those who live under its sway but outside its walls, and the New Testament more commonly asserts that in Christ a new citizenship has been established, which is indeed a present reality. In Ephesians 2:12, the Gentile readers are reminded that they formerly were excluded from God's πολιτεία, but have now been granted membership as fellow-citizens (συμπολῖται) with the saints (2:19). Similarly, 1 Peter 2:9f reminds its readers, 'once you were no people but now you are God's people' (λαὸς θεοῦ), and confers on them epithets appropriate to Israel, 'a chosen race, a royal priesthood, a holy nation', though by immediately appealing to them 'as aliens and exiles' (ὡς παροίκους καὶ παρεπιδήμους, 2:11) the inescapable tension of their status is restored. In this eschatological perspective, too, Philippians 3:20 loses its apparently Platonic character: 'our citizenship (πολίτευμα) is in heaven' and 'from it we await our Saviour', but the context is the transformation of 'our lowly body' through participation in Christ's resurrection, not the earthly exile of heavenly souls.

It is the burden of the argument of Hebrews that salvation is present as well as future, that the 'age to come' is already a reality: the Christians have already tasted 'the powers of the age to come' (6:5); they are entering God's sabbath rest (4:3); they have a high priest of the new order (4:14; 8:1; 10:21). In searching for an adequate vehicle for this message, it seems that this author, too, was wary of asserting too often or too unambiguously the visible existence of so solid an object as the heavenly city; on the other hand citizenship, though more conceivable, is perhaps too abstract to effect its purpose. The *household*, though, provided a term through which the author could pursue simultaneously a literal and a metaphorical description of the church as the end-time community.

The household of God

Οἶκος, οἰκία and their cognates have a wide range of meaning, of which the centre is the extended family and its dwelling place.[58]

---

[58] On the household and its Christian function, see Meeks, pp. 75–7; Judge,

Since the family would regularly include several generations, a constellation of nuclear families, together with domestic slaves and, in poor households, cattle, all under one roof,[59] the word could by natural extension mean clan, tribe, the whole 'house of Israel'. The values it touches on are similarly varied, and we shall need to consider related language of property and inheritance, genealogy and authority, sharing and responsibility. The persistence of the household as the basic unit of Mediterranean social and political organisation is one of those factors early lost sight of among the dominant republican ideals of the city. In Palestine and other rural areas, even if economic conditions tended to lead to the break-up of the multicellular family on its independent smallholding,[60] and to the formation of large estates run by stewards and worked by hired labourers, the household still provided the focus of personal values with certain distinctive tendencies: the blending of economic, family and friendship relations; stability over time; intimacy and a relative lack of class-distinctions; the authority of customary morality and of the head of the family.

This is to cast it as an ideal. Of course intimacy, stability and absolute authority may as easily be experienced as squalor, stagnation and parental tyranny, but there is much to suggest that, whatever the empirical reality, it was indeed functioning, in the first century, as an ideal of a lost harmonious way of life. For instance, it may be argued that the Caesars, in establishing their dynasty, were reasserting for the Roman aristocracy and urban proletariat the ancient authority of the paterfamilias and a familial ordering of society, over against the imported and never naturalised Greek republican virtues.[61] Likewise, in Palestine the Hellenistic cities were much distrusted, and seldom visited by Jesus, whose teaching assumes an older set of values: God as Abba, Father; his disciples as sons and brothers bound to him and to each other by a common meal; an ethic of mutual service and brotherly love. This is the dynamic of the parable of the Prodigal Son, and the basis of Paul's theology of adoption as sons. In physical terms, too, the Christian church originated in

'Social Identity', pp. 215–17; Judge, *Social Pattern*, pp. 30–9; Malherbe, *Social Aspects*, pp. 66–70; Tidball, *Introduction*, pp. 79ff.

[59] MacMullen, *Roman Social Relations*, pp. 7ff, cites two contemporary Egyptian households with twenty-six and twenty-four members each, the latter comprising three related nuclear families plus a tenant and his wife and children.

[60] On the decline of peasant farming during the Empire, see M. I. Finley, *The Ancient Economy* (London, 1973), pp. 105ff.

[61] Judge, *Social Pattern*, pp. 31ff.

such a group, small enough to gather in an upper room; and the domestic setting of early Christian worship, unlike the synagogue with its gallery and its customary distinctions of status, encouraged the recognition that among the baptised 'there is neither Jew nor Greek, there is neither slave nor free, there is neither male nor female' (Gal. 3:28). The conversion of whole households together (Acts 11:14f; 16:33; 1 Cor. 1:16; 16:15) and the assimilation of individual converts, for the purposes of worship, into household groups under the leadership of the wealthier members as hosts and patriarchs (Rom. 16:3–5, 23; 1 Cor. 16:19), laid the foundations of the first Christian communities.[62]

Not only in theory, then, the Christian gospel was offering a revolutionary return to a personal ordering of society, based neither on hierarchy nor on equality but on sharing, belonging, as slaves and sons (the distinction no longer mattering) of the same heavenly Father.[63] In the light of this argument, it is necessary to review the value of the *Haustafeln*, which it is now usual to regard, when they appear in the ethical sections of the later epistles, as a sign of the reabsorption of the church into the world of bourgeois Hellenistic morality. This view has never commanded universal assent, and an alternative (well argued by Elliott in relation to 1 Peter[64]) is to see the household code, though frequently couched in conventional terms, as an expression of the obligations intrinsic to living together in the most natural and God-given way, as a household of all ages and types, and therefore as a proper and positive enunciation of the principles of Christian discipleship.

We may envisage these 'Hebrews', then, like other local churches, meeting in private houses in mixed groups of relatives, friends and servants, each one a quasi-household. Whether these households are isolated to the extent of being one to a town, or whether each locality might contain several, is unclear, but οἶκος is certainly the author's primary group-concept, for it appears in Hebrews ten times (more than in any other letter) and in contrast to Paul the term ἐκκλησία occurs only twice: in the first instance, quoted from Psalm 22:22, it refers to the assembly of God's people (Heb. 2:12); in the second

---

[62] F. V. Filson, 'The significance of the early house churches', *JBL*, 58 (1939), 105–12, is a pioneering and still extremely valuable study of 'the actual physical conditions under which the first Christians met and lived'. See also Judge, 'Social identity', pp. 215ff; Malherbe, *Social Aspects*, pp. 60ff.

[63] See Malherbe, *Social Aspects*, ch. 4, especially pp. 85ff.

[64] Elliott, *Home*, pp. 208ff. See also Malherbe, *Social Aspects*, pp. 51–3.

(12:23) it is describing what we may call the plenary session of the church, the heavenly assembly of the saints and angels. When referring to the church as a present reality, it is always a *house*. But does it not have a figurative, cultic sense? Despite the fact that the New Testament does elsewhere refer to the church under the metaphor of a new Temple (1 Cor. 3:16; Eph. 2:18ff) and the fact that the Temple can be called the 'house of God' (οἶκος τοῦ θεοῦ), and despite the fact that Hebrews is very interested in cultic matters, the term refers here to the community, without any cultic overtones, except where these are made explicit.[65] None of the ten appearances conveys an unambiguously cultic sense. In 11:7, when Noah's οἶκος is saved from the Flood, it means 'family'; in 8:8–10, when a new covenant is promised to the House of Judah and the House of Israel, it means 'nation'. In 3:2–6 the word appears five times as *God's house*, formerly ruled by Moses, the faithful steward, but now by Jesus, the Son – the same house, which formerly was Israel, but now 'we are his house' (3:6). Moses is not acting as a priest, though, and nor, though he has just been described as 'apostle and high priest' (3:1), is this part of Jesus' *priestly* role: like Moses, Jesus is here acting as a secular leader of the 'nation'. The only apparently cultic use of the term appears in 10:21 where, at the conclusion of the central priestly argument, the author announced 'we have a great priest over the house of God'; yet it is precisely at this point that the hortatory language of 3:6 is reappearing, so that the readers are addressed simultaneously as suppliants approaching their mediating priest (οἶκος = heavenly sanctuary) and as God's people (οἶκος = the new nation of the saved) advancing confidently under Jesus' leadership.

As well as the cultic, the physical side of houses is mainly avoided in the letter: Christians should accept loss of their property joyfully (10:34); should have no homeland (11:14) nor city (11:13,16; 13:14) except in heaven; should regard Abraham the tent-dwelling exile as their model. On the other hand, households as communities and as genealogies are strongly stressed, and affect much of the epistle's thought. This distinction is embodied, for instance, in the concept of 'faith' set out in chapter 11: becoming God's house by putting no trust in earthly houses. That chapter offers also a celebration of the ancient nomadic way of life of the Hebrew people, with an interest in the blessings bestowed by fathers upon sons, and the natural

[65] See Elliott, *Home*, pp. 241f (n. 29), pp. 249f (n. 99). In this respect, Hebrews and 1 Peter are very close.

affection of kinship such as is displayed by Moses and his parents. Yet family as such can be as much a false 'homeland' as anything, and Christ's priesthood is derived not from Aaron's line but from God, like Melchizedek who was 'without father, without mother, without genealogy' (7:3). The blessings mentioned in Hebrews 11 are equally unnatural: those of Jacob and Esau, of Joseph's sons, of Cain and Abel, were all reversed, the younger receiving the firstborn's blessing, for this is *God's* house, and divine election and sonship is not the same as human. Furthermore, *all* mere bodily descent is relativised by Abraham's willingness, at God's command, to offer up Isaac, his only hope of founding a 'house'. The value of the house is affirmed, but membership is by divine election, not by birth.[66]

On the ethical plane, too, the church is conceived as a household, and much of the language construed as the 'fraternal ethic' of the sect, in an earlier section,[67] is equally applicable to the extended family settlement in which, within a patriarchal structure, adult males meet and work together as brothers, adult females as sisters, precise details of blood relationship being less important for practical purposes than active membership of the group. The readers are 'sons' (12:5) and 'children' (2:14), and Jesus is their 'brother' (2:17), the 'firstborn' (1:6) − though indeed they are all to be among the assembly of the firstborn (ἐκκλησία πρωτοτόκων, 12:23), unless like Esau they sell their birthright (τὰ πρωτοτόκια, 12:16). They are also Jesus' 'comrades' (μέτοχοι, 1:9) and he shares (μετέσχεν) the same nature with those who have their 'flesh and blood' in common (κεκοινώνεκεν, 2:14). Similarly, there is a major emphasis on the gifts they share with each other (a heavenly call, 3:1; Christ, 3:14; the Holy Spirit, 6:14; God's fatherly discipline, 12:8), and the sufferings they should share with imprisoned and persecuted brothers, thus displaying their 'brotherly love' (φιλαδελφία, 13:1). Hospitality to strangers is urged too in 13:1, and in 11:31 it is implicit in the praise of Rahab the harlot whose 'friendly welcome' is, surprisingly, no commercial transaction but faithfulness to the laws of hospitality (a point echoed in 1 Clement 12).[68] All these are intrinsic to the idea of the church as household. So too, though they have not appeared in detail before and might be regarded as merely conventional appeals to bourgeois values, are the other ethical topics of chapter 13: the

[66] On election, see pp. 156−60, 177−86, 203−9 below; on the sacrifice of Isaac, see further ch. 5, pp. 173−81 and ch. 6 *passim*.

[67] See p. 20 above.

[68] On Rahab, see further pp. 153−6 below.

need to respect leaders (13:7, 17), and to avoid marital infidelity and
the dangerous fascination of money and novel teachings (13:4, 5, 9).

Symbols of identity

So far as we can reconstruct it, and whatever their precise situation,
the community revealed in the letter seems to be a group of small
churches suffering from persecution from outside and disillusionment
and doubt within, and which is therefore tending to lose its hard
edges and its firm centre. In these circumstances, these Christians
need more than the verbal assurance that, as voluntary exiles, they
share the experience and the promise of Abraham and the patriarchs
– for this 'exile', though currently critical, is only a part of their
experience, and not the defining part. More positively, as a vehicle
for their sense of identity, the author offers them the rich concept
of the household, a household of God in the intimate sense and,
on the larger scale, a nation which has replaced Israel in divine favour.
For these legitimating manoeuvres[69] to be effective, it is essential
that the readers should recognise that they are *already* a household,
and identify themselves as such, even if negatively – a mere family
of Christians among a thousand hostile pagans and Jews. On this
basis the author is able to develop, as we have seen, a positive understanding of what it means for the church to be a family, and beyond
that to offer a theological proof that this is truly the house of *God*
and therefore a 'kingdom of priests' (Exod. 19:6) able to accompany
Christ into the heavenly sanctuary.

Unlike 1 Peter, Revelation and the Dead Sea Scrolls, the author
desists from actually calling the readers a 'kingdom of priests',[70] but
the book offers a view of the fulfilment of the Torah in Christ which
has much in common with these others. The vexed question of influences and associations cannot be pursued here,[71] but it is no

[69] On legislation, see Berger, *Social Reality*, pp. 29ff.
[70] See further below, pp. 234–7, 258f.
[71] On the general question of the relation of early Christianity to the Scrolls and
the Qumran community, see M. Black, *The Scrolls and Christian Origins* (London,
1961); W. D. Davies, *Christian Origins and Judaism* (London, 1962), pp. 97–117;
D. Howlett, *The Essenes and Christianity* (New York, 1957); D. Flusser, 'The Dead
Sea sect and pre-Pauline Christianity', *Scripta Hierosolymitana*, 4 (1958), 215–66.
On the place of Hebrews, see Y. Yadin, 'The Dead Sea Scrolls and the Epistle to the
Hebrews', *Scripta Hierosolymitana*, 4 (1958), 36–55; F. F. Bruce, ' "To the Hebrews"
or "To the Essenes"?', *NTS*, 9 (1963), 217–32; L. D. Hurst, *The Epistle to the
Hebrews: Its Background of Thought* (Cambridge, 1990), pp. 43–66. See further the
discussion on Melchizedek below.

accident that, in looking for a renewed and purified cultus, Hebrews, like the Dead Sea Scrolls and like Stephen's speech in Acts 7, refers exclusively to the Tent and not the Jerusalem Temple; nor that Acts 7, in denouncing the idea that God dwells in a 'house made with hands' (7:48) makes much of the multiple senses of οἶκος and its cognates, as does the Old Testament source of this critique, Nathan's denunciation of David in 2 Samuel 7. In sum, the true 'house of God' is not a princely palace nor a princely dynasty (however messianic), nor a temple or a priesthood, but the community (not in itself either princely or priestly) which identifies itself by him who, like Melchizedek, is both priest and king, and whose palace and sanctuary is in heaven.

Further, lest this spiritualised cultus seem more abstract and distant than the old, corrupt earthly one, Hebrews insists that it has also been personalised, and become closer and more immediate. In place of a subpersonal transactional system based on 'blood', there is the sole mediation of Jesus himself as High Priest, who bids people to 'draw near', and who is himself 'beset with weakness', 'only without sin' (10:22; 5:2; 4:15). Jesus is thus the restoration of the individual and informal priestly mediation witnessed to in early parts of the Old Testament (for example, Eli in 1 Sam. 1:6–18). But behind the time of local shrines the Old Testament reflects an even more primitive right of the *householder* or clan chief to act as priest for his people and make offerings on their behalf (Gen. 31:54; 46:1), a right retained later by the king (1 Sam. 14:31–5; 2 Sam. 6:17–20; 24:25; 1 Kgs. 3:15).[72] The symbol for this understanding of priesthood is the figure of Melchizedek (though confirmed in the depiction of Moses and Abraham) – Melchizedek who, both historically and Christologically, represents a time when the priest-king rules a nation of secular priests.[73]

To a community conscious of itself as cut off from its social and religious past and uncertain of its future, the author offers a three-fold identity, by means of three stories so intertwined as to become three phases or aspects of one story, their own continuing past and present pointing to a possible future. The three narratives are, first, the tales of ancient Israel, especially Abraham, Melchizedek and Moses; second, the suffering, death and heavenly intercession of Jesus; and third, the readers' own sufferings, remembered and

[72] On this alternative conception of priesthood, see below, pp. 104f, 256–60.
[73] On Melchizedek, see further below, pp. 164–8.

present, with their responses. These do not represent a contrast between past and present, however, as each story contains a present aspect: the readers' current sufferings, Jesus' intercession in the heavenly shrine on behalf of those who suffer, and the experienced identification of the persecuted readers with the homeless patriarchs, and with their trust in God's promise.

All these narratives are full of tension and contradiction: the joyful suffering of the readers (10:34) and of Jesus (12:2); his being at once the reflection of the glory of God (1:3) and of flesh and blood in its weakness (2:14); the faith of the patriarchs which sustains and contradicts their 'aimlessness'. In all of these, God's tradition and his community are under threat, and survive only through faith. The first and third tales carry dire warnings in the death of Moses and the wilderness generation, and in the vehement promise to those now tempted by apostasy that 'our God is a consuming fire' (12:28); in the second and defining story, however, death is transformed into hope (2:14–18; 5:7–9; 12:2). There are tales of good things possessed here, too, but never wholly without a continued seeking: the city seen by the patriarchs 'from afar' by faith and to which this genera-tion, if it too has faith, has come; the throne at the right hand of God that is the reward of enduring the cross; the 'good things' that 'have come', according to some, or perhaps are still 'to come' (9:11).[74]

These stories are fullblooded enough to found a community on, but none of them is easy, and in that way they symbolise the tense place of these churches, between hope and fear, salvation grasped and lost. In chapter 7, Abraham, the exile and yet the bearer of God's tradition and his promise for Israel (6:13–15), meets Melchizedek, who stands outside all genealogies, communities and traditions and yet is king and priest of God Most High: on such enigmatic moments, and what they say about the character of God's anointed and his people, the text bids these vulnerable Christians meditate, and so maintain their point of balance.

---

[74] See the discussion by H. W. Attridge, *The Epistle to the Hebrews* (Philadelphia, 1989), pp. 244f τῶν γενομένων ἀγαθῶν seems to be the harder reading, and to accord better with the eschatology of the letter (despite Montefiore, *Hebrews*, p. 151). Thus Johnsson, 'Defilement and purgation', p. 290; Westcott, *Hebrews*, pp. 255f.

PART II

STRUCTURALISM

2

HEBREWS AND STRUCTURAL ANALYSIS

Contexts and meanings

Chapter 1 has offered, as an alternative to historical criticism, one way of reading Hebrews which seeks to be holistic and intratextual, via the community presented in the text. In this chapter it will be argued that the sacrificial symbolism of the book cries even more stridently for an holistic approach, such as can be provided by anthropological studies of religion. To do so, it is necessary to enter into the debate about contexts of interpretation. Contextual issues reach far down into the interpretative process, from exegetical questions about cultural, historical and philosophical 'background' to methodological discussions about the disjunction between the 'horizons' of ancient texts and their modern readers, and whether it is necessary, or possible, for these horizons to become 'fused'.

One recent provocative proposal about contexts in Biblical criticism is that of Brevard Childs. Since he also reaches the conclusion that historical criticism, however excellent, has not materially assisted the reading of Hebrews,[1] it will be helpful at the outset to show why 'canonical criticism', though likewise holistic, integrative and hermeneutical in form, is not the solution towards which this argument is tending.

In *The New Testament as Canon*, Childs questions the adequacy of critical scholarship in general in four main respects:[2] first, its assumption that 'the historical critical approach is suitable, indeed, mandatory for every correct reading of the Bible'; second, the failure of a 'uniformly historical-referential reading of the Biblical text' to deal with the 'multi-dimensional theological reality' to which the Bible bears witness; third, the domination of 'an approach which identifies the key to a text's meaning with a determination of its historical origin'; fourth, the separation of the 'descriptive' from

---

[1] B.S. Childs, *The New Testament as Canon: An Introduction* (London, 1984), pp. 400–18.
[2] *Ibid.*, pp. 35–7.

the 'hermeneutical task of interpretation ... as if to determine what a text meant and what it means could be neatly isolated'. All these assumptions about the primacy of the historical have been called into question here, in the course of reviewing the problems of scholarship on Hebrews; nonetheless, Childs' concept of 'canon' will not help, for several reasons. When Childs identifies the 'canonical sense' of a text with its 'plain meaning',[3] he shifts the ground of signification from history to theology, but retains a unitary conception of 'meaning', making no allowance for the necessity of a plurality of meanings in the development of theological interpretation over time – unless, inconsistently, it is this that he is envisaging when he says the scriptures 'do not serve as a frozen deposit of tradition or doctrine, but [as] a living vehicle through which the will of God is perceived'.[4] Second, he equates the meaning of the Bible with conscious perception of meaning, as when he criticises Dunn for posing 'tensions within the canon which historically were often never thus perceived':[5] this not only reiterates his unitary concept of meaning, and the limitation of meaning to the contents of consciousness, but also, incidentally and paradoxically, expresses his preference for an historical reconstruction of 'how the material was actually heard' over a reading which allows it to be a complex 'multi-dimensional theological reality'.

Childs' comments on Hebrews itself, in the light of this conception of 'canon', do not carry us very far into the meaning of the book. One of the chief functions of the canon (not discussed by Childs) was and is to provide an overarching context of Christian meaning for the very varied contents of the New Testament. That is, the New Testament texts tend to operate at several levels of generality, from the specifically factual ('When you come, bring the cloak that I left with Carpus at Troas', 2 Tim. 4:13) through general commands ('Pray constantly', 1 Thess. 5:17) and doctrinal applications ('Have this mind among yourselves which is yours in Christ Jesus', Phil. 2:5) to symbolic theological reflection ('Christ is the image of the unseen God, the first-born of all creation', Col. 1:15), and reading the text involves some awareness of these levels and the way they interact. Even ruling out of account the lowest level of generality (abstaining from interpreting Paul's cloak) all the lower levels depend on being taken up into the higher levels for their value: thus St Paul's injunction that 'the women should keep silent in the churches' (1 Cor.

[3] *Ibid.*, p. 24.   [4] *Ibid.*, p. 40.   [5] *Ibid.*, p. 29.

14:34) has to be related, not only to other such statements and to the philological and social background, but also to general principles of Christian social and sexual organisation, and to the anthropology implicit in Christ's incarnation 'in the likeness of sinful flesh' (Rom. 8:3). Since few New Testament books can provide the full range of this coherence on their own,[6] the church has always treated individual books as part of the higher unity of the canon, and so leaves open the possibility of a low-level command in one book being supported by a theological principle in another. Such a procedure is called in question by critical awareness of the historical development of the New Testament, and the differences between its authors – though it may still be legitimate if we can argue that, say, James *would* have supported a remark in a certain fashion (and given the fragmentary and unsystematic nature of the literature this is an expedient to which we are bound frequently to turn). The canon acquires the function of providing a larger unity, a doctrinal control-system by which the idiosyncrasies and omissions of individual authors can be adjusted and redressed. But, whether the synthesis at which we arrive is pre- or post-critical, it is an artificial construct.

The claim for the distinctiveness of Hebrews, by which is meant its need of special treatment, rests on two foundations. First, it can stand alone, in virtue of its historical isolation and having in itself (in common with a small number of other New Testament books) a coherent relation between all its levels of generality; second, the control-system operative at its highest level appeals beyond any system of 'Christian doctrine' to the divinely authorised symbolic network of the Old Testament sacrificial cultus.

The final chapter provides a good test for the claim of coherence. Those who believe it to be an addition to the main body of the book have sometimes understood this passage as a bid for Pauline authorship,[7] due less to its reference to Timothy (13:23) than to its lapse, characteristic of the Pauline corpus, into detached advice and commendations. Whatever the merits of this argument, it does highlight the difference of the first twelve chapters in this respect. They contain much hortatory material (comprising at least 2:1–4, ch. 3f, 5:11–6:12, 10:19–39, ch. 12) and indeed the letter is described (though in chapter 13) as a 'word of exhortation' (13:22), yet all of this is closely

---

[6] This is particularly true of the later epistles with their tendency to append lists of moral platitudes only loosely related to Christian theology (compare Col. 3:18–4:6 and 1 Tim. 5 with Eph. 5:21–33 in this respect).

[7] For example, W. Wrede, cf. Moffatt, *Hebrews*, p. xxix.

integrated with the (chiefly cultic) patterns of symbolism, that is, rooted in the church and the redemption offered by Christ. Only in Hebrews 13 is there any suggestion of a neutral and free-standing morality to which Christians should subscribe.[8] The hortatory and discursive sections belong together: the exhortations are not practical applications of a theological theory; nor is the theology an abstract development from the concrete advice. We see here a thoughtful application to this specific situation of a fully formed theological outlook: hence the 'sacrificial' conception has given rise to specific theoretical and practical arguments to meet a concrete need. Whether the 'outlook' preceded the author's knowledge of the situation cannot be perceived, but of the text as it stands only the scriptural quotations can be said to have had a prior existence. The book is conceived and written as a whole, the hortatory passages so fully involved with the theological thought as to seem to create it.

When their classical background predisposed an earlier generation of biblical scholars to see in Hebrews' echoes of Philo an underlying Neoplatonic outlook, they were responding to the same impulse to read the book in isolation from the rest of the New Testament as a self-contained treatise; and its attitude to time, different in several respects from St Paul's, made it possible to think of the book as using, without really belonging to, the Jewish tradition. But the Philonic influence is relatively superficial. Though Hebrews exhibits Alexandrian terminology and a dualistic thought-pattern of earthly and heavenly, copy and real, many and one, in every case the substance of the thought is Jewish: these are really comparisons of the sinful and the holy, the provisional and the permanent.[9] As well as having an historical aspect it is essentially concrete, concerned with human persons, not souls; Jesus Christ, not a redeeming spirit; a new covenant between humanity and God, not escape from the material. The Hellenistic element overlays a mind thinking in the categories of the Old Testament cultus, with its contrasts between

[8] Only the possibility of assigning a separate origin for this chapter, however, makes this 'morality' even a 'suggestion': if the book is read as a unity, only v. 4 and vv. 17–19 receive no explicit or implicit support from Heb. 1–12.

[9] The best study of the book's eschatology is still Barrett, 'Eschatology'. For differing views on the 'Philonic' character of the letter's thought, compare Spicq, *Hébreux*, vol. I, pp. 39–91, with R. Williamson, *Philo and the Epistle to the Hebrews* (Leiden, 1970), and Hurst, *Hebrews*, pp. 7–42. See also Barrett, 'Eschatology'; Bruce, *Hebrews*, pp. 1ff; A. Snell, *A New and Living Way* (London, 1959), pp. 36–40; L. K. K. Dey, *The Intermediary World and Patterns of Perfection in Philo and Hebrews*, (Missoula, 1975).

the near and the unapproachable, the manifest and the hidden, the sinful and the holy, and with its stress on the sacred time and place, on wrath, on the purifying power of blood and the sacred functions of priest and victim. In short, it depends for its presuppositions, not on a fashionable form of philosophic idealism, but on those portions of the Old Testament which are in appearance most 'primitive' and uncongenial, not only to the nineteenth and twentieth centuries but to the educated Jew and Greek of the first century too.

The real difficulty, however, is not so much distaste as distance. Both Hebrews and the texts in Leviticus it is based on take the power and efficacy of sacrifice for granted, for both know that in purificatory rites and holocausts God is encountered and his grace experienced: Hebrews does not decry sacrifice, but offers a 'better' and final rite. Whereas we are so far from their understanding that we must be glad of the least passing remark as to the function of it all, for both ancient authors this understanding belongs with direct perception and action and is therefore seldom given conscious, conceptual utterance. When, however, a partial explanation is offered, as in Leviticus 17:11, it seems that the priestly author shares with us the extreme difficulty of verbalising its meaning.

If the author's attitude to the death of Christ and the Christian's situation is based on a particular understanding of Israel's cult, we can hardly expect to reach the former without passing through the latter. Plainly, this involves more than piecemeal inquiry and annotation. The cultus is essentially a system of actions mediating between humanity and God, so 'understanding' it must involve entering into the assumptions and thought-patterns intrinsic to that relationship but seldom made explicit in the procedural details set down in the text or retrieved by archaeology.

In seeking to penetrate through the ritual phenomena and their conscious interpretations to the unconscious roots we shall need, in addition to the resources of social anthropology, psychology and comparative religion, a strategy to guide us through the mass of materials this brings into view. The theme of the argument so far has been that distinctive benefits can be expected to flow from treating Hebrews, and the Old Testament cultus, as integrated wholes rather than as bundles of contingent particulars, so the strategy which commends itself is the essentially holistic approach of structuralism. That term is used to label many different activities, but one of the questions which it raises is whether interpretation itself can be a whole: whether it is possible to frame a methodology capable of dealing even-handedly with Hebrews' interpretation of the Old Testament and with our interpretation of Hebrews. Is there really a homology between these activities, and, if so, can it be succinctly displayed?

Structuralism and Biblical study

Structuralist analyses of New Testament texts have been numerous in recent years, but they have mostly been concerned with small units – a parable, a few chapters – and mainly with narrative, using narratological techniques derived from Propp and Greimas.[10] Hebrews does contain, and concern itself with, stories, but the centre of its interest (and, it has been suggested earlier, of the modern readers' difficulty), is not in this but in its use of sacrificial symbolism. Several Old Testament scholars, however, have found in the work of Lévi-Strauss a valuable methodology for interpreting the symbolic language of the Pentateuch, including the sacrificial symbols of Leviticus interpreted by Hebrews, and it is this anthropological line that will be followed here.

There has been some debate about whether 'structuralism' should be thought of as an investigative method or as an ideology, and whether, therefore, it can be used as a tool in Biblical studies.[11] Others have abridged that discussion in order to test the method in practice. It is, in any case, not only in theology that questions about ideology arise. Many of the writers cited in chapter 3 stand in the Anglo-Saxon empiricist tradition, and few would describe themselves simply as 'structuralists'. Within social anthropology, Lévi-Strauss is only one contributor to long-standing debates about the nature and importance of symbolic classification, and about the interpretation of ritual.

---

[10] See R. Barthes, 'Introduction to the structural analysis of narratives', in *Image–Music–Text* (ET Glasgow, 1977), pp. 79–124; J. Calloud, *The Structural Analysis of Narrative* (Philadelphia, 1976). On the application of these techniques to Biblical criticism, see D. Patte, *What is Structural Exegesis?* (Philadelphia, 1976); W. G. Doty, 'Linguistics and biblical criticism', *JAAR*, 41 (1973), 114–21; and the essays in A. M. Johnson (ed. and trans.), *The New Testament and Structuralism* (Pittsburgh, 1976).

[11] A short general discussion is given by A. C. Thiselton, 'Structuralism and biblical studies: method or ideology?', *ExpT*, 89 (1977–8), 329–35; D. Greenwood: *Structuralism and the Biblical Text* (Berlin, 1985) surveys a range of methods and issues from a critical perspective, though the level of argument is erratic. The question of structuralism and the historicity of the gospel is discussed by A. M. Johnson, in A. M. Johnson, (ed.), *Structuralism and Biblical Hermeneutics* (Pittsburgh, 1979).

This is not the place for a full discussion of structuralism,[12] nor even for describing the particular analytic methods to be used in this study, which will be set out in chapter 3. What is needed at this point is to show why it is appropriate to the problem of holistic interpretation raised by Hebrews, and to survey some problems and objections. The characteristic concern for treating data as systems, as wholes, stems from the central axiom of the structuralist linguistics of Saussure, the 'arbitrary nature of the sign'.[13] Just as a phoneme is an arbitrary division of the continuum of sound, so a concept is an arbitrary division of human experience; and at each level these linguistic units are defined not by an essence but by the space they occupy between other sounds and concepts, that is, their relation to other elements in a conceptual or phonemic system. Meaning is therefore a function of relationships within a pattern, rather than of correspondence between a word and its object (between a 'signifier' and its 'signified'). This has obvious application to anthropology and literature; less so, perhaps, to the interpretation of discourse.

The other fundamental contributions of Saussure are equally systematic in nature. Taking language to be the model for all culture, similarly characterised as a system of conventions for ordering perception and action, Saussure expressed the relation of the whole to the parts as that of *langue* to *parole* (others would say 'code' to 'message').[14] He distinguished between two sorts of relatedness within the system, the syntagmatic or horizontal relations of signs in sentences, sequences, institutions, and the paradigmatic (he would say 'associative') or vertical relations of metaphor and synonymy;[15] more controversially, he argued that the historical or diachronic dimension has no explanatory power, and that interpretation is necessarily synchronic, alterations of a system in time being considered merely as shifts from one fixed, synchronic state to another.[16]

We have already seen that Hebrews invites treatment as a whole on the grounds of the high level of internal integration of its parts and its relative lack of external reference. What is proposed is that it should be read as a self-contained symbolic system, whose meaning should be located in the whole rather than in the parts. This should not be conceived as a rigid enclosedness, however. Like any text,

---

[12] The unity of 'structuralism' is in any case a matter of dispute. See S. Wittig, 'The historical development of structuralism', *Soundings*, 58 (1975), 145–66; J. Sturrock (ed.), *Structuralism and Since* (Oxford, 1979), pp. 3ff.
[13] F. de Saussure, *Course in General Linguistics* (ET Glasgow, 1974), pp. 67ff.
[14] *Ibid.*, p. 17ff.   [15] *Ibid.*, pp. 12ff.   [16] *Ibid.*, pp. 79ff.

Hebrews makes ostensible reference to outside matters, but these references will be interpreted not as the isolated correspondence of certain signs in Hebrews with particular features of the world but as an appeal which Hebrews makes to be placed, as a whole, within the context of a wider whole – the Christian Church, the Old Testament cultic theology, the human condition. It is in the conjunction of these overlapping *langues* that Hebrews speaks a single, complex *parole*.

The preference for synchrony seems very applicable to a book which, as we have seen, detaches itself from historical process and identity. Although its internal associations are constantly representing movement, time, tradition, its argument is largely cast in terms of transition from one fixed, synchronic state ('the old covenant') to another ('the new covenant'), and it exploits very directly concepts of timelessness borrowed from ritual. Nevertheless, it exists in time, and we shall find that historical issues keep pressing in at the periphery of the inquiry. The internal structure of the work's argument and the formal relations of its parts have been frequently discussed,[17] and to these syntagmatic questions this study will contribute only indirectly, focussing instead on the associative or paradigmatic meaning of symbols within the religious 'culture' constituted by Hebrews and the wider contexts it appeals to, on the manner of its *bricolage* of random elements into significant wholes, on the 'meaning-world' which is composed of the text's inner relations. It will be shown, for example, that the importance and meaning of the strange figure of Melchizedek, which syntagmatically is unnecessary and confusing, lies in its paradigmatic relation – as a type of Christ, the counter-systematic force – to many of the central symbols of the book.

Structuralism is thus a highly suggestive and comprehensive methodology for dealing with the symbolic elements in cultures and in literature, and therefore doubly applicable to Hebrews, which in a self-consciously artistic fashion recreates and reshapes the cultus of the Old Testament. However, this application of structural linguistics to different areas and disciplines is not without its opponents, and the questions they raise must be dealt with before we go further.

---

[17] The most ambitious is that by A. Vanhoye, *La Structure littéraire de l'Epître aux Hébreux* Analecta Biblica (Rome, 1963); see also discussion in W. G. Johnsson, 'The cultus of Hebrews in twentieth-century scholarship', *ExpT*, 89 (1978), 105f.

The methods to be used here follow the anthropological path of which Lévi-Strauss is the chief spokesman and theorist. His work has been criticised on a number of counts, which may be grouped under two headings. There is, first, what many would regard as the undue emphasis he has placed on the classification of experience by means of binary opposition as a defining characteristic of primitive thought, to the extent that, as he presents them, the cultures of primitive peoples become a pure, formalist system of conceptual oppositions. And second, there is the question whether his system is an *a priori* conceptuality divorced from the reality of specific social, cultural and economic conditions.

Is binary-opposition in fact a feature of primitive thought? Some anthropologists, while accepting that it is, question whether it is also a feature of the thought patterns of 'civilised' cultures, and therefore whether the very general argument which Lévi-Strauss builds upon it can be sustained;[18] others argue, conversely, that 'binary-opposition' is an analogy derived from a computer logic of the twentieth-century West, and not at all true of 'primitive' thought, which is rather 'organismic and synthetic',[19] and based in a perception of fundamental unity. In answer to this last point it should be said that the meaning-bestowing power of association (paradigmatic transformation) is equally a part of Lévi-Strauss' work, even where his dominant rationalism throws the emphasis on the creation of patterns of binary opposition. It is here that the work of Eliade is an especially valuable complement: beginning from a quite different philosophical standpoint he presents a logic of symbols and myths based in association, demonstrating the essential unity of concepts and pratices which to the typical 'Western' mind seem wholly distinct.[20]

There is some validity in the charge of intellectual wilfulness levelled against Lévi-Strauss, for his tendency to see in every difference an 'opposition', imposing an Hegelian scheme of thesis-antithesis-synthesis,[21] and for his use of highly selective material, when

[18] T.K. Seung, *Structuralism and Hermeneutics* (New York, 1982), pp. 59f; R. Barthes and F. Bovon, *Structural Analysis and Biblical Exegesis*, Pittsburgh Theological Monograph Series 3 (Pittsburgh, 1974), p. 11.

[19] B. Morris, *Anthropological Studies of Religion* (Cambridge, 1987), p. 289.

[20] See M. Eliade, *Patterns in Comparative Religion* (London, 1958) and *The Myth of the Eternal Return* (London, 1989).

[21] See E.R. Leach (ed.), *The Structural Study of Myth and Totemism* ASA Monograph Series (London, 1967), pp. 61f, 113; R. Girard, 'Differentiation and reciprocity in Lévi-Strauss and contemporary theory', in R. Girard, *'To Double Business Bound'*, London, 1978, pp. 155–60.

necessary forced into shape.[22] However, as a way of ordering experience, binary-opposition can be found in cultures at every stage from 'primitive' to 'modern', and there is no question that it has, at times if not universally, explanatory power.

It seems, though, that Lévi-Strauss will be satisfied with nothing less than a universal and invariant thought-process, and he has therefore been subject to considerable criticism for the inherent and deliberate determinism of his approach.[23] If his aim is to describe rules of language as rules of thought, such that every aspect of primitive culture can be explained; or if, to put the same point a different way, the mythologies of peoples widely scattered in space and time are held to exhibit at a deep level unvarying congruence – then both the intentions of agents and the specificity of cultures are only superficial manifestations of a fundamentally similar, regular and predictable structure of thought, and all human belief and action can in principle be explained without remainder. But, whether or not such an explanatory attempt is a desirable aim – to Geertz, the Lévi-Strauss 'structure of myths' is 'an infernal culture-machine'[24] – few anthropologists would accept that, even over the limited range of cultures he has studied,[25] Lévi-Strauss has achieved it. Always there is too little hard data to construct a systematic model of a type at all similar to those of the natural sciences.[26]

[22] See Leach (ed.), *Myth and Totemism*, pp. 67f. R. C. Culley, 'Some comments on structural analysis and biblical studies', *VT*, Supp. vol. 22 (1972), 129–42, criticises Leach in the same terms.

[23] C. Geertz, *The Interpretation of Cultures* (New York, 1973), p. 346, quotes Lévi-Strauss' avowal (in *Tristes Tropiques*, Paris, 1955) of the aim of 'the reintegration of culture into nature and generally of life into its physico-chemical conditions'. For criticism, see Geertz, *Interpretation of Cultures*, pp. 345–59; P. Ricoeur, *The Conflict of Interpretations* (Evanston, 1974), pp. 51ff; G. Steiner, *Language and Silence* (Harmondsworth, 1969), pp. 257f; J. Bowker, *The Sense of God* (Oxford, 1973), pp. 98–103.

[24] Geertz, *Interpretation of Cultures*, p. 355.

[25] Ricoeur, *Conflict*, pp. 40f and 57 (n. 19), points out that Lévi-Strauss restricts his view to totemist and non-European cultures. N. Dyson-Hudson, 'Structure and infrastructure in primitive society', in R. Macksey and E. Donato (eds.), *The Structuralist Controversy* (Baltimore, 1972), pp. 218–41, criticises his retreat from field-work into book study and his corresponding tendency to use 'poetic' generalisations (pp. 224ff). See also the remarks of M. Douglas in Leach (ed.), *Myth and Totemism*, pp. 66–8.

[26] That this, with its hard facts and experimental method, is the goal of Lévi-Strauss' work, is the point of his use of the model of linguistics, which is, he says, 'probably the only [social science] which can truly claim to be a science and which has achieved both the formulation of an empirical method and an understanding of the nature of the data submitted to its analysis' (Lévi-Strauss, SA, p. 31).

Besides, one of the reasons why linguists after Jakobson have not been attracted to the semiological project bequeathed to them by Saussure has been the perception that meaning is only very partially to be accounted for as a product of the classification of given experience, and that a more interesting question is how, within the rule-system laid down by a language, new meanings are generated, meanings which cohere with the existing pattern of thinking, but could not have been predicted from it.[27]

Yet even within the more restricted process of creativity as described by Lévi-Strauss, the *bricolage* of cultural units into myth, the question arises of the source of these materials.[28] 'The arbitrary nature of the sign' is a Saussurian axiom which, even if it can be considered absolute in the field of phonology, has much less straightforward application to the constituents of human experience: it may be form which gives meaning, but signs, insofar as they are (necessarily) drawn from human experience, must have some substance, and that substance has an irreducible specificity which must be taken into account.[29] Whatever is specific is subject to change across time as well as space, of course, and this therefore reintroduces into the discussion the element of diachrony, which tends to be excluded – not so much, in fact, by the structuralist preference for synchrony (since synchrony, properly understood, is not incompatible with history, but rather studies history as an aspect of the present state) – but rather by the 'timelessness' sometimes attributed to primitive cultures, a presupposition which excuses the researcher from looking too closely into what a culture's past has actually been – and from looking at the experience, not of generalised 'humanity', or 'the tribe', but of particular individuals.[30]

The issue here may be clarified by taking a Biblical example: the Passover. The structures of myth and sacrifice as we find them in the Old Testament are of course far from being primitive, unconscious

---

[27] See E. Leach, *Lévi-Strauss* (rev. edn, Glasgow, 1974), pp. 27f, 112f, 120 (n. 5).

[28] Lévi-Strauss, *SA*, pp. 208ff Cf. Geertz, *Interpretation of Cultures*, pp. 352ff.

[29] Levi-Strauss qualifies his argument on this point, however, when he says: 'the linguistic sign is arbitrary a priori, but ceases to be arbitrary a posteriori. Nothing existing a priori in the nature of certain preparations made of fermented milk requires the sound-form *fromage* ... On the other hand, it is in no way certain that these phonemic options, which are arbitrary in relation to the *designatum*, do not, once the choice has been made, imperceptibly affect ... their position within a semantic environment' (*SA*, p. 91).

[30] See Derrida's critique of what he regards as Lévi-Strauss' romantic and primitivist presuppositions, in *Of Grammatology* (ET Baltimore, 1976). On the relation of abstract structuralism to individual minds, see Leach (ed.), *Lévi-Strauss*, pp. 83–7.

phenomena. They are the result of a long historical development and conscious reinterpretation in a culture with a high degree of organisation and a strong historical sense. Biblical scholarship has concentrated on the search for the historical development of Israel's institutions, without being much concerned to attribute 'meaning'; nonetheless, we shall not be justified, conversely, in seeking a meaning without reference to history and to the question whether history has not merely changed that meaning but become part of it. Historical study reveals that the feast of Passover has had varied forms: thus, in modern Jewish practice, and as described in Exodus 12, it is a family celebration, but in New Testament times, following Deuteronomy 16:1–8, it was a Temple feast. Whatever form it took, though, all Biblical references agree in describing it as a narrative commemoration of a saving event in Israel's history, salvation from Egyptian slavery by God's merciful deliverance. However, on the basis of certain features of the rite discordant with that account, and by comparison with ancient and modern near-Eastern parallels, it is generally accepted that it originated in fact as an apotropaic Spring festival of pre-Israelite pastoral nomads.[31] Should we identify the 'real' meaning of the rite as that given by its origin, or by its traditional form? The fact that, in the Christian reinterpretation of the Passover through the symbols of the cross and the Lamb of God, both aspects are present, suggests that a different and more open method is in order; for alongside the continuity of conscious meaning (that is, the eucharistic narrative celebration of a new saving event) arises a buried unconscious significance (the cross as apotropaic offering of blood to avert the power of universal evil) which is equally important for the development of Christian theology.[32]

    In what follows, we shall see how little it is possible, in a society

---

[31] See R. de Vaux, *Studies in Old Testament Sacrifice* (Cardiff, 1964), pp. 1–19; but compare J. Rogerson, *Anthropology and the Old Testament*, (Oxford, 1978), pp. 38f., and H. H. Rowley, 'The meaning of sacrifice in the Old Testament', in H. H. Rowley, *From Moses to Qumran* (London, 1963), pp. 68f, for criticism of de Vaux's position.

[32] Young, *SI*, p. 156. There is, of course, no mystery about how Christian theology rediscovered these primitive elements, since both the blood and its purpose of warding off the Destroyer remained part of the Passover narrative of Exod. 12, though not included in the account in Num. 9:1–14, nor part of its annual re-enactment in New Testament times. (Num. 9:6ff, however, contains an interesting, 'structurally' identical, procedure for protecting the ritual purity of the feast against defilement by contact with death.) The theological interpretation of this ancient rite within Yahwism left some of its symbols understressed, but available for realisation in the context of some further reinterpretation.

about which we have real information, to extricate questions of meaning which might have cross-cultural applications from those which are rooted in conditions specific to that culture alone. If so, will our method be properly 'structuralist'? It is certain that, for some, 'structuralism' implies operating with a closed and entirely self-referring system: in the next chapter we shall see how Piaget's concept of structuralism is inseparable from stable and self-regulating wholes. Lévi-Strauss, however, denies that this is his aim. In the 'Overture' to *The Raw and the Cooked* he protests:

> I do not hope to reach a stage at which the subject matter of mythology, after being broken down by analysis, will crystallise again into a whole with the general appearance of a stable and well-defined structure.[33]

The reasons he gives for not entertaining this hope are apparently empirical: the obscurity of the available data, the effect of diachrony which means that 'we are dealing with a shifting reality', and therefore the impossibility of ever knowing enough about another culture to reduce plurality to unity.[34] But, having said this, the goal of the operation does after all emerge as a search for unity, not at the surface level of the myths themselves but in the 'constraining structures of the mind', the 'laws operating at a deeper level',[35] which generate a 'pattern' of mythology of which any individual myth is a 'limited application':[36] 'I therefore claim to show, not how men think in myths, but how myths operate in men's minds without their being aware of the fact.'[37]

In a famous essay,[38] Derrida has criticised Lévi-Strauss' argument here because in denying the fundamental unity of mythology his empiricism covers up (and in doing so reveals) a nostalgia for the 'Presence' of a centre in the structure, an ordering essence, the universal mentality which is the transcendental signified of the system. This closure for which Lévi-Strauss is criticised by empiricists, and which he denies, is here asserted as a more truthful outcome of his thought. Lévi-Strauss offers a luxuriant description of the

[33] C. Lévi-Strauss, *The Raw and the Cooked* (ET Harmondsworth, 1986), p.3.
[34] *Ibid.*, p.3. To achieve total knowledge of a culture may well be called an impossible task and a 'meaningless' hope. Lévi-Strauss appears to regard such total knowledge as a prerequisite for making any general statements, although elsewhere (p.7) he says that for such an aim few facts are sufficient.
[35] *Ibid.*, p.10.   [36] *Ibid.*, p.13.   [37] *Ibid.*, p.12.
[38] J. Derrida, 'Structure, sign and play in the discourse of the human sciences', *Writing and Difference* (ET London, 1978), pp.278–95.

'code' of human culture, a code which has as its signified 'Humanity';
in contrast, post-structuralist writers offer a code without any
message, a 'relentless intertextuality', which they would claim is the
unacknowledged drift of structuralism itself. Therefore any attempt
to apply structuralism as a method to the Bible, in the hope of
demonstrating here another 'Great Code', whose signified is God,
has to be aware of the danger that by the process of 'slippage' the
'signified' will be annihilated, and leave only (as in the work of
Lindbeck) a sectarian ideology without external reference.[39]

Not surprisingly, therefore, there are those who would question the
applicability of Lévi-Straussian analysis to Biblical texts.[40] Indeed,
Lévi-Strauss himself has criticised an early essay by Leach, in which
he applies structuralist principles to Genesis, on the grounds that
Biblical ethnographic data is 'almost entirely lacking', and that the
myths have been 'deformed' by editors,[41] whose 'purpose ... was
different from that of the originators of the mythical material'.[42]
This argument seems curious: while the processes of transmission and
the varying forces at work in shaping the Biblical material necessitate
special treatment,[43] they are not such as to disqualify it as genuine
information about the culture it represents. In his essay on 'The
Structural Study of Myth', Lévi-Strauss argues that a myth consists
of all its variants, primitive and sophisticated, direct and indirect,

[39] G. A. Lindbeck, *The Nature of Doctrine* (London, 1984). See further below,
pp. 58ff.

[40] Greenwood, *Structuralism and the Biblical Text*; R. A. Spivey, 'Structuralism and
biblical studies – the uninvited guest', *Interpretation*, 28 (1974), 133–45. Ricoeur,
while critical, insists on the indispensable role of structuralism in dialectic with
hermeneutics ('a necessary intermediary between symbolic naïveté and hermeneutic
comprehension', *The Conflict of Interpretations*, p. 61). Other positive evaluations
of its use can be found in Doty, 'Linguistics and biblical criticism'; F. Bovon, 'French
Structuralism and Biblical Exegesis', in Barthes and Bovon, *Structural Analysis*,
pp. 4–20; R. Jacobson, 'The structuralists and the Bible', *Interpretation*, 28 (1974),
146–64; Johnson (ed.), *Biblical Hermeneutics*; Rogerson, *Anthropology*, pp. 102–14.

[41] Johnson, *Biblical Hermeneutics*, p. 13.

[42] Greenwood, *Structuralism and the Biblical Text*, p. 21. The debate was originally
reported by Lévi-Strauss, under the title 'A confrontation' in *New Left Review*, 62
(1970), 7–74; see Johnson, *Biblical Hermeneutics*, pp. 12ff, and Greenwood,
Structuralism and the Biblical Text, pp. 21f. For another criticism of Leach's essay,
see Culley, 'Some comments on structural analysis and biblical studies'.

[43] Compare Leach's wilful use of the AV despite the additional distortions it gives,
on occasion, to his view of the Biblical material (e.g. E. R. Leach and D. A. Aycock,
Structural Interpretations of Biblical Myth, Cambridge, 1983 p. 100), and his unqualified
introduction of plainly post-Biblical ideas (e.g. the 'City of God' and the 'pangs of
sacrifice', in Leach, *CC*, pp. 72, 93).

all equally relevant to establishing the myth's meaning;[44] if so, the second criticism, with its concept of an authorial 'purpose' denying rather than adding to the plurality of meanings, seems to be particularly bizarre from this source, unless he is tacitly placing an unbridgeable gulf between the nature of oral and written myth.

There is certainly a question about the relevance of structuralism in the detailed analysis of small textual units, with which Biblical exegesis habitually deals, and it is not always clear, once the hidden structures of the text have been identified, what has actually been achieved. Are these structures held to constitute the text's 'meaning', and if so, why? Lévi-Strauss' techniques, in particular, were developed for use in exploring relations between families of myths and exchange systems, not for minute analysis of composed texts; in this they differ from those of Greimas and Barthes, which are essentially literary methods, and most structuralist Biblical criticism, especially that applied to the New Testament, has followed that literary, syntagmatic route.[45] Lévi-Straussian analysis is only really appropriate where it is possible to identify a text as an enunciation of an existing myth or symbol-system, and though there has been good work done on Old Testament topics, the New Testament consists more obviously and inescapably of composed literature with discursive intent (even its chief narratives are categorised as statements, 'good news'), and critical practice to date has been frankly disappointing.[46]

---

[44] Lévi-Strauss, *SA*, pp. 216ff (see further chapter 6 below). According to Barthes, 'the structural analysis of a text ... does not look for the secret of a text ... Of course, if there is a meaning, a monosemy, or an anagogical process in the text ... we will treat this anagogy as *one* code of the text, among other codes ...' (Johnson, *Biblical Hermeneutics*, p. 119).

[45] T. Collins, in his essay, 'Decoding the Psalms − A structural approach to the Psalter', *JSOT*, 37 (1987), 41−60, attempts to unite the two streams. He first analyses the psalter as a system of divine−human relations with ten or eleven fixed motifs found in variable combination, interacting through binary oppositions (the special feature of Ps. 119 being that it deploys the whole set, and thus displays the complete system in miniature); less successful is the attempt to supplement this with a Greimasian analysis, which forces the psalter into the mould of heroic narrative.

[46] The emphasis on 'method' often seems disproportionate to the results obtained (see Greenwood, *Structuralism and the Biblical Text*, pp. 24f), and the application of supposedly 'scientific' principles has often an air of arbitrariness (cf. Thiselton, 'Structuralism and biblical studies', p. 334); these problems have affected, for example, the analysis of Gal. 1:1−10 in D. Patte, *What is Structural Exegesis?* (Philadelphia, 1976), pp. 59−76 and D. O. Via's 'A structuralist approach to Paul's Old Testament hermeneutic', *Interpretation*, 28 (1974), 201−20. More supple examples can also be found, however, for example, J. Starobinski's essay, 'The Gerasene demoniac' (in Barthes and Bovon, *Structural Analysis*, pp. 57−84) and F. Kermode's study of Mark, *The Genesis of Secrecy* (Cambridge, 1979).

However, the importance of the question of the presence of discursive intentionality in much of the Biblical material has less to do with the nature of structuralism and its applicability to certain types of literature, or even with the refining of our critical expertise, than with the status of *revelation*. Paul Ricoeur asks whether it is appropriate to the nature of kerygmatic literature to read it in a structural way.[47] The canon of the Old Testament has preserved a conscious emphasis on the theological standpoint of its latest editors, and there has been a traditional impulse to harmonise scriptural reading with the overall interpretation they impose; the New Testament is similarly shaped throughout by a gospel very much at the forefront of its authors' concerns. But if, according to structuralist principles, no element can claim priority on historical or theological grounds, 'intended' meaning cannot take precedence over unintended, and the final editing of a Biblical text cannot be abstracted from the wealth of material in which it is couched. A synchronic reading of the canon must do justice to the full variety of meanings which the Bible preserves, whether these are understood as 'semantic richness' providing a quarry for successive reinterpretations,[48] or as contradictions which deconstruct the unity of its discourse.

Is there, ideally, some complex unity in revelation which hermeneutics should aspire to state, or should we be led by the variousness of God to prefer to affirm an ultimate plurality of readings? If we choose the latter, are we, with Barthes, practising 'the infinite deferment of the signified',[49] or is pluralism disguising an ultimately single, non-negotiable conclusion?[50] Perhaps we are not obliged to choose between these options, provided we pursue a method which at every point affirms the reality of the question.

Structuralism and hermeneutics

Though it is hoped that the argument of this book will succeed in itself in holding that question open, it will be helpful here to outline some of the features of the post-war hermeneutical debate which underlie the choice of structuralism as a methodology. It is a choice

---

[47] Cf. Ricoeur, *Conflict*, pp. 27–61, and the debate cited in n. 42 above.

[48] Ricoeur, *Conflict*, pp. 47f.

[49] Barthes, *Image–Music–Text*, p. 158.

[50] As in the 'Supplemental theses' of Alain Blancy (Johnson, *Biblical Hermeneutics*, pp. 179–82), where we are told: 'The meaning is always plural. It is always an interplay of reflections between signifiers without a final signified who worked it out (except for God)' (p. 180). But presumably this is ironic in intent.

which automatically sides us with those who identify the meaning of an utterance not with that of its originator but with the utterance itself. Without denying that what a speaker or author says he or she 'meant' is a datum relevant to the interpretation of an utterance, that datum can have no absolute authority. Barthes would go further. In the essay quoted above,[51] he contrasts a 'text' with a 'work', defining a 'work' as the object of bourgeois literary production and consumption, existing in clearly defined genres, with (ideally) a single demonstrable meaning; by contrast the text 'exists only in the movement of a discourse', in a playing, and activity; it is irreducibly plural, 'free of the determination of an author', as it 'practices the infinite deferment of the signified'. Signification is therefore an activity generated in the reading of a text, not an 'over-rich' content to be retrieved or discovered by any interpretative 'method'. It is the product of contradictions which render meaning finally 'undecidable', the text 'illegible'. Thus not only the Bible but the world (considered as a 'text') has to be played with, enjoyed, without expecting certainty, direction or purpose, still less an authorial Presence.

Such a conception of meaning is grounded in the high value placed on *writing* as that which gives freedom to the word by detaching it from the author, in a way that speech can never be detached from its speaker. But is it not possible to be true to the objectivity of the text and yet allow it to refer outside itself? In the essay, 'What is a text?', Ricoeur contends that the separation of sense and reference entailed by this detachment is not final, that it is 'intercepted not suppressed'.[52] Resisting the naïveté of romantic hermeneutics, in which the text is regarded as a vehicle for transferring ideas from one mind to another, he resists also the inverted romanticism of structuralism and its successors, 'the ideology of the absolute text'.[53] The value of structuralism in hermeneutics, in his view, is as an analytic methodology to be applied to the text as a closed system, a *langue*, exploring the way in which its sense arises. Through its objectivity it offers, as a necessary preliminary to an understanding of the text itself, an explanation of how it works. But this detachment is a methodological stance, and not a feature of the texts under consideration. Ricoeur points out how 'impure' in fact are the basic units of sense which Lévi-Strauss identifies, the 'mythemes' out of

[51] Barthes, 'From work to text', *Image–Music–Text*, pp. 155–64.
[52] Ricoeur, *Hermeneutics*, p. 148. In addition to this essay (pp. 145–64), see related discussions in *ibid.*, pp. 131–44, 197–221.
[53] *Ibid.*, p. 148.

which the structure is built, carrying over into the structure, as was argued above, values from the world context in which they arise;[54] and he maintains that it is this dealing in living questions, and not the pure formal beauty of the structure formed from these atoms, that makes both the texts and structuralism as a methodology worthwhile.

In declaring his preference for the 'semantic richness' of the units over the dynamic of interaction, Ricoeur shows himself antipathetic to structuralism's most basic tenet, that meaning is not positive but relational. But this does not mean that in his view texts have a single determinable meaning – on the contrary they need to be constantly re-read to do justice to their 'surplus of meaning', so meaning is irreducibly plural.[55] Always there is more to be discovered. And yet meaning cannot be permanently detached from the world of readers: the pursuit of the 'sense' of the text is one movement in a larger process of reading, a process which remains to be completed by a movement of 'appropriation' into the life of the reader.

There is therefore no inherent contradiction between reference and textuality.[56] The 'world' which appears in a novel is not the world, any more than the 'author' is the author, but it is through the medium of the text that the halves of those pairs relate and interact. Thus, for example, Lindbeck is right to argue that the gospels seek to bring the reader into conformity, not with 'the Jesus of history' or 'the metaphysical Christ' or anything else 'behind' the text, but with 'the Jesus Christ depicted in the narrative'.[57] It is necessary to move *in* the Bible as a text, not to treat it as a disposable pointer, moving immediately *through* the text to a definable meaning or conclusion 'God'. And yet to move in and not through the Bible and Christian tradition is to dwell in a world which sees itself as under pressure from transcendent mystery. The 'Jesus Christ depicted in the narrative' is a figure whose identity the gospel-writers cannot, it seems, depict, except in relation to the undepicted God. For even if God seldom appears directly in the tale (narrative modes adequate to that depiction being hard to sustain), always the question of God's being and nature, God's justice and will, is present in the world of the text: without needing to be a 'character' in the story, God is the inseparable, problematic reference point of its world. Therefore to ask the question of the being of God is not to move outside the text, turning aside from

[54] *Ibid.*, pp. 160f; cf. the discussion above, p. 53 and n. 29.
[55] Ricoeur, *Conflict*, p. 48.
[56] See Ricoeur, *Hermeneutics*, pp. 131–44.
[57] Lindbeck, *Nature of Doctrine*, p. 120.

hermeneutics to metaphysical speculation, but to dwell fully in it, taking the text seriously in allowing it to interpret us. The contention that hermeneutics is the process of letting texts interpret us is at the heart of the philosophy of H.-G. Gadamer, as firm an opponent of 'method' and as firm a proponent of 'play' as Derrida, but for opposite reasons.[58] To Gadamer the basic datum is Tradition, by which he means the totality of human meanings carried in the stream of language, which 'speak themselves' through those who form a linguistic community. Hermeneutics is not found in a detached and critical analysis of objects but in 'conversation', in the act of entering into immediate relation with Tradition through the texts, art-works and concepts which are its vehicles, participating in its life and letting ourselves be shaped by it.[59] In his positive evaluation of 'prejudice', Gadamer thus offers an alternative to the post-Enlightenment, 'scientific' myth of the detached observer, positing a Self formed by and able to know itself in its historical and relational identity, through participating in the shared ground of Tradition.[60]

Yet hermeneutics cannot claim to speak of truth unless it retains an element of critical detachment. Gadamer's account of understanding is larger and more persuasive than Ricoeur's, setting texts within the context of Tradition as the bearer of Being, but he has been justly criticised for allowing too little room for scientific methodology within this conversation. This negative attitude to science implies the danger that 'Tradition' is so all-encompassing that it cannot be criticised or its validity as communicator of 'Being' questioned. Yet are there not false traditions? Are there not, anyway, rival traditions? Here he has been subjected to the criticism of Habermas,[61] with his neo-Marxist critique of ideology, of all non-self-reflective speech and action, his projected 'depth-hermeneutic' of religious consciousness through psychoanalysis.

Here also Gadamer's thought requires the complementary determination of Ricoeur to construct a Christian hermeneutic which can address the critical philosophies, the 'counter-disciplines', which have developed since the Enlightenment in explicit opposition to religious

---

[58] H.-G. Gadamer, *Truth and Method* (ET, 2nd edn, London, 1979).
[59] *Ibid.*, pp. 321ff.　　　　　　[60] *Ibid.*, pp. 245ff.
[61] See J. Habermas, 'The hermeneutic claim to universality', ET in J. Bleicher, *Contemporary Hermeneutics* (London, 1980), pp. 181–211; and for discussion of this issue see Bleicher, *ibid.*, pp. 152–8; Ricoeur, *Hermeneutics*, pp. 62–100; Q. Skinner (ed.), *The Return of Grand Theory in the Social Sciences* (Cambridge, 1985), pp. 32–8.

thinking. In speaking of the work of Freud, Marx and Nietzsche, as well as Lévi-Strauss, as a 'hermeneutics of suspicion', he is seeking to appropriate them, within the double movement of 'explanation' and 'understanding', as elements in the widest tradition of Christian culture.[62] To do so is not to tame these critiques, but to affirm the religious value of the post-Enlightenment critique of religion, in insisting that religion be related to the whole of life and in resisting every tendency towards retreat into the private, spiritual realm, into religious consciousness, into myth, by emphasising also the social and material, the unconscious, the historical. Coming to terms with the potentially destructive elements in such philosophies is necessary for any religion, any interpretative act claiming to speak the truth, and Ricoeur's introduction into the notion of 'conversation', which in Gadamer is essentially the (subjective) relation of mind and tradition, of the strong objective pole of (potentially) reductive explanation, by deliberately distancing the interpreter from the received tradition, serves both to test and to enlarge it.

In this critical process, theology comes to stand outside itself, to see itself as a symbolic construct, and to take hold of the irreducibly symbolic character of all human thinking. What this leads towards, though, is not a reductivism but a condition of 'second naïveté', a critical openness to 'Tradition' in its widest sense. Ricoeur shares with Gadamer a reverence for human culture as a preserver and transmitter of precious meanings, through which knowledge of being is conveyed: in insisting that language has a referring function he contends that symbols are not self-contained systems but means for the enlarging of language to encompass new possibilities. What a myth, a novel or a symbol offers – once we have engaged with it in a participation that includes critical reflection – is a 'possible world' through which our sense of reality is enriched and enlarged, to be appropriated by means of imagination, which he calls 'the capacity for letting new worlds shape our understanding of ourselves'.[63] The Bible has in this no privileged status, no authority except the life-enriching power of the symbols it offers; thus for Ricoeur 'revelation' is a function of testimony, of recognising in the Bible 'a world I may inhabit and wherein I may project my ownmost possibilities',[64]

---

[62] Ricoeur, *Hermeneutics*, pp. 145–64; *Conflict*, pp. 27–61. For analyses of some of these styles of 'explanation', see Bowker, *The Sense of God*.

[63] Ricoeur, *Hermeneutics*, p. 181.

[64] P. Ricoeur, *Essays on Biblical Interpretation* (London, 1981), p. 102.

and to treat this recognition seriously demands the appropriating of that world in responsive action.

In this study, then, we shall approach the Bible as 'text', free of determination by the intention of any author, human or divine, whose meaning is not to be 'read off' but discovered, first in a movement of critical inquiry which seeks to show what the Bible 'says' regardless of what it 'intends', and second in the process of dwelling in the 'possible world' it opens up, in the hope of finding it to be a bearer of truth of being. The Letter to the Hebrews, as a self-contained text which forms part of the Bible's overarching text, will be approached with the same double movement of criticism and participation through which we both interpret and are interpreted. The task is made more complex by the fact that Hebrews is itself an interpretation of the Old Testament – a critical revaluation, a 'hermeneutic of suspicion' which deconstructs the sacrificial system – and yet it is at the same time a participation in the God-bearing world of scripture, a representation of its living Voice. In this hermeneutical task we begin with the critical movement of structuralism.

The hope of a structural interpretation of the Bible is to obtain access to perceptions of God which, failing to find a place in any level of the conscious tradition, are yet retained unconsciously in the text, held, as it were, in symbolic solution. In taking as our focus the Letter to the Hebrews, the procedure will involve weighing together the author's deployment of scriptural material with the fullest understanding we can achieve of what it meant and means, and the book's pastoral and theological purpose with our synchronic reconstruction of the 'world' it shapes around the transformative event of Christ. By setting the text fully in the contexts of the symbolic structures to which it appeals, it may be possible to deepen our knowledge, not only of the 'meaning' given to the work by its author, but of what, in the fullest sense, that anonymous author 'had in mind'.[65]

[65] See J. Culler, *Saussure* (Glasgow, 1976), p. 112: 'What one "has in mind" while speaking or writing is not a form and meaning conjured up for a fleeting instant but the whole system of a language, more permanently inscribed.'

3

SACRIFICE AND COVENANT IN THE OLD TESTAMENT

The previous chapter has related the particular problems of Hebrews to wider questions of interpretation; by contrast, this chapter moves from general issues in anthropology to particular features of Biblical religion, in preparing for the extended discussion of Hebrews to follow in part III. Its purpose is threefold. First, it seeks to demonstrate in practice that recent structuralist studies in the field of anthropology have relevance and value also in the study of the Bible, taking as an example some interesting interpretations of aspects of Leviticus.[1] Second, it employs the principles used in these writings to survey from a structuralist point of view the Old Testament material most prominently referred to in Hebrews. Third, it locates structuralism alongside other methodologies in an inclusive view of the Old Testament. While the first two purposes provide the substance of the chapter, and will be worked out in parallel in its central sections, the third is the subject of some brief opening and closing remarks, which carry the hermeneutical discussion forward into later chapters.

Methodology in Old Testament interpretation

Anthropology differs from most methods used in Old Testament study, not only in being largely synchronic in its interests, but also in its fundamental concern with discerning and describing phenomena as wholes. To some extent, this is due to the historical origins of these studies: where anthropologists have been seeking to demonstrate an underlying unity and order, and therefore comprehensibility, in masses of apparently random customs, beliefs, folktales and the

[1] See Douglas, *PD*; Leach, *CC*; D. Davies, 'An interpretation of sacrifice in Leviticus', *ZAW*, 89 (1977), 387–99; J. W. Rogerson, 'Sacrifice in the Old Testament', in M. F. C. Bourdillon and M. Fortes (eds.), *Sacrifice* (London, 1980).

like, Old Testament scholarship has been using techniques borrowed from the study of languages, history, archaeology and so on, to explore the relation of Biblical data to non-Biblical, and in so doing has broken up the precritical conception of the Bible as a revealed whole. This apparent opposition conceals a deep similarity in method, in fact: the trends of historical development, cultural influence and theological order which Old Testament scholarship discusses are arrived at, like the cultural constructs of anthropologists, by inductive accumulation of data into patterns which are assumed to be not only provisional but contingent. Thus the break-up of the traditional unified conception of the Bible has followed Geertz' description of ethnography as providing an approximation to the organisation of a culture, a pattern which is 'intrinsically incomplete': 'the more deeply it goes the less complete it is'.[2] Israelite religion, Icelandic saga and Trobriand marriage customs are revealed in their contingent particularity, as alternative ways in which cultures have happened to 'create themselves' out of the interaction of their common humanity and their specific situations.[3]

The empirical method has, of course, its enemies in both theology and anthropology. Does it depict the ways in which God works through the limits of his creation, or deny the reality of his transcendence and revealed will? Does it celebrate the infinite variety of human creativity, or achieve only the pointless accumulation of unrelated facts?

> Are we condemned, like new Danaids, to fill endlessly the sieve-like basket of anthropological science; in vain, pouring monographs over monographs without being able to collect a substance with a richer and denser value?[4]

So cries Lévi-Strauss, whose programme has been to demonstrate that cultural patterns are essentially variant expressions of certain universal regularities of mental ordering, 'deep structures' which are in principle completely describable and more (not less) coherent than the surface patterns, so that once the contingent particularities derived from specific geographical and social situations are removed a comprehensive and universal order can be discerned. Though we have seen that this determinist presupposition has earned structuralism

[2] Geertz, *Interpretation of Cultures*, p. 29.
[3] *Ibid.*, pp. 40ff; Lévi-Strauss, *SA*, p. 23.
[4] R. Cohn and J. Middleton (eds.), *Comparative Political Systems* (New York, 1967), p. 46, quoted by Rogerson, *Anthropology*, p. 104.

opposition from anthropologists, and equally from theologians when they perceive it being applied to Biblical material,[5] our concern now is not to discuss the theoretical issue. The claim of structuralism is to be able to penetrate the meaning of some of the most difficult areas of human behaviour,[6] and thus to explain what other methods can only describe. Whether it does so in a reductive fashion remains to be seen, but it is as a plausible hypothesis that it has attracted the interest of Biblical scholars, in both its literary and its anthropological manifestations.[7] Our approach will focus on the latter, as it has been applied to the elucidation of the sacrificial regulations and related material.

The structuralist method is perhaps not as new as some of its proponents, and some of its critics, would claim. R.M. Polzin has shown how 'structuralist' are some established classics of the historical-critical method;[8] support for this approach can even be derived from the procedures of the Old Testament's Deuteronomic and Priestly editors. The argument of the Deuteronomist for the centralising of the cultus and the purification of Yahwism from its Canaanite elements, and the process by which historical and legendary material has been shaped to a more uniform pattern, reveal the strongly systematic urge behind the Deuteronomic redaction: only insofar as Israel conformed to a divinely given pattern of activity would its behaviour have validity. The Priestly document, in response to the post-exilic situation, goes further in addressing Israel as though it did in fact exhibit such an ideal order.[9] In simplifying and falsifying the empirical historical reality of Israel, it presents it as displaying the three features which, in Piaget's definition, characterise a 'structure':[10] wholeness, self-regulation and internal transformation. It will be useful to explore this point briefly:

[5] See above, pp. 52, 56–8.

[6] See, for example, Lévi-Strauss, *SA*, pp. 31ff.

[7] See the discussion in ch. 2 above, and Rogerson, *Anthropology*, pp. 102–19.

[8] R.M. Polzin, *Biblical Structuralism – Method and Subjectivity in the Study of Ancient Texts* (Philadelphia, 1977), pp. 126–201.

[9] See von Rad, *OTT*, vol. I, pp. 69ff.

[10] J. Piaget, *Structuralism*, (ET New York, 1970), cited by Polzin, *Biblical Structuralism*, pp. 1–5. Piaget's psychologically based 'structuralism' is different in many respects from the linguistic tradition derived from Saussure. See the comparative discussions of H. Gardner, *The Quest for Mind* (London, 1976), especially pp. 165–212, and Kee, *Christian Origins*, pp. 101–5. Here we are concerned only with the common interest in conceptual wholes.

Wholeness: literary, legal and cultic materials which historical study shows to be disparate in origin and theological
tendency are combined by P into a single Torah, governed by
a particular conception of Yahweh and his ritual institutions,
under which variant tendencies are eliminated or submerged.
Self-regulation: this order is divinely revealed and necessarily
antagonistic to any rival conception, whether arising within
Israel (rebellion) or outside (idolatry). Israel is symbolised
as a Camp surrounded by Wilderness, having no commerce
with any neighbours except by war.
A system of transformations: between the elements of this
whole a series of law-like relations exists which both enlarges
and delimits the meaning of individual units. Hence the
wilderness narratives of Exodus and Numbers both demonstrate the divine ordinance of the legal system and show it
at work; and the divine–human relation is expressed in
several complementary modes, as in the juxtaposition of
cultic laws with social laws, and apodeictic laws with
customary laws.

Insofar as it takes seriously this synthesising effect which has
created the final form of the Hexateuch and the prophetic-historical
corpus, structuralism bears a resemblance to recent 'canonical
criticism'. However, the two are very different in style. To elucidate
this relation, we may turn to the criteria used by Polzin.[11] He argues
that a structuralist analysis is characterised by three kinds of self-
consciousness in its approach: about its object, its conceptual model
and its subject. Its *object* is regarded as a whole (defined by him
in the Piagetian terms used above); its *conceptual model* is a
hypothetical–deductive methodology; its *subject* is self-reflexively
present in the analysis (rather than being rigorously excluded, as in
the objective–inductive model) as the 'structure structuring'. In
part III of *Biblical Structuralism*,[12] Polzin applies these criteria to
the work of Wellhausen, von Rad and Noth. He shows how well the
first two criteria fit Wellhausen's study of the Pentateuch (1878)[13]
and the form-critical work of von Rad (1938),[14] since both aim to

[11] Polzin, *Biblical Structuralism*, pp. 1–43.
[12] *Ibid.*, pp. 126–201.
[13] J. Wellhausen, *Prolegomena to the History of Ancient Israel* (ET Cleveland,
1965).
[14] G. von Rad, *The Form-Critical Problem of the Hexateuch* (ET London, 1966).

construct coherent and satisfying holistic interpretations of the material by applying to it conceptual structures whose intrinsic significance is not argued for but presupposed. In each case, that is, the concept represents a 'personal structure' in the author, and the success of these writings is due as much to the communication of this personal structure to the reader as to the detailed relation of this hypothesis to the facts. Where Polzin criticises both authors (from the point of view of these criteria) is in their lack of methodological self-awareness, due to a false adherence to empiricism, which led Wellhausen to assume that the Hegelian pattern of historical development he traced arose inductively from the facts, and von Rad similarly to treat a priori assumptions as though they were empirical data.[15]

These two examples, of course, are only fairly typical representatives of the long-standing but questionable presupposition of the primacy of induction in 'scientific' methodology generally, carrying with it the necessity of claiming that every hypothesis is an 'objective' reflection of the empirical data.[16] The Biblical Theology movement was perhaps particularly vulnerable to criticism at this point, its writers struggling to argue that the bold theological principles by which they organised the text were simply 'there'.[17] Canonical criticism, though genetically related to that movement, is less naïve in this respect.[18] Alongside the historical-critical analysis of the Bible it sets its holistic–synchronic reading of each unit in relation to other units and to the whole: it thus treats the Bible as a self-regulating transformational system, by applying to its contents the hypothetical unity of the *canon*. Like the older studies mentioned above, it fits the first two criteria, and it may be merely an accident that self-styled structuralists have shown little interest in the canonical ordering of the Bible. However, with respect to the third criterion, canonical criticism differentiates itself sharply from structuralism, and on the deliberate, dogmatic grounds of the *givenness* of the final ordering of the Old and New Testament as the *scripture* in which the

[15] Polzin, *Biblical Structuralism*, pp. 144–9, 166–73.

[16] For criticism of this presupposition, see M. Polanyi, *Personal Knowledge* (London, 1962), pp. 1–17.

[17] See the argument in J. Barr, *Explorations in Theology 7* (London, 1980), pp. 1–17.

[18] See B. S. Childs, *Introduction to the Old Testament as Scripture* (London, 1979), especially the rationale set out in pp. 69–83. For a useful discussion and bibliography, see J. Barr, *Holy Scripture* (Oxford, 1983), pp. 75–104, 130–71, 172–5. See also pp. 43f above.

community has enshrined its perception of God:[19] it is therefore this perception, or this received revelation, which forms the 'structure structuring' the text, and emphatically not the 'deep subjectivity' of its author, editor, interpreter or reader. We cannot here resolve the question whether this antagonism represents a real difference, or whether canon-criticism too is dependent on the 'personal structures' of its practitioners expressed in an understanding of the concept 'canon'. In the structuralist writings to be employed in this chapter, the symbolic systems through which men and women have experienced and expressed the presence of divine power are analysed as expressions of a deep pattern of human ordering, which, as well as being internally coherent and applicable to the data, reach through the subjectivity of the analysts of various disciplines, to claim a common (perhaps a universal) power of signification.

The form and function of sacrifice

Order and chaos

We have seen that the fundamental axioms of anthropological structuralism are Saussure's concept of 'the arbitrary nature of the sign' and the semiotic argument that a culture is a language-like communication system.[20] Being arbitrary, a sign has meaning not in itself but in its relations, its difference from other signs; and the same is true at every level of culture. The same arbitrariness which attends the segmentation of the phonic continuum to create phonemes, and the assigning of these sounds to particular conceptual categories, characterises also the creation of all cultural categories, in the process Leach calls 'mapping'.[21] Experience 'raw' is thus regarded as chaotic, made manageable only by being segmented, classified and named in language, and, in analogous fashion, human society is created by the segmentation of space, of time, of social relations, by means of a symbolic code.

Though the whole system of a language or culture may be extremely complex, it is reducible to a series of binary distinctions: a sign's 'most precise characteristic is in being what the others are not'. The maintenance of this meaning-system is dependent on the exactness

[19] Cf. Childs, *O.T. as Scripture*, pp. 75ff.
[20] Saussure, *General Linguistics*, pp. 67f.
[21] Leach, *CC*, pp. 33ff, 51ff; cf. H. Mol, *Identity and the Sacred* (Oxford, 1976), pp. 233ff.

of such distinctions, and simple oppositional relations play a great part in primitive linguistic and cultural codes, as Needham's work on the symbolism of right and left has shown.[22]

In *Purity and Danger* Mary Douglas has shown how important these devices for classifying and ordering experience are for the creation of value, and how deeply threatening most cultures find elements which are unclassifiable and ambiguous, leading to responses of horror, nausea and disgust.[23] The point here is a strictly structural one since it is not the content of the experience but the placing of that content which disturbs, and gives rise to rules of ritual purity. Dirt, as Mary Douglas argues, 'is matter out of place':[24] thus, to take common instances from our own culture, boots may be worn outside but not inside, or downstairs but not upstairs; and rotting vegetables are permitted in the kitchen if classified as 'waste' and confined to a bin. However arbitrary and conventional, contravention of such rules may cause deep-seated reactions, even while reason accepts that these boots worn inside are brand new, or the spilt bin has left no visible mess. She argues that such breaches are felt to threaten not only the particular rule in question but the whole system of rules, the entire rule-created order of existence.

A meaning-world is being visualised as an enclave carved out in the midst of chaos, which being an arbitrary and artificial construct must be constantly defended against the forces of natural ambiguity pressing in to dissolve meaning, blur distinctions and destroy the basis of order. This accounts for the intense emotion attached to conceptual distinctions, to borders and rules and categories. By extension, all persons, places and things which are unclassifiable evoke the arbitrariness of all categories and threaten disorder: hence the common fear of the half-caste, the hermaphrodite, the orphan, the Jew, the madman, the stranger, frequently expressed in the language of dirt; the taboos associated with thresholds, borders and crossroads; the power felt to reside in waste products such as smoke, ash, blood and saliva; the rules surrounding transformative acts such as cooking, sexuality and sacrifice.[25] Lévi-Strauss, in an influential essay,[26] has shown how such images are treated as interchangeable

---

[22] R. Needham, *Symbolic Classification* (Santa Monica, 1979). Cf. Leach, *CC*, pp. 55–64.

[23] Douglas, *PD*, *passim*, esp. pp. 32–40.

[24] Douglas, *PD*, p. 40. Leach, *CC*, p. 61, attributes the saying to Lord Chesterfield.

[25] Douglas, *PD*, pp. 94ff.

[26] C. Lévi-Strauss, 'The structural study of myth', in *SA*, pp. 206–31. See especially pp. 224ff.

(as 'paradigmatic transformations') in mythologies, as symbols of this area of experience through which myth can express a vision of life as ambiguous, caught between irreconcilable opposites (life/ death, individual/group), and seek to resolve that tension. One particular class of these marginal elements studied by Mary Douglas is concerned with the body, which, she argues, often functions as a symbol of the group, attention to diet and to bodily secretions showing the high significance attached to control of group membership.[27] In very many cultures blood, hair, semen, etc. are highly charged substances whose location on the border between the self and the not-self explains their symbolic equivalence to domestic waste (ash, smoke) and to margin-inhabiting substances such as mist and clothes.

It is not contended that the value of these images is in every culture the same, but that such ideas exhibit a family resemblance across diverse cultures and represent a 'universal means of organising daily experience'.[28] They occupy the central, 'liminal' area in the symbolic cosmos as depicted diagrammatically by Leach (see figure 1).[29]

Figure 1   The dangerous margin

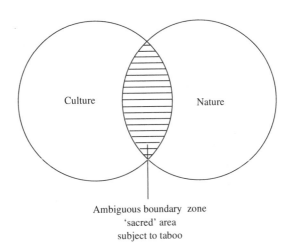

Ambiguous boundary zone
'sacred' area
subject to taboo

---

[27] Douglas, *PD*, pp. 32ff, 122ff; see also M. Douglas, *Natural Symbols* (London, 1973), pp. 95ff and Leach, *CC*, pp. 60ff, 71ff.
[28] Lévi-Strauss, *SA*, p. 225.
[29] Leach, *CC*, p. 35.

The innumerable binary distinctions embodied in language and custom each represent in miniature the one great distinction between the 'enclave' of ordered experience ('Culture') and the chaos of life without order ('Nature'). But, if the distinction is so important, how can the blurred boundary have positive value?

Though symbolic codes project the possibility of an ideal order, in real terms no absolute separation is sustainable since the continuance of ordered life depends on access to the disorderly power of 'Nature' working through climatic forces, sexual regeneration, the creation of soil through organic decomposition, and so on. The sphere of 'Culture' is necessarily open to a commerce with 'Nature' which both vitalises and threatens. In the margin is focussed this power of life which is also the power of death.

This fact of the *ambivalence of power* (together with its correlates, the precariousness of order and the potency of disorder) is a primary datum of all human society. It is the *mysterium fascinans et tremendum* of Otto's classic work, encountered at the 'edge' of the normal, in the place 'set apart', 'holy', 'taboo', both numinous and dangerous.[30] These are terms with very wide meanings, because the content of an experience of the 'holy' is highly variable and culture-specific; however, the relation between such experience and other experience is fairly stable across cultures, having the same limit-function, both defining and questioning the limits of normality. Therefore the 'religious' language with which it is often described will be avoided in this section, in order to treat as neutrally as possible this existential experience of unconditioned power, the 'potency of disorder'[31] which must be harnessed if life is to be enhanced as well as order preserved.

A basic strategy for achieving this is 'framing'.[32] By this is meant the positive control of disorder by containing it within conventional limits (that is, symbolic, humanly contrived categories) such as those of games, dance, drama, myth or ritual – activities in which the

---

[30] R. Otto, *The Idea of the Holy* (Oxford, 1950). Cf. Eliade, *Patterns*, pp. 1–33; Mol, *Identity*, pp. 202–6.

[31] Douglas, *PD*, p. 94.

[32] For the use of this term, see M. Milner, 'The role of illusion in symbol-formation', in M. Klein (ed.), *New Directions in Psychoanalysis* (London, 1955); for the logic of symbolic statements and actions 'in quotes', see D. Sperber, *Rethinking Symbolism* (Cambridge, 1975), pp. 90–112, esp. 110–12. See also Eliade, *Patterns*, pp. 32f; J. Fernandez, 'The mission of metaphor in expressive culture', *Current Anthropology*, 15 (1974), 119–47; Geertz, *Interpretation of Cultures*, pp. 87–125; E. R. Leach, 'Ritual', *International Encyclopedia of the Social Sciences*, vol. XIII, pp. 520–6; R. G. Lienhardt, *Divinity and Experience* (Oxford, 1961), pp. 252ff.

normal rules of behaviour are in some way set aside or reversed.[33] Thus in a dance the discharge of physical energy which might be destructive or divisive is made orderly, harmonious, corporate: a tension is released and group solidarity reaffirmed. Establishing and maintaining the 'frame', whether it be symbolised by a sacred space, sacred time, special clothes or special rules of behaviour, is essential for both releasing and containing the power which, in normal space or time, would be disturbing or positively evil. Hence to the frame attaches a sense of danger proper to the power it hedges in. But within the frame a new quality of experience is rendered possible, which is neither 'order' (normal experience) nor (destructive) 'disorder', but what we may call 'non-order':[34] though this quality is most easily described in negative terms, it is chiefly, though not universally, felt to be positive and life-enhancing. Two examples will make the point clear and conclude this general discussion.

The necessity and difficulty of structuring time, in its daily, monthly and annual cycles, and in the stages of a human life, give rise to many rituals designed to reduce the sense of time being a formless continuum and to strengthen the moments of symbolic transition.[35] This is the function of the 'timeless' moment of darkness and chaos commonly enacted at the New Year or Midsummer, an anamnesis of creation by which the power of disorder is acknowledged and human ability to order the world reasserted.[36] This is the function, too, of the more developed rites of passage. The use of physical and moral framing in these rituals has been commented on recently by Leach and Turner.[37] Thus initiation-rites commonly show a three-stage action, a symbolic death and rebirth through inversion of normality: temporary removal of the group of initiands into a place apart (typically, within a sacred enclosure or outside the settlement) which is a 'sacred space', that is, a place of 'holy disorder' or non-order, represented by the giving of special foods, clothes,

[33] For 'inversion' of the norm as a mode of framing, see M. Gluckman, 'Rituals of rebellion in S. E. Africa', in M. Gluckman, *Order and Rebellion in Tribal Africa* (London, 1963), pp. 110–36; Mol, *Identity*, pp. 243f; V. W. Turner, *The Ritual Process* (Chicago, 1969), pp. 166–205.

[34] Cf. D. W. Hardy and D. F. Ford, *Jubilate* (London, 1984), pp. 96–9.

[35] On 'sacred time', see Eliade, *Patterns*, pp. 388–408. On an equivalent ritual use of 'sacred space', see *ibid.*, pp. 367–87; also C. L. Albanese, 'The multi-dimensional mandala', *Numen*, 24 (1977), 1–25; B. Ray, 'Sacred space and royal shrines in Buganda', *History of Religions*, 16 (1977), 363–73.

[36] Cf. Eliade, *Patterns*, pp. 398–404.

[37] Leach, *CC*, pp. 77–9. Turner, *Ritual Process*, pp. 94–130; also V. W. Turner, *The Forest of Symbols* (New York, 1967), pp. 93–111. See also Mol, *Identity*, pp. 238–43.

names or language, and indulgence in behaviour associated with outcasts, children, madmen or savages; finally, after an act of purification, the initiates return to society transformed into their new status and its appropriate manners, customs and values (see figure 2[38]). In this transition from one status to another by passing through

Figure 2   The structure of initiation ceremonies

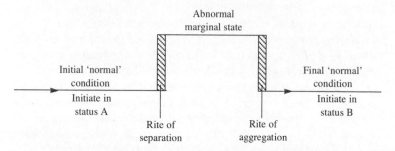

Abnormal
marginal state

Initial 'normal'
condition
Initiate in
status A

Final 'normal'
condition
Initiate in
status B

Rite of
separation

Rite of
aggregation

the margin, where all status is abolished, the danger of this event and the power it confers are recognised and contained.

The process of ritual 'inversion' of the norm is equally involved in sacrificial killing.[39] If an animal (or an offering of cereals, vegetables, wine or milk — the principle is the same) is given over to destruction, as in a holocaust, a deliberate loss is incurred by the donor, indistinguishable from waste except by the manner in which the action is performed, expressing the value attached to it by those involved. Even when the victim is to be wholly or partly consumed by the donor and his group in a communion-type meal, the death is still charged with significance, and in primitive cultures very rarely treated as routine or profane. To kill off part of the herd (even if apparently too old to calve or produce milk) is inherently risky destruction of productive capacity; yet meat is a source of health and vigour, and the reduced herd will have better access to food for its increase. Even utilitarian calculation, in these circumstances, treads the verge of mystery, and to take a life invokes disorder for the sake of creation. Thus death may be life-giving, but only in controlled conditions, with appropriate prayers and thanksgiving.

[38] Taken from Leach, *CC*, p. 78 (simplified).
[39] See J. van Baal, 'Offering, sacrifice and gift', *Numen*, 23 (1975), 161–78; H. Hubert and M. Mauss, *Sacrifice — Its Nature and Function* (ET London, 1964), p. 30.

In these ritual events, the spatial and temporal frames which enclose the 'inverted' activities, conferring on apparently anti-social acts altered and heightened meaning, paradoxically affirm and strengthen the bonds of order; as though the controlled inrush of chaos both recognises the ambiguity of our condition and affirms our ability to deal with it. A voluntary, socially sanctioned and highly specific breach of the rules affirms the system of rules.

Symbolic action

The range of phenomena to be included under the heading 'sacrifice' is so enormous it may be doubted whether any single theory can do justice to it all.[40] Participants in rituals seem peculiarly unable to explain what they are doing in ways that are either relevant or satisfactory.[41] Not surprisingly, then, modern anthropological theories have been very varied, and, like those of the participants themselves, they show a tendency to reduce rituals to a branch of some other and more comprehensible activity, such as technology, or gift, or (borrowing a model from the religious customs of our own culture) communion. These theories, exemplified in the writings of Frazer, Tylor and Robertson Smith respectively,[42] fail as general explanations because they seek to apply directly to this sphere a description in terms of the contents of ritual, derived from some other, value-charged but comprehensible, activity – which has then to be weakened or stretched to be sufficiently inclusive or precise to fit the facts.

By contrast, the structural model adopted here, though it does have analogues, aims to describe sacrificial action in terms of its form, and to be better able, therefore, to embrace a variety of culturally determined contents. It aims to define its function as a *system-affirming event*, whose precise purpose will be contextually established by the needs of any particular system. Finally, since a

---

[40] For surveys of theoretical treatments of sacrifice, see Bourdillon and Fortes, *Sacrifice*, pp. 1–25; E. O. James, *Sacrifice and Sacrament* (London, 1962), pp. 13–35. Recent studies include van Baal, 'Offering, sacrifice and gift'; T. P. van Baaren, 'Theoretical speculations on sacrifice', *Numen*, 11 (1964), 1–12; J. H. M. Beattie, 'On understanding sacrifice', in Bourdillon and Fortes, *Sacrifice*, pp. 29–44; V. W. Turner, 'Sacrifice as quintessential process – prophylaxis or abandonment?', *History of Religions*, 16 (1976–7), 189–215.

[41] Cf. Lévi-Strauss, *SA*, p. 18; R. G. Abrahams, 'Spirit, twins and ashes in Labwor, N. Uganda', in J. S. La Fontaine (ed.), *The Interpretation of Ritual* (London, 1972), p. 125; E. Bott, 'Psychoanalysis and ceremony', in La Fontaine, *Ritual*, p. 231.

[42] See Bourdillon and Fortes, *Sacrifice*, pp. 17–21; Rogerson, *Anthropology*, pp. 47–51 (on Frazer); van Baal, 'Offering, sacrifice and gift', pp. 161–78 (on Tylor).

sacrifice functions at the limit of a given cultural-conceptual system, its mode of operation will necessarily evade the understanding (cast *within* that system) of its participants, at least while they are engaged in its action. (In this respect, the claim of an outside observer to understand these matters better rests not on some supposed superiority but on the difference which being an outsider makes.)

In their essay on *Sacrifice* (first published in 1898),[43] Hubert and Mauss explored the meaning of rituals drawn from Hindu and Israelite tradition and identified a basic threefold form of symbolic action: Entry into sacred/significant space; a highly charged action there; and Exit now transformed.[44] By means of this action, and expressed most precisely in its central moment, there is a consecration, by which they mean a *communication* of sacred power. The weakness in their position arises from compromising this structural principle by a bias towards certain types of content, such as assuming the personal character of the divine power, and ascribing to the victim an exaggerated mediational role – both of which are very variable elements.[45] A more general description views sacrifice as essentially an *effective action* with typically the threefold shape noted above and illustrated in figure 2, a temporary transfer of the subject (or a representative) into the sacred marginal sphere, by which a *consecration* occurs, a transformation through sacred power.[46] So, although in content the action may well resemble a gift, an instrumental process, an act of homage, or whatever, in form it will have more in common with other transformational acts – especially those other 'framed' events already mentioned, myths, games and drama.

Among these, myth is distinguishable by its narrative mode, and game by its generally lower level of seriousness and higher degree of indeterminacy, but drama and rite are by no means easy to separate in every instance. Most sacrifice includes a word as well as an action, which may be the recital of a myth explaining the action, which thus presents it as renewing the mythical event, and turns the present into an anamnesis of the sacred past; or else it serves to bring about a dramatic identification of the object offered with its donor, or the god, or the recipient of the desired benefit.[47] This latter type, framing

[43] Hubert and Mauss, *Sacrifice*.

[44] *Ibid.*, pp. 30ff.

[45] *Ibid.*, pp. 51f, 95f. This confusion of the specific and the general is precisely their criticism of Robertson Smith's use of 'communion' as a principle (p. 7).

[46] Cf. Hubert and Mauss, *Sacrifice*, pp. 51ff; Beattie, 'On understanding sacrifice', pp. 29ff; Leach, *CC*, pp. 81–3.

[47] Cf. S. J. Tambiah, 'Form and meaning of magical acts: a point of view', in R. Horton and R. Finnegan (eds.), *Modes of Thought* (London, 1973), pp. 199–299.

by means of an explicit fiction, may take many forms: Hubert and Mauss quote a Hindu rite in which the donor is symbolically identified with the stake to which the victim is tied (being of identical height), anointed simultaneously, 'purified' by the devouring flames); S. J. Tambiah has described the 'persuasive analogy' by which a creeper is identified with a leprous limb in order to heal it; Elizabeth Bott has shown how the precisely ordained seating arrangements for the Tongan *kava* ceremony, by reproducing an ideal social order, serve to resolve conflicts arising between actual status hierarchies.[48]

In either case, both the action and the fiction by which it is buttressed have an outward and social character. The Tongan ritual exemplifies the fact that restoration of social solidarity is not necessarily secondary to commerce with divinity as an occasion for sacrifice, and that it is the function of prescribed rites, of appointed places, of sanctified priests, to ensure this social dimension even for, say, individual expiatory offerings: the rite reintegrates the individual sinner into the ordered system of divine–human relations. The public, conventional nature of the symbolism ensures that there is no such thing as a private sacrifice: even when being performed in seclusion, a public symbolic code is being employed and affirmed.[49]

A typology of the sacred

Before passing on to examine the sacrificial system of Israel, it is necessary to relate the abstract and formal concept of consecration set out so far to the range of possible contents of religious belief, the concepts of divinity by which in different cultures such acts are motivated at the level of consciousness, and the types of sacrifice appropriate to each.

The typology to be employed here is derived, with qualifications, from an anthropological essay by J. H. M. Beattie,[50] who views sacrifice similarly as an action bringing humans into relation with 'divine' power in the 'sacred sphere'. In terms of content he distinguishes two axes of experience: personal/impersonal and conjunctive/disjunctive. The basic model set out in the previous pages demands that the 'divine' be described in impersonal terms as unconditional power set over against the precarious human order, and

[48] Cf. Hubert and Mauss, *Sacrifice*, p.30; Tambiah, 'Form and meaning', pp.212–17; Bott, 'Psychoanalysis and ceremony', pp.217ff. See also Lévi-Strauss, *SA*, pp.207–27.
[49] Cf. Lienhardt, *Divinity and Experience*, pp.252–97; Douglas, *Natural Symbols*, pp.190f.
[50] Beattie, 'On understanding sacrifice', pp.37–43.

it may also, of course, be experienced as such; but since this power is the source of human personal life, personal conceptions of this life-giver are also widespread. Similarly, cultures differ in regarding this 'divine' power as a source of blessing to be sought or of danger to be avoided. These two axes thus yield four broad types of deity and four corresponding types of sacrifice (see figure 3):

Figure 3   A typology of the sacred

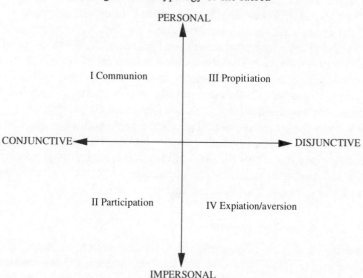

I.   *Personal-conjunctive*: This includes all rites aimed at personal contact with a god, such as mediumship and blessing; some forms of communion, the fellowship meal eaten in the god's presence or shared by him; also the gift, insofar as this expresses thanksgiving, homage, etc. It would also include the idea of dedication, and ideas of promise and covenant by which gods and humans enter into mutual (though more or less unequal) relations.

II. *Impersonal-conjunctive*: Here too the aim is to gain access to the divine, but conceived as impersonal power. It therefore includes theophagy, feasting not with but *on* the gods, by, for example, drinking their blood, in symbol, to acquire strength (this would apply even where a god thus impersonally consumed is conceived of as personal); also all ritual means by which people seek to harness themselves to the natural cycle, in fertility rites etc.; and sorcerous use of power.

III. *Personal-disjunctive*: This includes all actions motivated by fear of personal power, whether of dead ancestors, malevolent spirits, evil eye or wrath of a god: rites include exorcism, placatory gestures, and propitiatory offerings as quasi-personal means of restoring relationships.

IV. *Impersonal-disjunctive*: Divine power is here experienced as taboo or material impurity, a threat to personal life in the form of abstract evil, death or plague; responses include charms and other apotropaic gestures, expiations, purifications and boundaries to keep evil at bay.[51]

It will be noted that the two axes are not quite comparable in form. The horizontal (conjunctive/disjunctive) axis represents two sharply opposed relational orientations and forces (attraction/repulsion), variable but distinct, and giving no real value to the middle ground (which represents the sphere of 'normal life', in no direct contact with the divine); the vertical axis, though, offers potentially infinite gradations from pure impersonal Energy to the highly personalised concepts of Christ or Krishna, and including a wide middle area of variability and uncertainty, from which even these extremes are not wholly removed.

The distribution among these four types is of course very variable: almost certainly, every culture responds to the ambivalence of the holy by having some function at either end of the conjunctive/ disjunctive scale, either by means of a pantheon divided, like the Hindu and Greek, between gods of beneficent and gods of terrible aspect, or by a simple dualism of light and darkness, or by the riskier attempt to reconcile these opposites in the personality (whether perceived as comprehensive, or as unstable) of a single deity.

The aim of this section is not to impose a rigid classification on data which certainly require subtle and sensitive interpretation, but to provide a vocabulary through which to assess the style of a culture, its strategy for achieving balance and economy in its relations with the divine. So the exact classification of any particular rite is less important than the overall pattern of rites in a culture and the conception of deity which together they express. This will now be applied to the culture and institutions of Ancient Israel.

---

[51] No distinction is made at this stage between expiation and aversion; both this and the extent to which they are confused in Israel's worship will emerge below.

Israel and the sacred

The previous section has tried to set out, using categories and evidence drawn from anthropology and the phenomenological study of religion, a perspective on life as lived in a precariously ordered enclave surrounded by the non-ordered power of the holy. It is now time to inquire whether Ancient Israel shared such a view. This will be done in two stages. In the first subsection, a phenomenological survey using material drawn from the Old Testament generally will show it to be a normal and natural part of Israelite religion; in the second, we shall examine the way this perspective was exploited and systematised by the Priestly redactors of the Pentateuch.

Marginality and ambivalence

Evidence for the concept of liminality in Israel is abundant, notably in the widespread use of the marginal imagery of smoke, blood, doors and so on, with the ambivalent value these give to the 'holy', and in the importance attached to purity and impurity.

These may be illustrated from the use of pollution-symbolism in relation to funeral-practices.[52] In Israel, the dead were buried outside the settlement at the edge of the open country, and therefore in a place lying in the same relation to the settlement as the communal ash-tips. The actions of mourning included placing dust and ashes on one's head, or sitting in ashes (Josh. 7:6; 2 Sam. 1:2; Jer. 6:26; Esther 4:1); fasting and wailing (1 Sam. 31:13; 1 Kgs. 13:30), adopting forms of nakedness by going shoeless or in sackcloth, or by shaving (or alternatively veiling) the head (Joel 1:13; Ezek. 24:12,17; Gen. 37:24); even by self-laceration (Job 1:20; Lev. 19:28). Mourners are identifying with the departed by symbolically sharing their state; they thus express the marginality, the vulnerability of their own condition, even while living, between death and the living God. Some of these manifestations, however, were expressly forbidden in the law-code, presumably because they were associated with an actual cult of the dead (Lev. 19:26–31).[53] At other times of grief, the same polluting actions are employed to identify one's state as *outcast*, as by Job's friends (Job 2:12), or by the distraught messenger who must report that the Ark of God has fallen into the hands of

---

[52] See de Vaux, *AI*, pp. 56–61; H. Ringgren, *Israelite Religion* (London, 1966), pp. 239–42.

[53] See below, pp. 102f, 106.

the uncircumcised (1 Sam. 4:12), or by those who lament their exile in Babylon (Lam. 2:10; Isa. 47:1). On the other hand, the ashes of burnt-offerings are sacred, and must be removed with elaborate precautions to a 'clean place' (Lev. 6:10f), a special ash-tip: to 'pour out' these ashes like any normal refuse would be a desecration of the altar from which they came;[54] and the purification for anyone who has come into defiling contact with a dead body is to be made by sprinkling him or her with water containing the ashes of a ritually slaughtered heifer (Num. 19:1–10). The very uncleanness of ashes, like that of blood, makes them efficacious in cases of gross defilement. It is the outlandish quality of the prophet, his garments, diet and dwelling-place fit only for wild animals, which makes him symbolically efficacious as a divine spokesman (1 Kgs. 17:4–6; 2 Kgs. 1:8; Isa. 7:15; Matt. 3:1–4). The same ambiguity of the sacred-polluting margin is shown by Abraham when he is permitted to act as intercessor for the doomed city of Sodom, as mediator between humanity and God: lifted high above the human sphere, he sees himself as 'but dust and ashes' (Gen. 18:27). In Isaiah 6:1–8, the prophet, caught up into God's presence, in a vision expressed in emphatically marginal imagery (the smoke, the lips, the shaking threshold) exclaims: 'Woe is me, for I am a man of unclean lips.'

These examples illustrate a further point. An influential line of criticism has argued that the sense of sinfulness in God's presence is a feature of the Priestly document, and not characteristic of Israel's early religion, which was joyful and unconcerned with questions of ritual purity.[55] The patterns traced above are drawn from every period and tradition in the Old Testament and demonstrate that, despite the ways in which Old Testament worship developed, in Israel as elsewhere humanity's relation to the unconditioned powers of God and death is conveyed in a broad pattern of highly charged imagery of margins and impurity. It appears in J, E, D and P; in prophets and psalms and histories; in primitive and late texts. Thus, to take an example of a different sort, *dew* is a liminal image here as in many cultures, sharing the seminal, life-giving properties of

---

[54] Cf. 1 Kgs. 13:3. Likewise the dead, though associated with ashes, were not, of course, buried among the rubbish dumps, but in a 'clean place' in the same symbolic sphere. Contravention of this rule has perhaps contributed to the horror associated with Gehenna (Jer. 19).

[55] See de Vaux, *AI*, pp. 424–32, for a critical review of Wellhausen's theory; for a contrary account, see R. J. Thompson, *Penitence and Sacrifice in Early Israel outside the Levitical Law* (Leiden, 1963).

rain, and therefore regarded as a heavenly blessing – all the more so for the mysterious manner of its appearance. It is found meaning the blessing of fertility in Isaac's benediction, Moses' song and Job's reminiscence (Gen. 27:28; Deut. 32:2; Job 29:19); its meaning is extended to represent the divine power of life over the unborn and the dead (Ps. 110:3; Isa. 26:19); and the creative mist in Genesis 2:6 is a variation of the same image. In Judges 6 it is one element in the ancient tale of Gideon's encounter with the angel, along with other liminal imagery: the angel-mediator, the threshing-floor, the ram's fleece (Judg. 6:36–40; 2 Sam. 6:6–10). By contrast, in Hosea 13:3 dew and mist are associated with chaff and smoke as worthless and evanescent substances symbolising the fate of the idolaters; and in Dan. 4:15ff to have one's head 'wet with the dew of heaven' is to be an outcast, living among the fields, associating with beasts and madmen. In a verse of the Song of Songs (5:2) these senses are mingled, the lover's 'head wet with dew' beautifully expressing both his importunity and the fertility he offers to his beloved.

When we turn to the legislative portions of the Pentateuch we encounter material of much greater concentration and systematic organisation, but the areas of experience invoked are closely related, overwhelmingly marginal in emphasis and imbued with the same sense of liminal power.[56] Laws are necessarily much concerned with boundary disputes, with proving definitions and judging relations. Thus much of the legal code of Exodus 20 to 23 and Leviticus 11 to 26 is to do with contracts of marriage and enslavement; the treatment of slaves, lepers, strangers and sojourners, widows and orphans; cases of sexual perversion and ritual uncleanness. Apart from worship, the most sensitive activities, those most hedged about with rules and prohibitions, are those connected with food and sex. But the rules are not so much interested in the events themselves (their content) as in making clear distinctions between one type and another: 'purity' means unambiguousness.[57] Thus the charge levied against the abominations of incest, adultery, homosexuality and bestiality is that they are *tebhel*, usually translated 'perversion' but more properly 'mixing' or 'confusion' – the confounding of conceptual order.[58]

Mary Douglas argues that the same urge to mental classification governs the lists of forbidden foods of Leviticus 11 and Deuteronomy 14, which are therefore part of a classificatory system symbolic of

---

[56] See Douglas, *PD*, pp. 41–57.   [57] *Ibid.*, pp. 53ff.   [58] *Ibid.*, p. 53.

the wholeness of Israel and the unambivalent worship of Yahweh. Thus the pig is forbidden, not because kept by the Canaanites,[59] nor because unhealthy,[60] but – as the texts indeed say – because it is *anomalous* in its physical properties, fails to fit into any of the categories and is therefore disturbing for the same reason as the eunuch and the transvestite.[61] There are strong reasons for favouring such a structural explanation.

Historical factors enter in, of course, to show why this one prohibition has received more attention than the rest of a long list, but seeking piecemeal explanations for these or any other laws leads to fragmentary and contradictory reasoning at just the point where clarity and consistency are being insisted on as the prime virtues, the sharp distinction between what is and is not acceptable to Yahweh which occupies Leviticus 10 to 15. Douglas argues that 'holiness' in Leviticus means wholeness, completeness, as the sign of Israel's being (wholly) 'set apart'. Israel is treated as a priestly nation which must therefore, like its priests above all, be uncontaminated by the relativities and confusions of ordinary life. So the nation's boundaries must be strictly defined: just as only Israelites and their circumcised slaves may participate in the covenant-celebration of the Passover (Exod. 12:43f), so, by analogy, one is rendered unclean by a number of bodily discharges, set out at length in Leviticus 12 and 15. Like the dietary rules of Leviticus 11, these serve to place a clear break between clean and unclean, and therefore between Israel and the nations.[62]

The same concern for wholeness has dictated the inclusion of the rules for first diagnosing and then cleansing leprosy (Lev. 13f). The skin as the body's boundary must separate without ambiguity what is inside from what is outside. The visible corruption and decay of the skin, the blurring of the edges of the self, rather than some supposed incurableness or infectiousness of the diseases here described under the name 'leprosy',[63] is the cause of the apparently instinctual horror it excites, and of the countervailing and deliberate precision of this long section in Leviticus. The leper is a visible reminder of the vulnerability of the margins, and the question whether a particular ailment is, or is not, leprosy, must be quickly decided, and by the priest as guardian of the community's wholeness. If it is, the one who is 'unclean' is consigned to the place of the dead in a mourning posture until healed, after which, by a complex progressive rite he is

---

[59] *Ibid.*, pp. 48f.   [60] *Ibid.*, pp. 30–2.   [61] *Ibid.*, pp. 51f.   [62] *Ibid.*, pp. 49ff.
[63] See de Vaux, *AI*, pp. 462–4; Davies, 'An interpretation of sacrifice in Leviticus', pp. 396f.

readmitted to the community (Lev. 13:45f, 14:1–20). It is impossible to tell what elements of medical precaution against infection might be presupposed by these devices for avoiding ritual defilement, but there is no evidence in the texts to suggest that there is any at all. The precision of the rules indicates a quite exceptional interest in the identification and cleansing of the disease; yet they fail (curiously, from a modern point of view) to discriminate between 'leprosy' as a human disease (whatever actual malady was meant) and 'leprosy' as a disease of garments and houses (Lev. 13:47–59, 14:33–53): the latter (presumably forms of mould) were to be cleansed by the same rite as laid down for humans. It would seem, then, that Douglas Davies, in his interesting study of this area from a structuralist point of view, is mistaken in arguing that it was because they 'disrupted social life' that leprosy for people and for houses demanded ritual action.[64] The logic of marginal impurity is working the other way: it is the symbolic uncleanness which makes the house uninhabitable, the garment unwearable, the person an outcast, and not vice versa. This is confirmed by the additional comments of the Mishnah, absurd from any practical point of view, that only Israelites and their houses are liable to contract leprosy, which does not affect Gentiles or sojourners, or houses outside Israel – nor, most revealingly, does it affect houses within Jerusalem.[65] Evidently, the nature of this problem of impurity, and the separation it demands, is neither medical nor social, but theological.

The theology of separation

One of the features of the methodology adopted here is its presentation of the *undifferentiated* function of the 'divine', as source of life and death over against the human domain. Bringing this into relation to the Old Testament presents a problem, since differentiating fiercely between what is and is not really divine is the ruling passion of most of the Old Testament's components. Inevitably, it questions the value of such a phenomenological survey, which appears to treat Old Testament material of great sophistication and theological self-consciousness on a par with customs observed among pre-literate peoples. The purpose of including, in the last subsection, alongside ancient rites and occasional imagery, items of carefully drafted

[64] *Ibid.*, p. 397.
[65] Mishnah Negaim 3.1, 12.1,4 (H. Danby (ed. and trans.), *The Mishnah* (Oxford, 1933), pp. 678f, 691). Cf. Davies, 'Sacrifice in Leviticus', pp. 396f.

legislation from the Priestly document, is not to reduce the whole to
the status of a primitive religion but to show that the latest sections,
being revisions of much older material, take up prerational rites and
beliefs into a higher order.

The rationale behind the Priestly code's interest in these areas of
marginal ambivalence, and its regulatory treatment, is its theology
of holiness understood as *separation*:[66]

Who shall ascend the hill of the Lord?
And who shall stand in his holy place?
The one who has clean hands and a pure heart. (Ps. 24:3f)

In setting out this perception, it employs three modes of organisation
which are transformations of each other: first, the construction of a
rigid conceptual 'map' of Israel as a theological community; second,
the definitional role given to the mediating function of the Aaronic
priesthood as occupants of the sacred sphere; third, the interrelation
of law and narrative as twin determinants of Israel's present. All three
display a reciprocal defensiveness in connection with the 'holy': a
desire to protect Israel against the dangerous force of God's holiness,
and to protect both Israel and God against defilement by the world.
As a result, there is a tendency for expiation – offerings made to God
to set right a relationship broken by sin – to be confused with aversion
– offerings made to demons to ward them off. This is a transition
with serious consequences for Israel and its understanding of God.

The Camp

In the ideal conception of Israel in God's presence which came to
dominate the Pentateuch, Yahweh is visualised as enclosed behind
numerous marginal zones: making his presence known only in the
inner sanctuary of the Tabernacle, which stands in the court into
which only the priests may go (Exod. 27:9ff). Around this sacred
area the Levites are encamped, preventing non-sacral tribes from
'drawing near' to defile God's presence, and simultaneously protecting Israel from the 'wrath' which any such approach would incur
(Num. 1:51–3) (see figure 4).

It might seem that under this scheme the ambivalence of the non-
ordered realm, as expressed in figure 1, should be reduced, since
from the point of view of the 'Camp' (that is, ordinary experience),
Yahweh and the 'Wilderness', good–holy and bad–holy, are placed
at opposite poles. This implied polarisation of Life and Death, as

[66] See von Rad, *OTT*, vol. I, pp. 203–12, 272–9.

Figure 4   The geography of the sacral community

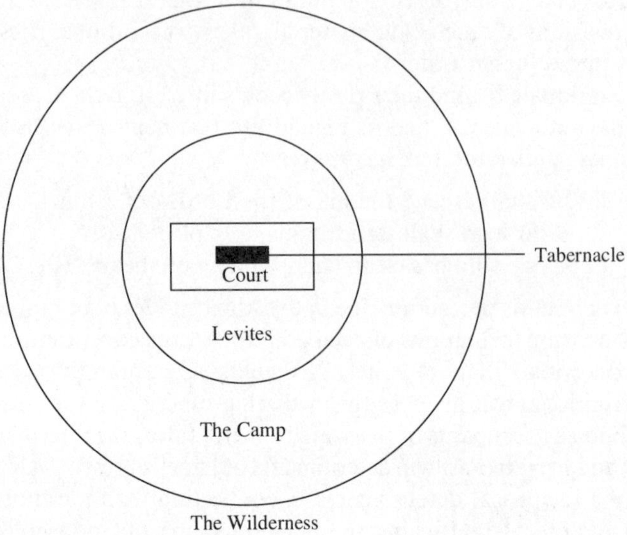

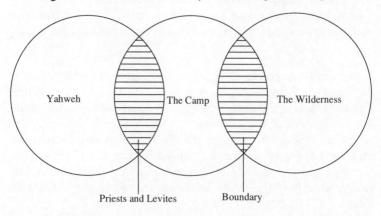

Figure 5   The sacral community and its dangerous margins

depicted in figure 5,[67] is not consistently maintained. In part, this is because the 'map' is inspired by interest in the Temple and its cultus, and therefore less attention is paid to the boundary of the

[67] Compare the schemas used by Davies, 'An interpretation of sacrifice in Leviticus', p. 394, and Leach, *CC*, p. 86.

Camp (in marked contrast to the outward-focussed exclusivism of Ezra-Nehemiah: for example, Ezra 9f). This scheme does operate in most of the sacrificial rituals, but the theology as a whole is not so fully integrated, nor so neat. The danger incurred by infringement of ritual purity (approaching Yahweh) is called 'wrath' or 'plague' interchangeably (Num. 1:53, 8:19); those who endanger God's holiness may suffer destruction in the vicinity of the sacred precincts, or expulsion into the 'Wilderness' (Lev. 10:2; Num. 12:15).

The actual wilderness as a real place and source of *physical* danger is of no interest to the Priestly authors, although those Israelites who show a preference for life there rather than make the risky passage into the "Land of Promise" bring upon themselves death in exile, beyond the borders of Canaan (Num. 14:20ff). Alongside this controlling idea of the central Tabernacle there stand, embedded in the P-narrative, several ancient texts reflecting an alternative conception of the desert sanctuary as a 'Tent of Meeting' situated *outside the Camp* in a sphere visited only by selected 'elders' (Exod. 33:7–11; Num. 11:16, 24–6, 12:4; Deut. 31:14f). The tent then stands in the same relation to Israel as Mount Sinai, and reflects an interest in personal encounter, rather than sacrifice, as the mode of communication.[68] The topographical inconsistency is outweighed, even in the narrative, by an identical thrust: both express theologies of divine manifestation, through the cloud and smoke, of a God whose holiness can have no permanent contact with humanity (as opposed to the Ark-theology of God's dwelling among Israel), and who must for Israel's sake be separated from the Camp, either by Levites or by physical distance. However, the standardised version (figures 4 and 5), by striving to separate good–holy from bad–holy, conveys also the fear that Yahweh must manifest himself in the centre lest he be himself threatened by the powers of destruction.

The priesthood
The practical expression of this encircling function of the Levites is the reserving to the priests of the right of entry to the court and sanctuary, and the repeated statement that it is the *priests* who 'make atonement' for sins (Lev. 4:20, 26, 31, 35; 5:6, 10, 13, 16, 18; 6:7 – but notably omitted at 4:12, 21). The latter point, which is unique to P, does not imply that the priests here usurp God's function;[69] rather the holiness of God is such that the priesthood is

established as a barrier endowed with sufficient holiness to communicate God's 'covering' of sin. The clear distinction between priest and layman, though not evidenced in the earliest Old Testament strata,[70] had doubtless obtained in the Jerusalem Temple long before the Exile, but the emphasis placed on it in P is correlated to the necessity of preserving the holiness without which this divine action cannot be discharged.

In the elaborate rites of ordination and purification are to be found the most markedly 'structural' means for separating clean from unclean, as well as some very primitive-seeming features, of apotropaic character. Leach has shown how, among the multiple sacrifices, the central action of the ordination-rite given in Lev. 8–9 exhibits the pattern of a rite of passage (figure 2).[71] Aaron and his sons are first *separated* from the congregation, by being washed, anointed and reclothed, and by presenting a pair of offerings (Lev. 8:1–21); next *consecrated* by a special blood-rite and secluded within the sanctuary for seven days in God's presence, living on the meat of the 'ram of ordination' (8:22–36); finally *reintegrated* with the congregation in their new status as sanctified priests by performing their first sacrifices on behalf of the people (9.1–21). The whole action is completed by a multiple manifestation of divine power: blessing, glory, fire, noise (9:22–4). Those who have been privileged to dwell in God's house now discharge this power, particularly that of 'covering' or 'atoning for' sin.

Law and narrative

The means by which such covering is made are chiefly the sacrifices to be examined in the next section. What these sacrificial rules presuppose is a holy priesthood, an institution endowed by God with his holy power: hence the system-creating function occupies a large place in the ordering of the material, and overflows from legal texts into narratives concerned with threats to purity and endangered boundaries. Immediately following the ordination of Aaron's sons as priests, Leviticus 10 narrates the action of two of them, Nadab and Abihu, who offer 'unholy fire' in their censers before the Lord, and upon whom 'holy fire' falls to consume them (Lev. 10:1f). The purpose of this, the only true narrative in Leviticus, is plain: the ban on 'unholy fire' (presumably incense offered in a manner

---

[70] For example, Judg. 17:5, 7ff. See de Vaux, *AI*, pp. 345–57.
[71] Leach, *CC*, pp. 89–91.

suggestive of pagan worship[72]) is paralleled by the prohibition laid on priests against performing mourning-practices associated with cults of the dead (Lev. 10:6, 21:10f). As a complement to this narrative of the misuse of priestly power, Numbers 16 and 17 recite the revolt of Korah and his Levitical party, a challenge from outsiders against the Aaronid privilege. The offence of Eldad and Medad, related in Numbers 11, can also be seen to be a transformation of the same theme into terms appropriate to the rival Tent of Meeting tradition.[73] The revolt of Korah is not an isolated event, but a major element in the structure of the book of Numbers. The profound crisis caused by this bid for priestly equality results not only in the death of the 250 insurrectionists (swallowed alive by the earth) and the 'plague' from Yahweh which devours 14,700 sympathisers before it is 'stopped' by the ritual mediation of Aaron (Num. 16:31−5, 46−50), but requires, further, the miraculous proof of Aaron's priestly authority in chapter 17 (the rod which sprouts almond-blossom, Num. 17: 8−10), and the divine reaffirmation in chapter 18 that the separated state of the priesthood is a *blessing* on Israel to protect it from defilement by contact with the sacred sphere: 'and anyone else who comes near shall be put to death' (Num. 18:7). For further emphasis, the whole section is given a symbolic frame, through material setting out the absolute penalties for high-handed defiance of God's holiness (the man gathering sticks on the sabbath, 15:27−41), and through the primitive rite for consecrating expiatory 'water for impurity' (19:1−10).

Similarly, in Leviticus, the question of who may 'draw near', and how, dominates chapters 8−16, that is, the entire section between the sacrificial rubrics (1−7) and the Holiness Code (17−26). This

---

[72] See M. Noth, *Leviticus* (London, 1965), pp. 84f; J. C. H. Laughlin, 'The "strange fire" of Nadab and Abihu', *JBL*, 95 (1976), 559−65.

[73] Num. 11:16f, 24−30. The parallels between these traditions may be set out in tabular form:

	Tent of Meeting outside camp	Tabernacle at centre of Camp
Shrine	Tent of Meeting outside camp	Tabernacle at centre of Camp
Leaders	70 Elders	Sons of Aaron
Crisis	Eldad and Medad prophesy in the Camp	Korah etc. approach shrine with censers
Comment	Moses: 'Would that all were prophets'	Korah: 'All the congregation is holy'
Result	Wind brings quails to Israel	Earth/fire consumes rebels

It is notable of course that in this prophetic tradition (see M. Noth, *Numbers* (London, 1968), p. 90; P. J. Budd, *Numbers* (Waco, TX, 1984), pp. 126f) it is God who breaks the monopoly by sending his spirit on the pair, and Moses supports them against Joshua. For the question of charismatic versus institutional legitimation, see below, pp. 103−5.

extended theme explains the otherwise artificial connection made in
16:1 between the rite for the Day of Atonement which follows and
the sin of Nadab and Abihu not mentioned since chapter 10. The
first half of chapter 16 (vv. 2–28) appears to be an addition to
chapters 8 and 9, and a revision of the situation envisaged there,[74]
with the priests in constant commerce between the Camp and the Tent
in its midst. Here, apparently in the light of the dangers attached,
Aaron is instructed 'not to come at all times into the holy place
within the veil' (16.2) but to do so, presumably, at special times only
(though the institution of this as an annual feast is a further addition,
16.29–34[75]), but, most important, he is to do so only after taking
elaborate ritual precautions against impurity (16:3–5). Between
chapters 10 and 16, leaving no doubt about the issue involved, has
been inserted the solid block of regulations about *purity* in relation
to foods (11), childbirth (12), leprosy (13f), and bodily discharges
(15).

The theme of purity, especially in relation to the creation and
maintenance of the priesthood as a holy institution logically prior
to the sacrifices it exists to perform, is thus made to dominate these
books through a variety of literary modes. At this point, one further
transformation may be briefly noted. Parallel to these narratives of
threats to priestly prerogative, by external challenge and internal
corruption, there are the *political* narratives of threats to Israel's
divinely appointed leadership: the revolt of the people at Kadesh/
Meribah (Num. 11, 13–14, 20) and of Miriam (Num. 12), with their
dire consequences (Num. 11:1, 14:22f, 20:1); and the failure of those
entrusted with the leadership, Moses and Aaron, and their deaths,
likewise, in the wilderness (Num. 20:24ff, 27:12ff). In all these cases
the nature of the sin is appropriate to the political sphere, personal
and moral, providing a complement to the impersonal and ritual sin
in the other stories. This rather different view of the nature of Israel
will be taken up again at the end of the next section.

Sacrifice in Israel

No attempt is made in this section to give a complete account of the
sacrificial practices laid down in the Old Testament or performed
in Israel. Its aim is to discover the dynamic of the priestly system by

[74] See Noth, *Leviticus*, pp. 117–19, 126.
[75] *Ibid.*, pp. 117, 126.

identifying the systematic function of the main types of sacrifice and the leading concepts these employ, and by relating them to the categories set out in pages 77–9 above.[76]

Types of sacrifice

Communion-sacrifices

In the *zebah shelamim* ('peace-offering', RSV)[77] a domestic animal of either sex and from either herd or flock was presented to Yahweh, and while its fat portions were burnt as 'an offering by fire, a pleasing odour to the Lord' (Lev. 3:5), and its blood 'thrown against the altar round about' (Lev. 3:2), the meat was consumed by the donor with his family or friends (though later supplements appoint certain portions to be set aside for the priests' maintenance (Lev. 7:28ff, 10:14f). In origin, it was a first-fruits offering, sacrificed by the family head at the local shrine on some occasion of communal or private rejoicing (Exod. 24:9–11, 34:15; Deut. 12:18; 1 Sam. 9:12f, 16:3ff; 1 Kgs. 8:62–6). This function largely fell aside when the Deuteronomic code centralised the cultus in Jerusalem, splitting it into a formal rite and a secularised slaughter; and by the removal of the priestly levies noted above it came to approximate to the holocaust. Whether, therefore, it retained in the Second Temple the character of a joyful household feast, motivated by gratitude and relaxed in its procedures,[78] may be doubted, but the meaning of the action is still evident in the form.

The *zebah* is a meal eaten in God's presence and, using our typology of the divine, is *personal-conjunctive* (Type I) in tendency. It has been argued that God was conceived as sharing the meal, united to the donors by co-consumption of the victim.[79] The idea of feeding God was widespread, but it appears in Israel only under foreign influence. The portions set aside for God consist of the blood and fat, both of which are in every instance sacred – impure substances

---

[76] For this simplified typology, see de Vaux, *AI*, pp. 415ff; de Vaux *Studies* pp. 27ff, 91ff; and Young, *SI*, pp. 35ff; however, vegetable and incense-offerings have been included with holocausts as *gifts*, as they add little of interest for our purpose.

[77] The rules are set out in Lev. 3. For comment, see de Vaux, *AI*, pp. 417f, 426–9, and *Studies*, pp. 31–51; Young, *SI*, pp. 35–40; von Rad, *OTT*, vol. I, pp. 257f.

[78] See, for example, the looser regulations regarding choice of victim (Lev. 22:23), presumably because economic factors could not be ignored. Only the supplementary regulations (Lev. 7:19–21) insist on the ritual purity of the participants; but cf. 1 Sam. 16:5.

[79] See W. Eichrodt, *Theology of the Old Testament* (ET London, 1961–7), p. 84, and discussion in de Vaux, *AI*, pp. 449f; de Vaux, *Studies*, pp. 38ff; Young, *SI*, pp. 37f.

which humans are forbidden to consume; they contrast instructively
with the profane value of the choice portions (breast and thigh) set
aside for the priests when they, as God's agents or representatives,
are held worthy of taking part in the feast.[80] In any case, though an
excessively anthropomorphic understanding may have been edited
out of the texts we possess,[81] that would not have affected the form
of the action: the essential point is an act of consecration of the
victim in the sacred place,[82] followed by communication of that
sacred power to the social group through the feast which, whether
eaten in a 'holy place' or at home, is reckoned to be in God's presence.
It expresses the sacredness of life and the solemnity of death, with
the minimum of sacerdotal overtones; in Leviticus, however, the
feasting is played down and the *zebah* becomes one of a number
of gift-offerings.

Holocausts

By contrast, the holocaust (*'olah* or *kalil*)[83] was regularly practised
until the destruction of the Temple, a daily morning and evening
sacrifice of this type being prescribed in Numbers 28:3f. The stipula-
tions are in some ways similar to those for the *zebah*, though more
precise as regards the choice of victim. The blood is, once again,
thrown against the altar by the priest, but the whole of the victim
is consigned to God to be burnt on the altar for 'a pleasing odour'.

It is most naturally understood as chief among gift-sacrifices.[84]
As a total offering, yielding no material benefit to the donor, the
'olah expresses vividly an unconditional homage to God, as the daily
offerings of the *tamid* expressed Israel's continued dedication to
the Lord. This understanding entails a quantitative element which
is at odds with the symbolic absoluteness of the offering, for if a
whole beast pleases God better than a part, would not several please
him still more? This idea, presumably exacerbated in popular belief
if God was thought to feed on the pleasing odour,[85] certainly contributed to a tendency, especially at times of crisis, to multiply

[80] For the significance of blood, see below. On fat, see especially Lev. 3:16: 'All
fat is the Lord's'; also Gen. 4:4; Lev. 3:3f, 4:8, 7:3. See also de Vaux, *Studies*, pp. 42, 50f.
[81] See *ibid.*, pp. 42ff.
[82] See de Vaux, *AI*, p. 453; Young, *SI*, pp. 35–7; von Rad, *OTT*, vol. I, p. 257.
[83] The rules are set out in Lev. 1. For discussion, see de Vaux, *AI*, pp. 415–17,
426–9; de Vaux, *Studies*, pp. 27–51; Young, *SI*, pp. 38–40; von Rad, *OTT*, vol. I,
pp. 255f.
[84] See de Vaux, *AI*, p. 452; de Vaux, *Studies*, p. 37; Young, *SI*, pp. 38–40.
[85] See de Vaux, *Studies*, pp. 40ff.

sacrifices in a way that is frankly propitiatory and against which the prophets inveigh (2 Sam. 24:24f; Amos 5:21–4; Isa. 1:11). In this process, a gift-rite which is basically personal-conjunctive (Type I) acquired a disjunctive character, aiming to avert Yahweh's anticipated wrath (Type III). It may be relevant to note that in Greek religion the holocaust was a part of the chthonic cult;[86] Leviticus 1:4 explicitly adopts the *'olah* into P's expiatory system by giving it a (general) atoning function.

Expiatory sacrifices

Though rarely attested before the Exile, the expiatory *hatta'th* and *asham* ('sin-offering' and 'guilt-offering', RSV)[87] are the most prominent components of the sacrificial rubrics in Leviticus, some of their features being, it appears, transposed also into the rules for offerings of different types,[88] and they provide the base for the many ancillary purificatory rites of the Temple system. Though it is less likely that they were innovations than revisions of ancient rites,[89] they introduce into this material a new element, in the focussing of all rituals through the key concepts of purity, sin and atonement.

Attempts to clarify the difference between the offences for which *hatta'th* and *asham* were appropriate have not succeeded.[90] Interest in the moral aspect of sin is hard to document, but sin as 'impurity' is fundamental to these rites: ritual uncleanness of a material, even contagious character.[91] Similarly, the moral and personal overtones of the English word 'atone' are misleading in this context, and translation of *kipper* by 'expiation' is to be preferred, not least in having likewise a restricted, technical sense which resists reduction to other concepts. Whatever its etymology, the word's meaning has to be derived here from the meaning of the cultic system in which it

[86] See de Vaux, *Studies*, pp. 48ff; Young, *SI*, pp. 13f, 38.

[87] The rules are set out in Lev. 4:1–5:13 and 5:14–6:7. For discussion, see de Vaux, *AI*, pp. 418–21, 429f; de Vaux, *Studies*, pp. 91–112; Young, *SI*, pp. 40–3; von Rad, *OTT*, vol. I, pp. 258ff.

[88] See Lev. 1:4 and Young, *SI*, p. 52n.

[89] See de Vaux, *Studies*, pp. 102ff.

[90] See von Rad, *OTT*, vol. I, p. 259; de Vaux, *Studies*, pp. 98ff; N. H. Snaith, 'Sin-offering and guilt-offering', *VT*, 15 (1965), 73–80.

[91] See J. Milgrom, 'Sin-offering or purification-offering', *VT*, 21 (1971), 237–9, where it is argued, on linguistic grounds, that *hatta'th* should be rendered 'purification-offering', the moral overtones of the familiar translation being a distortion derived from the LXX's use of ἁμαρτία. This conclusion seems probable (it is shared by the recent study of N. Kiuchi, *Purification Offering in the Priestly Literature* (Sheffield, 1987)); but it does not follow that ritual impurity is a merely technical problem, without theological, and therefore moral, implications.

functions and whose purpose it denotes.[92] Expiation takes on, in Leviticus, the impersonal character of the 'sin' which it exists to deal with, as an objective act of setting right. Since sin may put one in danger of God's wrath, expiation may acquire negative overtones of aversion, and these are prominent in P, which is concerned with the Godward and objective nature of the action. But equally its function is restoration of an individual to his or her place in the order of Israel, and it is reasonable to suppose that the subjective, moral sense of sin operated in the individual, who might experience expiation as forgiveness.

It is necessary to look in more detail at the working of the sin-offering, which provides the pattern for the other expiatory rites. Like the other sacrifices, the action of the *hatta'th* has three phases: the presentation; the blood-rite; the disposal of the flesh. Full discussion of the *blood-rite* will be reserved till later,[93] but we may note here that its manner is different from that of the *zebah* and *'olah* since the blood is not thrown against the altar but smeared on its horns and the rest poured out at its base. As with the others, however, the *slaughter* is a preparatory operation, relatively non-sacral in character and performed by the donor not the priest, to facilitate the blood-rite proper and the appropriate treatment of the flesh. It is not, of course, as though the death were unimportant, but rather that the animal is conceived, on the one hand, as being prepared for the blood-rite proper, and on the other, as having already passed within the sphere of death in the moment of being presented and accepted as a proper offering (see below), the slaughter only actualising at the biological level what is already the case. It might even be said to pass into death at the moment when it is picked out of the herd or flock, 'set apart' for sacrifice.[94]

The *presentation* includes up to four elements: bringing the victim (and other sacrificial material) to the altar; laying hands on its head; an act of confession; the priest's declaration of acceptance or rejection. In every rehearsal of the procedures for the *hatta'th*, the

---

[92] Cf. Young, *SI*, p. 42 and von Rad, *OTT*, vol. I, p. 262. Suggested root-meanings, based on possible etymologies, include 'cover', 'wipe away', 'purge'.

[93] See below, pp. 98f, and for its meaning see pp. 100–3.

[94] See de Vaux, *AI*, p. 452; Young, *SI*, pp. 54ff. Compare the following account of human dying: 'When man is beyond the possibility of praising God, he is truly "in death" ... Thus the dangerously ill, the accused who face the court without any support, the persecuted who are helplessly delivered over to their enemies, all these already belong to the world of the dead' (H. W. Wolff, *Anthropology of the Old Testament* (London, 1974), p. 111; see also pp. 106f, 109–13.)

donor is instructed to 'lay his hand on the head' of the victim and kill it. No doubt, this has the practical function of identifying the individual for whom this offering is to be made.[95] No explanation is offered, but it surely also means more than this. What meaning is it given by its structural function, in relation to the confession, declaration and consumption which follow?

In Leviticus 16:21, Aaron is commanded to lay his hands on the scapegoat and 'confess over it all the iniquities of the people of Israel'. Since confession is not commanded elsewhere as a specifically cultic act, it has been argued that this confession and transference of sin to the beast are, like its expulsion into the desert, special to this occasion. However, several texts command confession as part of the process of atonement for sin (Lev. 5:5; Num. 5:6f); and, given the purpose of the *hatta'th* as a means of dealing with *specific* offences, such a solemn acknowledgement of guilt, made in the holy place before the Lord, seems necessary. A simple, formal acknowledgement of error is what is intended, it appears, such as would very naturally accompany the act of presenting the sacrifice by laying one's hand on its head.[96] Such a view would add support to the argument that at this point, in response, one of a number of 'declaratory formulae' was uttered by the priest: 'it is unclean meat', 'it is (not) accepted', 'it is a sin-offering'.[97] If the priest's 'reckoning' extends beyond technical examination of the victim to include (especially in the case of the sin- and guilt-offerings) assessment of the donor, the ancient priestly function of giving *torah*, divine oracles, is here retained in stylised form, the priest enunciating to the sinner God's verdict and therefore, if favourable, his forgiveness.[98] The formula is more than a comment, it is an *illocutionary act*, for when the priest pronounces 'It is *hatta'th*' the sacrifice has begun.[99]

The fact that *hatta'th* means both the 'sin' and the 'sin-offering' has raised the question whether what happens in that little drama centred on the laying on of hands is the *transference* of the confessed

[95] See de Vaux, *AI*, p. 416; Young, *SI*, p. 53.

[96] See E. O. James, *The Nature and Function of Priesthood* (London, 1955), pp. 180–2, for examples; see also H. H. Rowley, 'Sacrifice', pp. 82f.

[97] Lev. 19:7, 22:23, 4:21. On the identification and interpretation of these formulae, see von Rad, *OTT*, vol. I, pp. 260–2.

[98] See von Rad, *OTT*, vol. I, pp. 260f, 271f.

[99] *Ibid.*, p. 262. On the concept of illocutionary acts, see J. L. Austin, *How to do Things with Words* (Oxford, 1965); J. R. Searle, *Speech Acts* (Cambridge, 1969); and see further chapter 8 below.

and accepted sin to the beast being presented.[100] This view, though controversial, is supported by the means of disposal of the flesh: following the slaughter and the blood-rite, and the burning of the fat portions on the altar (as in *zebah*), the rest of the flesh is consumed by the priests in the sacred precincts (Lev. 6:24–30). This is quite different to the tithing regulations appended to other offerings. The flesh is said to be 'a very holy thing' and when they eat it the priests 'bear the iniquity of the congregation' (Lev. 6:29, 10:17). As in the holocaust, the meat is consumed within the sacred sphere and therefore wholly removed from the profane, but this consumption by the priests rather than by fire identifies them as similarly vehicles of divine power, and mediators between human sin and God's holiness. The objection has been raised,[101] that the animal cannot be identified with the 'sin' formerly 'borne' by its donor since it is as a 'very holy thing' that the priests eat it. This sounds contradictory, but the ambivalence of the holy and the characteristic inversion entailed by ritual have altered the logic. Once the animal has been transferred into the sacred sphere it no longer participates in the *relative* condition of created things but is 'set apart' as bad–holy, utterly impure, 'sin'. Its impurity will contaminate any other person or object (including the pots in which it will be cooked (Lev. 6:28)), but is discharged, 'borne' by the priests, who are themselves 'most holy'.[102]

[100] See James, *Priesthood*, p. 148; Leach, *CC*, pp. 81–4; Rowley, 'Sacrifice', pp. 82–92. This view is contested by de Vaux (*AI*, p. 416, *Studies*, p. 94) and by Young, *SI*, p. 52. For discussion, see below and n. 102.

[101] De Vaux, *AI*, p. 419f, *Studies*, p. 94; Young, *SI*, p. 52.

[102] The discussion of this topic has been bedevilled by the introduction of theologically motivated irrelevancies, especially the association of 'substitution' with penal ideas or a supposed origin in human sacrifice, as by James, *Sacrifice and Sacrament*, p. 34. See pp. 101f below. Rowley, 'Sacrifice', p. 83, reads into the act a Christian moral significance ('death to sin', cf. Young, *SI*, p. 51); Leach, *CC*, p. 84, explains it by means of an analogy, alien to the Old Testament, of the separation of the soul from the body. What is proposed here is that the victim becomes, in the act of presentation, the *objective representative* of the sin, borne away into the holy place to be destroyed, annulled, 'covered', according to the divinely appointed rules. The victim dies, therefore, not in any sense 'in stead of' its donor, but 'on his behalf', to effect the cleansing: without this action he would continue to 'bear his sin' (Lev. 5:1) and therefore to provoke wrath, not only on himself but on Israel as a whole. See the extended discussion in von Rad, *OTT*, vol. I, pp. 262–72, which stresses Israel's belief in the *corporateness* and *objectivity* of sin, and its synthetic fusion with the sin-offering in this objective event.

Institutional expiations

In the first two types of sacrifice the priest's part is restricted to accepting the offering and bringing the relevant portions to the altar: he is appointed to perform an intermediary function. In the *hatta'th*, the priesthood as a whole stands as a human 'sacred zone', a holy fire to sanctify and expiate. Therefore ensuring the holiness of the institution is of paramount importance, and this is the purpose, explicitly or implicitly, of all the special expiatory rites given in the texts.

The point can be made clear by stating that the sin-offering for a priest is different from that for a layperson, but identical with that for a sin of the whole nation (Lev. 4:1–12, 13–21). It differs from the norm in each of the three phases mentioned above. The major offering of a young bull is prescribed; once it has been presented and killed its blood is, in an explicitly apotropaic gesture, taken within the sanctuary and sprinkled seven times towards the veil of the Holy of Holies, then rubbed on the horns of the incense altar there before the rest is poured out, as usual, at the base of the altar of sacrifice. But most important to notice here is the fact that the priest, being on this occasion tarnished with human sinfulness, is effectively 'profane' and unable to 'bear' his own sin so as to dispose of it. Therefore the flesh is not eaten but burnt, and not on the altar (as a holocaust) but 'outside the Camp' on the Temple ash-heap, which despite its function and location is regarded paradoxically as a 'clean place' (Lev. 4:12). Here this sin which threatens the holiness of the entire priesthood may be discharged, and chaos kept at bay.

In this movement the limits of the mediational system are sharply exposed. The holiness of the centre is so loaded with the function of removing sin that the system is crucially vulnerable to breakdown through the occurrence of sin at that point. A less sin-conscious source might have defined sin in such a way as to make it an impossibility for priests; but when the system fails only action in the holy place remains as a means of restoration. That is, as noted earlier,[103] the neat division of good–holy from bad–holy (figure 5) collapses under stress of sin into a more basic perception (figure 1). All these special, system-affirming rites involve an action 'outside the Camp', and reveal that the evil-averting function of expiation is rooted in a dark conception of God.

Thus, the purification rite involving the red heifer (Num. 19:1–10) is very unusual in its details, but can best be understood (in this

[103] See above, pp. 85–7.

context) as a transformation into the Tent-of-Meeting theology of the corporate/priestly *hatta'th* described above. Several features are identical, in fact or in emphasis: the focus on blood, with its colour-symbolism of the red cow and the scarlet cord, and the sevenfold sprinkling of blood 'before the Lord'; and the focus on purity, with the cedar, hyssop and running water as well as the burning of the victim 'in a clean place'. But other points are inverted: the Lord is located in the Tent of Meeting, and the entire action takes place (uniquely) outside the Camp. The crisis related in the central chapters of Numbers[104] calls in this primitive apotropaic rite to buttress a Temple system whose rationale it necessarily subverts.

The conscious commitment of the redactors of this system is unquestionably to the unity of the divine sphere, the worship of the One God who both gives and takes away, blesses and curses: evil is not a separate force, but the experienced wrath of God. If this unity is to be preserved in ritual expression, the range of symbolism at work in the culture must be shaped and integrated, till each part is a transformation of each, within an ordered whole. To this end, blood-rites of differing origin are combined into a set of complementary movements, as in the diagram:[105]

$$\frac{\text{upward}}{\text{downward}} : \frac{\text{inward}}{\text{outward}}$$

This is symbolised by the line or ledge which in contemporary altars divided the top of the altar from the base.[106] In *zebah* and holocaust the blood is dashed 'against the altar' above this line, while the smoke ascends (the root meaning of *'olah*); but poured away into a drain below the line in the expiatory rites. The former movement, expressing a simple dedication, is always brought inwards to the altar; the latter is always operating at margins, so that, though only exceptionally performed 'outside', in every instance it is anointing edges and extremities − the horns of the altar (= phallic representation of the god?), the toe, thumb and ear of the priest at his

---

[104] See above, pp. 89f.

[105] See J.M. Grintz, '"Do not eat of the blood"', *Annual of the Swedish Theological Institute*, 8 (1972), 78−105. De Vaux, *AI*, pp. 440f, argues that the two movements correspond to Canaanite and Arabic influences on the development of Israelite religion. Modern Arabic parallels have to be used with care, however: see Rogerson, *Anthropology*, pp. 35−45.

[106] For description and illustration, see 'Altar', in *Encyclopedia Judaica*, vol. II, pp. 759ff.

ordination, the veil of the sanctuary in the priest's *hatta'th*, the doorposts and lintels at Passover. The rite for the cleansing of a leper (Lev. 14) beautifully expresses these complementary movements in its multiple sacrifices, and in the margin-affirming rite of the pair of birds between which an arbitrary distinction is made, the one to be sacrificed, the other to be released 'into the open field' (Lev. 14:5). On the Day of Atonement the same arbitrary choice is made between two goats, the one to be sacrificed for Israel's sin in the Temple (and its blood taken in to the Holy of Holies itself), the other to be sent out laden with this sin into the wilderness (Lev. 16:7–10).[107] Here the priest stands, as Aaron stood on the day when 'the plague was stopped' (Num. 16:48), 'between the dead and the living'. These three actions, though binary in form, do not, however, display the full complementarity since they all remain marginal in location and avertive in aim: Aaron performs the single action of stopping the plague; the first pigeon in the leper-rite is killed *downwards* over running water, at the Camp's edge; the first goat, though it goes inwards, is killed as a sin-offering so that its blood is sprinkled and poured downwards, its flesh finally taken outside the Camp to be burnt (Num. 16:48; Lev. 14:5, 16:27).

In the multiplicity of its sacrifices, the Day of Atonement strives to achieve a balanced ordering, making offerings in both directions at once and at every level of its 'cosmos', from innermost centre, the darkened cube where God alone may dwell, to outer edge, the abode of 'Azazel'. It is the one action which really attempts to face and reconcile the contradictions in the Priestly theology, in a penitential mood which is deeply fitting; but the solution it provides still springs from, is indeed the culmination of, that same theology. The logic of the Day is the total breakdown of the mediational system, the utter defilement of all Israel, its priesthood and Temple, even the Holy of Holies itself, which must be reconsecrated with blood; conversely, the nation which was before utterly impure is at the end wholly purified and without sin. It provides a necessary admission that the priesthood, which dares to exercise God's expiatory prerogative, can do so only in dependence on the imparted holiness of God. But a rigorous examination of that logic must ask how even the high priest, who is also implicated in sin, can *begin* the reconsecration process: would it not require *God himself* to initiate the holy action?

[107] See de Vaux, *AI*, pp. 507–10. For comments, see Davies, 'Sacrifice in Leviticus', 394–6; Young, *SI*, pp. 47–50; James, *Priesthood*, pp. 161–5.

That question, which is not far from the mind of the author of
Hebrews, cannot be avoided. The primary symbol is blood, and the
rite will only work if divine action is rendered unnecessary by the
presence in blood of an intrinsic, purifying power – a power *independent of God*. Such a thought makes nonsense of the Priestly
theology, and raises a still deeper doubt about the vision expressed
here. When the high priest sprinkles blood on the mercy-seat itself
'to make atonement for the holy place' (Lev. 16:12–16) is this the
symbolic pleading for the abatement of God's wrath that it claims
to be, or is it, as it appears, a driving out of an evil force, some
plague which has invaded even the earthly locus of God's holiness?
Is he, in fact, *defending God*, by means of blood, from defeat at
the hands of the demonic?

The need for some more satisfactory representation of divine action is manifest. The Mishnah describes the high priest's preparatory
vigil in the Temple, the whole night being spent reading scripture.[108]
Many modern commentators stress the accompanying moral
penitence, noted in rabbinic texts, as evidence that the rite was not
regarded as having automatic efficacy,[109] though it is hard to say
when the moral element entered the rite or what transitions it underwent. Certainly some such moral theme was essential in order to
avoid theological distortion of an extreme kind. The argument of
the next subsection is that (quite apart from the subjective intentions
of the priests or the people) an objective corrective already existed
in the function the rite had within the larger whole of the covenant-
relation of Israel to God.

Sacrifice and the covenant

The meaning of 'blood'
Much misunderstanding of the nature of Israel's ritual has arisen
through excessive concentration on its use of blood. Blood has a
number of distinctive uses, but no single, intrinsic meaning, since it
features in a number of rites, each of which is a syntagmatic whole
defining the meaning of its parts. In this chapter, the meaning of
sacrifice has been expounded as the *consecration* of a person, animal
or object by means of a symbolic transfer into the sacred sphere,
and its transformation there, by the power of the 'holy', into an
object of sacred *power*: this may then be brought back into the

[108] Mishnah Yoma 1.5–7 (Danby, *The Mishnah*, p.163).
[109] See James, *Priesthood*, pp.163ff, and Young, *SI*, pp.48ff.

secular realm bringing with it life-giving power, or retained at the margin to ward off the power of death. In Israel, as we have seen, the *zebah* had originally the former function as a joyful thanksgiving feast in God's presence. The holocaust, too, seems originally to have been an event of this type, through the fictive motif by which the donor is deemed to stand in the holy place by virtue of his offering, and so to receive God's blessing. In Leviticus, however, the holocaust, like the sin-offering, belongs to the latter type. Historically, this witnesses to a general movement away from personal towards impersonal conceptions of God, and from conjunctive to disjunctive impulse.

This movement was reflected in the growing emphasis on the value of blood. Blood, as we have seen, is a feature of all the main types, though not more so than fire or sacred space. However blood, unlike fire, has no profane uses. Israel, denied the use of pictorial images, was bound to develop through natural symbols exclusively the means of expressing theological truth, and blood is always a substance of power, always open in meaning, always mysterious. Besides, the increasing concentration on animal rather than vegetable offerings, and on the sin-offering in particular, led to an emphasis on its peculiarities as though it were they alone which could carry expiatory power, apart from the total action in which they figure. Further, and harmfully, this process, by narrowing its focus on to the overtly apotropaic element in the expiatory rites, distorts the meaning of 'expiation' itself into 'aversion of evil' (which is one aspect) and conveys the impression that blood is efficacious in dealing with evil because it has intrinsic, sanctifying power.

The problem of achieving balance in understanding the expiatory complex, and the difficulty of avoiding theologically motivated abridgements, is illustrated in the controversy over the meaning of 'blood' between Leon Morris and Lindsay Dewar.[110] In this debate, Morris argued that in sacrificial contexts as elsewhere 'blood' means 'death' so that the killing of the victim is the central moment of the drama, Dewar that 'blood' means 'life-power', vital energy released in the symbolic manipulation of the blood. As stated, neither of these positions quite does justice to the evidence. Our structural perspective suggests that any answer which does not allow the

---

[110] The reference is to three articles entitled 'The biblical use of the term "Blood"', two by L. Morris (*JTS*, 3 (1952), 216–27 and *JTS*, 6 (1957), 77–82) and one by L. Dewar (*JTS*, 4 (1953), 204–8). A useful summary of the debate is found in Young, *SI*, pp. 53–6.

common pattern of all the rites in Leviticus to emerge is probably wrong: the first position, which identifies blood with death, places a far wider gulf between blood-rites and others, and between expiatory rites and the *zebah* and *'olah*, than Leviticus itself. It also relies implicitly on a substitutionary dynamic: either animal sacrifice is a substitute for human sacrifice, a view once widespread but now discredited; or sacrifice is a stylised form of divine punishment by which the donor acknowledges his guilt and so avoids the actual suffering of the due consequences. This punitive view has been widely canvassed but finds no support in the Old Testament. The most telling objection is the fact noted above,[111] that the slaughter is performed by the donor, not the priest, and is therefore not a part of the blood-rite at all, only a necessary preparation.

The alternative proposal, that blood represents life-power released in the ritual, can at least claim the support of the one explicit comment offered in the texts on the purpose of sacrificial blood:

> The life of the flesh is in the blood; and I have given it for you upon the altar to make atonement for your souls; for it is the blood that makes atonement, by reason of the life.
>
> (Lev. 17:11)

This invokes the elemental perception of blood as that essential and mysterious substance whose loss, meaning death, may paradoxically bring life. What the text does not permit, though, is a *quantitative* reading, as though each beast contains a given quantity of life (*nephesh*), which is released to replenish the common stock. That would be a plausible account of slaughter done for food, of course, but we have seen earlier[112] that the purpose of a first-fruits offering (such as the *zebah*) is to distinguish the secular, economic appropriation of energy (the feast) from the sacred symbols of life (the blood and the fat), and then to hallow the feast by juxtaposing, but never *confusing* them. The 'life' named here is not physical energy but something less determinable: as at any death (including human) the life-power present here is the sacred, ambivalent power of life-and-death, the divine.

In other words, blood has power only insofar as it participates in the power of God. The material conception which might support the opposite view is plainly rejected by the polemic against the practice

---

[111] See p. 94 above. Cf. Johnsson, 'Defilement and purgation', pp. 255ff.
[112] See pp. 91f above.

of eating blood, the force of which indicates that a deliberate cultic activity is being described, and not a 'secular' attitude to blood as 'neutral' (Lev. 17:1–13, 19:26; Deut. 12:16, 23f).[113] The ban on eating blood is rare in being a taboo (bad–holy) which is never, as most of them are, paradoxically commanded at some point as especially sacred (good–holy). It is associated in the texts with soothsaying and witchcraft, with sacrificing to satyrs and self-laceration (Lev. 17:7, 19:26–31). It was against this that the incoherent words of Leviticus 17:11 were directed, and not in recommendation of sin-offerings as such – against the blasphemy of taking into oneself the blood that should be offered up to God as holy-substance. Of the typology set out in pages 71 to 79 and figure 3,[114] this represents the only category not yet mentioned in connection with Israel: the *impersonal-conjunctive* attempt to gain access to divine power by direct consumption of divine substance. In relation to this class – which includes also the Canaanite fertility-rites by which humanity strives to unite itself to the rhythms of nature, through sacred prostitution and the worship of graven images (other taboos for Israel which are never relaxed) – no compromise could be permitted. What this indicates is that attributing intrinsic and quantifiable power to blood was not merely thinkable but very much a possibility in Palestine, and one from which Yahwism had to struggle to distance itself. It also indicates that one factor which laid Israel open to this alien influence was its own undue emphasis on the ritual use of blood. If 'life' means the incalculable and uncontrollable power through which humanity comes into knowledge of God, it cannot be understood or symbolised by ritual means alone.

The covenant

In tracing the meaning of the sacrificial rules we have necessarily been concerned with what is distinctive in the rather static version of the Priestly code, such as its emphasis on ritual purity and expiation, while noting occasionally that there are other matters which, even if

---

[113] See also Gen. 4:1–12, for the contrast between Abel's offering of 'the firstlings of his flock and of their fat portions' (4:4) and Cain's connection with 'downward' sacrifice, drinking blood, and material concepts of life-power (4:3: an offering of the fruit of the ground; 4:8: 'Let us go out into the field' (cf. Lev. 17:5); 4:10f: 'The voice of your brother's blood is crying to me from the ground . . . which has opened its mouth to receive your brother's blood'; 4:11f: 'Now you are cursed from the ground . . . it will no longer yield to you its strength'). Cf. Grintz, 'Do not eat of the blood'; and see further below, pp. 149–53.

[114] See above, p. 78.

not made explicit, must be taken into account. Alongside the penitence of Psalm 51, a survey of the psalter finds hymns in exuberant praise of God, in celebration of his historical concern for Israel and of his power over death.[115] The fact is that, in Israel's religion, 'one who has clean hands and a pure heart' *can* 'stand in [God's] holy place' (Ps. 24:3f). Deuteronomy and the prophetic movement affirm a religion of the heart and of moral obedience not always easy to align with cultic trends;[116] and in the centuries following the return from Exile the Jewish people recreated for themselves (beside the now centralised sacrificial cultus) an accessible 'sacred space' in the developing worship of the synagogue, and in the popularity and significance given to Passover and to late, family-based festivals, Hannukah and Purim.[117] The ritualist tendency towards an impersonal and disjunctive conception of God is balanced by the concept of 'covenant' which, from one point of view, formed the framework within which the priestly system operated. The Covenant-Lord was he who had drawn near to Abraham, to Moses, to David and Solomon, and whose 'wrath' was always the converse of the love which sought endlessly to establish rebellious Israel in his blessings.[118] A thoroughly personal conception of God sustains a personal conception of virtue and sin, too: the clean heart and loving obedience without which outward sacrifice has no value in God's eyes; the guilt of oppressing the weak which sacrifice is powerless to annul.[119] In narratives like those of the Red Sea and the wilderness, Israel's consecration in the holy and chaotic place finds expression in covenantal terms which offer a diachronic perspective to offset the static priestly vision.[120]

One point particularly concerns us. The Old Testament notion of the role and character of the priest is not confined to that promoted in Leviticus and Numbers.[121] If priests exist, in brief, for the dual purpose of representing God to humanity and humanity to God, we can see that the balance has shifted. Where P strongly emphasises the latter, the priest being essentially a *sacrificer*, standing between

[115] For example Pss. 150 and 47; 78 and 106; 22. Interesting light on the inclusiveness of the psalms is found in T. Collins, 'Decoding the Psalms' (see chapter 2, n. 45 above).

[116] See von Rad, *OTT*, vol. I, pp. 225f and 370ff.

[117] See Ringgren, *Israelite Religion*, pp. 327f; de Vaux, *AI*, pp. 510ff.

[118] See von Rad, *OTT*, vol. I, pp. 121ff, 219ff; Ringgren, *Israelite Religion*, pp. 115ff.

[119] See von Rad, *OTT*, vol. I, pp. 370ff; Ringgren, *Israelite Religion*, pp. 126ff.

[120] See von Rad, *OTT*, vol. I, pp. 175ff.

[121] See de Vaux, *AI*, pp. 345–57; James, *Priesthood*, pp. 68–79, von Rad, *OTT*, vol. I, pp. 93–102.

sinful human beings and the God they dare not approach, the early traditions suggest that previously the two sides were given much more equal place in their varied activities, though with some preponderance, in fact, of the former. Priests there are individual figures at local sanctuaries who act as God's spokesmen in a variety of mediatorial functions: giving oracles, delivering pastoral judgements (*torah*), perhaps most characteristically uttering *blessing and curse*. Since their authority was more charismatic in origin, it was more overtly political in its sphere of operation: thus, while Moses and David could offer sacrifices, Aaron and Samuel were also leaders of the people. The confusion of categories which is abomination to Leviticus is indispensable to the historical traditions. Above all Melchizedek, who as the first priest in Torah should present a perfect model of priesthood, is sublimely anomalous, in being king and priest at once, in coming from nowhere and leaving no dynasty, and in executing his priestly function not by sacrificing but by *blessing*, pronouncing God's favour on Abraham.[122] We have seen earlier that this and other functions survived as echoes embedded in the sacrificial rites,[123] even though in general the oracular role passed to the prophets and the traditions of certain historical individuals (Abraham, Moses, Elijah) through whom God's will was made known; later we shall see how Hebrews seeks to recapture the priestly character of such mediation.[124] But if the individual priest in Leviticus (and perhaps in post-exilic reality) was seldom seen explicitly representing God by transmitting his blessing or judgement, the Temple system as a whole certainly was: the repeated act of blessing had been largely superseded when God blessed Israel with his gift of the Temple and its sacred rites, by which people were able to find atonement and so live at peace.

The blood of the covenant

The Temple and the covenant are complementary conceptions, then; but complements can also contradict each other. The Temple, which from the point of view of the covenant is a blessing, a place for rejoicing in the presence of God, looks different from the inside. If the Temple is a blessing because it is holy, the prime duty of the

---

[122] Gen. 14:18–20; Ps. 110:4. See further F. L. Horton, *The Melchizedek Tradtiion*, SNTS Monograph Series 30 (Cambridge, 1976); J. A. Fitzmyer, *Essays on the Semitic Background of the New Testament* (London, 1971), pp. 221–67.

[123] See above, p. 95.

[124] See below, pp. 251–60, and compare pp. 37f above.

priests is to maintain that holiness against the miasma of sin; so the aversion which guarantees holiness is logically prior to the praise and gift which celebrate it. In the process, a space is created in which to praise, but that space is limited by the condition of its creation: to protect the holiness of God, humanity must not come too close. The urge to control access to divine power, which militates against household religion and vineyard festivals, and is fearful of the arrival of unknowns claiming Priestly descent and rights (such as Korah presumably represents), was directed with most firmness against the eating of blood. Why should this practice, as described above, be so vehemently condemned? Certainly it was associated with other dark practices of Canaanite folk-religion, and with the fertility-rites of the 'high-places', and all they implied: but was it not also because eating blood parodies too neatly the obsession with material, tangible holiness on which the Priestly rites depend?

The previous paragraphs have sought to show that there existed, in other areas of Israel's religion, ample resources for controlling the meaning of cultic symbols so as to harmonise and enrich theological understanding rather than diffuse it. The 'atoning' power ascribed to blood is not a product of the expiatory ideology, rather the reverse: it is a direct extension of the recognition of God's otherness, his holiness, we found expressed in the simple dedicatory blood-rite and first-fruits offering of the *zebah*. Blood, so understood, was well fitted to stand as symbol, not only for the individual's 'atonement' leading to forgiveness for specific sins, but for the given, corporate, diachronic 'atonement' of the covenant – and a symbol capable of uniting cult and narrative and the differing, not always harmonious, impulses they represent.

In Exodus 24, Moses seals the Sinai Covenant by performing the dramatic rite of throwing the sacrificial blood of *zebah* and *'olah* half over the altar and half over the assembled people, a symbolic binding of Israel to its new Lord (and paralleled in the text by the communion-meal on the mountain).[125] Arguments for the regular enactment of covenant-renewal ceremonies in Israel have not found evidence for the repetition of that particular act: what follows will

---

[125] See von Rad, *OTT*, vol. I, pp. 130ff; R. J. Daly, *The Origins of the Christian Doctrine of Sacrifice* (London, 1978), pp. 37f. Note that the other examples of double movement in Israel's ritual, described on p. 99 above, treat the members of an *identical* pair *differently*, symbolising the incomprehensible but actual *separation* of the sacred and profane at the appointed margin; here two *unequals* are treated *the same* in a ritual binding into one.

suggest that this may be because it is purely a *communion rite*, with no avertive element. *Circumcision*, however, is in many texts treated with an emphasis on the blood, as an individual's 'covenant-sacrifice'.[126] This is a symbolic act of *dedication*, binding the male individual simultaneously into relation with God and with the nation; but through the avertive significance of blood in conjunction with extremities, in a context of ritual 'death', it is also a sign of *separation*. Many texts illustrate this idea of standing poised between life and death at the moment of entering the covenant (drawing a boundary): for example, the covenant renewals in Joshua 24 and Deuteronomy 30, and in Genesis 15 and 17.[127] And the rite which admits one to the circle of divine mercy is widely understood to be itself expiatory, setting aside all past sin: see, for example, the targum on Exodus 4:25: 'Now may the blood of this circumcision atone for the guilt of my husband.'[128]

Among the many unusual features of the feast of the *Passover*, what specially concerns us here is its character as both a blood-sacrifice and a covenant-ceremony.[129] It has some markedly impersonal-disjunctive elements: the apotropaic smearing of the doorposts, the use of hyssop and the nocturnal performance; and in Exodus 12:23 the dangerous power against whom these precautions are taken, 'the Destroyer', is identified as God. Yet also, as a family meat-meal, it has similarity to the *zebah* as it must have been celebrated formerly (though with differences, such as the roast meat, derived from its nomadic origin (Exod. 12:8)). And this joyful communion is a covenant-feast: first, the blood-rite separates those inside, enjoying God's favour, from his enemies; second, no one may take part in the Passover except Israelites (slaves count as Israelites if circumcised, Exod. 12:43−9); third, it is in text and tradition inseparable from the salvation story of the Exodus.[130] The ambivalence of God is here dramatised in blood: he is not only the Destroyer whom blood is smeared on doorposts and lintel to drive away, but the Covenant Lord for whom it is a sign of homage and dedication.[131]

[126] See Daly, *Origins*, pp. 41−4.
[127] See von Rad, *OTT*, vol. I, pp. 168ff.
[128] Quoted by Daly, *Origins*, p. 42. See G. Vermes, 'Circumcision and Ex. 4:24−6', in G. Vermes, *Scripture and Tradition in Judaism* (Leiden, 1961), pp. 178−92.
[129] See de Vaux, *AI*, pp. 484−93, *Studies*, pp. 1−26; Young, *SI*, pp. 43−7; Daly, *Origins*, pp. 38−41.
[130] See Rogerson, in Bourdillon and Fortes, *Sacrifice*, pp. 54ff.
[131] The issue of divine ambivalence is treated in chs. 5−8 below; for the expression of this through the Passover, see especially pp. 158f, 177, 194f.

The avertive form of the blood-rite (sprinkling, 2 Chron. 35:11) was subsequently altered to conform to the throwing action of the covenant-sacrifice in Exodus 24.[132] Within the space marked out by blood, Israel feasts in God's presence. The connection with circumcision is further supported by the later 'Legend of the two bloods' in which the blood of circumcision is said to be mingled with that of the Passover lamb, uniting the individual and the corporate, and the present with the past.[133]

These symbols overlap closely in a common area, and display a striking homology of aversion/dedication, expiation/communion, sacrifice/covenant. They all also affirm God as the one who blesses Israel: in each case God is active, life-bestowing (though also acknowledged as source of death) and unthreatened by the presence of sin – as when the seventy elders on Sinai 'saw the God of Israel ... and he did not lay his hand on the chief men of the people of Israel; they beheld God, and ate and drank' (Exod. 24:9–11). It is this gracious initiative, conveyed in the objective assurance of the blood (reminding us that death has not been ignored but integrated), which sets up the possibility of forgiveness.

In the story of the Exodus and in Genesis 22, first-fruits offerings of a kind are made: the Egyptian first-born consecrate Israel to Yahweh's service; Isaac the first-born is offered up as a sign of Abraham's self-dedication to the covenant-promise of God. In Jewish tradition, the story of the Binding of Isaac, the Akedah,[134] was developed into a structural transformation of the Passover narrative, and associated with it, liturgically and theologically. The sacrificial death of Isaac the first-born (at the hands of an ambivalent deity who gives death as a sign of the life he promises), a death which is regarded as actual, and symbolised by his 'blood' and his 'ashes', is said to be the prototype and source of the efficacy of the Passover: the Passover is said to have atoning power for its participants because at it the Akedah is recalled, the virtues of Isaac's covenant-sacrifice being 'remembered' by God for the sake of the children of Abraham. In the targums and in later rabbinic writings a further step is taken: this 'blood' is accorded the status of foundational sacrifice, inaugurating and validating and empowering the entire covenant between

---

[132] Mishnah Pesah 5.1–7 (Danby, *The Mishnah*, pp. 141f); see Daly, *Origins*, p. 39.
[133] See *ibid.*, pp. 42f.
[134] See *ibid.*, pp. 47–52; R. J. Daly, 'The soteriological significance of the sacrifice of Isaac', *CBQ*, 39 (1977), 45–75; G. Vermes, 'Redemption and Genesis 22', in *Scripture and Tradition*, pp. 193–227. See further chapters 5 and 6 below.

God and Israel. It is in this sense, presumably, that the author of Hebrews says boldly (9:22): 'Without the shedding of blood there is no forgiveness of sins.'

Conclusion

This chapter began from the position that there is a *prima facie* case for applying structuralist techniques to the interpretation of the Torah. This was based on two arguments: first, that much of its material, and many of its interpretative difficulties, inhabit areas proper to anthropology, which can therefore be expected to assist understanding even though, as a thoroughly sophisticated expression of Israel's faith, it cannot be classed as 'primary' myth or as the relics of a 'primitive' culture; second, that P's conscious organisation of myth, legend, symbol and rite has been aimed at creating a synchronic pattern, a unified whole which – like music, dream and myth itself, those 'machines for the suppression of time' (Lévi-Strauss[135]) – contains history within itself and is therefore not subject to its flux.

The central sections have tried to show that many of its apparently random details, connections and organisational forms make sense in a system of divine–human relations, and that some 'irrational' features demonstrate the working of deeper organisational principles. Such are the dietary laws of Leviticus 11 and the leprosy laws of Leviticus 13f; the unity of ordination and atonement (Lev. 8–10, 16) and the function of Korah's rebellion (Num. 16) in the construction of Numbers; the patterns of liminal symbolism and consecratory action. Such, too, is the provision of a ground from which familiar antinomies in Old Testament interpretation – Does sacrificial blood mean 'life' or 'death'? How can 'holy' mean both 'pure' and 'impure'? Does the sacred sanctify the world or the world profane the sacred? – can be seen to be wrongly presented. In seeking to harmonise Israel's religious practices, the Priestly authors were inspired by an existential vision ('the Camp') which was not, as they understood it, devised, but rather found, given, revealed. In exploring this material, the benefit of historical-critical work on the formation of the Pentateuch has been an essential aid, even when not explicitly referred to, in searching for unities operative below the level of consciousness and outside the processes of history.

But the Pentateuch will not reduce to a simple unity without

---

[135] Leach's translation. Cf. Lévi-Strauss, *The Raw and the Cooked*, p. 16.

remainder, and time cannot be suppressed. As well as 'deep-structural' drives towards order, both D and P exhibit strongly rationalist aims (products of Israel's history) creating an alternative and rival tendency. The Deuteronomic restriction of Yahweh's cultus to Jerusalem was a reductive exclusion of ordinary, secular Yahwism, which was forced into furtive contact with cults of the dead; P's effort to explain the Exile in terms of divine wrath made sense of Israel's history while casting doubt on the faithfulness of God. In pages 105–9 we saw the post-exilic development of covenant-blood symbols, and their effect in healing this breach by uniting conjunctive and disjunctive impulses, personal and impersonal. Anomalies remain, however, and no perfect 'structure' is to be found, however many corrective elements are supplied to restore the balance.

Outside any ideal order of Israel there remain persons (such as Melchizedek, Job, Samuel, David, Balaam, Jeremiah), events (such as the Akedah, Meribah, the prophecy of Eldad and Medad, Jacob's wrestling with the Angel), and concepts (such as wrath, righteousness and promise) which war, in varied ways, against each other and against the theological system of which they are indispensable but also unassimilable parts. They exhibit that 'semantic richness', that 'surplus of meaning', which Ricoeur has identified as the driving force behind the continuous interpretative movement of the Old Testament's tradition-history.[136] Structural interpretation may certainly reduce the obscurity of these elements: about several of them something has been said above, and there are well known full-scale studies of Moses, Job, Jacob's wrestling and other puzzling features of Genesis.[137] When successful, though, these studies are valuable contributions to the scope of Biblical scholarship, and to the understanding of these items in particular: they do not reduce all particularity to a single, all-explaining system, nor abolish history. Structuralism is no more capable than the Priestly redactors of producing out of the richness of Israel's traditions an ideal conceptual order which would perfectly express the deep-structure of its 'world'. If such a structure exists – and of course linguistics is far from satisfied with so mechanical a view of the generation of meaning –

---

[136] See P. Ricoeur, 'Structure and hermeneutics', *Conflict*, pp. 44f.

[137] On Moses, see E. Leach and D. A. Aycock, *Biblical Myth*, pp. 33–66. On Job, see Polzin, *Biblical Structuralism*, pp. 57–121. On Jacob, see R. Barthes, 'The struggle with the angel', in Barthes and Bovon, *Structural Analysis*, pp. 21–33. On other features of Genesis, see Leach and Aycock, *Biblical Myth*, pp. 67–88, 113–27; also D. F. Pocock, 'North and south in the Book of Genesis', in J. H. M. Beattie and R. G. Lienhardt (eds.), *Studies in Social Anthropology* (Oxford, 1975), pp. 273–84.

it must be continually vying in the real world to unify contrary cultural structures and penetrate the web of historical forces. Whether conceived as interpretative development or 'homeostatic feedback',[138] as an intrinsic 'semantic richness' in the material or as the interpreter's 'rational overload',[139] cultures necessarily remain in need of new resolutions of anomaly, new appropriations of their own 'surplus of meaning', new attempted closures of their conceptual systems.

Is it possible to conceive a perfect resolution, a non-provisional closure, beyond which no openness is necessary or desirable? The author of Hebrews is convinced that Jesus *enacted* such a resolution or transformation of Israel's meaning; one which, though still for the book's Christian readers provisional, is nonetheless final, and about to be accomplished in that 'perfected' relation between humanity and its ultimate reality which constitutes the 'new covenant'.

---

[138] Cf. Ricoeur, *Conflict*, p. 49.
[139] See D. Sperber, 'Is symbolic thought prerational?', in M. L. Foster and S. H. Brandes (eds.), *Symbol as Sense* (New York, 1980), p. 38. For a more general discussion, see Sperber, *Rethinking Symbolism*.

PART III

RENEWING THE COVENANT

4

A LITURGY FOR THE DAY OF SALVATION

Religious language and the genre of Hebrews

In the previous chapter it was argued that the Pentateuch contains materials springing from what has been called the 'liminal-sacral' mentality, and that the coherence of these phenomena owes at least as much to an attempted rational systematisation, undertaken by the Deuteronomic and Priestly editors in particular historical circumstances, as to some hypothetical 'deep-structural' coherence. Doubt was cast by this on the sufficiency of any pure 'structuralism' to replace the historical element in Old Testament exegesis; however, it was noted that, in certain sorts of material, where the rational system of the Priestly code worked against the tendencies inherent in the liminal-sacral (on the question of the ritual meaning of 'blood', for example), intertestamental developments show the gradual establishing of a pattern in accord with that logic and its 'deep structures'. The employment of structuralist techniques was therefore justified by its ability to explain particular non-rational elements in the Old Testament and in subsequent developments.

The question before us now is a 'structural transformation' of the previous question: in common with the other books of the New Testament, the Letter to the Hebrews exhibits signs of a liminal-sacral world-view, most obviously in relation to elements of Israel's cultus − the new covenant being presented in imagery drawn from the old. Structuralist methods have been fruitfully applied to elucidate such elements, but whereas other New Testament texts exhibit these incidentally or in isolated and fragmentary fashion, Hebrews alone attempts a systematic interpretation of Christian salvation as fulfilment of the Old Testament sacrificial cultus. The starting point for this study, as argued in the Introduction, is the failure of conventional historical exegesis to discover, at certain crucial points, the book's meaning − whether 'meaning' is taken in the subjective sense of 'speaker's meaning' or 'reader's meaning' (restricted as these are by the elusiveness of both the author and the readers), or in the objective sense of 'text's meaning'. As with the Priestly code, it is hoped that the methods of anthropological structuralism will enable us, at particular places, to understand the book 'better than the author himself',[1] and better than the first readers too.

Yet caution is necessary, because the book is not merely manifesting but consciously *interpreting* the Levitical material: this writer too is claiming to understand it better than its 'authors', or rather the Aaronic priestly caste who edited and transmitted it. It is not only that a reference to, say, the Day of Atonement, represents, in Hebrews as in Leviticus 16, a further link in the chain of interpretation of a 'primitive' rite, but that it may represent a different type of interpretation of some or all of this tradition, a 'hermeneutic of suspicion'. In relation to the Old Testament it was argued that the Priestly editors were employing rational and conceptually clear criteria to distinguish one 'primitive' element in their culture from another, and to declare one to be part of divine order, another 'abomination' or idolatry;[2] yet at several points their orderly aims were undermined by the force of the symbols' own logic, perceptually grasped if not conceptually understood, with results which are contradictory, though illuminating.[3] Hebrews, likewise, is both master and slave of the symbolism it aims to interpret. We shall need to inquire whether, like P, and despite this critical principle, this author accepts certain sacral phenomena as *given*, and therefore good, or whether the book's argument, though couched in such language, is directed to the exclusion from Christian consciousness of the whole sacral perspective and all its manifestations.

What arises here is the recurrent question whether sacrificial language is employed as an extended simile, strictly subordinate to the argument (of which it forms the vehicle) that it is no better than a partial offer of salvation and therefore ultimately worthless; or whether it is intended to reaffirm the form of sacral logic while revising its content. If the latter, we are bound to ask whether the result is in tune with the radical newness of the Christian

---

[1] See I. Kant, *Critique of Pure Reason*: 'It is by no means unusual, upon comparing the thoughts which an author has expressed in regard to his subject ... to find that we understand him better than he has understood himself.' Quoted by E. D. Hirsch, *Validity in Interpretation* (London, 1967), p. 19n. Schleiermacher's development of this principle is discussed by Gadamer, *Truth and Method*, pp. 169–73; cf. A. C. Thiselton, *The Two Horizons* (Exeter, 1980), pp. 300–2.

[2] See above, pp. 81–4.

[3] See above, pp. 85–7, 97–100.

revelation as proclaimed elsewhere in the New Testament; if the former, we must ask whether a superficial exploitation of material very deeply rooted in the human consciousness could hope to be outweighed by the force of a rational argument, and whether, therefore, the mere use of such terms has not justified later readers in finding their sacral apprehensions given canonical status. Whether sinister or merely naïve, on either view the book is potentially so misleading that ascribing to it the authority of scripture is highly dangerous.

The argument which follows will hope to show that such questions about the theological coherence of the book derive from misunderstanding of the logic at work within it, a logic, shared by the author and by many intertestamental and post-Christian Jewish interpreters (whether or not any of these parties 'understood' it), which accounts for many of the most 'original' points in Hebrews. Although historical questions are of course involved in this, it will be contended that the anthropological methods employed here enable us to override certain difficulties which refuse to yield to strictly historical and discursive-rational criticism. It will be helpful to illustrate this claim, before going further, and this can best be done by reference to two prominent and problematic features of the book, its use of paradox and of axiom.

First, axioms. It is one of the most striking features of sacrificial customs that they persistently defy explanation, yet this author repeatedly refers to ritual matters without explanation or with only a dogmatic reason which itself demands to be explained. Not all of these are equally problematic, of course. In one sense, at least, the author could expect readers to know why the outer sanctuary contained a particular collection of objects (9:1–5), why 'the priests go continually into the outer tent' (9:6) and why 'every priest stands daily at his service' (10:11); why 'the bodies of those animals whose bodies are brought into the sanctuary as a sacrifice for sin are burned outside the camp' (13:11); why it is only the high priest who enters the inner shrine, why he does so once a year only, and why he enters 'not without blood' (9:7). All these, though mysterious, are matters of fact prescribed in the divine law, but other things are less straightforward. For though 'it is beyond dispute that the inferior is blessed by the superior' (7:7), it is less easy to say why it should be so (or what is meant in this context by 'superior'); or why it is that 'under the law almost everything is purified with blood'; or, still harder, why 'without the shedding of blood there is no remission of sins' (9:22). Understanding why such purification of material things is needed, we might come nearer to understanding why the heavenly shrine too needs purifying (9:23) – a 'necessity' which has troubled nearly all modern commentators as either nonsensical or verging on blasphemy, but which this author presents without argument or clarification.[4] It will be contended later that it is the same curious logic that is appealed to when the book sets out its Christology, with its dependence on what is asserted (but not shown) to be 'fitting' (ἔπρεπεν 2:10, 7:26), and when it states baldly that 'it is impossible to restore again to repentance those who have once been enlightened ... if they then commit apostasy' (6:4).

Alongside these unintelligible 'necessities' may be set a number of unresolved paradoxes, contraries juxtaposed without comment as though harmonious partners. Perhaps these collocations too are 'obvious', if regarded from the right point of view. An important example of this tendency is again provided by the book's Christology, which is at the same time one of the 'highest' in the New Testament (ascribing to Christ in explicit terms pre-existence, the divine attributes of eternity and involvement in creation (1:10ff) as well as the divine titles 'Lord' (1:10) and 'God' (1:8), and also one of the 'lowest' (the author preferring to speak simply of 'Jesus' and emphasising his suffering and temptation through which 'he learned obedience' and was 'made perfect' (5:8f)). Both emphases are entirely consistent with the rest of the New Testament, and Paul and John likewise struggle to hold the two together, but for the explicitness of its treatment of each, and the sharpness of the contrast presented, Hebrews is certainly remarkable.[5] Another tension, not unrelated to that, is the simultaneous presentation of God as at once merciful, gracious, providing in Christ a high priest who is able 'to sympathise with our weaknesses' and who gives us access to the 'throne of grace' (4:15f; and yet also as a fierce and unrelenting judge, a 'consuming fire' (12:28).

A further contradiction appears in the literary structure of the work, particularly in its alternation between the contrasted styles of the 'cultic' sections (1:1–14, 2:5–3:6a, 4:14–5:10, 6:13–10:22, 12:18–24, 13:8–16) and the 'paraenetic' sections (2:1–4, 3:6b–4:16, 5:11–6:12, 10:19–12:17, 12:25–9, 13:1–25). These form distinctively different portions of the work, though there is some overlap

---

[4] See below, p. 232.   [5] See Westcott, *Hebrews*, pp. 424–8.

(4:14−16, for example) and readers are not entirely agreed about the precise points of transition, nor about how to construe the inner structure of each type of material. In a recent article,[6] W. G. Johnsson has pointed out that the tendency of commentators to focus on one or other of these strands has far-reaching consequences for interpretation. Those who focus on the 'cultic' tend also to attribute to the letter a Platonic or Philonic cosmology and eschatology (Spicq, Cody[7]), whereas those who focus on the 'paraenetic' tend to attribute to it a Palestinian or futurist eschatology (Bruce, Buchanan[8]). This choice of stance naturally affects the reading of its theology: is sin defilement or rebellion? Is the Christology a development from Judaism or radically discontinuous? It also tends to determine whether the book is understood as a theological meditation, abstract and speculative in form, obscure in content, a 'theologian's theology' (Scott, Cody), or as an exhortation to action, urgent in tone and unashamedly severe in its warning, a highly personalised expression of pastoral concern (Buchanan, Manson).

Graham Hughes locates the point of unity of the book in the author's Old Testament hermeneutic. He argues that the dislocation between the two main styles in the book occurs because a prior meditation on the gospel as a legitimate development from scripture is being applied by the author to a specific situation, one which demands a slightly different question, that of the continuing authority of the Old Testament for Christian congregations. Out of this conjunction the author develops a 'hermeneutic of eschatological existence'.[9] Schillebeeckx offers a not dissimilar fusion of the book's elements through a mystical 'Sinaitic spirituality' of sectarian Judaism, reflecting both Jewish apocalypticism and Platonic terminology.[10]

In the article already cited, Johnsson is in agreement with the present study in his conviction that the interpreter has to follow the author into 'the enigmatic world of the cultus' if the relations between the ideas are to be perceived: he identifies a number of problems relating to the 'logic of the cultus' and proposes that, since the

[6] W. G. Johnsson, 'The cultus of Hebrews in twentieth-century scholarship', *ExpT*, 89 (1978), 104−8.
[7] A. Cody, *Heavenly Sanctuary and Liturgy in the Epistle to the Hebrews* (St Meinrad, IN 1960).
[8] G. W. Buchanan, *To the Hebrews* (New York, 1972).
[9] G. Hughes, *Hebrews and Hermeneutics* (Cambridge, 1979), pp. 101−10.
[10] Schillebeeckx, *Christ*, pp. 237−93.

book's terminology is '"religious" rather than "theological"',
what is called for is an approach through the phenomenology of
religion.[11] There are several reasons why such an approach has been
unfashionable, largely connected to the distaste for sacrifice discussed
in the introduction and chapter 2, a distaste given rationale by
Robertson Smith's evolutionary anthropology,[12] which consigned
sacrifice to the 'primitive' stage of religious development and gave
higher status to the 'spiritual' language of St Paul. It was this presupposition which entitled E. F. Scott to speak of the 'sterility' of
Hebrews' theology of salvation, expounded as it is in the language of
sacrifice and not in terms of its 'moral and spiritual significance';[13]
his assumption that this soteriology could not really hold for the
author the significance apparently assigned to it allowed Scott to
praise the author's 'modern' and non-'mystical' temperament,[14]
and to claim that 'his place ... is with the great idealists'.[15] Likewise
Käsemann, in the absence of any convincing account of the cultic
language, argued that Hebrews 'never develops a real anthropology
at all'.[16]

Thus nineteenth- and twentieth-century idealism has compounded
the damage done by centuries of dogmatic eisegesis: the tendency
for Protestant interpreters to read Hebrews as a Pauline treatise
on faith, and to be interested in 'blood' only as equivalent to
'saving death'; while Catholic commentators have found here the
basis for a theology of ministerial priesthood and eucharistic sacrifice
– neither of which appears overtly in the work.[17]

What is necessary is to come a pre-understanding of cultic language
which will enable us to appreciate why it seemed important, and
to expound its meaning. This was a major feature of the commentary
of Westcott, who was well informed about the state of anthropology
and comparative religion in his own day. Despite its age, his work
retains its value because it is the product of profound reflection
on the symbolism of Hebrews, moved by a conviction that the
issues in it, far from being academic or obscure, are highly relevant
to contemporary Christian existence, and in a series of additional
notes he attempted to find 'general laws of religion' in relation

[11] Johnsson, 'Cultus of Hebrews', pp. 107f; cf. Johnsson, 'Defilement and
purgation', pp. 97ff.
[12] Robertson Smith, *Religion*; see pp. 6f, 46f above.
[13] Scott, *Hebrews* p. 74f.   [14] *Ibid.*, p. 84.   [15] *Ibid.*, pp. 203ff.
[16] Käsemann, *Wandering People*, p. 7.
[17] See Johnsson's critique of modern approaches to Hebrews, 'Defilement and
purgation', pp. 27–96.

to important matters such as priesthood, sacrifice, blood, blessing and covenant. This attempt is based on two important presuppositions: first the continuity, not only of New Testament religion with that of the Old Testament, but of Biblical religion with natural religion – so that exegesis could not be carried out as though Biblical texts exist in a vacuum; and second, the tendency of sacrificial customs to form a systematic whole, in which reference to any part implies the whole, and priority necessarily attaches to those forms of sacrifice which establish and maintain the whole covenantal system, over those which, though individually perhaps more striking, depend on the system's prior existence.

In his full-length study of Hebrews, Johnsson commends Westcott's commentary as the 'high point in the study of the cultus' and criticises writers influenced by the History of Religions School for losing sight of his achievement, and failing to come to terms with its essential conceptuality.[18] His admiration for Westcott's work leads him to accept uncritically some ideas which today seem to most writers less persuasive (for example, that 'blood' necessarily signifies 'life-power'[19]). He takes as his starting point the Phenomenology of Religion and its methodology of seeking to understand religious experience without judging, in search of the inner dynamic of the religious system:[20] *defilement* is identified as the fundamental religious problem, which sacrifice confronts by providing *purgation* by means of *blood*. Though Johnsson's work is restricted to discussion of this particular set of categories, and to the parts of the text where these are most active, particularly Hebrews 9 and 10, in its general outlook it has much in common with the present study. Both seek to develop a religious theory as a basis for an interpretative method; in both the method is structural, that is, synchronic, and ahistorical; in both religion is seen as the means by which humanity comes to terms with a 'sacred' reality. However, there are also fundamental differences of approach, both about the extent and validity of the accounts of religion offered and about the hermeneutical conception of the act of interpretation. For Johnsson, Hebrews is the vehicle of an *argument* expressed largely in religious symbols, and the function of exegesis is to seek to reconstruct the author's intention in deploying this argument; whereas it is the thesis of

[18] *Ibid.*, pp. 43f, 76ff.
[19] *Ibid.*, pp. 45f, 59; cf. Westcott, *Hebrews*, pp. 293–5. For example, he finds it 'incredible' that A. B. Bruce had read Westcott and yet equated 'blood' with death (p. 59).
[20] Johnsson, 'Defilement and purgation', pp. 97ff.

this present study that religious symbols have a logic which cannot be wholly subordinated to any conceptuality or 'argument', and that they have in themselves a meaning which resists subordination to an author's 'intention'. Johnsson's insistence that he is not concerned with the book's 'significance for modern man',[21] but only with enhancing the scope of historical-critical inquiry by means of phenomenology, is not only a limitation in his aims, but a fundamental inconsistency too: for if the religious patterns we discover have indeed the universality claimed for them, it is absurd to treat them, in interpretation, as though they were accidental features of an ancient author's world-view without relevance for today.

Despite its valuable exploration, therefore, Johnsson's study limits itself, both in its scope and in its outlook, to the work of exegesis and to the historical-critical frame whose deficiencies have already been surveyed. By contrast, the hope of this present work is to approach Hebrews in a thoroughly *hermeneutical* fashion. It has been argued that the central hermeneutical problem in Hebrews is identifying an adequate conceptual framework to which to relate its theology presented in symbols. What we require, then, is to find a non-discursive genre which can fitly contain the whole book with all its apparent contradictions, and which is a suitable medium for expressing its 'liminal' character. In this and the following chapters, Hebrews will be treated as if it were presenting us, not with an argument but with a *liturgy*, a sacral action, and our aim will be to develop ways of reading suitable for participation in such an action.

Precedents for this suggestion can be found in the way certain texts give us a symbolic deposit from ritual (the many sides of the Passover tradition reflected in the composite material of Exod. 12, for example) as well as in what seem to be conscious evocations of liturgy, such as Deuteronomy 29 and Psalm 81; in the New Testament, the first type might be illustrated by the imagery of the Johannine discourses,[22] the second by the supposed baptismal origin of 1 Peter.[23] The difference here is that Hebrews is not offering, consciously or unconsciously, any kind of reconstruction of an existing rite, although the elements of many rites will be

[21] *Ibid.*, p. 210.
[22] See O. Cullmann, *Early Christian Worship* (London, 1953).
[23] See J. N. D. Kelly, *The Epistles of Peter and Jude* (London, 1969), pp. 15–20; Kümmel, *Introduction to the New Testament*, pp. 419–21.

found here, drawn from the traditions and practice of Judaism and from the worship of the early Church. In the *Liturgy for the Day of Salvation* presented here we see, not a 'rite', but the life of the Christian community viewed as a liminal state, a *standing before God*, and as a sacral action, a *drawing near to the throne of grace*, a 'system-affirming event' by which the system of divine–human relations (the 'covenant') is renewed: that is, both affirmed and changed.

The covenant relation

The covenant as a symbol-system in Jewish tradition

In speaking of Hebrews as the representation of a system-affirming event, the 'system' in question is the more-or-less unified collection of covenantal symbolism already existing in Jewish practice and tradition. The chief elements in this system, and the way in which 'covenant' became an organising principle within it, were sketched at the end of chapter 3. The point was made there that contradictory tendencies within the sacrificial language of the Old Testament came to be treated as complements within an overarching symbol of 'covenant', chiefly by focussing attention on the most inclusive elements, and by merging or equating disparate symbols. Such a synthesis occurs, for example, when the 'Legend of the two bloods' associates the blood of circumcision with that of the Passover lamb,[24] thus reinforcing the covenant-affirming function of the Passover by blending individual and social aspects at a liturgical level.

Another development, the connection of ritual laws to events and individuals in the Pentateuchal narratives, can also be illustrated with reference to Passover. Thus it was on Passover night (according to PRE 32)[25] that Isaac blessed Jacob and rejected Esau, establishing in Israel the blessing and promise of God. In another text

---

[24] Targum Pseudo-Jonathan on Exod. 12:13, quoted by Daly, *Origins*, pp. 42f. Another text, PRE 29, relates that all of Israel was circumcised on the day they left Egypt, with the divine comment: 'By the merit of the blood of the covenant of circumcision and by the merit of the Paschal lamb ye shall be redeemed from Egypt, and by the merit of the covenant of Passover ye shall be redeemed at the end of the fourth kingdom' (G. Friedlander (ed. and trans.), *Pirke de Rabbi Eliezer* (New York, 1965), p. 210).

[25] *Ibid.*, p. 236.

(Tg. Ps-J.on Gen. 4:3)[26] the story of Cain and Abel is similarly associated with Passover:

> And it was at the end of the days on 14th Nisan that Cain brought of the fruit of the ground, the seed of flax, an offering of first things before the Lord.

Bowker points out that the reference to 'seed of flax' brings this offering into opposition to Leviticus 19:19, and may be intended to explain that Cain's offering was rejected because of the presence of 'two kinds of seed'.[27] Alternatively, by assigning to this event the date of Passover (as does PRE 21),[28] this text makes Abel's offering from the flock (it is the 'firstling' too) ritually appropriate, and Cain's not. This link with the Passover sacrifice is assisted by some suggestive apotropaic elements in the Genesis narrative – the downwards motion of Abel's blood into the ground, and sin 'couching at the door' (Gen. 4:7, 10).

In PRE 27, commenting on Genesis 14:5, Abraham is said to have defeated the four pagan kings by night, a night identified as that on which God defeated the Egyptians;[29] similarly, the memorable night of God's covenant-promise to Abraham (Gen. 15) is identified in PRE 28 as Passover;[30] and a variety of Jewish traditions associate the Binding of Isaac (Gen. 22) with Passover.[31] In the 'Poem of the Four Nights' (Tg. Neofiti on Exod. 12:42), by conflating Abraham's covenant (Gen. 15) with the Binding of Isaac (Gen. 22), and both with the act of Creation, the Passover in Egypt (Exod. 12) and the End of the world, this tendency to identify every night significant for salvation with Passover is carried up into a striking example of 'liturgical time'.[32]

---

[26] Translation in J. Bowker, *The Targums and Rabbinic Literature* (Cambridge, 1969), p. 132.

[27] Bowker, *Targums*, p. 137. For the phrase 'at the end of the days', also used in Heb. 1:2, see below, pp. 132f, 136.

[28] Friedlander, *PRE*, pp. 153f.

[29] *Ibid.*, pp. 193ff. Whether this night should be understood, more precisely, as the Passover or as the Red Sea crossing is not clear: these are very frequently conflated.

[30] Friedlander, *PRE*, p. 198.

[31] These include Jubilees, as well as targums and rabbinic texts: see Daly, *Origins*, pp. 47–50; Vermes, 'Redemption and Genesis 22', pp. 193–227; R. Hayward, 'The present state of research into the targumic account of the sacrifice of Isaac', *JJS*, 32 (1981), 127–50. Hayward, 'Targumic account', pp. 144f, and Vermes, 'Redemption and Genesis 22', p. 216, argue that the link with Passover is earlier than the established synagogal tradition which links it with the New Year.

[32] Translation in A. Diez Macho (ed. and trans.), *Neophyti I* (2 vols., Madrid, 1970–1), vol. II, pp. 441f; cf. Daly, *Origins*, p. 48; R. Le Deaut, *La Nuit pascale*,

The interrelation of these varied symbols can be illustrated also by the tendency to regard all altars (and by extension all sacrifices) as interchangeable – and, further, to identify them all with Mount Zion. As early as 2 Chronicles 3:1, Zion is (without comment) identified with Mount Moriah, on which Abraham offered Isaac to God, and the targumic evidence suggests that this tendency was well established before the Christian era. In Targum Pseudo-Jonathan, for instance, the altar built by Noah (Gen. 8:20) is identified as 'the altar which Adam had built at the time when he was cast out of the garden of Eden and had made an offering on it; and Cain and Abel made their offerings on it'.[33] According to the same text, Adam is said to have lived at Moriah,[34] a name interpreted as 'the land of worship' and therefore implicitly equated with Zion,[35] and it was there too, presumably, that Cain and Abel made their Passover offerings as described above.

In PRE 29 Abraham is said to have been circumcised by Shem (= Melchizedek) on Mount Moriah on the Day of Atonement:[36] thus not only are Zion and Moriah equated but, in this document at least, so also are circumcision and the Day of Atonement. Elsewhere, as we have seen, the link is established between circumcision and Passover, and on the whole Passover was the preferred liturgical focus. There is, however, no necessary consistency even within individual bodies of material, which are more concerned with enlarging the scope of the meaning of these symbols than with defining them or making them mutually exclusive. The ideal aim implied by these targumic and midrashic procedures must be to see every symbol in the light of every other symbol, each one thus potentially expressing the whole of Torah. Naturally, such an aim is nowhere achieved, but the data discussed at the end of chapter 3,[37] and amplified here, demonstrate a crystallising of theology around certain key sacrifices and stories. This process of symbolic association, which can equally well be described as 'liturgical' or as 'structural', has three particular features:

Analecta Biblica (Rome, 1963), pp. 73–129. Another of Abraham's ten trials, the abduction of Sarah by Pharaoh, is also said to have occurred on Passover night (PRE 26: Friedlander, *PRE*, pp. 189ff).

[33] Bowker, *Targums*, pp. 167f; cf. PRE 31 (Friedlander, *PRE*, pp. 226f).
[34] Tg. Ps-J. on Gen. 3:23 (Bowker, *Targums*, p. 123).
[35] Tg. Ps-J. on Gen. 22:2 (Bowker, *Targums*, pp. 224, 230).
[36] Friedlander, *PRE*, pp. 203f.
[37] See above, pp. 103–9.

(1) the *interchange* of ritual and narrative motifs, so that all
    stories become paradigmatic transformations of all other
    stories, all rites of all other rites, and the two genres become
    increasingly interdependent;
(2) the *fusion* or reconciliation of diverse symbolic impulses,
    such as personal with impersonal, conjunctive with dis-
    junctive, sacral with political;
(3) the creation of composite *system-affirming symbols* of
    the covenant (composed variously of rites, institutions,
    roles and narratives).

The Letter to the Hebrews adopts a comparable quasi-liturgical
style, taking its particular ritual framework from the Day of Atonement, incorporating other sacrificial symbols and narratives concerning Israel, Jesus and the book's addressees, and integrating them
into what might be the *mythos* of a Christian covenant-renewal rite,
a *Liturgy for the Day of Salvation* on which, rather than reaffirming
the old, the new and final covenant is established. The function
in this of the Day of Atonement ritual is immediately apparent in
a reading of the text, although very little is actually said about it
as an event. On the other hand, though the mass of other narrative
and symbolic allusions has little overtly systematic about it, they
provide an associative background which furnishes a meaning for
the Day of Atonement itself. In its short space, and within the
purpose of its argument, many of its references to laws, customs,
beliefs and events may appear arbitrary, in isolation from the ritual-
narrative system, deeply interfused with the covenant-symbolism
of Judaism, which is presupposed as the context of their meaning.
To articulate that system by making plain hidden connections is the
task of this chapter and the next.

Covenant-sacrifices and covenant-renewal

In Hebrews 9:15–22, in order to present Christ as 'mediator of
a new covenant', the author describes the rite by which Moses
instituted the (old) covenant and the necessity of the 'shedding
(or sprinkling) of blood'[38] which it enshrines. The shape of the

---

[38] The translation is controversial, and related to theories of atonement. See
T. C. G. Thornton, 'The meaning of αἱματεκχυσία in Heb. 9:22', *JTS*, 15 (1964), 63–5;
N. H. Young, 'αἱματεκχυσία: a comment', *ExpT*, 90 (1978–9), 180; Johnsson,
'Defilement and Purgation', pp. 318–24.

rite recalled here is drawn from the Sinaitic rite in Exodus 24:3–8
– the laws are read, the blood is brought into contact with symbols
of God and the people – but many of the details are borrowed
from elsewhere, so that what emerges is a composite *covenant-
ceremony*. As well as calves (μόσχων 9:19, compare μοσχάρια
Exod. 24:5) the slaughtered beasts include he-goats (τράγων):
these would be permissible for burnt-offerings and peace-offerings
such as Moses offered, but they are prescribed only for the Day
of Atonement (Lev. 16:5); however a female goat (αἶγα) is involved
in the unique covenant-sacrifice of Abraham (Gen. 15:9). Our
author gives to this sacrifice a distinctively expiatory character:
whereas in Exodus 24:6–8 Moses *threw* the blood against the altar
and over the people, here the people are *sprinkled* (ἐρράντισεν
9:19);[39] Moses takes not only the animals' blood but also 'water
and scarlet wool and hyssop', details drawn from the leprosy-rite
(Lev. 14:4f), the red-heifer rite for 'water of purification' (Num.
19:6f, a text echoed also at 10:22), and perhaps from a traditional
version of the Day of Atonement rite.[40] In place of the altar, in
Hebrews' version, blood is applied to *the book*, and additionally
to the tent and to 'all the vessels used in worship' (9:19, 21): these
items may be derived from Moses' consecration of 'the tabernacle
of the tent of meeting' in Exodus 40:9 (where, however, they are
anointed with oil rather than sprinkled with blood),[41] but the use
of τὸ βιβλίον as principal symbol of the covenant-promise aligns
this version with a very different stream of Old Testament theology.
Nonetheless, the covenant-sacrifice, as described here, has been
subsumed into the dominant ideology of expiation, as a type of
sin-offering, in line with a widespread intertestamental trend already
described, but with the specific purpose of showing how far, in this
author's view, the Mosaic covenant stands from the will of God.

For a more positive model of a covenant-rite, however, the
author turns to a different source, the Passover, giving a brief
but similarly synthetic account (11:28):

> By faith [Moses] kept the Passover (πεποίηκεν τὸ πάσχα)
> and the sprinkling of the blood (καὶ τὴν πρόσχυσιν τοῦ
> αἵματος) in order that the destroyer of the first-born
> might not touch them.

[39] See above, pp. 98f, and the discussion below.
[40] See Mish. Yoma 4.2 (Danby, *The Mishnah*, p. 166).
[41] But compare Josephus' account of consecration with oil, water and blood
(*Antiquities* III. 205).

Two points call for comment. (1) Although ποιεῖν τὸ πάσχα is used in the Septuagint to mean 'keep' rather than 'institute', it is plain that this *first* Passover must be distinguished from every act of repetition. Buchanan therefore translates it as 'instituted', and Spicq argues that the perfect tense 'suggests that this celebration effects the foundation of a definitive institution'. Westcott prefers 'kept', but adds: 'The Passover then instituted and kept remained as a perpetual witness of the great deliverance.'[42] (2) Most translations (including RSV, NEB, JB) render πρόσχυσις inadequately as 'sprinkling'. The noun does not appear in the Septuagint, but the verb is normally used to denote the act of *throwing* blood against the altar, proper to holocaust and peace-offering (Exod. 24:6, 29:16, Lev. 1:5, 3:2).[43] Although it translates *zaraq* ('sprinkle') in three cases (Lev. 17:6, Num. 18:7, 2 Chr. 35:11, the last of these being a reference to Passover), it never refers to the apotropaic 'smearing' commanded for Passover and priestly ordination (Exod. 12:7, 29:20). It is notable that in the Mishnah, whereas the act of sprinkling, with its expiatory overtones, had been introduced into the rites for whole-offerings and peace-offerings (Mish. Zeb. 5:4f),[44] the blood in the Passover rite was to be *tossed* against the altar (Mish. Pes. 5:6)[45] in a manner more reminiscent of the peace-offering or the unique covenant-sacrifice (Exod. 24) than of the sin-offerings. Moses, of course, did not have an altar at this first Passover, but the Temple celebration had never considered that an important objection to its procedures, nor did our author think to mention the altar when it did figure, centrally, in the event recalled at 9:19–22, preferring to speak of 'the book'.

In this verse, then, we see the author interchanging expiatory and covenantal motifs, and treating the Passover as an annual reenactment of a foundational covenant-sacrifice. Although a widespread desire for such a reenactment and renewal of the covenant-relation can be seen in the way Passover was used in the inter-testamental and Christian periods,[46] and it is probable that there was at least an element of covenant-renewal in the composite New

[42] Buchanan, *To the Hebrews*, p. 198, Spicq, *Hébreux*, vol. II, p. 359, Westcott, *Hebrews*, p. 374. See also Westcott, *Hebrews*, p. 177 for his comment on the use of the perfect tense in Heb.: 'in every case its full force can be felt'.
[43] See A. Nairne, *The Epistle to the Hebrews* (Cambridge, 1921), p. 93. Spicq, *Hébreux*, vol. II, pp. 359f, and Westcott, *Hebrews*, p. 374, adopt 'sprinkle'; Buchanan, *To the Hebrews*, p. 198, refers even more loosely to 'pouring'.
[44] Danby, *The Mishnah*, pp. 468f.   [45] *Ibid.*, p. 142.
[46] Daly, *Origins*, pp. 38ff; de Vaux, *Studies*, pp. 24ff.

Year feast in Solomon's Temple,[47] the Old Testament as it stands contains no set of explicit regulations for such an event. However, recent scholarship has revealed, in both Deuteronomy and the deuteronomic revision of Judaism, traces of such an action (Deut. 27–31, Josh. 24).[48] Though embedded in reports of particular occasions in the lives of Moses and Joshua, these passages are apparently based on a regular (perhaps annual or septennial) rite performed at Shechem in the days of the monarchy, which may have disappeared with the Northern kingdom and was certainly not revived at Jerusalem after the Exile. This ceremony, which has similarities also to ancient secular 'covenanting' procedures, contains, among other elements:

(1) a rehearsal of past benefits given by God as the basis for future trust and obedience;
(2) a command to loyalty;
(3) a reference to God as witness of the covenant, with formulae of blessing and curse pronounced upon those who either honour or disregard its terms.[49]

It presents in dramatic form a personal confrontation and mutual commitment between divine and human parties, and an application of unchanging divine will to specific human circumstances. This is seen most clearly in Joshua 24, which describes a reaffirmation of the Sinaitic covenant made by the elders of Israel at Joshua's behest, following the conquest of Canaan: the renewed covenant takes into account altered circumstances and promises unchanged loyalty to Yahweh who has brought about Israel's present state. Joshua 5 reflects a similar event, in the form of a national circumcision of Israel's males as they came out of the Wilderness.

Deuteronomy is also aware of the fact of covenant-renewal rites, though its use of them is more complex. They are presented partly

[47] The classic argument of Mowinckel and the subsequent debate are summarised by D. J. McCarthy, *Old Testament Covenant* (Oxford, 1972), pp. 6–9.

[48] Von Rad, *OTT*, vol. I, pp. 192f, 219–31, and *Deuteronomy*, (ET London, 1966); E. W. Nicholson, *Deuteronomy and Tradition* (Oxford, 1967); J. Muilenberg, 'The form and structure of the covenantal formulations', *VT*, 9 (1959), 247–65. For alternatives to this cultic derivation, see the influential essay by G. E. Mendenhall, 'Covenant forms in Israelite tradition', *Biblical Archaeologist*, 17 (1954) 50–76, who relates it to treaty-formulas; and M. Weinfeld, *Deuteronomy and the Deuteronomic School* (Oxford, 1972), who finds here a basically literary, rhetorical tradition. McCarthy, *O. T. Covenant*, provides a review of the arguments.

[49] See Mendenhall, 'Covenant forms', pp. 58–61; Weinfeld, *Deuteronomy*, pp. 59–81.

in the form of future reaffirmations, which Moses stipulates are to be made 'on the day when you pass over the Jordan' (Deut. 27:1–8, 11–26; 31:10–13), and partly in the form of past re-affirmations, made by Moses himself while in Moab (Deut. 1:1–4:43; 4:44–6:25; 29–30); but, more deeply, the entire book, comprising these rites and all the other laws and exhortations, has the character of a covenant-renewal in two senses: first, as a narrative, historical record of the second giving of the Law through Moses at the end of the forty years' wandering; and second, as an actual, theological representation of Yahweh's demand and promise to Israel in the circumstances of the monarchy.[50] This gives to Deuteronomy a dynamic and strongly marked liturgical flavour: a comprehensive exhortation to Israel to remember God's actions (29:2), to recall his laws, and to make a solemn choice, a commitment to obedience (30:15) in knowledge of both blessing and curse. Confession of failure, of having tested God in the past, 'in the wilderness' (Deut. 1:26–46; 9:6–29; Josh. 5:6), and being liable to do so again (Deut. 6:10–16; 8:11–20; 29:18–28) is a crucial element in this renewal. Psalms 81 and 95, standing in the same theological tradition, similarly refer back to the wilderness narratives of rebellion connected with 'Massah' and 'Meribah' (Exod. 17:1–7) in order to affirm, through a thoroughly liturgical characterisation of the present moment (Ps. 81:1–3, 95:1f, 7b), the possibility and necessity of obedience.

Hebrews has been influenced by these passages in a number of ways, and apart from detailed quotations and echoes, the most important of which are listed below, many of its leading ideas are involved with this Deuteronomic vision.

(1) Its descriptions of rebellion are heavily dependent on Deuteronomy 29:18ff. Compare Hebrews 3:12 (Βλέπετε, ἀδελφοί, μήποτε ἔσται ἔν τινι ὑμῶν <u>καρδία πονηρὰ ἀπιστίας</u> ἐν τῷ ἀποστῆναι ἀπὸ θεοῦ ζῶντος) and 3:10 (<u>ἀεὶ πλανῶνται τῇ καρδίᾳ</u> = Ps. 95:10) with Deuteronomy 29:18f. (<u>μή τίς ἐστιν ἐν ὑμῖν</u> ... <u>τίνος ἡ διάνοια ἐξέκλινεν ἀπὸ κυρίου τοῦ θεοῦ</u> ... <u>ἐν τῇ ἀποπλανήσει τῆς καρδίας</u>). Compare also Hebrews 12:15 (<u>μή τις ῥίζα πικρίας ἄνω φύουσα ἐνοχλῇ</u>) with Deuteronomy 29:18 (<u>μή τίς ἐστιν ἐν ὑμῖν ῥίζα ἄνω φύουσα ἐν χολῇ καὶ πικρίᾳ</u>). Note also

[50] For discussion of the origins of Deuteronomy see von Rad, *Deuteronomy*, pp. 23–30; Nicholson, *Deuteronomy*, pp. 119–24.

how references to God's curse (ἀρά) and his burning anger (ἐκκαυθήσεται ὀργὴ κυρίου καὶ ὁ ζῆλος αὐτοῦ) in Deuteronomy 29:19f (LXX) and the description of the burnt and sterile land in verse 22 (LXX) are reflected in Hebrews 6:7f (κατάρας, καῦσιν etc.), while πυρὸς ζῆλος (Heb. 10:27) echoes Deuteronomy 29:20, and that the similar description of God's wrath as 'consuming fire' (πῦρ καταναλίσκον 12:28) is quoted from Deuteronomy 4:24 and 9:3. The grounds for condemnation at 10:28 are borrowed from Deuteronomy 17:6.

(2) Deuteronomy 31:6, God's commission to Joshua, is quoted at Hebrews 13:5, where it is applied to the individual Christian: 'He will not fail you nor forsake you.'

(3) Hebrews 4:11 reflects the circumcision rite at Joshua 5:2,[51] and the language of the covenant ceremony in Joshua 24 ('assemble together', v. 1; 'I and my house', v. 15) is found in Hebrews 10:19f.

(4) The remarkable passage Hebrews 12:18ff is based on Israel's approach to Yahweh to receive the first covenant, as described at Deuteronomy 4:11–14 and Exodus 19:12ff.[52]

On a larger scale, the relation between disbelief (disobedience) and Moses' failure to enter the land of promise (Deut. 32:48ff) forms the major theme of Hebrews 3–4 and provides the theological underpinning for the paraenetic strands within which all the detailed examples above are to be found.

Perhaps most striking, though, is the way Hebrews picks up from this Deuteronomic literature the ideas of 'liturgical time' and 'liturgical space': seeing all times as one time, the *time of worship*, and all places as one place, the *place of worship*. The Old Testament never gives up the notion of 'sacred place', though we can trace within it a transition from thinking of the sanctuary as the place of God's dwelling to thinking of it as the place of meeting with God.[53] If God has no local dwelling, he can be met with anywhere, not necessarily in a sanctuary and therefore not necessarily through recognisable cultic institutions. Without such a non-spatially oriented

---

[51] See below, pp. 171f.
[52] See below, pp. 144–6.
[53] See de Vaux, *AI*, pp. 326f. On the other hand most putative divine dwellings would seem to be first identified by some theophany, that is, an encounter. See Eliade, *Patterns*, pp. 367–70; de Vaux, *AI*, pp. 276ff.

theology, Deuteronomy's campaign for the centralising of the cultus at Jerusalem would be intolerable. What matters in these Deuteronomic texts is not whether the participants are standing in the ancient sanctuaries of Shechem (Josh. 24) or Gilgal (Josh. 5) or merely in the plains of Moab (Deut. 1:1), but that 'they presented themselves before God' (Josh. 24:1) and are told 'You stand this day all of you before the Lord your God' (Deut. 29:10). Actual space is subsumed within divine space. Hebrews is employing the same device when it announces boldly, 'You have come to Mount Zion and the city of the living God' (12:22),[54] and in the spatial language of its appeal to the readers to 'draw near' to God (4:16, 10:22) and its warnings to them not to 'drift away' or 'fall away' (2:1; 3:12).

Hebrews has two ways of describing the present time. There is, first a more general term: 'at the end of these days' (ἐπ' ἐσχάτου τῶν ἡμερῶν τούτων 1:2). Most current translations ('in these last days' (RSV), 'in this the final age' (NEB), 'in our time, the last days' (JB)) miss the subtlety of its phrasing which suggests an end-time now drawing to a close, reflecting the use of the phrase in the Septuagint (without τούτων) in contexts of eschatological prophecy,[55] and also at the covenant-rite in Josh. 24:27 (LXX) where the stone is said to be a witness to Israel's renewed covenant both 'today' and 'to the end of the days' (ἐπ' ἐσχάτων τῶν ἡμερῶν). It is probably within that time-scale that the conventional reference to 'the Day drawing near' (ἐγγίζουσαν τὴν ἡμέραν 10:25), to Christ's second appearance (9:28, 10:37) and to God's shaking the world 'yet once more' (12:26) should be placed. But second, elsewhere, discussion of a particular present day has a different meaning, and replicates the liturgical usage of Deuteronomy, in which the day of encounter with God is consistently 'Today' (σήμερον Deut. 27:1, 29:10, 30:11, Josh. 24:15, 27) or 'this day' (ἐν τῇ ἡμέρᾳ ταύτῃ Deut. 5:1, 26:16, 27:9f): *this* is the day of hearing God's commandments (in fact, the whole of Moses' exhortation (Deut. 5:1)), the day of Israel's decision, for Yahweh or against him

[54] Superficially, this appears to be a reversal of the regular procedure, but in moving from named actual places to an unnamed place-of-encounter, in the Old Testament examples, and moving from an unnamed actual place to a named place-of-encounter, in this verse in Hebrews, the matter of naming is secondary to that of encounter.

[55] J. Héring, *The Epistle to the Hebrews* (ET London, 1970), pp. 2f, quotes Num. 24:14, Jer. 23:20, Dan. 10:14. See also H. W. Attridge, *Hebrews*, p. 39; and Bruce, *Hebrews*, p. 3n., who comments that 'the use of the phrase here implies an inaugurated eschatology'.

(Josh. 24:15), the day of the solemn covenant. 'Today' is also the time of encounter and repentance in Psalms 81 and 95, and enters Hebrews through its quotation of Psalm 95:7–11:

> Today when you hear his voice
> do not harden your hearts as in the rebellion
> on the day of testing in the wilderness.

The phrase is repeated at 3:15 and again at 4:7, where especially it is treated not at all as a mere manner of speaking, but as denoting a specific time, the time appointed by God for his people to enter his rest.

Hebrews is not interested in recreating ancient liturgical practices any more than Deuteronomy but, whether consciously or not, both books exploit a dramatic or liturgical pattern with a particular perception of time and space (one which appears, in fact, to have a particular historical antitype), to give a highly charged intensity to their message and to its urgent demand for a response. Like Deuteronomy, Hebrews alternates between rehearsal of God's saving actions, especially in Jesus (1:1–4, 2:1–4, 5:7–10, 6:17f) and exhortations to respond to these with obedience (3:6, 10:19, 12:25), marking the transition from one mode to another by repeated use of 'because', 'therefore' and their cognates.[56] The presence of God as witness and judge is strongly emphasised (4:11–13, 10:26ff, 12:18ff), and the outcome of the decision is presented as either blessing (4:1ff, 6:13–20, 8:1f, 10:18, 13:20f) or curse (4:12, 6:4–8, 10:26–31, 37–9, 12:12–17, 25–9). The background of previous failure and divine judgement, which Psalm 95 takes as its particular focus, has a double importance for Hebrews: as an offer of a 'new covenant' (7:12, 8:6–13, 9:15) the failure of the old is a necessary condition; but for Hebrews, as for Deuteronomy (considered as a seventh-century text), this is not the first presentation of this new covenant, either, and its aim, however didactic its appearance, is really paraenetic. Its appeal is made in full awareness that this offer too may be rejected, and therefore heavy with consciousness of the judgement which disobedience would entail.

Another resemblance between the dramatic 'occasions' of the two books may be noted in passing. One significant historical

---

[56] For example: γάρ 2:5, 10, 6:13, 7:1; διὰ τοῦτο 2:1, 9:15; ὅθεν 3:1; διό 3:7, 6:1, 12:12, 28; τοιγαροῦν 12:1: compare Deut. 4:1, 11:1, 29:9; Josh. 24:14. See Hughes, *Hermeneutics*, pp. 54ff, for the importance of this technique in the paraenetic use of scripture.

occasion of ceremonies for renewing the covenant-commitment
was at a change of spiritual or political leadership, as seen in
Deuteronomy 31ff and Joshua 23f, both of which are attempts
by dying leaders (Moses and Joshua respectively) to secure from
Israel a commitment to continued obedience. In Deuteronomy
31:1 – 15, 31:23 and 34:9 this is fused with Moses' naming of Joshua
as his successor. A major theme of Hebrews is the failure of both
Moses and Joshua to secure the 'rest' for God's people, and the
fulfilment of this task by the new 'Ιησοῦς (4:8). Whether or not
this helps to explain the anonymity of the letter, it is certainly
not to its author but to *Jesus*, as pioneer and leader, that the book
urges obedience.

Writing about Deuteronomy, von Rad asks: 'When and where
was Israel ever again able to clothe a great literary work in so
completely uniform a style and diction?'[57] His question is made
the more pertinent by the fact that Deuteronomy is, as he says,
generally acknowledged to be 'an artistic mosaic' made up of
interspersed strands of narrative, cultic and paraenetic material;[58]
some have argued further that its present form is the result of a
fusion of two streams of covenant-theology, one Judahite, Davidic
and cultic-institutional, the other Ephraimite, Mosaic and prophetic-
political.[59] Both the distinction and the fusion are highly suggestive
for the study of the varied strands in Hebrews and the tightly
structured and consistent whole into which it welds them, sufficient
perhaps to offer an answer to von Rad's question. However the
relation between Hebrews and Deuteronomy is in reality less literary
than functional, in each case an attempt to articulate God's call
and challenge to his people, not only in an authoritative preaching
but, through the re-presentation of an event, in the celebration
of a divine personal presence and the possibilities which that
presence opens up: the renewal of history.

Sacred time and sacred place

We have seen that one technique which both Deuteronomy and
Hebrews use to profound effect is the theological redescription
of time and space. Wherever Deuteronomy's hearers are, they are
'before Yahweh', and the occasion is always 'today', the moment

---

[57] Von Rad, *OTT*, vol. I, p. 220.   [58] Von Rad, *OTT*, vol. I, p. 221.
[59] Mendenhall, 'Covenant forms', pp. 63 – 76.

of choice: they are simultaneously in the past and the present, dwelling in the syncretistic cities of seventh- or eighth-century Palestine, encamped at the foot of Mount Sinai, and standing in the plains of Moab waiting to enter the Land. Hebrews too addresses its readers 'as if' located in several places and times at once:

Place	Time
The Edge of the Land	Today
Mount Zion	The Eve of the Sabbath
At the door of the Tent of Meeting	The Day of Atonement

Not only the method but two or three of these six items have in fact been borrowed from Deuteronomy, or anyway point us back towards that book. In examining each of these in detail, we are not concerned with identifying sources, however, but rather with exploring the particular range of associations which each brings into Hebrews, and the means by which the book seeks to invite us to identify with them, to participate in its liturgical-dramatic 'as if'.

Sacred time

Today

It is a feature of sacred time to be at once all times (or all significant times) and no time – but emphatically not one particular and non-significant time.[60] Whenever the author of Hebrews was writing, the book is written in God's *'Today'* (3:13). This 'Today' is considered as both the time of creation and the time of the end: in it, Christ is 'the same' (1:12) from creation to the world's end, 'the same yesterday and today and forever' (13:8). Melchizedek likewise 'continues a priest for ever' in a perpetual now, 'without beginning of days or end of life' (7:3); his appearance signifies the renewing of all things, so that it is as though creation were new-begun, and humanity could choose over again whether the earth would be blessed or cursed by its actions (6:7f). Past succession is occasionally recognised – God spoke his word about 'Today' after and because Joshua had failed to realise the divine promise (4:7f); chapter 11 follows chronological order in telling of Israel's heroes of faith; the readers are bidden to 'recall the former days' (10:32) – but what matters about the past is being gathered up into the present. Hence Abel still 'speaks' (11:4, 12:24), and God's past speaking

[60] See Eliade, *Patterns*, pp. 388–409.

through the prophets is fulfilled in speaking now through the Son (1:1f). To stand still, content with past achievements, is effectively to fall back (5:11–6:2).

Similar reasoning applies to the future. Jesus Christ is eternally 'the same' (ἐχθὲς καὶ σήμερον ... καὶ εἰς τοὺς αἰῶνας 13:8). There is a tomorrow, but in the earthly sense only one: 'the Day' when Jesus will come a second time (9:28) to complete the process of salvation begun 'today'; Christians are urged to see this Day approaching (10:25) and to hear now God's promise that 'yet once more' (ἔτι ἅπαξ 12:26), but only once, he will shake both heaven and earth. 'These days', as the idiom of 1:2 suggests,[61] have been numbered in advance; they have been brought to an end by the fulfilment of the prophecy made through Jeremiah:

> This is the covenant that I will make with the house of Israel after those days (μετὰ τὰς ἡμέρας ἐκείνας), says the Lord.   (Jer. 31:31; Heb. 8:10)

'Today', then, is the day of the making of the new covenant, in which therefore the old covenant is 'ready to pass away' (ἐγγὺς ἀφανισμοῦ 8:13), though not yet vanished. More specifically, in the letter's terms, 'Today' is the day of the begetting of Christ as Son:

> 'You are my Son,
> today have I begotten you,'

in the words of Psalm 2:7 quoted at 1:5, and quoted again at 5:5, where they are treated as equivalent to Psalm 110:4:

> You are a priest for ever
> after the order of Melchizedek.

The Son who brings creation (1:2) and the past (πάλαι 1:1) into the present is the high priest who makes 'Today' the beginning of the new age, and by making expiation for all sins makes today the Day of Atonement, at least for those who heed the exhortation: 'O that today you would listen to his voice.'

The eve of the sabbath

The concept of the 'sabbath' has equal possibilities for simultaneity. If 'the sabbath-day' means one particular day in any week, it means

---

also one day in every week; one sabbath is like every sabbath, and therefore points back to creation and the first sabbath, and forward to the completion of God's purpose in the new age. From the concept of the weekly sabbath as divine blessing of rest from labour (Exod. 34:21) there developed the ideal image of the sabbatical year (in which, mysteriously, 'the sabbath of the land shall provide food for you' Lev. 25:6) and the Jubilee as sabbath of sabbaths, commencing on the Day of Atonement and signifying, not only extended holiday, but the righting of all wrongs. In rabbinic tradition this was taken further to become an archetype of eternal rest in God's presence, whether for individuals (cf. Rev. 14:13) or for the whole world: 'an image of the world to come' (Gen. R.17).[62]

In speaking of 'a sabbath rest for the people of God' (4:9), Hebrews is playing off the hope of eternal rest against the failure of the Promised Land to offer genuine fulfilment (4:8). This 'rest' is at once the new age and the rest which God enjoys. A rather different stream of contemporary thought counted the six days of creation as 6,000 years (based on Ps. 90:4) and therefore looked forward to the seventh day, a thousand years in which God and all creation would rest together, 'the Day of the Lord' yet to come;[63] for Hebrews it is a heavenly ideal, the rest into which God entered on the seventh day of the world, when he finished the work of creation, and into which his people too will enter at the coming of the new age.[64] The rabbinic 'liturgical' conception is here placed in an eschatological context (though the text shows no interest in counting the days or developing a chronology of the end-time), to affirm that while God's rest 'remains' (ἀπολείπεται 4:9) so does his promise that some shall enter it (καταλειπομένης 4:1). This Day is to be seen drawing near (10:25), but it is not yet here, and the question of who shall enter remains an open one. 'Today', when God is once again heard speaking (4:7, 12:24f), is the critical time, the sabbath-eve.

According to a widespread Jewish tradition, there were 'ten things' made by God at the very end of his Creation, on the eve of the first sabbath 'between the evenings' (or 'between the suns'),

---

[62] Gen. R. 17, quoted by Montefiore, *Hebrews*, p. 85. Cf. H. Freedman (ed. and trans.), *Genesis Rabbah* (London, 1939), p. 136, where it is rendered as 'the incomplete form of the world to come'. See also Barrett, 'Eschatology', p. 371n.

[63] Ep. Barn. 15:1–5, 8f; similar 'millennial' views are found in Rev. 20; 2 Esd. 7.

[64] Barrett, 'Eschatology', pp. 366–73 distinguishes this view sharply both from the chronology of 'Barnabas' and from the speculative, non-eschatological references to 'sabbath' by Philo.

that is, at the ambiguous marginal time when the sixth day had not ended nor the seventh begun. The lists vary, and so does the actual number of items, but here is one typical listing (from Mekilta Vayas. 6):[65]

> the rainbow
> the manna
> the rod of Moses
> the writing
> the shamir (to cut the altar)
> the tables of stone
> the tomb of Moses
> the cave of Moses and Elijah
> the opening of the earth (to swallow the wicked, Num. 16:30)
> the mouth of the ass of Balaam the wicked.

The same document refers also to another list which includes 'the rod of Aaron' (= rod of Moses?) and 'Adam's garments'. Other items listed elsewhere include:

> the well (Num 21:16) (= the Rock, 1 Cor. 10:4?) (PRE 18; B.Pes. 54a)[66]
> the alphabet (PRE 18)[67]
> the ram of Isaac (PRE 18, 40; Tg. Ps-J.on Gen. 22:13)[68]
> the ass ridden by Abraham (in Gen. 22) (PRE 40) (= ass of Moses/Messiah, PRE 31)[69]
> the shekinah and
> the demons (Tg. Ps-J.on Num. 22:28)[70]
> the land of Cain's exile (Tg. Ps-J.on Gen. 4:16) and
> the wine given to Isaac by Jacob (Tg. Ps-J.on Gen. 27:25).[71]

Though the items are of very varied kinds, they are all mysterious and in some way numinous objects involved at crucial points in God's converse with his people in the narrative portions of the Pentateuch. Either centrally (like the manna) or more peripherally (like the wine) they are instruments of the covenant. Our author refers, directly or indirectly, to several of these items:

[65] Bowker, *Targums*, pp. 113f.
[66] Friedlander, *PRE*, p. 124; Bowker, *Targums*, pp. 114f.
[67] Friedlander, *PRE*, p. 124.
[68] *Ibid.*, pp. 124, 312f; Bowker, *Targums*, pp. 225, 233f.
[69] Friedlander, *PRE*, pp. 312f, 224f.
[70] Bowker, *Targums*, p. 115.
[71] *Ibid.*, pp. 115, 133.

the manna (9:4)
the rod of Aaron (9:4)[72]
the tables of stone (9:4)
the opening (mouth) of earth (sea) to swallow the wicked
(11:29, 10:27, 12:29)[73]
the land of Cain's exile[74]
the ram of Isaac.[75]

We cannot conclude from these examples that Hebrews makes use of such a list, but only that it shares a common valuation of these particular symbols, springing from a common concern with the covenant, and that its strategy demands that a presentation of the 'new covenant' take full notice of the shape and contents of the old. The use made of these otherwise obscure symbols will be shown below, but it should be plain, at least, that their association with sabbath-eve and creation 'between the suns' would suit this book's liminal perspective.

The Day of Atonement

The ideal character of the Day of Atonement in Jewish tradition needs no exposition. More even than the Passover it attracted to itself description as 'the Day' in which the covenant of salvation is complete. As with sabbath, one Day of Atonement 'is' every Day of Atonement and points, not backward to creation, for there were then no sins to need atoning, but forward to the final atonement in the new age. It was said, 'like the ministering angels, Israelites are innocent of all sins on the Day of Atonement'.[76]

A number of covenantal narratives are associated with this day, especially in PRE. It is the day when Melchizedek circumcised (= 'blessed') Abraham on Mount Moriah (= Zion) and thereby inaugurated the covenant (PRE 29);[77] it was on this day that

---

[72] On Aaron's Rod, see below, pp. 160–4.
[73] See below, pp. 153, 155f, 160f.
[74] On Cain, see below, pp. 149–53.
[75] On the Binding of Isaac, see ch. 5, pp. 173–83, and ch. 6 *passim*.
[76] PRE 46 (Friedlander, *PRE*, p. 364).
[77] Friedlander, *PRE*, p. 204: 'Every year [God] sees the blood of our father Abraham's circumcision, and he forgives all the sins of Israel ... It says also "I said unto thee, In thy blood, live, yea, in thy blood, live" (Ezek. 16:6).' This repetition is the basis of the 'legend of the two bloods' (see Daly, *Origins*, p. 48). The connection with some significant details of the cultus is made even more explicit: 'In that place where Abraham was circumcised and his blood remained, there the altar was built, and therefore "and all the blood thereof shall he pour out at the base of the altar"'.

Abraham, as high priest, made a unique offering of his son Isaac (PRE 31);[78] it was on this day that Moses descended from Mount Sinai and gave Israel the Law (PRE 46).[79] It is called 'the sabbath of sabbaths which does not pass away' and stands both 'in this world and in the world to come'.[80] Though perhaps intrinsically less comprehensive in its resonances than Passover, the inclusiveness of its symbolic action secured its place as the principal covenant-feast,[81] at least while the Temple stood. While Hebrews has material relating to Passover, as to almost every aspect of the cultic system, its central argument straightforwardly expounds the death and exaltation of Jesus as fulfilment of the Day of Atonement ritual, and in particular (ignoring the scapegoat rite) the entry of the high priest into the Holy of Holies. In speaking of the 'high priest' (9:7) Hebrews here shows knowledge of the Temple ritual, breaking with its normal practice of referring only to the scriptural texts, in order to make a clear distinction between the one priest and the many, in preparation for its description of Jesus as a priest of a different (and unique) kind, 'high priest' as well as 'priest for ever after the order of Melchizedek' (9:11, 7:20f). The once-a-year event is treated as anticipation of the once-for-all (9:7–12), and, taking seriously the cosmic properties of the Temple, the entry into the shrine is fused with Jesus' entry into heaven. The symbolic value of this definite physical movement, 'drawing near', is very fully exploited in the letter, as is the movement's goal, the *personal encounter* of humanity with God in his holiest place, which is contrasted with the impersonal symbolism more generally employed (9:9f, 10:4) as well as with the disjunctive ideology it expresses (9:18–22, 12:18–21).

The complex procedures of the Day are for the purpose of the argument reduced to this one entry of the high priest bearing (his own) blood. The atoning sacrifice is therefore a single, completed, past event (9:11, 27f), but 'Today' is still the Day of Atonement, for time has stood still. Whereas the old covenant was marked by multiple and repeated sacrifices (9:6f, 10:11), so that a cycle of time was intrinsic to its operation, the new covenant has one sacrifice already made once for all on this day, and the continuation of chronological time has no interest for the author. The final event is yet to occur, and is plainly imminent, but any calculation of

[78] Friedlander, *PRE*, pp. 226ff.   [79] *Ibid.*, pp. 362f.
[80] *Ibid.*, pp. 362f.   [81] See above, pp. 107–9.

times and seasons would conflict with the central theme of faith and endurance.

Thus the present is *penultimate*, pointing beyond itself, whether 'Today' is thought of as the Day of Atonement or as the eve of the sabbath. According to the solar calendar in use among the Qumran covenanters, the Day of Atonement fell always on a Friday, the sabbath-eve.[82] Though the confluence of these two symbols of time has no need of such an empirical basis, if a positive connection between Hebrews and Essenism or the Dead Sea Scrolls were to be established[83] it would offer for the author and for the first readers a further level of resonance and integration.[84]

Sacred place

The edge of the Land

Of at least three distinct 'theological locations' for the readers of Hebrews, this first one, corresponding to some extent with the first two notions of time described above, visualises them as the people of Israel standing at the edge of the Land of Promise (or the 'rest', Ps. 95:11), just as they were when Moses delivered to them that great address in Moab which forms the book of Deuteronomy, looking back to the fate of the rebellious generation which left Egypt and died in the desert (3:16f) and urging them to believe that 'the promise of entering his rest remains' (4:1).

---

[82] See G. Vermes, *The Dead Sea Scrolls in English* (Harmondsworth, 1975), p. 43.

[83] On this question, see the literature listed in ch. 1, n. 71.

[84] As a possibility, this raises two questions: (1) May we legitimately discover in this significance attached to Friday the idea of *crucifixion*? To argue this, we would need to take into account the fact that the same solar calendar placed Passover regularly on a *Wednesday*, so that for anyone using it crucifixion could hardly be associated (as it is in the gospels) both with Friday and with Passover. On the other hand it is noteworthy that in Heb. − in contrast to the synoptics, John, Rev., and 1 Cor. 5:7 − Passover when mentioned is given no *Christological* interpretation. (2) Supposing the Day of Atonement already possessed in this circle a 'sabbath-eve' association, would such a resonance be welcome or unwelcome to the author of Hebrews? The connection as it establishes itself in the course of the work is essentially eschatological, a single and climactic salvation-event, and any hint that the book was here describing a merely (that is, literally) liturgical fusion of symbols, to be repeated annually, would immediately undermine its argument. Whether singly or together, the author is not interested in these feasts as anticipations of the new age (though this background is unquestionably assumed) but in the *new age* itself, demonstrated to be the fulfilling of all such hopes and anticipations. Hebrews is certainly not suggesting that any previous calendar is fulfilled in some Christian *liturgical* cycle, and however far the book may be responsible for the evolution of 'Good Friday' as a Christian 'Day of Atonement' that would (I suggest) be the very antithesis of its author's hopes.

Time has stood still: that distant past is still 'Today'; a voice urged perseverance; Joshua (ὁ 'Ιησοῦς) is still ready as pioneer (ἀρχηγός) to lead his people into the Land.[85]

Several features of the presentation help to convey this historical fiction. In 4:2 the author says 'we received the good news just as they did', a remark which is normally understood as a contrast between 'we', the present Christian readers, and 'they', the generation of Moses, but there are other possibilities. The anachronistic use of εὐηγγελισμένοι, which suggests that the 'good news' received is none other than the *gospel*, raises the question whether the contrast is rather (or also) between two groups of contemporaries (perhaps two fragments of one original group), who responded to the preaching of the Christian gospel in different ways. Or equally the contrast may be between two groups of contemporaries in the past: since 'they' have already been named as 'those who left Egypt under the leadership of Moses' (διὰ Μωϋσέως, 3:16), 'we' whom the good news benefits may be identified with the next generation, those 'born on the way', with whom God made a new covenant untainted by sin. The dramatic tension, which is both between 'us' and 'them', and between the present and the past, is best represented by taking both these pairs of contrasting contemporaries together, a current dispute seen in the light of the ancient ἀντιλογία in the desert.[86] In characterising the sin of those who have fallen away, Hebrews develops a comprehensive notion of 'Rebellion' by conflicting the incident at Meribah (= rebellion, ἀντιλογία, Num. 20) with others from the Kadesh cycle, Korah's revolt (Num. 16) and Israel's refusal to enter the land at the spies' behest (Num. 13f),[87] while omitting any mention of the specific subject of Numbers 20 (the people's demand for water) and instead widening God's refusal to allow Moses to enter the Land 'because you did not believe in me' (Num. 20:12) into the 'unbelief' and

---

[85] A. Vanhoye, 'Longue marche, ou accès tout proche? – La contexte biblique de Héb. 3:7–4:11', *Biblica*, 49 (1968), 9–26, also proposes this understanding of the dramatic location of the readers in his interesting critique of the 'pilgrimage' interpretation.

[86] Such a view favours (but does not depend on) the textual reading: μὴ συγκεκερασμένους τῇ πίστει τοῖς ἀκούσασιν ('since they were not united by faith with those who heard') (with Spicq, NRSV, JB) rather than the subjective reading (συγκεκερασμένος) preferred by most commentators and versions (RSV, NEB, Moffatt, Bruce, Montefiore, Westcott) ('since it did not meet with faith in the hearers').

[87] Compare particularly 'those whose bodies fell in the wilderness', Heb. 3:17, with Num. 14:32, 16:41ff; and 'disbelief', Heb. 3:18, 4:6, with Num. 14:11, 22.

'disobedience' of the whole people which bars them from entering God's rest (3:7–4:10). The letter's view of Israel's subsequent history is also affected. Throughout the book, the author writes about 'the Tent' rather than the Temple (like Stephen in Acts 7), and makes no direct reference to the institutions of Israel's settlement in Canaan, such as Jerusalem[88] or the monarchy. In chapter 11, Abraham and his descendants are portrayed as present in the land, but as sojourners only, 'living in tents' (11:9). Later in the chapter, the historical sequence which should proceed from the Exodus into the conquest of Canaan is ended abruptly at the fall of Jericho (vv. 30f) without any mention of the part played by Joshua; the achievements rehearsed in the list which follows, though in many cases derived from the scriptural narratives of the monarchies, are detached so as to look like the exploits of private individuals, while the way in which they are piled up indicates beyond argument that there is here no 'rest'. It is all written as though Israel had never entered the Land – or anyway had never managed to expel its enemies, to settle down, to establish the institutions of peace – as though it were still waiting on the other side of Jordan, with the constructive task of Joshua yet to be done.

On the other hand, this historical fiction, so skilfully built up, is at certain points deliberately undercut by drawing attention to the pastness of some of the events. At 4:7f, for example, the author points out that Joshua *did* not give them rest (εἰ γὰρ αὐτοὺς ... κατέπαυσεν), and that the psalm which names 'Today' as the moment of opportunity was written 'so long afterward' (μετὰ τοσοῦτον χρόνον) – the latter being the one reference to the historical character of the composition of the scriptures by a writer who is elsewhere studiously vague in these matters (διεμαρτύρατο δέ πού τις λέγων, 2:6). This is deliberate because it is after all essential, for Hebrews as for Deuteronomy, that the reality of past unbelief and its consequences should be fully in view, and that this return to the moment of entry should have a totally different outcome.

---

[88] Jerusalem is not offered in translation of 'Salem' in 7:1ff, for example, though this was commonplace among contemporary writers: Josephus, *Antiquities*, I.180; cf. Bowker, *Targums*, pp. 193f. 'King of Salem' also received allegorical treatment, as 'king of peace' (Philo, *Legum allegoria*, III.80) and as 'whole [i.e. circumcised] king' (Gen. R. 43.6; Freedman, *Genesis Rabbah*, p. 356).)

Mount Zion

The most overt instance of the author's liturgical or symbolic use of space occurs at 12:22, when it is asserted boldly, 'You have come [or drawn near – προσεληλύθατε] to Mount Zion and the city of the living God.' Few contend that this should be understood literally,[89] but in order to assess the force of the metaphor we must decide whether 'Mount Zion' should be thought of as a heavenly (that is, ethereal) city, or as the concrete earthly Jerusalem seen from a sacred point of view.

As sacred space, 'the True Place', Jerusalem can be thought of as 'Centre of the Earth' or as 'Divine Abode'. The first idea appears chiefly in Canaanite imagery of the ideal or sacred mountain (Ps. 48:2, Isa. 2:2, 14:13, Ezek. 38:12; cf. Judg. 9:37 on Mount Gerizim as 'centre'), and is the source of the concept of the 'Jerusalem above' (2 Bar. 20:2; 2 Esd. 7:26);[90] the latter in texts which describe God's dwelling in the city or Temple empirically described (Ps. 46:4, 84:1). These ideas are not necessarily held in isolation. Ezekiel, who draws a sharp contrast between God's holiness and the abominations currently practised in the Temple (Ezek. 8–10), can still envisage God dwelling again in the earthly shrine, once purified (43–6, 43:7), though his hope is also accompanied by visions of a paradisal city (28:13–19, 47:1–12, cf. Isa. 54:11–14). In the New Testament a similar interaction is expressed in John's vision of the new Jerusalem described in ideal terms (Rev. 21:1–22:5) for the point is that the heavenly city descends to earth, and then 'God's dwelling is with humankind' (Rev. 21:2f, 3:12; cf. Gal. 4:26, Phil. 3:20).

These accounts show differing emphases in their cosmologies – whether the Real is a present but heavenly ideal or a future earthly perfection – but both stand firmly in the Jewish apocalyptic-eschatological tradition; neither shows any trace of Platonic dualism. Reasons are given elsewhere for believing this book also to be thoroughly eschatological in its outlook, yet it may be that this view has not commanded general assent because this author, eschewing the elaborate pictoriality of the apocalyptic tradition represented by Ezekiel and Revelation, offers a very mild and

---

[89] But see Buchanan, *To the Hebrews*, pp. 222f, 258f.

[90] See Eliade, *Patterns*, pp. 374ff; C. Rowland, *The Open Heaven* (London, 1982), pp. 133, 167ff; A. T. Lincoln, *Paradise Now and Not Yet*, SNTS Monograph Series 43 (Cambridge, 1981), pp. 18ff; A. J. Wensinck, *The Ideas of the Western Semites concerning the Navel of the Earth* (Amsterdam, 1916).

'spiritualised' description of Mount Zion and its life.[91] The sensory impact of the supposedly positive presentation of Mount Zion in 12:22–4 is minimal in comparison with that of the negative presentation of Mount Sinai which precedes it (vv. 18–21), in language borrowed from Exodus 19 and Deuteronomy 4. The imagery can be compared in table 1, with the more vivid images in italic type.

Table 1. Imagery of the holy mountain

	Mount Sinai	Mount Zion
Visual	*Blazing fire* *Darkness and gloom* *Tempest, tremble* Mountain, beast 'So *terrible* the sight'	Mount Zion, Jerusalem City, enrolled *Sprinkled blood* *Angels in festal array*
Tactile	*blazing fire, tempest* 'What may be touched' Touch mountain, *stoned*	Sprinkled
Auditory	*Sound of trumpet* *Speaking voice* and its message	*Blood speaks*

The sensory power of the words used in the second list, already slight, is further distanced by the application of vague qualifiers: *heavenly* Jerusalem, enrolled *in heaven, spirits* of the just, *myriads.* On the other hand, verses 25–9, in asserting the readers' situation as perilous, increase the concreteness with strong and terrible imagery (*shake the earth, no escape, consuming fire*), so that these Christians seem, after all, to be confronted with a blazing fire, with gloom, and with a message to make mere humans tremble. The assurance of freedom from terror, of the festal gathering, appears to be hollow. By comparison with the immediacy of such language, the attempt of the argument to assert that not Sinai but *Zion* is the readers' present reality is feeble; and in verses 18–21, too, the force of the images used to describe where 'you have not come' is far stronger than the logical negative 'not': merely by *naming* the tangible realities of Sinai, we as readers

---

[91] See pp. 31f above. On the concept of Temple in Hebrews, see Barrett, 'Eschatology', pp. 373–6, 383ff; C. F. D. Moule, 'Sanctuary and sacrifice in the church of the New Testament', *JTS*, 1 (1950), 36ff; G. W. MacRae, 'Heavenly temple and eschatology in the Letter to the Hebrews', *Semeia*, 12 (1978), 179–200, finds in 9:8ff the eschatological belief in a heavenly temple conjoined with a Philonic conception of the world as temple.

'come' there. However, the imaginative movement in this complex passage is not all one-way: the 'spiritual' values of the central section (vv. 22–4) also interpret the physical and fearful strength of both outer sections. To stand in God's presence *is* terrifying, as the first and third parts insist, but within the terror is promise of joy; the word of heavenly mercy, which seems so feeble to humanity in its need, is not weak, but has all the strength of the awefulness of the God of Beth-el, Mount Moriah and the burning bush.

This stylistic issue is deeply significant for the book's religious purpose of presenting the new covenant as no novelty but the inner reality of the old, though its subordination of discursive logic to imaginative power is liable to misunderstanding. That which is heavenly must be presented as *more* real than the earthly, even if this can only be done by employing physical language with all its risks. Thus in describing the action of the new covenant, too, the author derives the necessary concreteness and numinous quality not from fantasy but from the real power of the old. Writing that Jesus entered the holy place 'taking not the blood of goats and calves but his own blood' (9:12) gives a concreteness to 'his own blood' and to its result ('securing an eternal redemption') by association with 'the blood of goats and calves', irrespective of the difference expressed by the 'not'. Conversely this author can, on another occasion, describe the earthly sanctuary and its activities (as in 9:1–10) with a bluntness, a matter-of-factness, which makes them hardly evocative or numinous at all, but merely curious. However, these things too have been named, and we shall see later that, despite this apparent casualness, there is a discernible reason for the inclusion of every element.[92]

At the door of the Tent of Meeting

In a number of passages, the readers are addressed as if they had not only approached Mount Zion but were inside the Temple, at the very edge of the holiest sphere – 'in the Holy Place' or 'at the door of the Tent of Meeting' – and being bidden to go still further into the centre, the Holy of Holies itself.[93] This location is obviously

[92] See below, pp. 101–4.

[93] There is a significant ambiguity in the verb in 12:18, 22, usually translated (e.g. RSV, JB, NIV) 'you have not come ... but you have come'. Προσέρχομαι appears five times more in Hebrews (4:16, 7:25, 10:1, 22, 11:6), always in the context of *approaching God*, as suppliant or as intercessor, and with overtones derived from its

related to the previous one, but not identical, since it involves not only a change of place but a change of role: it was as Israel, the people of God, that they stood over against the mountain (Mount Zion); it is as God's priests that they are urged to 'draw near to the throne of grace' and to 'have confidence to enter the sanctuary' (4:16, 10:19–22), assured that the 'hope' which has 'entered into the inner shrine behind the curtain' is to be *seized* because Jesus has gone there 'as a forerunner on our behalf' (6:19f). The model presupposed in these passages is not so much the inauguration of a new covenant as the ordination of a new priesthood (7:12, 10:9–18), as in the ceremony set out in Exodus 29 and Leviticus 8, which involved the enclosure of Aaron and his sons for seven days 'at the door of the Tent of Meeting' (Lev. 8:31ff), literally 'dwelling in God's house' (Ps. 23:6, 84:4), in transition from a secular to a sacred status.[94] They are God's people now purified and able to dwell in his presence (his οἶκος (household) dwelling in his οἶκος (house)), a 'royal priesthood' (1 Pet. 2:9, echoing Exod. 19:6) though the term does not appear in Hebrews.[95] Whereas the Mount Zion passage is very sparing in its use of sacrificial language (including only the 'festal throng' and the 'sprinkled blood of Jesus'), these passages, though no less insistent that the atoning sacrifice is completed, express vividly the awesomeness of approaching God – as well as its gracious permissibility – in sacrificial terms: sanctuary, blood, curtain, priest, house of God, sprinkled, washed, pure, ἐπισυναγωγή (10:19–25); high priest, sin, grace, mercy, throne, gifts and sacrifices, περὶ ἁμαρτιῶν, τὰ πρὸς τὸν θεόν (4:14–5:3).

The use of such language is risky, however. Like Jesus (7:14, 8:4), the readers are not, in fact, priests under the old covenant,

use in LXX to signify *priestly* approach charged with danger for those who are not worthy (Lev. 21:17, 21, 22:3). When in Deut. 4:11 (a verse echoed at 12:18) the people 'approached and stood at the foot of the mountain' they were putting themselves at risk; and any nearer approach, as the warning contained in Exod. 19 indicates, would be trespass into the realm of God. Though it is not used in Exod. 19 in the sense of approaching God, in the command 'do not approach a woman' (v. 15) it signifies that which renders unclean in approaching God's presence. For this reason the verb should probably be rendered in both these verses '*drawn near*', to emphasise that approach is in both cases to that which is *holy*, but charged in one instance with fear, in the other with grace. NEB's rendering 'stand before' is a successful attempt to convey both this contrast and the ambiguity implied in the Greek. Or perhaps a differential translation is required to make the distinction more strongly still: instead of 'drawing near' fearfully to Sinai, you have '*come*' with joy to Zion.

[94] See Leach, *CC*, pp. 77–9, 89–91, for discussion of this ceremony within the framework of a transitional rite.

[95] See below, pp. 234–7, 258f.

and may even be Gentiles.[96] If a priesthood is needed to 'serve' the new covenant it is a priesthood whose membership is coextensive with the covenant itself and whose 'service' is just the faith and obedience demanded of all. In 13:11−14 the familiar image of 'drawing near' is inverted and the same idea expressed in terms of movement *outwards*, going 'outside the camp' to the place of Jesus' suffering, a transformation of expiatory language which comes closer to recognising the distinctiveness of Jesus and the covenant he offers. If the invitation to 'draw near' expresses an invitation, it expresses also an unrealised hope. Being 'at the door of the Tent of Meeting' − like being 'on the edge of the Land' − it is as easy to go back as to go forwards, perhaps easier. These express spatially, in complementary cultic and political terms, the question which the author puts before the readers 'today'.

[96] Bruce, *Hebrews*, p.273n., suggests that προσεληλύθατε in 12:18, 22, is a deliberate echo of the cognate term προσήλυτος.

5

THE NARRATIVES OF THE COVENANT

There is a great deal in the Old Testament which, for whatever reason, appears arbitrary and strange, even though scholarship shows that the text we possess is the end product of a long history of editing laws and traditions in accordance with preferred patterns of practice and theology. In Hebrews as in Jewish tradition we see at work the continuing process of interpreting the arbitrary contents of cultural memory into conformity with a unified system of thought and practice, in which the concept of 'covenant' functions as an organizing principle. Within the overlapping and interacting contexts supplied by the six spatio-temporal locations described in chapter 4, Hebrews develops its theology of covenant less by direct discursive argument than by reference or allusion to a network of ritual and narrative symbols drawn from this memory (written and oral), selected and deployed in a fashion which itself, however, often seems arbitrary. The aim of the exposition which follows will be to show that the real difficulty is caused by interpretative overload rather than arbitrariness, too much rather than too little meaning. This is material which has been formed and reformed, and appropriated to new contexts, several times before it reached Hebrews. It functions here as the quasi-liturgical recital of the covenant-traditions, the history of the 'covenant-people' which the letter addresses; though not organised chronologically, but through theological and symbolic association, it is the memory appropriate to standing before God.

Cultic traditions

Cain and Abel

Although these brothers appear in scripture as a pair, Cain is in Hebrews particularly associated with themes of judgement, exile and the possibility of repentance, while Abel, who is named twice in the letter (11:4, 12:24), prefigures Christ in being both sacrificer and victim, and in continuing to speak after death. In 12:24 this is made explicit when Christ's 'sprinkled blood' is said to speak 'more graciously' (κρεῖττον) than Abel (or, than Abel's blood). Recalling that in Genesis 4:10 Abel's blood 'cries from the ground' for vengeance on his slayer, the author is here apparently buttressing the comparison between Sinai and the heavenly Jerusalem by setting the vindictiveness of the old covenant against the graciousness offered by the new. This idea of vengeance relates to the judgement theme of the letter, restated in the immediately following verses (12:25–8): those who ignore 'the one who is speaking' (that is, Jesus, or perhaps God)[1] bring on themselves the judgement of the 'consuming fire'. When the same theme is stated at 10:26–31 the sinner is called ὁ τὸν υἱὸν τοῦ θεοῦ καταπατήσας (10:29), literally, 'he who has *trampled underfoot* the son of God', a strong and strange image which should perhaps be related to the account of Abel's guilty burial (Gen. 4:10). The still earlier statement of this theme (6:4–8) ends with a comparison between fruitful land and unfruitful – land which, 'if it bears thorns and thistles, is worthless and near to being cursed; its end is to be burned'. The Fragment Targum comments on Genesis 4:16, that the earth was fruitful like Eden until Cain killed his brother, but then 'because he turned about and killed his brother Abel, it turned about to produce for him thorns and thistles'.[2] In allusions like these, and in the image of burning, which appears in all three passages, we find a shadowy but consistent connection between this archetypal murder and the most uncomfortable theme in Hebrews.

The role of Cain as cursed by God and sentenced to perpetual wandering is also to be found underlying the presentation of Israel in Hebrews 3–4 as wandering endlessly without finding rest, as a result of its primal act of disobedience or disbelief; and perhaps, too, in the unexplained fact that those who wander on the face of the earth, despite their acknowledged faith, do not 'receive the promises' (11:40). Yet Cain seems to stand under judgement even before his crime, otherwise why should his sacrifice be rejected? One probably contemporary attempt to explain this rejection, found

---

[1] For the reading of this as 'God', see Attridge, *Hebrews*, p. 379; Bruce, *Hebrews*, p. 381; O. Michel, *Der Brief an die Hebräer* (Göttingen, 1949), p. 321; for 'Jesus', see Montefiore, *Hebrews*, pp. 233f. Moffatt, *Hebrews*, p. 220, prefers Moses. Perhaps Westcott gets the right balance: 'he who "spake in a Son" (1:2) still speaks in him' (*Hebrews*, p. 418).

[2] FT (P) on Gen. 4:16 (M. Klein, *The Fragment Targums of the Pentateuch* (Rome, 1980), p. 9).

widely in the targums, may shed light on our author's not otherwise lucid explanation that Abel's 'more acceptable' sacrifice was offered 'by faith' (11:4). This version records a theological dispute between the brothers in which Cain denies the justice of God's order, even so far as asserting that:

> Neither is there judgement nor is there a judge, nor is there a world to come; and there is no giving of good reward to the righteous nor is retribution exacted of the wicked; and the world was not created with mercy, nor is it conducted with mercy.[3]

It is when Abel affirms his faith in all these unseen realities that Cain rises up and kills him, and thus becomes the archetypal atheist as well as manslayer. If that is relevant to the meaning of 'faith' in 11:1–3, and to the meaning of 'disbelief' in Hebrews 3 to 4, we find in the figure of Cain, though only named once, a confluence of a number of themes of deep interest to our author: faith and rebellion; judgement, wandering and ultimate rejection. According to a number of Jewish versions Cain subsequently repented and was forgiven by God;[4] this author is notorious for denying that possibility in general, and through the parallel figure of Esau (likewise the eldest of two brothers; rejected; a wanderer) he confirms (12:15) that since his readers will have *chosen* their part (either as rebels or as people of faith) no turning back will be possible.

In a passage of the Quran,[5] the Jews and the Christians are addressed as those who, having lost heart because of the long delay, may be about to fail to seize God's promise now, when it is at last being offered to them through Mohammed, just as the wilderness generation of Israel refused to enter the Land in fear of the giants (Num. 13f). To them, according to this passage, Moses was instructed by God to recite the story of Cain and Abel. The details of the story as given are closely similar to the targumic tradition quoted above, but the paraenetic application of this story to those who are in danger of 'falling away' from salvation at the crucial moment offers an interesting parallel to Hebrews.

---

[3] FT (V) and Ps-J. on Gen. 4:8 (Klein, *Fragment Targums*, p. 93; Bowker, *Targums*, pp. 132f).

[4] Tg. Ps-J. on Gen. 4:13f, Gen. R. 22:11,13 (Bowker, *Targums*, pp. 133, 139f); Josephus, *Antiquities*, I.58.

[5] 5:19–31 (M.M. Pickthall (trans.), *The Meaning of the Glorious Koran* (New York, n.d.), pp. 98f).

Abel's speech has so far been understood as a cry for vengeance, in the most natural reading of 12:24.[6] In 11:4 however, Abel is presented as a man of 'faith', approved by God as righteous, either because of his faith or because of his sacrifice (πλείονα θυσίαν παρὰ Κάϊν: a 'more abundant' sacrifice, or simply 'better'?), and 'through this' (through his faith, or through his sacrifice?) 'he is still speaking'. His speaking must therefore be more than a demand for vengeance on his brother, long since wrought by God: it may be *warning* of judgement to those who follow the way of Cain; it may equally be words of *intercession*, especially if 'through this' refers not to his faith but to his acceptable sacrifice.[7] Criticism has long recognised in Abel's blood crying 'from the ground' the traces of a chthonic sacrifice, appropriate to Cain the tiller of the soil, performed like the red-heifer rite outside the settlement, 'in the field', and with avertive overtones.[8] On this reading, Hebrews has in these two verses fused into one Abel's 'acceptable sacrifice' (11:4) and his 'blood' (12:24), to present Abel as a forerunner of Christ the priest-victim. As the Akedah tradition attaches to the event of Genesis 22 expiatory value and sees it as a single sacrifice 'remembered' in the Temple cultus, especially Passover, so this author gives to Abel's blood, shed in imitation of the sin-offerings (downwards, outside the Camp), expiatory and covenant-establishing power − but a power which anticipates the 'better' blood of Jesus (12:24) and gives way before it.

Confirmation of this reading can be found in the benediction at 13:20f:

> May the God of peace who brought back from the dead (ὁ ἀναγαγὼν ἐκ νεκρῶν) Jesus our Lord, the great shepherd

[6] See Moffatt, *Hebrews*, pp. 218f, and Bruce, *Hebrews*, pp. 378f, who refer to 1 Enoch 22:6f, where Abel's voice is said to be still crying to heaven for vengeance on Cain 'till his seed is destroyed from the face of the earth and annihilated from among the seed of men'. This is confirmed by adopting (with Montefiore and Bruce) the reading κρείττονα λαλοῦντι (p46) instead of κρεῖττον: the voice of Jesus 'speaks of better things'.

[7] Against the consensus of modern commentators (Moffatt, *Hebrews*, p. 163, Bruce, *Hebrews*, pp. 285f, Spicq *Hébreux*, vol. II, pp. 342f, Héring, *Hebrews*, pp. 99f), Westcott (*Hebrews*, p. 354) takes δι'ἧς to refer to his sacrifice, though he agrees that δι'αὐτῆς refers to his faith; however, Héring (*Hebrews*, p. 117) supports the idea of intercession in 12:24, Jesus' voice differing from Abel's in that 'it cries out more loudly than Abel's, and it has more far-reaching effects'.

[8] For example, 'Sin couching at the door' (Gen. 4:7); and in the Quranic account Abel's words to Cain: 'Allah accepteth (sacrifice) only from those who ward off (evil)' (5:27) (Pickthall, *Glorious Koran*, p. 99; or 'from those that fear him', J. M. Rodwell (trans.), *The Koran* (London, 1909), p. 489).

of the sheep (τὸν ποιμένα τῶν προβάτων τὸν μέγαν), in the blood of the eternal covenant, make you perfect in every good work.

The first two phrases are rightly connected with the reference to Moses in Isaiah 63:11 (LXX): ποῦ ὁ ἀναβιβάσας ἐκ τῆς γῆς (θαλάσσης) τὸν ποιμένα τῶν προβάτων; – where γῆ, if that is the right reading (MT and some LXX texts have 'sea'), means primarily the land of Egypt but is certainly amenable to an understanding as 'earth' (= place of dead = sea). There is also a reference to Joshua in these terms at Numbers 27:17. But Abel too is described in the Septuagint as ποιμὴν προβάτων (Gen. 4:2), and he was certainly regarded as *living* after his death, as 11:4 also contends;[9] however, his 'blood' (his covenant-sacrifice) was certainly surpassed by that of Christ, '*the great* shepherd of the sheep', 'mediator of a *new* covenant', 'in the blood of an *eternal* covenant'. This conforms to the Western liturgical tradition of juxtaposing Abel, Abraham and Melchizedek as types of Christ the high priest;[10] it also conforms to the association of Abel with Abraham and Noah in offering on the altar built by Adam (Eden = Mount Ararat = Mount Moriah = Mount Zion) foundational sacrifices for Israel's worship. This verse (13:20) serves to remind us that the function of sacrifice was to enable humanity to *live* before God and was therefore open to interpretation through some idea of resurrection. Isaac was certainly believed to have died and been restored, but it is significant that he is received back, here, ἐν παραβολῇ (11:19);[11] Abel too 'lives' in his blood, though not in himself; Jesus fulfils both their sacrifice and their rising and thereby establishes the *eternal covenant*.

Rahab

'Rahab the harlot' is placed among this list of sacrificial types because, though little is said in the single verse in which she is named, a great deal more may be inferred. Explicitly, Rahab's 'faith' is displayed in her having 'received the spies in peace' (11:31); 1 Clement 12:1

[9] Philo, *Quod deterius potiori insidiari solet*, 14; cf. Westcott, *Hebrews*, p.355. Perhaps because of the apparent contrast between Jesus and Abel in 12:24, this connection between them in 13:20f has received little notice among commentators.
[10] Westcott, *Hebrews*, p.354. Spicq (*Hébreux*, vol.II, pp.409f) quotes Matt. 23:35 to point out that Abel anticipates Christ in being an *innocent* blood-victim; this interpretation is denied by Moffatt (*Hebrews*, p.209).
[11] See below, pp.177–9.

likewise commends her for her 'faith and hospitality', and James says that by her action of 'receiving' the Israelites she was 'justified by works' (2:25). Hospitality (φιλοξενία) is an important virtue, especially for those who 'sojourn' and 'wander in faith', and our author associates it particularly with the hospitality of Abraham who (in Gen. 18) 'entertained angels unawares' (13:2); so does Clement who, in a passage (chs. 9–12) which apparently draws on Hebrews 11 or a parallel tradition, in praise of Enoch, Noah, Abraham, Lot and Rahab, commends Lot and Rahab in particular for their hospitality (Lot having protected, in Gen. 19, two of the same angels who had visited Abraham); and so perhaps does James who, in the verse already quoted, praises Rahab for receiving the messengers, that is, 'τοὺς ἀγγέλους'.[12]

Why is Rahab specifically named here as 'the harlot' (ἡ πόρνη)? Only two women are named in Hebrews (both in ch. 11), the other being Sarah: why these two? Though the connection is not brought out here, Rahab is in some sense a complement to Sarah, as she appears in the intriguing narrative of Genesis 12:10–13:1 (paralleled in Gen. 20, and again, through the person of Rebekah, in Gen. 26:6–11): Sarah the Israelite princess turned pagan concubine; Rahab the pagan prostitute turned Israelite protector (and, according to some traditions, ancestor of the royal house of David (Matt. 1:5)).[13] Perhaps our author is interested in Rahab above all as an *outsider*, like Melchizedek and Jesus, from whose entry into Israel, threatening though it seems, salvation flows, and with whose excluded situation the readers need to identify themselves.

However this may be, the chief overt function of Rahab here is in relation to the *Passover*. The commands given to Rahab for her protection in Joshua 2:18ff are to bind a scarlet cord in her window, to gather her whole household into her house and to ensure that none pass the doors while the Israelite army destroys Jericho around them.

---

[12] Cf. Midr. Teh. on Ps. 37:1, where the acts of hospitality of Melchizedek (Shem) and Abraham are treated together (Bowker, *Targums*, pp. 197f).

[13] See 'Rahab' in *Encyclopedia Judaica*, vol. XIII, pp. 1,514f; A. T. Hanson, 'Rahab the harlot in early Christian tradition', *JSNT*, 1 (1978), 53–60; J. D. Quinn, 'Is 'Ραχαβ in Matt. 1:5 Rahab of Jericho?', *Biblica*, 62 (1981), 225–8, and the reply by R. E. Brown, '*Rachab* in Matt. 1:5 probably is Rahab of Jericho', *Biblica*, 63 (1982), 79f. A further parallel may be noted, between this incident involving Sarah and the treatment of Moses in ch. 11: the child Moses is hidden by his parents because he is beautiful (ἀστεῖος) and becomes 'a son of Pharaoh's daughter' tempted by the 'treasures of Egypt' (11:23–6); Sarah is hidden by Abraham because she is beautiful (εὐπρόσωπος, Gen. 12:11) and is taken into Pharaoh's household, but the plagues which result cause Abraham's expulsion by Pharaoh, in an anticipation of the Exodus.

There is a striking similarity to the Passover rules, with the family enclosed by liminal blood-symbolism from the destroyer outside, and Christian interpretation has followed 1 Clement in seeing the scarlet cord as 'typifying the redemption ... through the blood of the Lord' (1 Clem. 12:7). For our purpose, the specific detail of the cord is less important (since it is not mentioned by the author) than the whole pattern of paschal symbolism called up by the mention of her name, and reinforced by its place in a sequence of four salvific events with which the main list of faith-heroes in chapter 11 concludes. These are related in verses 28–31, and have a chiasmic shape:

(1) *Passover* instituted with application of blood;
    Israel saved from 'the Destroyer of the first-born'.
(2) *Movement through* the Red Sea (boundary vanishes);
    destruction of the pagans (Egyptians).
(3) *Movement round* city walls (boundary vanishes);
    destruction of the pagans (Jerichoites).
(4) Rahab's '*passover*' (with scarlet cord);
    the faithful saved while 'the disobedient' perish.

In addition to the contrast between two (saving) ritual actions and two (boundary-crossing) motions, notice that the first two acts of 'faith' comprise *leaving Egypt*, while the second two comprise *entering the Land of Promise*. Between these should fall the forty-year period of wilderness wandering, but to that time no acts of 'faith' are attributed. It has already been described as the time of disbelief (ἀπιστία 3:12) and disobedience (τοῖς ἀπειθήσασιν 3:18), and the latter word, used there of Israel, is used here to describe the Gentiles who perished in Jericho. Thus although, historically speaking, the Israelites and the Gentiles are enemies in this story, the *pattern* identifies the Gentile Rahab with the Israelites who earned divine protection 'by faith', and conversely identifies the Egyptians not only with the citizens of Jericho but also with the 'disobedient' Israelites who fell in the wilderness (Heb. 3f).

A further set of associations confirms this last point. In verse 29 the Egyptians are said to have been 'swallowed' in the sea (κατεπόθησαν), a word which echoes a phrase in Moses' song (Exod. 15:12): κατέπιεν αὐτοὺς γῆ. Notice here the interchangeability of sea and earth, witnessed already in the variant texts of Isaiah 63:11 (LXX),[14] both perhaps subordinate to a mythological image of

[14] See above, p. 153.

Death (or 'the Destroyer', v.28) as a monster opening its huge jaws to swallow. When we look at the role of Korah's rebellion, we shall find that in Numbers 16:32 'the earth swallowed' (ἡ γῆ κατέπιεν) Korah and his associates, while *fire* 'came forth from the Lord and consumed' (κατέφαγεν 16:35) the 250 men offering incense;[15] in the other occurrence of this motif, in Leviticus 10:3, again the false priests are 'consumed' (κατέφαγεν) by fire, and the image is repeated, though in different words, in the paraenesis of Hebrews, 'our God is a consuming fire' (ὁ θεὸς ἡμῶν πῦρ καταναλίσκον 12:29, cf. πυρὸς ζῆλος ἐσθίειν μέλλοντος τοὺς ὑπεναντίους 10:27).

In these four short but carefully structured verses several major symbolic motifs are integrated in a way which represents the covenant-theology in a 'Priestly' perspective: outside the defended circle of the new covenant (= Rahab and Moses) dwells the 'fury of fire', the 'Destroyer' who swallows the disobedient.[16] However the priesthood in question is certainly not Aaronic, and the beneficiaries of the covenant, as presented here, do not include Israel.

Twin-birth and divine election

The reference to Rahab, and the specific description of her as 'the harlot', point to another motif from scripture and tradition which underlies the author's thinking. Although Hebrews distinguishes between those who consciously rebel against God (Esau, 12:11; the wilderness generation, 3:7−4:11; some of the book's readers, perhaps, 6:4−8, 10:26−31, 12:25−8) and those who, by faith, obey him (the heroes of chapter 11; Jesus, 5:7−10, 12:1−3; Moses, 3:2−5, 11:24−8; most of the readers, hopefully, 10:32−9), there remains a sense of mystery about this division, almost a fatalism, as though the choice is not after all so firmly in human control. Esau wishes to repent but cannot (12:17); the Old Testament heroes despite their faith 'did not receive what was promised' (11:39f); the author's denial implies that there is indeed a possibility that God might, after all, overlook the readers' good works (6:10). It seems that God chooses according to rules of his own devising: if he causes others to suffer he might as easily have inflicted it on the readers (13:3); whatever they might think about their condition, they may in the end be 'judged to have

---

[15] See below, pp. 160f.
[16] See below, pp. 194ff.

fallen short' of salvation (4:1).[17] Such a theme, if too overtly stated, would completely undermine the value of the author's exhortations to faith and perseverance, but the question of election, and even more fundamental, the question of the *righteousness* of God's judgements, are necessary to a complete and honest theology such as this author is attempting, as the following two chapters will show.

The older strata of the Pentateuch abound with twin-births and other sibling pairs, with the characteristic motif of the younger son favoured over the elder: for example, Cain and Abel (Gen. 4), Ishmael and Isaac (Gen. 21), Esau and Jacob (Gen. 25–7), Zerah and Perez (Gen. 38), Manasseh and Ephraim (Gen. 48), and a variant female pair, Leah and Rachel (Gen. 29f). Karl Barth has pointed to the theological connection of this motif with the arbitrary choice between two birds in the leper rite (Lev. 14) and between two goats in the Day of Atonement (Lev. 16);[18] in chapter 3 it was argued that this action of making a distinction where by definition there is none has a powerfully order-creating effect, appropriate to those occasions when vital distinctions have been put under threat.[19] Whatever the origin of these stories, in their present form they express the incalculability of the will of Yahweh ('I will have mercy on whom I will have mercy', Exod. 33:19), and his protection of the weak and disregarded.

The story of the birth of Zerah and Perez, sons of Judah and Tamar, has similarities to that of Esau and Jacob – Perez like Jacob supplanting his elder brother in the womb itself – with the curious addition that when Zerah puts out his hand from the womb the midwife ties round it a scarlet thread (Gen. 38:28), such a scarlet threat (κόκκινος) as was to be used in the leper-cleansing and the red-heifer rite (Lev. 14:4, Numb. 19:6), and which, according to Mishnah Yoma 4.2,[20] was to be tied around the head of the scapegoat (and around the throat of the other goat) on the Day of Atonement; it was also what Rahab tied in her window (Josh. 2:18). The significance of this blood-symbol attached to extremities is not the rejection of the bearer, however, but the setting-apart by God of this particular liminal object or figure as the means for the reaffirming of the

---

[17] Reading δοκεῖν in an objective sense ('be judged' rather than 'seem') with RSV, NIV, Moffatt (*Hebrews*, p. 50); against NEB, Bruce (*Hebrews*, p. 70), Spicq (*Hébreux*, II, p. 81), Westcott (*Hebrews*, p. 93).

[18] K. Barth, *Church Dogmatics*, vol. II–2 (Edinburgh, 1957), pp. 357–66.

[19] See above, pp. 67–75, 82–91.

[20] Danby, *The Mishnah*, p. 166.

covenant: as such it may entail divine protection.[21] The scapegoat which goes into the wilderness by divine decree, like Cain and Ishmael, goes there to serve God's purpose not to be cast away utterly: hence its death is not disorder but life-bringing sacrifice, and at the moment of its death, according to Mishnah Yoma 6.8,[22] the scarlet cord in the Temple turned white. Like the leper whose hand and forehead are anointed with blood to signify his return from an ambiguous status to rejoin the living, with his margins redefined, the blood of Passover separates those who are brought clear of chaos even when (or perhaps especially when) they seem undeserving.

God is the protector of the outcast, like Rahab the harlot, and like Moses, who though 'son of Pharaoh's daughter' and heir to 'the treasures of Egypt' has chosen self-exile, preferring 'to share ill-treatment with the people of God' and 'the reproach of Christ' (or 'of the anointed one') (11:24−7). Moses should probably be understood here as a 'first-born son' who for God's sake loses his security as first-born of his parents and later, likewise for God's sake, surrenders his royal inheritance in Egypt, in explicit contrast to Esau who, 'having sold his birthright (πρωτοτόκια) for a single meal', is dismissed as πόρνος ἢ βέβηλος (compare Rahab ἡ πόρνη!), and 'found no chance to repent' (12:16f). Isaac too is a first-born (ὁ μονογενής 11:17, Ishmael not being mentioned), the son through whom Abraham's progeny is to come, but he too is offered up to God in faith and (symbolically) received back from the dead (11:17): it is presumably such as these who comprise 'the assembly of the first-born (ἐκκλησία πρωτοτόκων) enrolled in heaven' (12:23), since God's disregard for primogeniture as such is clearly reflected in his preference for Abel and in the references, slight but pregnant, to Isaac's blessing of Jacob and Esau (in that order) and, in the next verse, to Jacob blessing the sons of Joseph (Gen. 48:13f), in which again, as is well known (though it is not stated here), the order was reversed.

When Moses gave up his privileged position he exposed himself to 'the anger of the king' and 'the destroyer of the first-born' (vv.

---

[21] Rahab's window-cord = Passover blood on lintel = blood on ears and toes of priests in ordination (Lev. 8) = blood on tail and wing of the live bird in the leprosy rite, and on the leper's hand (Lev. 14) = 'mark of Cain' (Gen. 4:15) = divine favour of Ishmael despite his banishment (Gen. 21:12−21) = (?) red colour of Esau (Gen. 25:25). In Ep. Barn. 7:8ff, the bush on which the wool is placed is said to be a bramble, signifying by its thorns the trials of discipleship and by its berries the reward; the identical goats signify the identity of Christ as both sufferer and Judge.

[22] Danby, *The Mishnah*, p. 170.

27f), two terms which function here as a single objective destructive force ready to fall on him but for the protection of the πρόσχυσις of the Passover.[23] But what is this force, this 'wrath'? There are good grounds for relating it to the impersonal 'wrath' or 'blow' or 'plague' of the Priestly editors, and therefore identifying this 'destroyer of the first-born' with God as he appears in this letter, the God who is – at least sometimes – a 'consuming fire'. We recall that there is in the Passover tradition itself a profound ambiguity about the role of God, who appears there as both protector and destroyer.[24] For how is the figure of 'the Destroyer' in the Passover pericope to be understood? Does it signify:

(a) *Egypt*, seeking to attack God's chosen people (but finally destroyed by God)?

(b) *Death*, attacking all first-born sons (but, being prevented by God from attacking those protected by paschal blood, it kills only the Egyptians)?

(c) *God*, exacting vengeance on Egypt but sparing his people Israel?

(d) *God*, attacking all mortals or all first-born sons (but, being prevented by the avertive power of blood from killing Israel, he kills only Egyptians)?

While the course of the exodus narrative as a whole is non-problematically represented by (a), and the present text of Exodus 12 takes (c) as its standpoint, again non-problematically, there remain, it seems from earlier recensions, references to 'plague' (v. 13) and 'the destroyer' (v. 23) which God will not allow to enter the Israelites' houses, presumably an impersonal power of death (b) kept under control by God. The possibility (d) finds no place in the text, except in the irremovable importance attached to the apotropaic actions themselves, a theme which reappears in this verse of Hebrews – Moses instituted the Passover and the blood-sprinkling 'that the destroyer of the first-born might not touch them' – and which the structural argument above contends should be understood in the verse about Rahab and the perishing of the disobedient too.

The issues which this raises will be developed in later chapters. All this material is impersonal-disjunctive in type, and conveys a

---

[23] Compare the parallel tale (Exod. 1–2) in which Moses is cast away on the waters, and thus delivered by God's hand from the decree of Pharaoh directed against 'every son that is born to the Hebrews' (Exod. 1:16, 22).

[24] See above, pp. 107, 154–6, and below, pp. 177, 194f.

profoundly avertive attitude towards God, which unquestionably colours the text of Hebrews even though little of it appears at the surface level; on the other hand, and adding to the ambiguity which faces us, what does appear on the surface is a motif of the election of the inferior and the protection of the weak, a motif which is potentially subversive of any system of inheritance or institutional authority, even those sanctioned by God.

Korah's rebellion and Aaron's rod

Though Korah and the rebellion he led (Num. 16) are nowhere mentioned in Hebrews, there are significant echoes of the language of that narrative, and specific references to related material, such as Aaron's Rod (Heb. 9:3, Num. 17) which bring it within the scope of our inquiry. This is not an isolated incident. It was argued in chapter 3 that it is central to the Priestly redaction of Numbers, or certainly to chapters 11−21 which narrate the complaining of Israel against the leadership of Moses and Aaron.[25] Corresponding to the different roles of these two brothers, as civil and religious leaders respectively, the complaints tend to have either a political or a cultic character: on the one hand the objections to manna and Moses' rule (Num. 11), the abortive (because half-hearted) raid into Canaan (Num. 13f), and the rebellion met by Moses' production of water from the rock (Num. 20); on the other hand, Korah's uprising (Num. 16f), the Priestly laws of chapters 15, 18 and 19, the man sinning on the sabbath (15:32−6), the averting of the plague of serpents (21:4−9). The division is not absolute − there is, for example, the mixed event of Miriam's objection to Moses' leadership resulting in impurity (leprosy) in chapter 12 − and chapter 16 is revealed by analysis to be a blend of two complementary traditions, a civil revolt of Reubenites against Moses, who are finally swallowed by the earth (vv. 1f, 12−15, 25−34), and a cultic revolt of a group of Levites under Korah, against the cultic monopoly of the Aaronids, resulting in their consumption by holy fire (vv. 1−11, 16−24, 35−40). In the present version of this story the civil strand has been subordinated to the cultic, making of the whole a challenge to the divine authority of the priesthood:

[25] See above, pp. 88−90.

so that no one who is not a priest, who is not of the descendants of Aaron, should draw near to burn incense before the Lord, lest he become as Korah and his company.

(Num. 16:40)

Hebrews is deeply concerned with the subject of rebellion against God, and likewise approaches it from both social and cultic angles. In social terms, it deals at length with the revolt of the wilderness generation and its descendants through the medium of Psalm 95, and the possibility of its reproduction in his readers. What links this line of argument explicitly to Korah is the common conception of the wrath of God: the 'swallowing' of God's enemies by the earth (11:29), their 'consumption' by fire (10:27, 12:29), and the vision of God as 'living' and terrible (4:12f, 10:31).[26]

On the cultic side, apart from making use of imagery from the related Numbers 19 (compare Heb. 9:13, 19; 10:22), our author lists in 9:3−5, among the contents of the sanctuary, as signs and guarantees of the covenant, the ark, the tables of the law, and three objects derived from this portion of Numbers: the manna (cf. Num. 11:4ff), Aaron's rod (Num. 17) and a mysterious χρυσοῦν θυμιατήριον. This last term is usually translated 'the golden altar of incense', although the reference is vague (there is no article in the Greek) and the altar in question stood, not in the Holy of Holies but in the outer sanctuary, whose contents have already been listed in verse 2. The alternative is to translate it as 'golden censer'. Scripture records no such object kept within the sanctuary, but the Mishnah (Yoma 4:4)[27] speaks of a golden censer used by the high priest to make his once-yearly offering of incense within the Holy of Holies on the Day of Atonement: though it is not said to be kept there, its associations with this place, this figure, this action and this day fall squarely within the author's area of interest.

However, there is another censer to which this might refer, that used by Aaron in stopping the plague which came forth from Yahweh to attack the people when they objected to the fate of Korah and his company (Num. 16:41−50). The word θυμιατήριον does not appear in the Septuagintal version of that chapter, which prefers πυρεῖον ('fire-pan'); however θυμίαμα is used there frequently in speaking of incense (Num. 16:7,40,46) and Josephus uses θυμιατήριον in recounting Korah's revolt.[28] Aaron's action is a powerful symbol of

---

[26] See above, pp. 155f.   [27] Danby, *The Mishnah*, p. 167.
[28] Josephus, *Antiquities*, IV.32, 54, 57.

atonement through separation: by it the boundary between the camp and the 'plague', the force of destructive holiness coming from God, is re-established, and the mediating function of the priesthood is set between the sin of the people and God.

This censer, therefore, is in symbolic terms a transformation of 'Aaron's Rod which budded' (Num. 17), the indisputable testimony to Aaron's divine priestly authority and power. The equation of the object named in Hebrews 9:4 with both Aaron's censer and the 'golden censer' used, according to tradition, on the Day of Atonement cannot be conclusive while there is no known precedent, but our author's interests prompt the reference to Aaron's Rod – which, despite the remarkable fact of its budding and being said to be preserved in the sanctuary, is mentioned nowhere else in scripture – and along the line being pursued in the book there are powerful reasons for framing such an association if it did not already exist to be remembered.

The word ῥάβδος appears twice more in the letter, and this repetition casts light on the author's reference to Aaron's rod here. In 1:8, quoting Psalm 45:6 (44:7 LXX), it names the *sceptre* of the messianic king; in 11:21, quoting the Septuagintal mistranslation of Genesis 49:31, Jacob, when he blessed the sons of Joseph, is said to have bowed in worship (προσεκύνησεν) on the head of his *staff*. The priestly rod and the royal sceptre are plainly sacred objects, while the staff, if not being actually worshipped, is named in a context of deep reverence. They share a background in tradition rich in covenantal and messianic associations which makes them fit objects for veneration: ῥάβδος not only connotes a sacred object made by God 'between the suns' to be an instrument of salvation appropriately preserved in the sanctuary, but also a sign of the messianic kingdom now won by Christ ('descended from Judah' 7:14) who *is* the living, sprouting staff.[29] When Jacob 'worshipped', therefore, he was

[29] The fact that ῥάβδος is used in LXX to render several Hebrew terms helps to fuse the association of the king's sceptre, the priestly rod and the staff with which Jacob crossed the Jordan (Gen. 32:10)). In Jewish tradition the rod created 'between the suns' (PRE 40) is passed down in succession through Adam, Enoch, Noah, Shem, Abraham, Isaac, Jacob, Joseph, and thence to Moses; this is the rod with which Moses parted the Red Sea and struck water from the rock, and appears to be interchangeable with the rod used by Aaron. Gen. R. regards the staff given to Judah (Gen. 38:18) as definitely *messianic*, and equates it with that in Ps. 110:2, 'the Lord sends forth from Zion your mighty sceptre'; in Greek this in turn is one with the kingly (messianic) sceptres of Ps. 2:9 and Ps. 45:6, a connection which cannot have been lost on our author, who quotes Ps. 45:6 and gives to other verses from Pss. 2 and 110 a central place in his argument. There is also the remarkable use of ῥάβδος to translate the living *shoot* coming forth from the stump of Jesse (Isa. 11:1 LXX).

bowing before the staff as symbol of the divinely secured succession which he had just pronounced in his blessing, and as symbol of the Christ to whom it leads.

This complex of otherwise curious objects and events has a two-fold significance for Hebrews. First, it is presenting an argument against the efficacy of the Aaronic priesthood and its sacrifices (7:11,19,23,27; 8:7; 9:9f; 10:1f,11) which denies the authority given in these chapters of Numbers; second, by describing Jesus as 'high priest' and by urging its readers to 'draw near' Hebrews casts him and them in the role of Korah and his insurrectionists flatly opposing that divine institution:

> And you and your sons with you shall bear iniquity in relation to the sanctuary ... I give your priesthood as a gift, and any-one else who comes near shall be put to death (Num. 17:1,7).

Merely repeating that, unlike Korah, Jesus' claims to priesthood are not based on earthly, genealogical qualifications (7:14, 8:4) does not absolve the book of its responsibility for confronting this issue head-on. Its treatment is perhaps deliberately cavalier: having named the contents of the shrine, baldly, and with no attempt to explore their symbolic meaning, they are dismissed as matters of no intrinsic interest ('of these things we cannot now speak in detail' (9:5));[30] their value is further diminished when the entire daily ritual cycle of the cultus is subordinated to a single annual rite conducted in the inner shrine (9:6f), which is in turn devalued by being accorded efficacy only for 'purification of the flesh'.

All this contrasts with the positive arguments advanced for the efficacy and validity of the priesthood and sacrifice of Christ, though the book nowhere argues against the validity of the Aaronic institution as such − it is in any case grounded in scripture − and is even content to adduce forgotten proofs of its power such as the budding rod and (perhaps) the censer. Hebrews shares the fundamental view-point of that Priestly text: there *is* a sin-bearing, and there *is* a necessary separation between humanity and God which only the appointed priest can bridge; but it will argue for the superiority, even the absoluteness of Jesus' atoning sacrifice over all others, including that of Aaron, and show from scripture (Ps. 110:4) that there is an *eternal* priesthood which evacuates the role of Aaron

---

[30] As by Philo, *Quis rerum divinarum heres sit*, 221, who uses a similar phrase (Montefiore, *Hebrews*, p. 146).

and his sons but allows laypeople, by holding fast to Jesus through faith, to 'draw near'. The book can even remind its readers about Aaron's rod, presumably, because those who have 'tasted the heavenly gift' (6:4) have proofs as solid and sensible in their own experience to confirm the reality of the new covenant and its mediator.

Melchizedek

By contrast with the cultic materials just described, which are deeply woven into the fabric of the Pentateuchal traditions, and feature in Hebrews in a wealth of fragmentary and associational glimpses, Melchizedek appears here, as in much contemporary literature, as a conscious symbol being consciously interpreted. Introduced in the Old Testament in exalted and suggestive terms which invite speculation, but confined to one verse of Psalm 110 and a few verses of Genesis 14, the absence of associational development within the Bible contrasts sharply with the abundance elsewhere. This figure was exercising a fascination on the Jewish imagination at the beginning of the Christian era, and appears in numerous contemporary writings, including Jubilees, the Genesis Apocryphon, Philo, Josephus and the Dead Sea Scrolls, as well as in midrashic literature. No one has established the indebtedness of Hebrews to any of these; indeed it seems that many putative influences on Hebrews are more likely to be reactions, and that Hebrews itself provided the main boost to further developments in the centuries which followed.[31] Desire to undercut its argument, that in Melchizedek is to be found the scriptural basis for a divinely authorised non-Aaronic (and even non-Jewish) priesthood, would seem to be the best reason for the identification of Melchizedek with Shem son of Noah, as when 'he shall dwell in the tents of Shem' (Gen. 9:27) is read as 'Shem shall dwell [= serve] in my tent [= sanctuary]' (Midr. Teh. on Ps. 76:3);[32] for the etymology of 'Melchizedek' as 'whole king' by which it is argued that he was already circumcised at birth (Gen. R. 43:6ff);[33] for the statement that Shem (Melchizedek) circumcised Abraham

---

[31] On Melchizedek and 11Q, see Fitzmyer, *Semitic Background*, pp. 245–67; A. J. B. Higgins, 'The priestly Messiah', *NTS*, 13 (1966–7), 211–39; J. W. Thompson, 'The midrash in Heb. 7', *NovT*, 19 (1977), 209–23; Horton, *Melchizedek*, pp. 167–70. For the argument that Hebrews is the cause rather than the heir of the traditions concerning Melchizedek, see Horton, *Melchizedek*, pp. 152–72; J. J. Petuchowski, 'The controversial figure of Melchizedek', *HUCA*, 28 (1957), 127–36.

[32] Bowker, *Targums*, p. 198.

[33] Freedman, *Genesis Rabbah*, p. 356.

(= 'blessed him') on Mount Moriah (Zion) on the Day of Atonement (PRE 29);[34] for the idea that Psalm 110:4 was addressed by God to Abraham, thereby making *him* the 'priest for ever after the order of Melchizedek' and qualifying him to offer the sacrifice of Isaac 'like a high priest' on the Day of Atonement (Gen.R. 55:7, PRE 31).[35]

Two features of Melchizedek led to this special interest: his representation of ideal priesthood and his integration of priestly and kingly functions. Both can be understood in historical terms: the former was naturally attractive in an age when the purity of Aaronic descent had been so muddied, and the abuse of the political power of the priesthood had become so scandalous, with consequent loss of confidence in the priesthood as atoning barrier between humanity and God; the latter arose in the same context, in the ideology of the Hasmonean kings and that of their opponents, expressed in the hope for the two-messiahs or single priest-king messiah found in Qumran texts.[36] A certain tension between real and ideal, or historical and heavenly, is inseparable from the Melchizedek verses. For this reason it is amenable to a variety of differing treatments, emphasising either his historicity − as, for Josephus, he was the historical founder of the Jerusalem cultus[37] − or else his ideality − as, for Philo, he is an image of a pure 'unlearned priesthood' and of the just king.[38] For the authors of 11Q Melchizedek he is concrete but eschatological, a heavenly figure, encountered by Abraham but otherwise reserved in heaven till he should appear at the last to establish the true Day of Atonement and usher in the final cosmic Jubilee.[39]

By contrast to the general abundance of speculation which this figure aroused, and by contrast to this author's usual tendency to link every sacrificial or quasi-sacrificial act and personage into a comprehensive symbolic system, the treatment of Melchizedek in Hebrews is extremely restrained. F. L. Horton has argued that the current interest in Melchizedek as a model of priesthood derives largely from his historical priority as *the first priest* in the world because the first named in scripture (on the principle: *Quod non in*

---

[34] Friedlander, *PRE*, pp. 203f.

[35] Gen. R. 55:7 (Freedman, *Genesis Rabbah*, p. 488); Friedlander, *PRE*, p. 227.

[36] See Vermes, *Dead Sea Scrolls*, pp. 47−51.

[37] Josephus, *Antiquities*, I.181; see Horton, *Melchizedek*, pp. 81f.

[38] *Leg. all.*, III.79f: ἱεροσύνης ἄξιον τῆς ἑαυτοῦ πρῶτον ... βασιλεὺς δίκαιος; see Horton, *Melchizedek*, pp. 54−60.

[39] See Horton, *Melchizedek*, pp. 64−82; for the text of 11Q Melchizedek in translation, see Vermes, *Dead Sea Scrolls*, pp. 265−7.

thora non in mundo);[40] but no hint of this appears in Hebrews, in which, if anyone, this honour ought to fall to Abel. In fact, he is hardly an historical figure at all. The author's motif of ignoring the existence of the Temple inhibits the possibility of arguing that Melchizedek, rather than Moses, Aaron, David or Solomon, was the true establisher of worship at Zion. Besides, such an argument would subordinate Christ to Melchizedek, whereas he is, as Horton has pointed out, really Christ's *antitype*:[41] 'resembling the son of God he remains a priest for ever'. Like Philo, this author offers a grandiose etymology for Melchizedek's name and title, but refrains from finding there pointers to an immanent manifestation of God, as Logos or Wisdom.[42]

The author's principal object in introducing Melchizedek (at least as far as the argument goes) is to furnish the book's Christology with an image of priesthood in contrast to Aaron's: whereas Aaron and his sons are ἀποθνήσκοντες ἄνθρωποι ('dying men' rather than merely 'mortal'[43]), this priest 'lives' (7:8) and 'remains a priest for ever'; whereas the Levitical priests receive tithes from the 'descendants of Abraham' they *pay* tithes to this priest of a wholly different order. However, the Christological aspects of these motifs are pared very thinly. Melchizedek is proclaimed to be 'without father or mother or genealogy, without beginning of days or end of life', yet *these* are not features Hebrews wishes to juxtapose too closely with that Jesus of whom it says bluntly, in the same chapter, 'it is evident that our Lord was descended from Judah' (7:14), a frank admission of a fact which ought to link Jesus with the other 'descendants of Abraham', including the Levitical priests, rather than with Melchizedek. Jesus' priesthood is 'Melchizedekian' only in an oblique sense which permits him, 'when he came into the world', to proclaim, ' "a body hast thou prepared for me" ' (10:5), a body firmly related to the 'blood and flesh' of his humanity by a complex of references to sharing and participation (2:14–18, 5:5–10) and by its role in his sacrifice (9:14, 13:11f). Presenting Melchizedek in ideal terms appears to pose for this author no threat, either to the divine character of the

---

[40] Horton, *Melchizedek*, pp. 157–60.

[41] *Ibid.*, pp. 161–3.

[42] Gen. R. 43:6 (Freedman, *Genesis Rabbah*, p. 356) brings together Melchizedek's gifts to Abraham (Gen. 14:18) and the words of Wisdom (Prov. 9:5), 'Come, eat of my bread and drink of the wine I have mixed' (i.e. the Torah). Cf. *Leg. all.*, III.82, where Philo speaks of Melchizedek as Logos, giving Reason's wine which produces 'divine intoxication' (ἵνα κατάσχετοι γένωνται θείᾳ μέθῃ).

[43] Westcott, *Hebrews*, p. 178.

event being accomplished through Christ, or to Christ's human historical identity. He provides a ground on which to argue that *as a priest* Christ has neither father, nor mother, nor genealogical qualifications; nor any 'end of life', continuing to minister for ever in the 'true tent'; nor, by the same token, any 'beginning of days'. Debate continues concerning the point at which, according to this writer, Jesus *became* high priest, whether before, or during, or even after his sacrifice; at the crucifixion or the ascension, or earlier at his baptism, or his birth, or at creation.[44] Such a debate has importance if we wish to determine what sort of theology, in a conceptual sense, the author holds. For the theology of the letter, however, Christ's appointment is simply dated '*Today*' (5:5f), in the eternal now which is the letter's time, and therefore both event and eternal state.

Melchizedek is important to Hebrews neither as an historical figure, nor as an eschatological redeemer, nor even as a pure ideal if that phrase suggests some completed alternative to the actual. He is primarily a bringer of non-order. Thus symbolically he functions in the letter in the paradoxical role of Priest-Stranger as a double of Christ, both like and unlike. Appearing and disappearing again, his achievement is to leave a space to be occupied by Jesus the high priest, and his main interest lies in his being *anomalous*, an agent of dissidence to unsettle the fixed structures of conceptions of priest-hood – not in having anomalies which are themselves particularly relevant to the nature of Christ, though some capital of this sort is in fact made.

As priest and king, Melchizedek necessarily has something to con-tribute towards the letter's fusion of cultic and political symbolism, but is allowed to do so only in an entirely understated way, as an abstract ideal focussing concepts developed concretely through other media, such as the blessings pronounced by the patriarchs and the sacrificial offerings of Abel, Abraham and Moses. What is opened up through these, though, is something at least as important as the negative work of devaluing the Aaronic system by showing how far it falls short of perfection – an alternative type of priesthood which is active not in sacrifice but in *blessing*.[45] This idea, though only suggested here and always developed indirectly, is the image of priesthood towards which the book is pointing, an image of Christ's

---

[44] See the discussion by D. Peterson, *Hebrews and Perfection*, SNTS Monograph Series 47 (Cambridge, 1982), appendix 2, pp. 191–5.

[45] See pp. 104f above and pp. 251–9 below.

ministry at God's right hand now that the atoning sacrifice has been offered once for all.

Moses, Joshua and the wilderness generation

Moses

His function as Lawgiver in Jewish tradition and the overarching echoes of Deuteronomy give to the figure of Moses an authority and a many-sidedness disproportionate to the space he receives. Several of these references have already been discussed. In chapter 11, Moses functions as a model of faith in his willing self-exile, in choosing solidarity with the sufferings of the 'people of God', which are 'the reproach of Christ', and in finding greater reality in the invisible God than in the tangible wrath of the king. This last aspect, it was suggested, is symbolically represented as the institution of the Passover, the separation of the first-born under God's protection from the Destroyer (as confirmed in v. 29: at the Red Sea the people cross, but the Egyptians fail). Elsewhere, Moses appears again as a priest (9:19–22) and as a faithful leader (3:2–6), but the covenant he institutes has been superseded and he has failed in his task as leader. In his ambivalent status he is perhaps an emblem of Judaism as it appears from the point of view of this author.[46]

At his first mention (3:2–5) Moses is described as 'faithful in God's house ... as a servant, to testify to the things that were to be spoken later'. If these things are, as they seem, the speaking through Jesus as Son and Word of God (1:1f, 2:1–4), Moses who points the way to the truth is being given high praise, though such a role subordinates him finally to Christ. The epithet quoted here is from Num. 12:7 (LXX): 'my servant Moses who is faithful in all my house; mouth to mouth I speak with him, clearly and not in dark speech, and he beholds the glory of the Lord'. This tradition of Moses as the man who met God face to face is probably echoed again at 12:21: 'so terrible was the sight (τὸ φανταζόμενον) that Moses said "I tremble with fear" (ἔκφοβός εἰμι καὶ ἔντρομος)'. The 'sight' here is certainly a manifestation of God's holiness such that anyone, even Moses, is bound to tremble; though outward signs such as fire and darkness have been named in verse 18, the use of the strong word φανταζόμενον

---

[46] See above, pp. 126–31, 158f. For a recent full-length study of Moses' role, see M. R. D'Angelo, *Moses in the Letter to the Hebrews*, SBL Dissertation Series 42 (Missoula, 1979).

and the return to the visual, after a main emphasis on words, may imply a more specific *appearance* of God himself, such as Moses received on other occasions (Exod. 3:1–4:17, 33:11–23). In confirmation of this, ἔντρομος is found in Acts 7:32, in Stephen's account of Moses' encounter with God in the burning bush,[47] while ἔκφοβός εἰμι is quoted from Deuteronomy 9:19, in the incident of the golden calf. In all these cases, Moses is cast as representative of humanity, aware of his sinfulness as he comes into God's presence, but it is not clear that his response should be understood, as Hebrews 12:21 suggests, as a sign of his failure. This might be so if he were trembling at the mere outward signs, but the references to Numbers 12:7 and (perhaps) Exodus 3:1–6, imply that he trembles before the divine presence, indicating Moses' *privilege* 'as seeing him who is invisible' (11:27), a privilege which puts him, in the world of this book, in a class whose only other member is Jesus. Besides, his response to this event, though it seems to be rejected by comparison with the joyful approach to Mount Zion, is, as has been argued above, not clearly distinguishable from the 'reverence and awe' soon afterwards commended to the readers as the fitting way of approaching God (12:28).[48]

These detailed signs of praise are overlaid with adverse criticism, however, for the law which Moses establishes is declared to be provisional and deficient in several respects: given by angels, not by the Son (2:2); not 'written on the heart' (8:10); a 'copy or shadow' of the real law (8:5, 10:1); merely 'regulations for the body imposed until the time of reformation' (9:10); consisting of blood-sacrifices which God has 'not desired' (10:5) and which 'can never take away sin' (10:11). Moses' reputation is diminished by association, as mediator of such a deficient covenant.

Alongside this argument for the provisional character of the Mosaic law is a totally different argument: that the law, though perfect, failed because of Israel's disobedience, located classically in the wilderness. In this tradition, Moses is a servant who, whatever his good qualities, failed to lead those who left Egypt into the land of Promise and was himself barred from entering it. This view of Israel's history is expressed in many places, including Psalms 81 and 95 and the central narrative section of Numbers, which contains several transformations of a basic rebellion motif, as in the Korahite crisis (Num. 16f). It was, in fact, in response to Miriam's challenge to Moses' leadership that the divine testimony to Moses' worth as a

[47] See Bruce, *Hebrews*, p.372. [48] See above, pp.144–6.

faithful servant was given (Num. 12:7, quoted in 3:5). In Hebrews
3 to 4 two other major incidents are referred to, the Meribah revolt
(Num. 20) and the failed attempt to enter Canaan (Num. 13f). The
former, in both its versions (Exod. 17, Num. 20) is a challenge to the
leadership of Moses and Aaron and to God's sovereign providence
('Is the Lord among us or not?' Exod. 17:7), in response to which
Moses strikes water from the rock. Here is a classic image of God's
covenanting love and Israel's contentiousness: it is this incident which
is repeatedly named (although no reason for it appears in the texts)
as the occasion on which Moses and Aaron also show *disbelief* in
God (Num. 20:12,24, 27:12–14, Deut. 32:51) and are therefore
condemned to die outside the borders of the Land; and the divine
oath directed against 'this generation' that 'they shall never enter
my rest' is equally firmly associated with 'Meribah' by Psalm 95,
though it is not in fact pronounced here but at Numbers 14:20–35:

> None of all those who have seen my glory and the signs
> which I wrought in Egypt and in the wilderness ... shall see
> the land which I swore to give to their ancestors.   (14:22f)

In that context, it is a direct response to Israel's failure to listen to the
favourable report of Caleb and Joshua, in timidity shrinking back
(compare Heb. 10:36–9) from the venture of entering Canaan from
the south to possess the land. This symbolic refusal to grasp the promise God offers, while complaining that it has not been given, of which
these separate stories are quite generally treated as complementary
accounts,[49] is the source of the motif of the 'forty-years', and, for the
author of Hebrews, taking a cue from Psalm 95, the source of the
image of Israel as perpetually wandering, on the edge of the Land,
awaiting a leader, a 'great shepherd of the sheep' who can succeed
where neither Moses nor Joshua nor any other leader has succeeded.

Joshua

Bearing the name of Ἰησοῦς, as both model and contrast, Joshua's
role in the book is ambivalent in much the same way as that of
Moses, in whose shadow he mostly stands. Tradition names Joshua
with Caleb as a man of courage who opposed Israel's timidity in
the face of the difficulty of entering the Land, and it is he who is

---

[49] Cf. T. W. Mann, 'Theological reflections on the denial of Moses', *JBL*, 98
(1979), 481–94.

promised 'I will not fail you or forsake you' (Heb. 13:5, quoting Deut. 31:8; Josh. 1:5); as such his character should surely be present to our minds when this theme is in view, in Hebrews 3 to 4, representing the alternative to 'disobedience'. It is curious, then, that his only mention is not a commendation but a criticism for failing to 'give Israel rest', and we saw earlier that in chapter 11 this is interpreted implicitly as a failure of military as well as spiritual leadership.[50] When Jesus is described as an ἀρχηγός (12:2), his virtues as a pioneer or route-leader are being compared directly with those of Joshua. If, on the other hand, we pick up echoes of his great covenant-ceremony (Josh. 24) to be found in 1:2 and 9:19, he will be seen to occupy the role of covenant-mediator also filled by Moses, Abel, Abraham and Jesus.

One further example of this can be given here, in a verse which serves to confirm the symbolic location of Israel and the readers 'on the edge of the land'. It is a detail in the much-discussed passage 4:11−13. One of the difficulties which that short passage poses is that it introduces into the letter a number of new images which are not sustained and for which the appropriate interpretative context is not clear. This particularly affects the meaning of λόγος and the image of the sword. A full exegesis is not in place here, but there is one set of associations, commonly overlooked, which links these verses to the theme of Joshua and his attempt to mediate God's salvation, to 'give them rest'. The word of God is likened to a two-edged *sword* which, being sharp, is able to penetrate deeply:[51] this conveys a threat, as of judgement. Where does this sword image come from? The suggestion being made here is that in the μάχαιρα δίστομος to which the λόγος is compared, being sharper (τομώτερος) and 'piercing even to the division of soul and spirit' should be heard an echo not only of the military sword (as in 11:37) but also, perhaps primarily, the priest's ritual knife: in particular, a knife associated with Joshua.[52] In Joshua 5:2−9, Joshua took 'sharp flint knives'

---

[50] See above, p. 143.

[51] The likening of (divine) words to a sword occurs fairly frequently in the Old Testament, e.g. Isa. 49:2; Wisd. 18:15f; see Bowker, *Targums*, p. 41, n. 3, for a rabbinic example of Torah as a two-edged sword.

[52] See J. Swetnam, 'Jesus as Λόγος in Heb. 4:12f', *Biblica*, 62 (1981), 214−24. The strength of Swetnam's article is his attempt to give a less disunified interpretation to these verses than is usual (different sense of λόγος in vv. 12 and 13, for example); however his directly Christological reading cannot be sustained. The earliest explicitly Christological use of Josh. 5:2−9 is by Justin Martyr, *Dialogue with Trypho*, 24: 'Jesus Christ circumcises all who come with knives of stone' (quoted by Bruce, *Hebrews*, p. 81n.).

(μαχαίρας πετρίνας ἀκροτόμους) and circumcised all the males of Israel at the moment of entry into Canaan. The whole generation who left Egypt having now died and all this generation being uncircumcised, he was effecting a ritual renewal of the covenant at the moment of passing into the sacred sphere. This is to be compared with the *verbal* covenant-renewal effected in chapter 24. Immediately following the account of that later ceremony, Joshua's death is reported, in the course of which we read (though in the Septuagint version only) that when he was buried there were buried with him 'the flint knives with which he circumcised the sons of Israel at Gilgal ... and they are there to this day' (ἕως τῆς σήμερον ἡμέρας, 24:31b LXX). If the motifs 'Today' (σήμερον) and covenant-renewal have in fact the significance attributed to them in the argument of chapter 4 above, this comparison occupies a mediating position between the 'word of God' (whether or not it means Jesus, as some maintain[53]) and the 'two-edged sword' of judgement; associations with ritual purification should probably also be found to run through τετραχηλισμένα into the overtly cultic imagery of verses 14ff.[54] Such a detail serves only to add to the manifest function of Joshua as a covenant-establisher, and to press a little more acutely the contrast between the 'Ιησοῦς of 4:7 and 4:11 who could not give rest despite all such fleshly acts, and the 'Ιησοῦς of 4:14 who has 'passed through the heavens', and invites his followers to 'draw near to the throne of grace'.

Abraham, Isaac and the heroes of Israel

The picture of Abraham which emerges in Hebrews is broadly in line with the treatment found in post-exilic Jewish scripture and tradition, and in the New Testament, as the *man of faith* above all others, through whom God established his covenant relationship with Israel.[55] Hebrews agrees with these traditions in commending four acts of faith:

---

[53] On the identification of the Logos in this passage with Jesus, see Swetnam, 'Jesus as Λόγος', and the patristic references in Westcott, *Hebrews*, p. 101.

[54] For Chrysostom's sacrificial understanding of this term, see Westcott, p. 104. Spicq (vol. II, pp. 90f) argues that this word implies the (spiritual) circumcision of those who are stubborn or 'stiff-necked' (σκληροτράχηλος Exod. 33:3, 5, Deut. 9:6, 13) as in Deut. 10:16: περιτεμεῖσθε τὴν σκληροκαρδίαν ὑμῶν καὶ τὸν τράχηλον ὑμῶν οὐ σκληρουνεῖτε; however, he does not connect this idea with the μάχαιρα in v. 12, which he takes to be a sword of judgement.

[55] See J. van Seters, *Abraham in History and Tradition* (London, 1975).

(1) Abraham's obedience to God's call to leave his home (Gen. 12:1, Heb. 11:8);
(2) his trust in God's promise to give him children (Gen. 15, Heb. 11:11);
(3) his obedience in sacrificing his son Isaac at God's command (Gen. 22, Heb. 11:17);
(4) his hospitality as the archetype of those who have 'received angels unawares' (Gen. 18, Heb. 13:2).

Hebrews also agrees with the common tradition that through this obedience a covenantal relationship is established, first between Abraham and God (as 'friend of God', 2 Chron. 20:7, Isa. 41:8, and as 'he whom God has chosen', Neh. 9:7), and then between God and those who call Abraham 'Father' and worship 'the God of Abraham' (Exod. 3:6, Matt. 3:9, 22:32, Luke 16:24): thus Abraham 'having patiently endured obtained the promise' (Heb. 6:15, though compare 11:13) and he received through Melchizedek (7:1 – 10) God's blessing; and in this letter, when salvation from death is in question, it is 'the seed of Abraham' that Jesus is concerned to save (2:16).

Abraham therefore functions as the *mediator* of a covenant, which is neither the new covenant established by Jesus nor the 'old covenant' given through Moses but, for Hebrews as for Paul, a pointer through the old to the new. Though Abraham was regularly given sacerdotal attributes in Jewish literature as high priest and sacrificer,[56] and also as intercessor (Gen. 18:22 – 33), this way of characterising a covenant and its mediator is understated here. Instead, *faith* is the hallmark of this covenant: Abraham dominates chapter 11 as an example of one who, by 'going out' from security and (more importantly) remaining in this vulnerable and marginal condition as a tent-dwelling sojourner (11:9f, 12 – 16), commends 'faith' as a mode of living and shows that 'going out' = 'drawing near to God'. The two ideas, of faith and sacrifice, come together, though, in the story of the 'Binding of Isaac', a theme which has vastly greater significance, not only for this chapter but for the theology of the letter as a whole, than its rather brief appearance (11:17f) would suggest. Its fundamental importance for the letter's Christology will be developed in chapter 6 below; our concern here is to show how it acts as the organising centre of Hebrews 11 and as a 'foundation-sacrifice' for the faith-covenant established through Abraham and renewed through Jesus.

[56] See above, pp. 139f.

The Akedah in Jewish tradition

In its developed form, the tradition of the 'Akedah' or 'Binding' of Isaac contains numerous elements present only tacitly, if at all, in the text of Genesis 22.[57] In one targum, for example, Isaac, who is thirty-seven years old, goes voluntarily to the altar;[58] he is identified as the 'lamb' which, as Abraham says, 'God will provide' for a burnt-offering, and he begs his father to bind his legs to prevent him from struggling and so impairing the physical perfection of the sacrificial victim;[59] he sees a vision of angels who show him the 'uniqueness' of this event.[60] In other versions Isaac prays to God to 'remember' his offering and to treat it as an atoning sacrifice for the sins of Israel, and it is regularly presented as the 'foundation-event' underlying the central rite of the Jerusalem cultus (whether this is Passover, Day of Atonement, or the daily burnt-offering (*tamid*)).[61] Although

[57] On Gen. 22, see C. Westermann, *Genesis 12–36* (ET London, 1986), pp. 351–65; van Seters, *Abraham*, pp. 227–40; T. D. Alexander, 'Genesis 22 and the covenant of circumcision', *JSOT*, 25 (1983), 17–22; H. C. White, 'The initiation legend of Isaac', *ZAW*, 91 (1979), 1–30. It has attracted a good deal of attention recently from a literary, and frequently a structuralist, point of view: see E. Auerbach, *Mimesis* (Princeton, 1953), ch. 1; G. W. Coats, 'Abraham's sacrifice of faith (a form-critical study of Gen. 22)', *Interpretation*, 27 (1973), 389–400; J. L. Crenshaw, 'Journey into oblivion: a structural analysis of Gen. 22', *Soundings*, 58 (1975), 243–56; R. Lack, 'Le Sacrifice d'Isaac – Analyse structurale de la couche élohiste dans Gen. 22', *Biblica*, 56 (1975), 1–12; and several contributions to F. Bovon and G. Rouiller (eds.), *Exegesis* (Pittsburgh, 1978). On the Akedah, see R. J. Daly, 'Sacrifice of Isaac', 45–75, and Daly, *Origins*, pp. 47–52; Vermes, *Scripture and Tradition*, pp. 193–227; le Deaut, *La Nuit pascale*, pp. 131–212; J. Swetnam, *Jesus and Isaac: A Study of the Epistle to the Hebrews in the Light of the Aqedah*, Analecta Biblica (Rome, 1981), pp. 23–79; P. R. Davies and B. D. Chilton, 'The Aqedah, a revised tradition history', *CBQ*, 40 (1978), 514–46; B. D. Chilton, 'Isaac and the second night', *Biblica*, 61 (1980), 78–88; R. Hayward, 'The present state of research into the targumic account of the sacrifice of Isaac', *JJS*, 32 (1981), 127–50, and R. Hayward, 'The sacrifice of Isaac and Jewish polemic against Christianity', *CBQ*, 52 (1990), 286–306; S. Spiegel, *The Last Trial* (New York, 1967). On the Christian use of this tradition, see further below.

[58] Tg. Ps-J. on Gen. 22:1 (Bowker, *Targums*, p. 224).

[59] Tg. P.-J. on Gen. 22:8, 10 (Bowker, *Targums*, pp. 225, 231–3). FT is even more explicit: 'And Abraham said: "From before the Lord will the sheep for a burnt-offering be chosen my son and if not then you are the sheep"' (Klein, *Fragment Targums*, pp. 16, 103). Cf. Tg. Neofiti (Diez Macho, *Neophyti I*, vol. II, p. 551); PRE 31 (Friedlander, *PRE*, pp. 226f).

[60] FT on Gen. 22:10 (Klein, *Fragment Targums*, pp. 16, 103); cf. Tg. Neofiti (Diez Macho, *Neophyti I*, vol. II, pp. 551f) and Ps.-J. (Bowker, *Targums*, p. 225).

[61] For the Passover, see Jub. 17:15ff, Tg. Neofiti on Exod. 12:42 (Diez Macho, *Neophyti I*, vol. II, pp. 441f); for the Day of Atonement, see PRE 31 (Friedlander, *PRE*, p. 227), Lev. R. 21:11, 29:9f (J. Israelstam and J. J. Slotki (ed. and trans.), *Leviticus Rabbah* (London, 1939), pp. 274, 376); for the *tamid*, see Lev. R. 2:10f (Israelstam and Slotki, *Leviticus Rabbah*, pp. 29–31). The motif of 'blood' also links the Akedah indirectly, through Passover, to circumcision: see Daly, *Origins*, pp. 41–4.

in the Genesis version Isaac's sacrifice is completed by the holocaust of a ram, in several late versions he is regarded as having actually died on the altar. Some texts speak of 'the blood of Isaac' and his 'ashes',[62] and though in various ways they indicate that these expressions should not be understood literally,[63] they should certainly be understood as describing an efficacious sacrifice, the remembrance of which has atoning power.[64] In 4 Maccabees, drawing on Isaiah 53:10, Isaac is regarded as 'alive to God' (16:25), and the source of the hope of resurrection to immortal life for all who are truly 'sons of Abraham' (9:22, 18:23).

In the light of this material it has been argued that many features of the Christian proclamation of the cross were taken over from – and intended to replace – an existing complex of ideas about Isaac: the cross as voluntary and atoning sacrifice;[65] Christ the 'son' handed over by the loving 'father'; Christ the paschal 'lamb'; the eucharist as ἀνάμνησις of the 'blood' of a foundational sacrifice. The direct source for the Christian use of many of these ideas was probably Isaiah 52f, yet this passage itself seems to be based in part on the Isaac story, with its image of the sacrificed servant (Isa. 52:13: παῖς LXX) who went 'like a lamb' to his death (53:7) and so 'bore the sins of many' (53:12), and who by becoming a 'sin-offering' will see the long life of his 'seed' (53:10). It is an indisputably early example of a theme found otherwise mainly in texts of the first century AD or in the targumic and midrashic material, so difficult to date precisely, but in its present form post-Christian.[66] Others have

---

[62] 'Blood': Pseudo-Philo, *Biblical Antiquities*, 18:5 (Bowker, *Targums*, p. 311); Mekilta de R. Ishmael on Exod. 12:13: 'And when I see the blood I will pass over you – I see the blood of the Binding of Isaac' (quoted by Vermes, *Scripture and Tradition*, p. 206). 'Ashes': see Lev. R. 36:5 (on Lev. 26:42): God 'remembers' Abraham and Jacob 'and the ashes of Isaac, as it were, heaped on the altar' (Israelstam and Slotki, *Leviticus Rabbah*, p. 462).

[63] Lev. R. 36:5 speaks of 'Isaac's ashes as it were'; Ps.-Philo, *Bib. ant.*, 32:4f (Bowker, *Targums*, pp. 313f), says Isaac was reprieved to become the father of two sons.

[64] See, for example, Abraham's prayer 'that when the children of Isaac my son enter into an hour of oppression, that you will remember for them the binding of Isaac their father, and absolve and forgive their transgressions, and rescue them from every distress' (FT (P) on Gen. 22:14 (Klein, *Fragment Targums*, p. 17).

[65] By Vermes, *Scripture and Tradition*, who reviews earlier literature; also by Daly, 'Sacrifice of Isaac', and N. A. Dahl, 'The Atonement – an adequate reward for the Akedah (Rom. 8:32)?', in E. E. Ellis and M. Wilcox (eds.), *Neotestamentica et Semitica*, Studies in honour of M. Black (Edinburgh, 1969), pp. 15–29.

[66] For recent discussions of the issue of dating, see S. A. Kaufman, 'On methodology in the study of the targums and their chronology', *JSNT*, 23 (1985), 117–24; G. Vermes, *Post-Biblical Jewish Studies* (Leiden, 1975), pp. 88–90; A. D. York, 'The dating of targumic literature', *JSJ*, 5 (1974), 49–62. On the contribution of Isa. 52f

argued that the degree of similarity between the Akedah and the Christian kerygma increases with the probable lateness of the texts, and that the influence is the other way about, the Akedah being developed in rabbinic Judaism as a deliberate alternative to the now desecrated Temple, and in opposition to the claims of the church.[67]

This debate, which still continues, has not been free from confessional bias and has been further muddled by a tendency on both sides to treat 'sacrificial' and 'expiatory' as equivalent terms,[68] whereas many of these developments are non-expiatory and the earliest evidence (Gen. 22) describes Isaac's projected death as an *'olah*, a burnt-offering. This is a form of sacrifice which we saw in chapter 3 to be fluid in its meaning, having both personal-conjunctive associations (the outward act accompanying human encounter with God) and also avertive undertones in its relation to the chthonic cultus in Greek worship and to the maintenance of the expiatory system of the Temple (Lev. 1).[69] In Canaanite religion the *'olah* was the form taken by child-sacrifices, and comparison of Genesis 22 with the sacrifice of Jephthah's daughter (Judg. 11:30–40) is very instructive:[70] in both, an only child is offered as *'olah* in fulfilment of the father's relations with God (Abraham's obedience, Jephthah's vow), and both are 'pure', the girl being a virgin and going voluntarily to her death; Isaac, whether as a child or as an adult, going obediently to his death. When a Moabite king offered his eldest son on a city wall (2 Kgs. 3:27) it was in an attempt, which succeeded, to renew the favour of his gods; Jephthah's daughter's death was the price of the vow in return for which God gave victory over the Ammonites; Abraham's offering is taken as the ground for a renewed promise of divine blessing (Gen. 22:15–19). All three could be described, like the Passover, as sacrifices for securing or renewing a covenant on the basis of the death of the first-born. If so, Genesis 22 is a parallel or transformation of the rite described in Genesis 15 by which the first giving of the promise of descendants was sealed.

to this development, see R. A. Rosenberg, 'Jesus, Isaac and the "suffering servant"', *JBL*, 84 (1965), 381–8.

[67] See Chilton, 'Isaac', and Davies and Chilton, 'The Aqedah'; also Bowker, *Targums*, pp. 231–3.

[68] A point insisted on by Davies and Chilton, 'The Aqedah', pp. 514ff. Against this Hayward, 'The present state of research', pp. 128f, objects to their definition of what they call 'the Aqedah doctrine' as a 'vicariously atoning sacrifice of Isaac', a definition which recognises only one (late) form of the Akedah, in place of a fluid and developing haggadah.

[69] See pp. 92f above.

[70] Compare Ps.-Philo, *Bib. ant.* 50:2 (Bowker, *Targums*, p. 314).

Alternatively, the motif of the endangered child may suggest a different origin in *initiation-rites*. Did the act of 'making your son pass through the fire' which in our texts refers to a pagan holocaust (2 Kgs. 16:3, 21:6) once refer to an initiation-by-fire?[71] There is ample evidence that circumcision should be understood in a similar fashion as a symbolic death.[72] In Genesis 22, though Isaac is to be sacrificed by fire, the narrative emphasis falls at least as strongly on Abraham's ritual knife (μάχαιρα): this tale can therefore be understood as a dramatised variant of the 'death' symbolised in circumcision, and a transformation of the circumcision of Abraham himself, on the occasion of which the covenant-promise was renewed, with explicit mention of Isaac (17:19). These should probably not be considered as alternative interpretations. If Genesis 17 = Genesis 22 as initiations into the covenant, Genesis 15 = Genesis 17 = Genesis 22 as covenant-sacrifices. By means of these symbolic links, the marginal and avertive elements in the 'Binding' pericope, which are not strong on the surface, are made plain.

It is by a similar process of symbolic association that many texts, as we have seen, relate the Akedah to the Passover, picking out 'Passover' themes already present: the offering of a lamb, the death and preservation of the first-born, the ambiguity of God's role as both preserver and destroyer. The ambiguity is explicit in Exodus 12 and gives to the Passover a dual character, both personal-conjunctive (covenant-feast in the presence of God the protector) and impersonal-disjunctive (aversion of the Destroyer by means of blood); the narrative of Genesis 22 likewise presents God as ambivalent, both giving Abraham 'seed' and testing his faith by demanding that 'seed' as sacrifice. In chapter 6 the significance of this ambiguity, and its relation to the Akedah, will be explored.

The Akedah in Hebrews 11:17−19

Arguments about the influence of the Akedah on the Christian concept of the Cross as an atoning sacrifice regularly name twenty or more New Testament references to the Akedah, with varying degrees of probability.[73] It is a point worth noting that, of the texts named, there are only two which actually speak of Abraham's offering of

---

[71] See White, 'The initiation legend of Isaac'; G. C. Heider, *The Cult of Molek* (Sheffield, 1985).

[72] See Daly, *Origins*, pp. 41−4; Vermes, *Scripture and Tradition*, pp. 178−92.

[73] Daly, 'Sacrifice', 66−74.

Isaac (Heb. 11:17–19, Jas. 2:21–4), and neither of these shows any interest in expiation. In Hebrews 11 it is introduced as one example of Abraham's 'faith', which has already caused him to obey God's call to 'go out' and to sojourn in 'the land of promise' as a tent-dwelling πάροικος, and which made possible, through Sarah, the birth of Isaac the promise-bearer. The language of these verses is sacrificial, but renders certain details of the narrative precisely: προσενήνοχεν τὸν 'Ισαὰκ καὶ τὸν μονογενῆ προσέφερεν, translated by RSV, 'he offered up Isaac and was ready to offer up his only son', though the distinction between the perfect and imperfect tenses might be paraphrased, 'he had made Isaac a sacrificial victim, and was in the process of offering him on the altar'.[74]

Every treatment of this event which wishes to find here a complete and efficacious sacrifice, of whatever sort, has to find its own way of reconciling that aim with the fact that, as related in Genesis 22, the offering of the son was interrupted. Swetnam argues that for some Abraham's *intention* to sacrifice Isaac in accordance with God's will is sufficient,[75] whereas for others some actual death is necessary, whether it be the burnt-offering of the ram (Gen. 22), or the annual offering of the Passover lamb (Jubilees 17:15, 18:18f), or the faithful deaths of the martyrs of Israel (4 Macc.), or that of Isaac himself (targums[76]). Both Hebrews and James come into the first group, showing no interest in the death as an efficacious event but emphasising Abraham's obedient willingness to do what God commands, and the ground of that obedience in 'faith'. Hebrews does, however, refer to the theme of Isaac's resurrection. Throughout this chapter faith is linked to death: it is mortality which restricts humanity within the limits of created existence, the 'appearances' which fill the vision, hiding God and causing people to doubt even his existence, but life comes to those who penetrate through the screen of death. Abraham's faith in God's power to raise people up 'even from the dead' is the ground on which 'figuratively speaking' (ἐν παραβολῇ) he 'received Isaac back' (11:19). Another reading could find in the use of ἐν παραβολῇ a reference to the developed Akedah tradition of Isaac's 'blood', which also preserves some distance from it: just as Isaac both was and was not sacrificed, he

---

[74] For discussion of the significance of the stages in blood-sacrifice, see above, pp. 94–6.

[75] According to Swetnam, *Jesus*, p. 78n., this is true of Ps.-Philo, the Mekilta and Lev. R. 36:5 (see n. 62 above).

[76] See n. 59 above; Daly, *Origins*, p. 48.

both was and was not raised up from the dead. Alternatively, more strongly, the author may find in Isaac's symbolic return from the dead a parable or foreshadowing of the real resurrection of Jesus.

Genesis 22 is not the only text in view here, though. In verse 17 the 'promise' refers back to Genesis 15:4f; the use of ὁ μονογενής and the quotation 'through Isaac shall your descendants (σπέρμα) be named' refer back to the exclusion of Ishmael following Isaac's birth in Genesis 21:9–12. 'Faith', shown in Genesis 22, was equally involved in 'receiving the promise' and in Isaac's birth (15:6, 21:7), and in Hebrews 11:11f it is made clear that it is faith in 'life-from-death': Abraham is 'as good as dead' (νενεκρωμένος v. 12) because of his age, yet trusted God's faithfulness to his promise. If this is the ground of Abraham's faith in God's ability 'to raise people even from the dead' (καὶ ἐκ νεκρῶν ἐγείρειν, v. 19), it may be that verse 19b should read 'whence [i.e. from the dead] he [previously] received Isaac, as a foreshadowing [of the resurrection or the seed-giving to come]': that is, this may refer, not to Isaac's sacrifice but to his *birth*, taking ἐκομίσατο to mean simply 'received' (as it does in 10:36, 11:39 and some MSS. of 11:13, and in each case in the context of receiving the 'fulfilment of the promises'). Romans 4:16–25 provides a parallel case of Isaac's birth expounded as 'life-from-death', and there are similarities in the language: not only the use of νεκρός, νέκρωσις, νενεκρωμένος (Rom. 4:17, 19), but also God 'calling what does not exist into being' (Rom. 4:17, compare Heb. 11:3) and the juxtaposition of this event with the resurrection of Jesus (Rom. 4:24).

The covenant sacrifice

In short, while 11:17 contains a plain reference to Genesis 22, verses 18f place that event in the context of Abraham's whole history of receiving promises, especially in relation to the birth of Isaac already described in verses 11f. It is therefore doubtful how much weight the author is placing on the Akedah and on Isaac as an anticipation of the atoning sacrifice of Jesus. The emphasis is squarely on Abraham's act of volition, responding to 'being tested' by a further show of 'faith', and there are here no expiatory associations at all. On the other hand, the references to the 'promise', to 'receiving' and to Isaac's figurative 'resurrection' indicate that we have here more than an arbitrarily chosen 'act of faith'. To appreciate its function as a *covenant-sacrifice* we must look at these few verses in the light of the whole history of Israel as this chapter relates it.

Isaac's sacrifice falls at the end of a list of Abraham's acts of faith (vv. 8–19), in which it appears to furnish one more example of something well established in verses 8–12, but it also inaugurates another important list of acts of faith (vv. 17–23), by which the aged pass on divine blessings to succeeding generations, the 'descendants' named 'in Isaac'. More precisely, Abraham, in 'going forth' and bringing Isaac to birth (vv. 8–12), establishes 'sojourning in the land of promise' and 'succession through divine promise' as the conditions of faith-living, in which neither the mode of living nor the form of descent are 'natural' but come directly and exclusively from God. These verses are followed by two sections on the patriarchs in general:

(a) verses 13–16 (anticipated by v. 9) describe their sojourning 'in faith' in a *synchronic* fashion, treating them all as contemporaries;

(b) verses 17–23 describe the patriarchs' succession 'in faith' *diachronically*, through the divine election of the younger sons and the lesser people.

Seen in this way, verses 17–19 are describing, not just another act of Abraham, but the act of transmission of the divine promise to his son, and thereby to all succeeding generations (σπέρμα). It is appropriately a ritual act − the offering up of the 'seed' to God − as also the blessings which follow are quasi-priestly acts of 'sacred speech'.[77] It seals the covenant made between Abraham and God and points (ἐν παραβολῇ) to its future and final fulfilment in Christ.

What kind of sacrifice is it? Sin and its expiation are not of prime concern here, and up to this point in the chapter even death is present rather as a limit and barrier to perception than as an enemy; but it has this in common with all the covenant-sacrifices so far dealt with, that it is expressly *marginal*. The covenant-community is established by the movement outwards from the place of security into the place of danger, or equally by the priestly movement inwards to the sacred sphere. Noah's building of the ark (11:7) was a 'going out' into the void in which the ark was the one place of perilous security; Abraham 'went out' into a land promised but not possessed, to sojourn there, and on the border between life and death begot 'descendants as many as the stars of heaven'; Moses went out from 'the treasures of Egypt' and a royal dynasty to 'share ill-treatment with God's

---

[77] See below, pp. 245ff.

people'. For all these the margin is the place of God's dwelling, as the readers also are urged in chapter 12 to find God in the place of their suffering, and in chapter 13 to 'go forth' to share Jesus' abuse 'outside the camp'. Abraham's other action fits this pattern too, surrendering to God the only security he now possessed, his son, given by God: he gave up his son into the place of death, where God dwells, and there he 'received' him alive.

The martyrs of Israel

Behind this and the other liminal acts just named there lies a strong martyrological tradition, which is invoked explicitly in the torrent of heroes in verses 32–8, with passing references to motifs developed elsewhere, including resurrection (v. 35), fire and the mouths of lions (vv. 33f), persecution (vv. 36f) and those who are 'destitute, afflicted' and 'wandering' (vv. 37f). It was suggested earlier that the author's purpose in interrupting the orderly narrative at verse 32 is in part an attempt to present Israel's history as one of constant striving without fulfilment;[78] it achieves this by presenting that history synchronically, throwing together incidents derived indifferently from the period of the Judges or that of the Maccabees to suggest not only a constant battling against enemies but also an absence of change or chronological movement. It points insistently forward in hope to a new possibility of movement, resulting in 'rest', which Jesus brings. Seen from another angle, though, the list, taken as a whole, is a continuation of the covenant-affirming actions of Abel, Noah and everyone down to Rahab. As such it is an example of the *martyrology*, characteristic of the intertestamental literature and reflecting its view of the struggle between Israel and Hellenism,[79] a genre which has the purpose of relating in outline the entire history of Israel-before-God, by means of particular heroes and their characteristics, and so inspiring in the present generation action loyal to that covenant tradition. Such a list functions like a recital of God's mighty acts in a covenant-renewal rite, invoking a 'cloud of

---

[78] See above, p. 143.
[79] G. W. E. Nickelsburg, *Jewish Literature between the Bible and the Mishnah* (London, 1981), pp. 78f, 119f. For a comprehensive account of the Hellenisation of the Palestinian upper classes, see M. Hengel, *Judaism and Hellenism* (ET London, 1974). In the second century BC, opposition to this process was voiced particularly by Ben Sira and Hasidic groups (Hengel, *Judaism and Hellenism*, p. 131ff, 175ff). On the crisis, in what was perceived to be an attempt to extirpate the worship of Yahweh, see Hengel, *ibid.*, pp. 286ff, 292ff.

witnesses' *to* God's faithfulness and *of* whatever response (faith-ful or faith-less) it meets with in the present readers.

Sometimes this sacral aspect of the covenant is made explicit, as in the long list in Sirach 44–50 beginning 'Let us now praise famous men' which makes special mention of the *covenants* established by God with various heroes (Noah 44:18, Abraham 44:19ff, Moses 45:5, Aaron 45:7,15, Phinehas 45:23f, David 45:25f, 47:11) and the *blessings* given to Israel through them (Jacob 44:23, Aaron 45:15, Simon 50:20f). In this list the high priests Aaron (45:6–22) and Simon (50:1–21) receive the longest descriptions, with lavish dwelling on the symbolism of their clothing and their actions. Hebrews, with its interest in images of ideal priesthood, appears to share some of these ideas: here, as in the Melchizedek pericope, the divinity is 'God Most High' (ὁ ὕψιστος 44:20, 46:5, 50:7,21); Simon the high priest emerges ἐν ἐξόδῳ οἴκου καταπετάσματος (50:5, compare Heb. 6:19); Aaron as ideal priest, is contrasted with Korah and other 'outsiders' (45:18f); Phinehas for his atoning zeal is granted 'the dignity of the priesthood for ever' (ἱεροσύνης μεγαλεῖον εἰς τοὺς αἰῶνας 45:24, compare Heb. 5:6);[80] the emphasis on blessing is in harmony with the 'Melchizedekian' concept of priesthood found in Hebrews 7:1.[81]

Such overtly cultic elements, though echoed elsewhere in the letter, are not to be found in Hebrews 11, however, which looks for its surface details to a different but parallel type of list of covenant-heroes, more secular in tone, several of which are found in the Maccabean books (1 Macc. 2:51–60, 3 Macc. 6:2–8, 4 Macc. 16:16–23, 18:11–19). The first of these is typical in its contents: Abraham, Joseph, Phinehas, Joshua, Caleb, David, Elijah, the three in the burning fiery furnace and Daniel, each commended for a specific virtue (Abraham 'was found faithful', Joshua 'kept the commandments' and so on), each faithful to God in the face of pagan persecution or Israel's rebellion or both (with the important exception of Abraham who, in a reference to Genesis 22, was simply 'tested' (ἐν πειρασμῷ 2:52)). The sacral and the secular tend to interact in this literature, however, and in 2 Maccabees and 4 Maccabees in particular the presentation of persecution, whether in lists or in

---

[80] Phinehas frequently occupies in tradition the role of Aaron (Num. 16:41–9) standing between the punitive 'plague' and the sins of the people: Num 25:6–13, Ps. 106:30, 1 Macc. 2:54, 4 Macc. 18:12, PRE 47 (Friedlander, *PRE*, pp. 370f).

[81] They also share an interest in the fate of Joseph's bones: Sir. 49.15, Heb. 11:22.

narratives, acquires a specifically *sacrificial* character which brings it close to the manner of Hebrews.

Two motifs demand comment here. First, the instruments of torture are conformed to cultic symbols, and vice versa. Thus, among references to the torture of Eleazar, the three young men in the furnace and Daniel among the lions, we are told: 'when Isaac saw his father's hand wielding a sword (ξιφηφόρον) and descending upon him he did not cower' (4 Macc. 16:20): the Akedah here becomes a 'torture' from which Isaac had sufficient courage not to flee. Conversely, fire as a torture is given sacral associations with initiation-rites by the conflation of the three in the furnace, Isaiah's promise (Isa. 43:2) that 'even though you go through the fire the flame shall not consume you' and 'Isaac who was offered as a burnt offering' (4 Macc. 18:11–15). Similarly, the seven brothers in 4 Maccabees who are represented as a 'holy chorus' (13:8) offering intercessions for their nation even in the hour of death (6:28, 12:17), are said to be 'consecrated' (ἁγιασθέντες 17:20) and by their 'blood' became a 'ransom' (ἀντίψυχον 17:21) and 'expiation' (ἱλαστήριον 17:22) through which the land was 'purified' (1:11). There is also a persistent association of ritual purity with those who go out from civilisation and even from humanity itself to live 'as animals do' for God's sake (1 Macc. 2:29, 2 Macc. 5:27, 6:11, 10:6) which reappears in Hebrews' commendation of those who 'went about in skins of sheep and goats ... of whom the world was not worthy' (11:37f).

The second motif, already touched on above, is the treatment of Isaac as prototypical martyr, who showed courage and was 'sacrificially slain (σφαγιασθείς) for the sake of religion' (4 Macc. 13:12, cf. 16:20, 7:14), as a result of which he overcame death and lives 'to God' (7:19), as shall all who do likewise (16:25, 18:19,23, 17:18), who are truly, with Isaac, 'sons of Abraham'. This theme of the 'sacrificial' testing of the 'seed of Abraham', developed through reflection on the life and death of Jesus, becomes, as we shall see in the next chapter, a *mythos* for the life of the covenant people. To prepare for that discussion, this section will conclude by asking what Abraham's 'seed' means in its occurrence in chapter 11.

The seed of Abraham

Nearly all the persons named in chapter 11 are physical descendants of Abraham, the exceptions being Abraham's ancestors (Cain and Abel, Enoch, Noah) and the two women, Sarah his wife and Rahab the Canaanite harlot. Although this adds up to an impressive sacred history, through the first half of the list runs a theme of *endangered succession*, most obviously in the cases of Abel, Noah and Abraham. What the two women have in common is the endangering of this descent by sexual relations with foreigners: in Sarah's case both through some uncertainty about her parentage (not mentioned in Gen. 11:29, but of which nation is she a 'princess'?) and through the Egyptian-princess theme of Genesis 12, though the present text gives prominence to the less complex and less threatening explanation of barrenness; in the case of Rahab because she is a Gentile and a harlot, though included by other genealogies in the ancestry of King David. On the male side there is constant interference with 'natural' (that is, primogenitive) descent through God's choosing of younger sons, as well as by God's 'testing' of Abraham in demanding the sacrifice of his son.

The 'seed of Abraham' is therefore quite strongly characterised as a *divine gift* rather than a natural progeny (though they are in fact all Abraham's physical descendants), a theme derived from the Genesis tradition of Isaac's wondrous birth through divine promise. This is how that birth is reported in Hebrews 11:11:

> By faith Sarah herself (καὶ αὐτὴ Σάρρα) received power to conceive (δύναμιν εἰς καταβολὴν σπέρματος ἔλαβεν) even when she was past the age, since she considered him faithful who had promised.   (RSV)

This verse contains no less than three unsettled exegetical problems. The chief of these is: (i) the attribution to Sarah of power εἰς καταβολὴν σπέρματος, that is, to the male production of seed rather than the female ὑποδοχή, though (ii) commentators have difficulty identifying her 'faith' too, and (iii) the meaning of καὶ αὐτὴ Σάρρα is unclear.

A suggestion which would solve all three problems at once is to make Abraham, rather than Sarah, the subject of the sentence, either by removing καὶ αὐτὴ Σάρρα as a marginal gloss, or by reading it as a dative (καὶ αὐτῇ Σαρρᾷ: 'together with Sarah')[82] however there is no authority for such an emendation in either case, and we shall see that it is unnecessary to conjecture one. The problem of Sarah's

---

[82] See Moffatt, *Hebrews*, p. 171, and the literature cited there. The second view has been favoured recently by Attridge, *Hebrews*, p. 325, Bruce (*Hebrews*, pp. 301f) and Michel (*Der Brief*, p. 262), and apparently by R. McL. Wilson, *Hebrews* (Basingstoke, 1987), p. 207, though he also suggests that these words might be placed in parenthesis.

'faith' (ii) is that Genesis gives no grounds for it − apart from her dubious ventures into pagan harems, her main action is to laugh at the promise of God (18:12). Montefiore suggests, rather desperately, that the author must have forgotten these incidents, and accepts her as a mother of faith and model of piety:[83] yet curiously she is seldom so regarded in Jewish tradition. In the Old Testament only Isaiah 51:2 mentions her ('look to Abraham your father and to Sarah who bore you'); in the New Testament she appears three times in connection with the birth of Isaac (Rom. 4:19, 9:9 and here), but in 1 Peter 3:6 she is named as one of the 'holy women who hoped in God' and showed this by her wifely submissiveness; 'and you are now her children if you do right and let nothing terrify you'. 1 Peter thus treats her as a female counterpart of Abraham, but whether this is the meaning of Hebrews is the point at issue. The phrase καὶ αὐτὴ Σάρρα (iii) can be read as 'even Sarah' without emendations or psychologising: even she who laughed at the promised seed was given power 'by faith' to become Isaac's mother in her barrenness and old age. This faith might be Abraham's faith (but there is no need to speak of his 'influence', as Westcott does[84]), or it might be a conviction which, despite the physical impossibility which causes her quite naturally to laugh, makes Sarah cooperate with the will of God 'since she considered him faithful who promised', as a result of which she gives birth to Isaac. The odds against her faith need to be fully in view, and not argued away, for in Hebrews the difficulty of faith is precisely the ground of its necessity.

As regards the use of καταβολή (i), also, the most obvious reading is the most satisfactory, though harder: it is better to accept a deliberately paradoxical use of language than to find here either a lexical error[85] or a special theory of generation.[86] Literally, in describing generation, it is Abraham who produces seed, Sarah who is ('by faith') given power to receive and nourish it. But the basic sense of καταβολή is *'foundation'*,[87] and it is widely used in this

[83] Montefiore, *Hebrews*, p. 194.

[84] Westcott, *Hebrews*, p. 360.

[85] Moffatt (*Hebrews*, p. 171), Montefiore (*Hebrews*, p. 194) and Westcott (*Hebrews*, p. 361) all follow the Vulgate by giving to this term a passive sense: 'power to conceive'.

[86] See Spicq (*Hébreux*, vol. II, p. 349) and Héring (*Hebrews*, p. 101) for the idea, attributed to pagan or rabbinic authors, that the woman has an active role in generation, which Spicq over-hastily fuses with the 'seed' of Eve (Gen. 3:5).

[87] See Buchanan (*To The Hebrews*, p. 190); Héring (*Hebrews*, p. 102), 'to create a posterity'. Westcott, however, dismisses this translation, 'for the foundation of a race', as 'altogether unnatural' (*Hebrews*, p. 361).

sense in Hebrews (4:3, 9:26) and elsewhere in the New Testament (among others Matt. 25:34, John 17:24, Eph. 1:4, 1 Pet. 1:20). Admittedly, in all these other cases it refers to the 'foundation of the world', but the immediate context here is the *foundation of a commonwealth* (as confirmed by the image of the city built on physical 'foundation-stones' (θεμελίους), in the preceding verse): this is the end in view, to which sexual generation is only the means. Sarah receives from God power to found a posterity, a 'seed' through which the promises of God will be carried to completion (11:12).[88] This is a sacred action, the foundation of Israel through the divinely promised 'seed', first manifestation of a 'blessing' to be fulfilled ultimately by and through Jesus. Rather than smooth out the linguistic difficulty, it is better to see in this hint of trans-sexuality another expression of liminal perception, the 'strangeness' which is normal in the presence of God.

The nature of this 'seed', and its implications for the New Testament in general and the Christology of Hebrews in particular, will be the chief subject of chapter 6.

Conclusion

The 'narratives of the covenant' explored in this chapter encompass a great mass of material, including much that is not apparent at the surface of the text. Some of these 'hidden' elements (for example, Korah) have a wider function in the text, and therefore receive more extensive treatment here, than others actually named (for example, Enoch). And even this long account cannot claim to be complete, for no associational method can ever hope to paint a complete picture of its subject-matter. Nor can it expect to be tidy without dressing up the evidence. The theology of the covenant which emerges from this battery of interlocking allusions is not reducible to an argument, though it complements the argument of the letter. Rather, it points to the dense interweaving of apparently dissimilar strands, so that even the distinction between cultic and non-cultic material, so clear in the text's outward structure, turns out to be chiefly a matter of convenience. Thus, the theme of rebellion and judgement, which appears overtly in the paraenetic material and in the sections about Moses, is found to be buttressed by a range of hieratic and apotropaic symbols: Cain and Esau, Korah, Passover and twin-births. In addition

---

[88] Cf. the 'seed' of Eve, Gen. 3:15.

to the obvious Christ-types in the book, Melchizedek, Moses and Joshua, other less likely candidates must be considered also: Abel, Isaac, Korah and even Rahab. There are outsiders, good and bad, in every corner: Cain, Esau and Korah; Rahab, Melchizedek and the younger sons. The quality of 'faith', which is exemplified by the heroes of chapter 11 culminating in Jesus, draws us through the motif of the Akedah towards Isaac and all who understand themselves to be 'children of Abraham'.

With the exception of Melchizedek, all of these symbol-clusters contain expiatory material with a distinctly apotropaic cast, particularly the themes of blood, and the sacrifice of the first-born, and the image of God as fire and mouth and sword; but each of these also offsets the apotropaic. In the figure of Abel, vengeance is complemented by grace; in Rahab, a Gentile validates the exclusivist ideology of the Passover; in the inscrutable logic of election, both those offered up as first-born and those cast off are part of God's plan; and the pro-Aaronite propaganda concerning Korah's assault on the cultic monopoly essential to the Priestly system is approved in order to provide support for the high-priesthood of the one who was 'descended from Judah' (7:14). In the subtle presentation of Abel, Rahab, Moses, and Abraham-Isaac; of Passover and Akedah; of the Exodus and the martyrs of faith, God is shown to be both fearful and graciously approachable.

The figure of Melchizedek is distinctive also in being employed here, quite consciously, to present a pattern against which to set Jesus. This function is appropriate in that his isolation in the literature tends to make him a two-dimensional figure, and therefore either opaque or else a fit subject for free speculation, whereas the other motifs, drawn from the deeper strata of the scriptural material, have become many-sided by the interaction of originally disparate symbols and stories until they have acquired an ambiguity, a suggestiveness capable of representing – certainly in the case of Moses and Abraham–Isaac – all sides of Israel's traditions and beliefs. Presumably that is why these figures receive more explicit treatment in the book, but the whole range of 'cultic' traditions, taken together, adds up to an equally many-sided and equally inclusive pattern. Inclusiveness is an essential quality if the 'covenant' is to be more than an outward and artificial contract. Through the development of these stories and symbols it acquires a very particular character: the whole culture of 'Israel', re-presented in the light of Christ.

6

THE TESTING OF THE SON OF GOD

The rich traditional materials relating to Abraham and Isaac were set out in the last main section of the previous chapter according to the associational method being employed there. It was argued that, for Hebrews, the developed tradition of the Akedah provides not only an important symbol of *faith-discipleship*, in the person of Abraham, but also a symbol of a *non-expiatory covenant-sacrifice*, in which the mysterious birth of Isaac is fused with his 'death and resurrection' into a composite symbol which is central to the letter's presentation of the faith-life of the covenant-people. The purpose of this chapter will be to take up that motif again and to develop the argument, this time through an analysis of its character as 'myth', in order to show that the Akedah gives also a basis for the letter's Christology.

The argument will proceed in three stages. First, it will use a method of myth-interpretation borrowed from Lévi-Strauss to present the Akedah as the *mythos* of covenant-sacrifice in inter-testamental Judaism (developing the point made earlier[1]), and an important element in the Christology of the New Testament; second, it will show how the New Testament (and Hebrews in particular) appropriated the related concept of the 'seed of Abraham' in its understanding of salvation; and third, it will show by exegesis of specific passages that this myth and the concepts it carries with it are foundational for the Christology of Hebrews.

A pattern of mythology

Myth and mediation

In his essay on 'The Structural Study of Myth', originally published in 1955,[2] Lévi-Strauss presented and illustrated a number of principles which have proved seminal and provocative for many others since:

[1] See pp. 181–3 above.   [2] Lévi-Strauss, *SA*, pp. 206–31.

(i) 'If there is a meaning to be found in mythology, it cannot reside in the isolated elements which enter into the composition of a myth, but only in the way those elements are combined';[3]
(ii) 'A myth is made up of all its variants';[4]
(iii) 'Mythical thought always progresses from the awareness of oppositions towards their resolution.'[5]

In relation to the first two points, he argues that what is distinctive about *myth* as a cultural phenomenon is not contained in the *words* in which a particular myth is recounted, since 'the mythical value of the myth is preserved even through the worst translation';[6] nor is it contained in the *story* as a unilinear syntagmatic structure, since different versions of the same myth can show quite marked omissions and divergences in their story-line while other myths with wholly different stories can yet be seen to be 'about' the same thing. In Saussurian terms, these are both parts of *parole*, whereas the *langue* of a myth emerges when its elements are considered simultaneously, not as moments in a narrative but as units in a structure of symbols. It is this structure, and what it is 'saying', which remains constant through the many transformations of a single myth found in different cultures and at different historical periods. It is therefore possible, taking his own example, to consider Freud's interpretation of the myth of Oedipus as one authentic version of the myth alongside more 'classical' versions,[7] and to be open to the possibility that what is new in Freud's version may be making explicit something always covertly present in the myth's structure. Whether this entitles us to ignore the historical and cultural environments in which myths are retold, and to dispense with the question of influences, is a more contentious matter, leading into an area of generalisation uncontrolled by empirical data where few anthropologists have been willing to follow.[8]

The usefulness of these principles in discussing the Jewish tradition of the Akedah will be apparent, and so will its dangers. In the last chapter we saw that some of the features found in targumic and midrashic retellings of the story of Abraham and Isaac appear to be rediscoveries of underlying symbolic elements (such as the child-sacrifice), while others (such as the idea of an expiatory

[3] *SA*, p. 210.   [4] *SA*, p. 217.   [5] *SA*, p. 224.
[6] *SA*, p. 210.   [7] *SA*, pp. 216f.   [8] See pp. 51–6 above.

sacrifice) seem to be genuinely new.[9] Freedom in such comparative
study of its variants has to be limited by the effect of the privileged
canonical status given to one version, that in Genesis 22, and by
the fact that there is a discernible relation between at least some
features of the later versions and preceding historical events. Taking
account of these, it was argued that what unites these versions is
the idea of a composite *covenant-sacrifice* already demonstrated
in relation to Jewish tradition in general (for the Akedah is only
part of a wider interpretative culture),[10] of which child-sacrifice,
expiation, circumcision and Passover are all historically conditioned
variants. On this basis it was possible to show the foundational
role of this material in Hebrews 11.

The third of Lévi-Strauss' principles defines myth as a vehicle
for resolving the conceptual problems which arise in perceiving
contradictory features of the world: life/death, nature/culture,
youth/age. As such, myth is analogous to the 'liminal' character
of ritual already discussed, mediating between irreconcilable opposites
by creating an area of significant ambiguity in which different
rules of logic apply. Myths tell stories about situations and characters
which effect such mediations: 'two opposite terms with no intermediary always tend to be replaced by two equivalent terms which
admit of a third one as a mediator' and so on, yielding a structure
of the kind shown in table 2.[11]

Table 2.   Symbolic mediation in myth

Initial pair	First triad	Second triad
Life		
	Agriculture	
		Herbivorous animals
		Carrion-eating animals (raven; coyote)
	Hunting	
		Beasts of prey
	Warfare	
Death		

In this chapter the Akedah will be treated as one variant, or group
of variants, of a myth of covenant-affirming sacral death, a myth
springing from the experienced ambiguity of God in the face of
death and developing in Israel's conflict with Hellenism in the

---

[9] See pp. 174–7 above.   [10] See pp. 123–6 above.   [11] Lévi-Strauss, *SA*, p. 224.

pre-Christian period. We shall see that the two central concepts, the ambivalence of God, and the testing of the 'seed of Abraham', are of deep concern to Paul, Luke and other New Testament writers. In Hebrews, too, Jesus, identified with the 'seed of Abraham', in passing through death, resolves the question of the nature of God and becomes the 'pioneer and perfecter of salvation' for the people of the covenant.

The Akedah and the covenant

Since we are dealing with material which is in principal historically datable, and the argument presupposes that the major alterations to this narrative tradition took place in response to the crises in the life of Israel brought on by the Exile, the Maccabean revolt and the fall of Jerusalem in AD 79, a necessary condition for the permissibility of this approach to the Akedah as a 'mythic pattern' is a demonstration that it rests on a defensible construction of the sequence of historical developments. Commentators are agreed that the story found in Genesis 22:1–19 is a late element in the Abraham-cycle of Genesis, and that its theme of *testing* and the *fear of God* associates it with late periods of Israel's history, the end of the monarchy (Westermann) or the Exile (van Seters);[12] however, this version is probably a revision of an earlier account directed principally against the Canaanite practice of human-sacrifice, especially in the related forms of the initiation-rite and the foundational child-sacrifice.[13] The protagonist here is Abraham, but in the third and second centuries, when the mounting threat from an aggressive Hellenism made martyrdom the likely result of loyalty to Judaism, the *trial-of-faith* motif gained renewed religious importance, and at some point the figure of Isaac re-emerged from behind that of Abraham, giving prominence to the idea of the voluntary self-offering. In this form the Akedah appears in texts of the first century AD (Pseudo-Philo and 4 Macc.) and the later recensions of targum and midrash; it may even be alluded to in the much earlier book of Judith (Judith 8:25–7).[14]

---

[12] See C. Westermann, *Genesis 12–36*, p. 355; Swetnam, *Jesus*, p. 76. Van Seters, *Abraham* (pp. 309ff) dates the entire Abraham cycle from this period.

[13] See Heider, *The Cult of Molek*, pp. 273–7; White, 'The initiation legend of Isaac'; Swetnam, *Jesus*, p. 20n. For a different view see van Seters, *Abraham*, pp. 227–37.

[14] See Swetnam, *Jesus*, pp. 34f.

To what extent was this story given a sacrifical interpretation? The link between the Akedah and the New Year feast does not appear earlier than AD 70, but midrashic links to the *tamid* and the Passover pick up references, contained in the story itself, to the 'binding' of the victim of the *'olah* and to the sacrifice of the first-born.[15] Attempts have been made repeatedly in recent literature to treat the sacrifice as necessarily *expiatory*, and to argue that it is a defining characteristic of the Akedah on this account.[16] It is said, for example, that because, in 4 Maccabees, Isaac is an exemplary martyr, and the martyrs' deaths are counted as having atoning value, Isaac's 'death' must be implicitly an atoning sacrifice too.[17] The text of 4 Maccabees avoids this obvious conclusion, probably for the good reason that its purpose is to encourage its readers, beleaguered by the forces of pagan Rome, to reproduce behaviour like Isaac's, whereas arguing for the efficacy (still more the completeness) of Isaac's self-offering would tend to defeat this plan by rendering its reproduction unnecessary. It is far more likely that this expiatory reading was a late development, a response to the Christian claims for the cross as atoning sacrifice, and perhaps, also, to a need, felt in Judaism, for an efficacious sacrifice to replace, at least in imagination, the destroyed Temple cult. However, this does not warrant the conclusion, drawn by Davies and Chilton, that the Akedah as such is a post-Christian development.[18]

What was firmly embedded in the story before Jesus' birth, whether Abraham or Isaac is seen as the central figure, is the pattern of a *testing* which is also a *sacrifice* determining the character of the covenant-relation between Israel and God: more than an historical illustration of faith-triumphant-under-duress, it is a *system-affirming event*, through which the covenant is established and renewed. The other feature of the story so deeply embedded it appears in every version is the *ambivalence of the divine nature* which created both good and evil – an ambivalence manifested, as we have seen, in the Passover tradition, where God appears as both Protector (God of Abraham, Isaac and Jacob) and as Destroyer intent on killing the first-born of both Israel and Egypt.[19] This is the fundamental opposition

---

[15] For examples, see Daly, 'Sacrifice of Isaac', 53f.

[16] Vermes, *Scripture and Tradition*, pp. 210f; Bowker, *Targums*, pp. 231–3.

[17] Daly, 'Sacrifice of Isaac', 56f.

[18] Davies and Chilton, 'The Aqedah'.

[19] See Coats, 'Abraham's sacrifice of faith'; Swetnam, *Jesus*, p. 24. And see pp. 158f above.

out of which the myth springs, provoking the question: how can the God who brings us into temptation be trusted and obeyed? The alternative is to ask: how can one who brings us into temptation be God? Kant wrote:

> There are certain cases in which man can be convinced that it cannot be God whose voice he thinks he hears; when the voice commands him to do what is opposed to the moral law ... he must count it as deception ... Abraham should have said to this supposed divine voice: that I am not to kill my beloved son is quite certain; that you who appear to me are God, I am not certain, nor can I ever be, even if the voice thunders from the sky.[20]

The Abraham of the Genesis narrative, receiving the moral law directly from God, has no such means of relaxing the tension but has to struggle with the first question and the dilemma it poses; the whole history of Israel, from the Exile to the Holocaust and beyond, can be described in terms of this intolerable wrestling with a God who cannot be categorised but demands assent.

In Genesis 22, the tension arises from the fact that God who gives Abraham a son, and (because of his faith) blesses him with the promise of infinite progeny through that son, is the same God who now demands that he show his faith by sacrificing his son as a burnt-offering. Yet the dilemma appears in this form only when Genesis 22 is related to one of the earlier accounts of the covenanting (Gen. 15, 17).[21] In itself, the story of Genesis 22 can be represented as a clash between love and obedience, a conflict which is unbearable but, as the story shows, only apparent, since God is loving and provides a resolution to this painful personal dilemma. In this subjective form, it is a story told in praise of Abraham, who is found true when tested. A different dimension is added when Genesis 22 is taken in conjunction with the earlier chapters, for why is this event necessary at all? The promise of seed given in Genesis 22:15–19 is identical with that given in 15:6: had it not been, in fact, a *promise*, but only a conditional offer, to be withdrawn if Abraham should fail to pass this (hitherto

[20] I. Kant, 'The dispute between the philosophical and theological faculties', quoted by Westermann, *Genesis 12–36*, p. 354. S. Kierkegaard, *Fear and Trembling* (ET New York, 1954), offers a very different way of struggling with the same event. See n. 24 below.
[21] See Alexander, 'Gen. 22 and the covenant of circumcision', pp. 17–22.

unmentioned) test? If so, what faith can be placed in the second pronouncement of this same 'promise'? In what new circumstances might it yet be withdrawn? Seen in this light, the story takes a different shape. In accordance with Lévi-Strauss' pattern, an initial opposition gives rise to a further pair of opposites, between which resolution is possible (see pattern I below).

I. God gives a son (Blessing)
      Abraham trusts in God's promise
          Isaac restored and the promise of 'seed' reaffirmed
      Abraham gives up his son as sacrifice
   God demands the son (Testing)

What is depicted here is not a private virtue, the faith of Abraham,[22] but the meaning of the covenant-relation with God in which Israel lives: the private dilemma of Abraham (love versus obedience) is only a subjective reflection of the objective ambivalence of God.[23]

Attempts are occasionally made to relax the intolerable tension which this presents, as when in several texts the command comes to Abraham from, or at the behest of, an evil angel (Mastema or Satan).[24] Passover, too, can be interpreted dualistically, as a struggle between Yahweh and an evil force (the Destroyer, or Egypt). That the paradoxical, monistic view of Passover is not only permissible but a more coherent interpretation is shown by the fact that the distinction between God and the Destroyer is not always maintained,[25] and by the form of the ritual resolution (see pattern II below).

---

[22] Faith is in fact not mentioned here, but at 15:6. See Nickelsburg, *Jewish Literature*, pp. 75f.

[23] Compare Spiegel's rabbinic exegesis of the names of God used in the passage, the two faces of God as *Elohim* (he who puts to the test) and *Yahweh* (he who is merciful), *The Last Trial*, pp. 121ff.

[24] J. L. Crenshaw, in his Introduction to J. L. Crenshaw (ed.), *Theodicy in the Old Testament* (London, 1983), p. 15, (n. 35), remarks that 'Kierkegaard's difficulty in "imagining" such a monstrous test prompts him to describe the griefstruck father as eager to protect God's honour, even at his own expense. Abraham reasons that it is better for Isaac to think him a beast than to think God one.' The alternative is to find an unambiguously evil being at work: in B. San. 89b (Bowker, *Targums*, p. 228) the protagonist is Satan; in Jub. 17:16 it is 'Prince Mastema' who says in the heavenly court (a scene 'reminiscent of Job 1–2', Nickelsburg, *Jewish Literature*, p. 75): 'Behold, Abraham loves Isaac, his son. And he is more pleased with him than everything. Tell him to offer him as a burnt-offering upon the altar. And you will see whether he will do this thing. And you will know whether he is faithful in everything in which you test him' (J. H. Charlesworth, *The Old Testament Pseudepigrapha* (2 vols., London, 1983–5), vol. II, p. 90).

[25] See pp. 158f above for the oppositions implicit in the accounts of the Passover.

II. God the Protector (God of Abraham, Isaac and Jacob)
   Covenant-meal shared by Israelites only
      Israel escapes (but Egyptian first-born die)
     Avertive action with blood of yearling lamb
  God the Destroyer (seeks death of first-born)

Here the contradiction − that it is the God who has established a covenant with his people who now seeks to destroy them − is reflected in the twin aspects of Passover as covenant-meal and apotropaic blood-rite, by which a boundary between the realm of life (Israel) and the realm of death is formed. The fact that the lamb provides both the meal and the apotropaic symbols causes the whole tension of the event (historical, liturgical and existential) to focus on it. In this connection we may recall also the strange incident in Exodus 4:24−6, in which Moses, having been commissioned by God to bring his people out of Egypt, is met by God 'at a lodging-place on the way', inexplicably intent now on killing him. It is Zipporah who turns God from Destroyer into Preserver by circumcising her son, visiting on herself in symbol the death of the first-born with which Moses was commanded to threaten Pharaoh in the immediately preceding verses (4:21−3), and making it also a symbol of Moses' circumcision/death, so that he becomes 'a bridegroom of blood' (see pattern IIa below).[26]

IIa. God the Protector (God of Fathers)
    'Death' of child establishes covenant-relation
  God the Destroyer (seeks Moses' death)

In this case, the ritual act of circumcision exists to make a direct mediation between Life and Death and to affirm the relation with the Lord who gives both. These parallels suggest why it is that the 'binding' of Isaac, which is both the sacrificial offering and the sign of Abraham's faith, is the centre of symbolic interest; they also suggest that if Abraham's 'faithfulness' is his acceptance of God as trustworthy, his conjunctive cleaving to God despite his own paternal love, the sacrifice should be understood as apotropaic, even though this is not apparent at the surface of the story.

    The fusion of narrative-ethical and cultic-religious elements in the Abraham cycle, of which Genesis 22 forms the climax, aptly represents the covenant-ideology of Israel-Judah in the pre-exilic

[26] See Daly, *Origins*, p. 42.

period.[27] However, both Israel's faith and the sureness of God's promises were capable of being falsified by experience. Though mild by comparison with the specifically religious-ideological opposition they were to meet from the Hellenistic kingdoms later, culminating in the Maccabean revolt, for the Jews the Babylonian captivity and its aftermath proved to be a renewal of God's testing, or a resurgence of awareness of God as 'Destroyer'.[28] The mediation found in pattern I then no longer settled the issue and left the unresolved opposition shown in pattern III below.

III. God's promise of blessing reaffirmed (Gen. 22)

God's promise threatened by the power of the Gentiles

This is a variant of the familiar anguished cry of disillusionment in the Psalms and the later Wisdom literature (Ps. 10, Job 21, 30): why do the wicked prosper while the righteous suffer? The collapse of the complacent Yahwism against which the prophets campaigned, the belief that God was Israel's protector in all circumstances, might even lead to this extreme form of the basic opposition (see pattern IIIa below).

IIIa. Yahweh is irreconcilably opposed to the idols of the nations

Yahweh is indistinguishable from the idols of the nations

However, no text goes so far as to state this paradox of despair. The Deuteronomic explanation, dating from before the Exile, that catastrophe is a punishment for national sin, was an attempt to justify God as the bringer of evil (see pattern IIIb below).

IIIb. Covenant of promise
  Israel has sinned against the covenant
    Repentance brings renewal of covenant-salvation
  Israel's persecution is punishment for sin
Power of the Gentiles

This account remained deeply influential (P.Az. 8). However, in the literature of the Hellenistic age the question why God allows his children to suffer persecution and ritual desecration for their faith received a new answer in the ideology of the *martyr* — that God permits such horrors in order to *demonstrate the faith* of his

---

[27] See von Rad, *OTT*, vol. I, pp. 129ff; Eichrodt, *Theology*, pp. 36–69; McCarthy, *O.T. Covenant*, pp. 1–9.
[28] Crenshaw, *Theodicy*, p. 5, von Rad, *OTT*, vol. I, pp. 391ff.

saints (1 Macc. 3:50–52; 2 Macc. 6:12ff; 4 Macc. 6:17ff) – and this naturally revived interest in the story of Abraham and Isaac, which is referred to with increasing frequency in the Maccabean literature. The 'classic' Maccabean tale of martyrdom (variants of which appear in 1 Macc. 2, 2 Macc. 7, 4 Macc. 8–18, Test. Mos. 9 and Josephus *Antiquities*, XIV.429f) tells of the unflinchingly faithful death of a parent and all his or her sons, and the faith of the 'fathers' is further illustrated by the obedience of wise old men (such as the death of Eleazar (2 Macc. 6:18–31, 4 Macc. 5–7) and the obedience of Abraham and Amram (Pseudo-Philo)); the martyrs are repeatedly identified in relational terms, as fathers, mothers, sons or brothers, and the question whether the sons will be faithful to the religion of the fathers is constantly in mind (2 Macc. 7:24, 28).[29]

In this material, and in the image of horrors perpetrated against children, there arises the spectre of *child-sacrifice*. In the Old Testament, this practice functions alongside 'drinking blood', 'adultery' and 'necromancy' as forbidden areas of cultic experience, the abominations of the Gentiles, and although there is no evidence of its occurrence in this period, the actual threat to the offspring of those who remained faithful raised the question whether God was now, in effect, demanding what he had hitherto forbidden; and with it the further question: can God, then, be distinguished from the false gods? The subject of the testing is increasingly frequently identified as Isaac, the son, rather than his father. In the first century AD we find Israel identifying itself in paschal terms as the threatened 'first-born' (2 Esd. 6:58, 5:21–30), and 4 Maccabees makes repeated reference to Isaac as the typical martyr, unflinching in the face of death, and now alive with God: those who imitate him are 'children of Abraham' (6:17, 22) and 'worthy of' (or 'son of') Abraham (9:21), 'true descendants of father Abraham' (17:6), a 'daughter of God-fearing Abraham' (15:28, cf. 14:20). Behind these texts, a developed form of the Isaac-myth is mediating the opposition between Israel's faith and its overwhelming experience, with particular interest in the 'sons' as agents of both faith and (self-) sacrifice (see pattern IV below).

---

[29] Compare this medieval account of a Christian pogrom during the hysteria of the first crusade (1096): 'And Zion's precious sons, the people of Mainz, were put through the ten trials like Father Abraham ... They too offered up their sons, exactly as Abraham offered up his son Isaac ... There were 1,100 victims in one day, every one of them like the Akedah of Isaac son of Abraham' (Spiegel, *The Last Trial*, p. 23).

IV. God the giver of life and covenant
    Faith of Abraham should lead to 'blessing'
        Faithful sons trust in God's promise
            'Sons of Abraham' inherit the blessing
        Sons die as atoning sacrifice
    Faithful sons obey covenant and die
God the destroyer of the first-born

As with Passover, we see here the ambivalence of God and of the sacrifice he commands. Pre-Israelite child-sacrifice was probably an avertive offering,[30] and reflection on martyrdom came, as in 4 Maccabees, to ascribe to it expiatory value as an offering for the sins of Israel;[31] but as a willing, and even glad, *self*-offering it acquires a conjunctive character perhaps best exemplified in the Song of the Three Young Men (often revealingly called the 'Three Children') (P.Az. 28–68),[32] who greet God amidst the flames in the form of his angel or son (ὁμοία υἱῷ θεοῦ Dan. 3:92(25) LXX). It is in the Danielic reflection on the 'Testing of faith' that resurrection emerges (Dan. 12:2), as a transformation of this pattern of mediation (see pattern IVa below).

IVa. Life
        New life beyond death
    Death

The Akedah and New Testament Christology

For the earliest kerygma of the Christian church, too, this myth-pattern provided a vehicle for uniting expiatory sacrifice and heroic martyrdom, and its transformations chart the chief options in New Testament Christology. There are many dualistic formulations, in which God defeats the powers of evil through the *coming of Christ* in Judgement (John 12:31, 1 Cor. 15:24f, Gal. 1:4), or through the resurrection understood as God's act of *vindication* of his

---

[30] See Heider, *Molek*, pp. 189–92, 383–400.

[31] See J. Downing, 'Jesus and martyrdom', *JTS*, 14 (1963), 279ff; Young, *SI*, pp. 67f. Daly, *Origins*, pp. 34f, finds in 2 Macc. 7:37f, 12:42–5; 4 Macc. 6:28f, the origin of the concept of *penal substitution* as a way of understanding atoning sacrifice. In the terms used here, this concept combines the Deuteronomic idea of divine punishment (IIIb) with the martyr's proven faith (IV), a broad base which perhaps accounts for its persistence in Christian thinking about atonement.

[32] Note that the Prayer of Azariah itself (P.Az. 1–22), though it mentions the Akedah (v. 12), is propitiatory in its tendency. See Nickelsburg, *Jewish Literature*, p. 28.

servant (Acts 2:23f, 36, 3:15, 5:30f; 1 Tim. 3:16b),[33] but it is possible to find also an expiatory *martyrological* scheme (see pattern IVb below).

IVb. God the giver of life and covenant
        Jesus is faithful to God
              Jesus gives salvation to those who trust in him
        Jesus gives his life as atoning sacrifice
    God the destroyer (demands Jesus' death)

This appears in numerous apparently primitive credal formulae (several of which are regularly included among proposed references to the Akedah[34]): 1 Corinthians 15:3f ('died for our sins' and 'raised the third day according to the scriptures'); Romans 4:24f; the ἀνάμνησις-theme in 1 Corinthians 11:24, Luke 22:19; the 'curse' in Galatians 3:13; the 'ransom for many' in Mark 10:45, 1 Timothy 2:6; the sacrificial language of Ephesians 5:1, 25ff, Titus 2:14. It is one strand in the Marcan Son-of-Man Christology, and finds new force late in the first century in the Christology of Luke.[35] In the religious climate of first-century Palestine, it was a natural way to speak of Jesus' mission and death, especially when held in conjunction with an apocalyptic eschatology which looked for the imminent fulfilment of God's kingdom bringing the resolution of these tensions.

Whether such a Christology did in fact hold the stage alone even for a time is hard to determine: what is certain is that within a few years a more radical type of Christology, based on the *mission of the Son of God* (Rom. 8:3, 32; 15:8f; Gal. 4:4; John 3:16), had come to complement and virtually replace it.[36] The strength

[33] See W. Pannenberg, *Jesus, God and Man*, (London, 1968), pp. 67f. He also (p. 68n.) raises the question whether this idea is 'in the background of Rom. 4:25'.

[34] For the Christian use of the Akedah, see the literature cited in nn. 57, 65 to chapter 5 above, and in addition J. E. Wood, 'Isaac typology in the New Testament', *NTS*, 14 (1967–8), 583–9.

[35] See R. H. Fuller, *The Foundations of New Testament Christology* (Glasgow, 1965), pp. 151–5, 167–74; Downing, 'Jesus and martyrdom', 279–93; J. A. T. Robinson, *Twelve New Testament Studies*, Studies in Biblical Theology 34 (London, 1962), pp. 139–53. On Mark, see Kee, *Community*, pp. 135–8; H. Tödt, *The Son of Man in the Synoptic Tradition* (London, 1965), pp. 144–7, 214–21. On Luke, see B. E. Beck, '"Imitatio Christi" and the Lucan passion narrative', in W. Horbury and B. McNeal (eds.), *Suffering and Martyrdom in the New Testament*, (Cambridge, 1981), pp. 28–47.

[36] See W. G. Kümmel, *Theology of the New Testament* (London, 1974), pp. 119–21; Fuller, *Foundations*, pp. 194–5; O. Cullmann, *The Christology of the New Testament* (London, 1959), pp. 290–305; J. D. G. Dunn, *Christology in the Making*

of this Son-of-God Christology, for the church's kerygma, lay in its assertion of the uniqueness and finality of Jesus, whereas the other was incapable of distinguishing symbolically between the many martyrs and the last, except by uniting itself to the simpler Christology of the vindicated prophet through an appended account of Jesus' ascension to God's right hand as Lord, a claim which itself would demand confirmation (Acts 4:29–31, 5:32). Yet these patterns are variants of the same myth, and seldom appear in total isolation from each other. The future lay with the Sonship-Christology, and its developments through the concepts of Adam and divine Wisdom, but in its train it took with it part of the expiatory ideology of the now displaced martyr-Christology.

New Testament references to the sending of the Son or Christ are allusive in a fascinating way: the identity of the Son, where he comes from, and how, and why, are plainly expected to be known by the reader of Romans 8:32, Galatians 3:24, Hebrews 1:2, John 1:18, 3:16, and there is in several of these verses a formulaic quality which causes many to doubt whether it is simply shared Christian knowledge, a common kerygma, that accounts for this. At one time a myth of a gnostic descending redeemer was postulated as an explanation,[37] while more recently the motif of the Akedah has seemed to many to provide a pre-Christian mould into which the proclamation of Jesus can fit: in either case the problem is to determine whether the allusiveness is a sign of tentativeness which prefers not to be explicit[38] or an assurance which knows it need not be.

The aim of the structural analysis used here has been to show that the fact that the New Testament allusions are to a *pattern of action*, rather than to narrative details, tends to confirm the presence, underlying the kerygma, of the Isaac-myth. But in which form? There is in the New Testament a dualistic form of the myth, consisting of the opposition between God and the powers of evil, which are vanquished by the sending of the Son, found in the

(London, 1980), pp. 36–46, 51–6. Whether this presupposes a concept of pre-existence, and whether the sending must imply incarnation, are controversial issues: compare Fuller (*Christology*, 194f and n. 34) with Dunn (who finds no such concepts in Paul, though he detects pre-existence (but not incarnation) in Hebrews).

[37] As by Käsemann, *Wandering People*, especially pp. 97–182. For a critical review of this approach, see Hurst, *Hebrews*, pp. 67–75; also Dunn, *Christology*, pp. 13–22.

[38] See, for example, Daly's curious explanation of the New Testament's sparse use of the Akedah: 'Perhaps also the early Christians were a bit reserved in the use of something which was obviously very "Jewish"' (p. 50).

parable of the tenants in the vineyard (Mark 12:1–12). One weakness of that story, however, is that it gives no compelling reason why the sending of the son should provide the logical resolution of the drama. There is also a reversion to the earlier and simpler pattern of Genesis 22 (pattern I),[39] though proposing a different conclusion (see pattern V below).

> V. God promises a seed (blessing)
>> God, as father, gives *his own son* as 'seed' and
>> paradigm of faith
> God demands faith (testing)

The Son stands in place of Israel in the earlier version, fulfils what it was not able to fulfil ('lives by faith in the promise'), and so vindicates the faithfulness of God. Unlike the martyrological pattern (IVb), this is able to show why salvation comes through *Jesus*: Jesus is saviour because he is God's Son, the 'Seed' for whom Israel had (whether it knew it or not) always been waiting.

But then how is the *death* of Jesus to be accounted for? Or, putting the question the other way round, given the fact of the crucifixion, which threatens the finality of the mediating event in the same way as the pagan ascendancy threatened the finality of its earlier form,[40] how can Jesus be *shown* to be the Son and salvation-bringer? One answer is to mediate this opposition through the idea of the 'son of Abraham' as it appears in the martyrological scheme (pattern IV). This produces a further development (see pattern VI below).

> VI. God gives his Son to fulfil his promise to Israel
>> Jesus shows faith in God's promise
>>> Jesus the Son, source of salvation for the faithful
>> Jesus gives himself as sacrifice
> God demands the death of the Son

By fusing the atoning death of the 'son of Abraham' with the sending of the 'son of God', the act of expiation with eternally prepared salvation, it shows why there is no need to seek pre-Christian models which ascribe atoning value to *Isaac's* death in order to explain this conception of the cross. This pattern is seen in operation in many places: in the idea of the lamb 'destined before the foundation of the world' (1 Pet. 1:19, cf. Rev. 13:8)

---

[39] See p. 194 above.　　　　[40] See pp. 196f above.

who now 'takes away the sin of the world' (John 1:29); in the juxtaposition of the Son, sent out of love for the world, with the apotropaic description of the son 'lifted up' like the bronze serpent in the wilderness (John 3:14−16); in the dual development of the concept of the 'Son of Man' as he who suffers 'for our sins' and he who 'comes down'; in the joyful benedictions with which Ephesians and 1 Peter begin; most concisely in hymnlike or credal passages, such as Philippians 2:5−11, Romans 1:1−4, Hebrews 1:1−4.

In the theology of Paul (though he also employs on occasions dualistic ideas) the same work of fusion is done on the basis of the Paschal pattern (II). For him the agonising question is how the God of Abraham, the lifegiver who promises so much, and has now sent his son to redeem that promise, can be reconciled with God the judge, the giver of the law whose wrath brings death. His answer is 'Christ our Passover' (1 Cor. 5:7), or as it is worked out more fully in Romans 1−5 (see pattern VII below).

VII. God of Abraham, Life-giver
            The Son sent to fulfil promise, bring life
                  Christ our Passover, ἱλαστήριον, sin-offering
            Sin to be expiated
      God the Judge, Law-giver, ὀργή

The vitality of the Passover theme, in Paul's writings and elsewhere, is that it integrates the expiatory offering with the creation of a new conjunctive covenant, frequently symbolised by the eucharist: 1 Corinthians 10 offers the eucharistic bread and cup as resolution of the opposition between God the Rock and God the Destroyer. This pattern depends on seeing the Law, or Judaism, as a manifestation of death, an idea (which in time became common to the whole church, especially Matthew and John) capable of simpler presentation than the narrative-based patterns described above, though these are of course necessary if the historical reality of Jesus (in which Paul shows so little apparent interest) is to be included.

The conclusions to which this excursion into Biblical theology points are that the Akedah is important in New Testament theology, not as a distinct and detachable motif, but as one expression of the fundamental theological perception that God is One and the source of all things, whether good or evil; and that it provides a model for resolving tensions between conjunctive and disjunctive elements in Israel's religion. In its developments it is able to relate to both the covenantal assurance that there is a promise which will some time receive concrete fulfilment (to be revealed), and the hope that those who display the faith of Abraham, or go the way of his son, are not far from God's kingdom. In Christian terms it explained why the Christ had to suffer, and why the death of Jesus can be proclaimed as final.

The salvation of the seed of Abraham

In view of the broadness of the mythic pattern which the last section has been designed to explore, there is little to be gained by trying to tie down with exact degrees of probability references in the New Testament and elsewhere to the Akedah, which are as often as not directly related to some other variant, such as Passover, or the sending of the Son, or Isaiah 52 to 53. Less has been written about the use in Jewish and Christian writings of the mythological role of the 'Son(s) of Abraham', but this too must be considered as evidence of the underlying presence of the Akedah and the whole pattern.[41]

Although, outside Genesis, there are not many references to Abraham in the Hebrew scriptures, he is more often named in the Apocrypha, and still more frequently in the New Testament.[42] The New Testament mainly reflects the Old Testament usage in referring to Abraham as 'our father' (often in conjunction with Isaac and Jacob), and as the source of God's covenant-promises (Exod. 2:24, 3:6; 1 Kgs. 18:36; 2 Chr. 20:7; Ps. 47:9; Mic. 7:20; Matt. 3:9 par.; Luke 1:55, 71; John 8:33; Acts 3:25, 7:2−32, 13:26; Rom. 4:1, 11:1; 2 Cor. 11:22; Gal. 3:16−18, Jas. 2:21). However, this basic theme is developed in two directions. First, who may call Abraham 'father'? The New Testament puts at the centre the personal characterisation of Abraham as God's friend (2 Chr. 20:7; Isa. 41:8), his servant (Ps. 105:66), his chosen one (Neh. 9:7),

---

[41] On the concept of the 'Seed of Abraham' see M. Wilcox, 'The promise of the "seed" in the New Testament and the targumim', *JSNT*, 5 (1979), 2−20; R. B. Hays, 'Have we found Abraham to be our father according to the flesh?' − Rom. 4:1, *NovT*, 27 (1985), 76−98; T. B. Dozemann, 'Sperma Abraam in John 8 and related literature − cosmology and judgement', *CBQ*, 42 (1980), 342−58.

[42] There are forty-two references in the Old Testament, half of them in five contexts (Exod. 2−4; Deut. 29−34; Josh. 24; 1 Chr. 1; Ps. 105) concerned with the renewal of the covenant; thirty-one references in the Apocryphal literature of which thirteen are in 4 Macc.; and seventy-four in the New Testament, of which forty-three occur in six limited contexts (Luke 16; John 8; Acts 7: Rom. 4; Gal. 3; Heb. 7).

and, more specifically, the one who showed *'faith'* (Gen. 15:6): to be heir of the 'man of faith' implies need for a similar outward and inward disposition, without which a person, though a Jew, is not after all a true 'son of Abraham' (Matt. 3:9 par.; John 8:31–40; Rom. 9:6ff)). In the face of Jewish resistance to the gospel and the existence of a sizeable group of pagan proselytes it became possible to conceive of the converse also, that if not all who are descended from Abraham are 'sons of Abraham' there may be those who are 'sons' without being descendants (Matt. 8:11f; Rom. 4:11–17; 2 Baruch 57:1f). But the New Testament also witnesses to a more conservative view of what constitutes sonship of Abraham, physical descent as a guarantee of God's blessing and concern, a view which is used defiantly and ironically by Paul (Rom. 11:1; 2 Cor. 11:22; Phil. 3:5f), but receives in Luke a non-ironic application to the nation (Luke 1:55, 73; Acts 3:24f) and to individuals (Luke 13:16, 16:22, 19:9).

Second, the relationship is conceived of as direct and personal. In Luke 19:9, it is not clear whether Zacchaeus shows himself to be a 'true son of Abraham' by his response to Christ, or whether it is because he is by birth a 'son of Abraham' that it is right that he should be brought back from the outcast state into which he has fallen; however, it is made plain elsewhere in the gospel (Luke 13:16, 16:22ff) that being a daughter or son of Abraham is in itself sufficient ground for God's concern, expressed through Jesus. This 'compassion' theme is distinctive to Luke and (as we shall see) to Hebrews (see also P.Az.12; 2 Macc. 1:2; 3 Macc. 6:3; Add. Est. 13:15), but it overlaps with the more common contemporary idea that Abraham, Isaac and Jacob were 'alive with God', found most notably in Matthew 22:32 (and par.) (the Sadducee's question) and Luke 16:22ff, but probably also in Matthew 8:11, Luke 13:28 (though the direct application of these is eschatological), and also in 4 Maccabees (5:37, 8:19, 16:25): the fathers are aware of the sufferings of their children, and filled with compassion on their account.[43] We may notice how often the term 'children of Abraham' is used in relation to bondage to the powers of evil: enslavement to sin (John 8:33–6), to the devil (John

[43] N. A. Dahl, 'The story of Abraham in Luke-Acts', in N. A. Dahl, *Jesus in the Memory of the Early Church* (Minneapolis, 1976), pp. 69f, comments on the similarity of outlook and terminology between Luke-Acts and 4 Maccabees which appears particularly in contexts concerning Abraham and Jewish martyrs, and reflects 'a common background' in relation to this material, despite the very different theologies of the books as a whole. See also Charlesworth, *O.T. Pseudepigrapha*, vol. II, p. 539.

8:36, 44; Heb. 2:14f), to 'elementary spirits' (Gal. 3:29–4:9), to death (Heb. 2:14f), to 'a spirit of infirmity' (Luke 13:11, 16), to the law (Gal. 4:21–31). Apparently because Abraham is the one through whom God enters into the covenant of salvation with humanity, the awareness of men and women as standing in need of salvation, in the face of death and of all the world's evils, seems to invoke this tender appellation of 'children of Abraham'. Most of the examples given above refer, in fact, to Jews, but Galatians 3:29–4:9 and Hebrews 2:14f (when seen in the context of 2:10ff) hint that, since the enslavement is a universal human state, God who is God of the Gentiles as well as God of Israel may consider them too to be 'children of Abraham'.

Through the Maccabean experience, which introduced into Judaism the martyr, the one who stands firm in his or her trust even in the face of death, in the furnace or lion's den or catapult, these two strands of thinking, initially contrasting, tend to coalesce. In the New Testament there is of course one particular 'son of Abraham' who by a sacrificial death and resurrection fulfils God's promise in Genesis 22:17f to bring blessing and salvation to Israel and indeed to 'all the nations of the earth'. The identification of Jesus as the 'seed' is most explicit in Galatians 3:16 ('seed in the singular, meaning Christ'), but it is found also in Matthew 1:1 ('Jesus Christ the son of David, the son of Abraham, cf. 1:17), Acts 3:13 ('the God of Abraham, Isaac and Jacob, the God of our fathers, glorified his servant (παῖς) Jesus, whom you delivered up') and Acts 3:25f (quoting Gen. 22:18, 'in your seed all the families of the earth shall be blessed'), and it is implied in John 8:56–8 ('your father Abraham rejoiced that he was to see my day ... Before Abraham was, I am').

The concept 'seed (sons, daughters, children) of Abraham' is used in the New Testament in four senses:

(A) Those physically descended from Abraham, the Jewish nation, Israel (but including (Ai) 'adopted sons', that is, Gentile proselytes);

(B) Those Jews whose plight calls down God's promised, covenanted compassion (a compassion which may perhaps also extend (Bi) to Gentiles in distress);

(C) Those Jews (but perhaps also (Ci) non-Jews?) who respond to God 'in faith', especially those whose faith stands firm in the face of death;

(D) One particular offspring, a son sent to fulfil the promise made to all Abraham's offspring (defined in any of the senses given above).

In 4 Maccabees both Isaac and the seven martyred sons (4 Macc. 8–14) are presented as 'sons of Abraham' in the first three senses, Jews faithful unto death who are promised salvation after death (18:23). Isaac is not regarded as filling sense D, nor as making an 'atonement', but as an archetype of A-C whom the young men imitate; and while their deaths are said to make atonement for Israel's sins (17:21f) it is not argued that their offering (which was in any case over 200 years in the past at the time of writing) had had any finality. The Christian claim, however, was that Jesus filled not only the first three categories, but by his death and resurrection fulfilled triumphantly the fourth as well, bringing about the salvation purposed by God even before Abraham, from the beginning (John 8:58; Eph. 1:3–10; 1 Cor. 2:7f). Hence the interest in Luke, and in Paul and John, in those to whom salvation is offered as 'sons of Abraham': it was as those in need (B) who recognised their hope in God and his covenant (C) mediated through Jesus (D) that they were able to be saved. Further, to be aware of Abraham as living is necessarily to be aware of the aliveness of God; his compassion is God's compassion; the redemption he represents is divine redemption. To be a 'son of Abraham' is to be also a 'son of God' in any of senses B-D. Further, if God is God of all, that is a title not intrinsically restricted to Jews: in Galatians 3–4 Paul expounds the logic by which he who is the 'seed of Abraham' (A–D) and 'Son of God' (D) enables the Gentiles to become 'sons of God' and 'Abraham's offspring' (B,C) heirs according to promise, without need of circumcision (A/Ai).

Hebrews shares much of this pattern. The book displays a conception of Jesus as Son of God, in both the 'high' sense (eternal salvation now arrived, 1:2–13) and the 'low' (Jesus as martyr 2:9f, 5:7–10, 12:1f); it characterises its readers as God's 'sons' (12:3–11) and brothers and sisters of Jesus (2:11–15) through sharing 'blood and flesh'; it presents Jesus as going through death in faith and urges its readers to do likewise (12:1–4). Those with whom Jesus is concerned, for whom salvation is worked, are specifically described as 'sons of Abraham' (2:16). The author is vividly aware of the plight of those who, being in flesh and blood (that is, the whole of humanity), are 'through fear of death subject to lifelong bondage' to the devil (2:14f), those to whom sin 'clings so close' (12:1), those who seek 'grace to help in time of need' (4:16), those who 'have fled for refuge' and need 'a strong encouragement to seize the hope' set before them (6:18). To 'human beings in their weakness' (7:28, cf. 5:2, 13:3), sons of Abraham in sense (B), God as a 'living God' (10:31) is largely an object of fear (2:1–3, 4:11–13, 6:4–8, 12:29), but his compassion is communicated through various intermediaries: angels (1:14), the agents of the Mosaic covenant (3:2, 5, 5:1–3), and emphatically now by Jesus as high priest (2:16–18, 3:1, 4:14–16, 7:25, 9:27f, 10:19–21, 12:24), on the ground that he has shared this nature of vulnerable flesh and blood. As 'pioneer of salvation' (2:10) he offers a model of faithful transcendence of death, which should enable others too to become truly sons of Abraham (sense C), imitators of his faith, even if they must first pass through torture to a 'better resurrection' (11:35).

We see that a 'Son of Abraham' martyrological scheme underlies the Christology and soteriology of Hebrews, meshing into its concepts of Jesus as 'Son of God' and 'high priest'. It is not correct, however, to understand 'seed of Abraham' solely in a 'spiritual' sense,[44] our sense (C), which is to say that what Isaac, Jesus and the readers share is retaining their faith in God in the face of death; this is the most difficult element, certainly, but it does not replace the need to fulfil the pattern as a whole. The author is at pains to point out that Jesus is 'son of Abraham' in the most physical senses: descended from Judah (7:14), sharing in blood and flesh (2:14), passing through death with 'loud cries and tears' as well as 'godly fear' (5:7). Likewise, as we have seen, the heroes in chapter 11 are, with one exception, all of the 'seed of Abraham' by physical descent as well as by faith. The significant exception to this rule is, of course, Rahab, though she is immediately included in the covenant people by means of the paschal pattern of the narrative.[45] Thus faith is defined in concrete terms, rather than through some hypothetical subjective state.

One other figure in Hebrews (Melchizedek) is explicitly *not* a 'son of Abraham',[46] but he is, in any case, offered as a model

[44] Swetnam, *Jesus*, pp. 93–7, 133–7.

[45] See above, pp. 153ff, and the literature cited in n. 13 to ch. 5.

[46] In rabbinic literature, Melchizedek is frequently identified with Shem son of Noah, and therefore regarded as one of Abraham's ancestors (Bowker, *Targums*, pp. 193, 196–9), but there is no hint of this here, Melchizedek being sharply differentiated

not for Christians but for Christ, and symbolises all those features of Christ which *differentiate* him from the 'sons of Abraham'. Whereas the Christ is 'son of Abraham' by descent (A), by being subject to the conditions of mortality (B), by greeting his death with faith (C) and through it conferring salvation (D) so that he is seen to be also the eternal Son of God, Melchizedek is not a 'son of Abraham' either genealogically (A: without father or mother) or existentially (B: neither beginning of days nor end of life), and he has therefore no need of 'faith' (C); nor is he 'son of God', though he 'resembles' him in continuing 'a priest for ever'.

How these contradictions are worked out will be explored below; the point here is that the author's use of Melchizedek does not affect the 'sons of Abraham', and what is *not* discussed is whether Christ, being a mediator 'after the order of Melchizedek' is a saviour for those outside as well as inside the Mosaic covenant. For Hebrews, as for 4 Maccabees, the question is only how those who are already sons of Abraham (A, B) can be 'truly' sons of Abraham (C). This is so because it addresses Christians of long-standing (2:3, 10:32, 13:7), whether they are Jews (by birth or conversion) who have hailed Jesus as the one Seed (D), or whether they are Christian Gentiles who have been adopted into Israel, perhaps by circumcision, more likely by baptism, as 'Abraham's offspring, heirs according to promise' (Gal. 3:29). Either way, they are treated as 'sons of Abraham' (A/Ai) and fall under the Jewish argument of the letter which is aimed at ensuring their perseverance in faith (C).

Although 'faith' is a key concept in the letter, and although its conviction that the old covenant no longer has salvific power is at least as emphatic as Paul's, the Pauline argument for the opposition of 'faith' and 'law' as modes of salvation is entirely bypassed: to use Sanders' terminology, Hebrews is all about 'staying in', not at all about 'getting in',[47] therefore it treats its readers as though they were all Jews by birth. This may, of course, be true, though we cannot exclude the possibility that 'those who draw near' (7:25) may include Gentiles too.[48] The point is that spiritual and physical modes of salvation are not contrasted but regarded as complementary elements in the totality of salvation which Christ offers. To see

from Abraham's other ancestors, who are treated, in effect, as 'sons of Abraham' before time (11:4–7).

[47] E.P. Sanders, *Paul, the Law and the Jewish People* (Philadelphia, 1983), pp. 6ff.

[48] See n. 96 to chapter 4 above.

why physicality is so important we shall turn next to a detailed examination of some passages where the death of Jesus, and his relation to those he saves by means of it, are explored.

Jesus among the children of God

The entry into death

In 2:10 we are told: 'It was fitting that [God] in bringing many sons to glory should make the pioneer of their salvation perfect through suffering.' This condensed statement raises many questions: what is meant here by 'perfect'? How does suffering 'make perfect'? Why is suffering a 'fitting' means of bringing about salvation? The first two of these questions, concerning the concept of 'perfection', will be examined later; at this point we shall look at chapter 2, verses 10–18, and the Christology implicit in the attempt made there to explain why suffering is 'fitting'.

Exegetes have found this a difficult passage. In particular, problems have been found in determining the meaning of σπέρμα Ἀβραάμ and ἐπιλαμβάνεται (v. 16), and in saying exactly what reasons the surrounding verses give for Jesus' association with the 'seed'. The view espoused by Swetnam, that in chapter 2 as in chapter 11 'seed of Abraham' has a Pauline 'spiritualised' sense, denoting 'those who have Abraham's faith', is taken also by Westcott, Bruce and Spicq, but roundly criticised by Buchanan,[49] whose defence of a more literal, physical sense of the term is, however, marred by his unconvincing attempt to read these verses (16–18) as the author's provision of a priestly pedigree for Jesus, the 'high priest'. The view adopted here is that the concept 'seed of Abraham', while open to the inclusion of Gentiles on grounds of faith (whether by means of baptism or circumcision), is not merely one of 'these archaic, biblical periphrases',[50] but on the contrary, a term which encapsulates much of what this author has to say about the human situation and divine providence.

Though they are a continuation of 2:5–9, verses 10–18 form a unified section of the text. Swetnam offers a formal analysis of this passage,[51] yielding a chiasmic structure in five parts, centred on verse

[49] Swetnam, *Jesus*, pp. 133–7; Westcott, *Hebrews*, p. 55; Bruce, *Hebrews*, p. 51; Spicq, *Hébreux*, vol. II, p. 46; Buchanan, *To the Hebrews*, pp. 36f.
[50] Moffatt, *Hebrews*, p. 37.
[51] Swetnam, *Jesus*, pp. 130ff.

13a (Christ's words, 'I will put my trust in him'), surrounded by the following pairings: verse 10 = verses 17f, verse 11a = verse 16, verse 11b = verses 14f, verse 12 = verse 13b. It has to be said that the pattern is not immediately obvious in the text,[52] and Swetnam's arrangement seems governed chiefly by the conviction that the affirmation of faith in verse 13a ('I will put my trust in him'), being theologically central, must be so structurally too. Nonetheless, there is a discernible correspondence in the logic and content of the verses he links. Both verse 10 and verse 17 begin with an axiomatic statement about Christ's death as the means of salvation, that it is 'fitting' (ἔπρεπεν, v. 10) and 'necessary' (ὤφειλεν, v. 17); second, both verse 11a and verse 16 are concerned with the origin or stock (whether literally or meta- phorically conceived) shared by Jesus and those he saves (ἐξ ἑνός, v. 11a; σπέρματος Ἀβραάμ, v. 16); third, both verse 11b and verses 14f describe the common state that he and they share, as 'brothers and sisters' (v. 11b) and 'children' (v. 14). Each of these units contains an important idea, with resonance elsewhere. We shall begin by examining what Jesus shares with those he saves, as expressed in the key terms ἐξ ἑνός and σπέρμα Ἀβραάμ.

Sharing blood and flesh

These are the relevant verses:

> verse 11a: ὅ τε γὰρ ἁγιάζων καὶ οἱ ἁγιαζόμενοι ἐξ ἑνὸς πάντες.
> verse 16: οὐ γὰρ δήπου ἀγγέλων ἐπιλαμβάνεται ἀλλὰ σπέρματος Ἀβραὰμ ἐπιλαμβάνεται.

What Jesus ('he who sanctifies') and 'those who are (being) sanctified' have in common is being 'from one' or 'out of one'. This may mean (i) 'from one *God*', indicating that, since sanctification is a divine prerogative, Jesus is not ὁ ἁγιάζων independently, but only as 'high priest in the service of God' (v. 17).[53] This, the most popular reading among commentators, establishes the unity of Christ and his people within the overarching divine order, but though it might

---

[52] This is partly because the units are very uneven in length, the second 'half' being in all but one case longer (and in one instance, vv. 11b/14f, five times longer) than the first 'half'; partly, too, because breaking the group of scriptural quotations put on Christ's lips into three parts seems less natural than taking them as one unit (or, if it must be broken up, taking them as four ideas, or two).

[53] Käsemann, *Wandering People*, p. 145; Michel, *Der Brief*, p. 80; Montefiore, *Hebrews*, p. 62; Spicq, *Hébreux*, vol. II, p. 41; Westcott, *Hebrews*, p. 50; Wilson, *Hebrews*, pp. 57f; Attridge, *Hebrews*, p. 89.

lead him to call them 'brothers' (v. 11b) it does nothing to elucidate the 'fittingness' of his suffering, asserted without explanation in verse 10. Besides, the angels too are 'from God', yet this author has hitherto insisted strenuously on the distinction between Christ and the angels (1:4–2:9), and in the corresponding verse (v. 16) will go on to emphasise the contrast, in God's perspective, between angels and 'sons of Abraham'. It must therefore be some aspect of *humanity* that Jesus shares with those he sanctifies, even if, in some way, this solidarity is to be located in the pre-incarnate nature of Christ.[54] To meet this, two suggestions are frequently made. 'From one' may mean (ii) 'from one *man*', that is, from *Adam* (cf. Luke 3:38; Acts 17:26; Rom. 5:15–19),[55] with a more metaphysical variant (iia) 'of one *race*'.[56] Alternatively, Buchanan suggests (iii) 'from one *ancestor*', that is, *Abraham*, chiefly on the basis of the connection with the 'seed of Abraham' in verse 16 and the 'many sons' in verse 10, but also the rather similar description of all Abraham's descendants as coming 'from one' (ἀφ' ἑνός) in 11:12).[57] The associations with Abraham are important, as we have seen, but this cannot be taken literally (as by Buchanan) to mean simply 'Jews by birth', or even to include circumcised Gentiles too, unless this letter is setting itself in positive opposition to the Pauline Gentile mission, of which there is no sign.[58] Swetnam surveys these options and goes on to propose a 'spiritualised' version of Buchanan's, which is in fact its converse: they are all (iv) 'of one *faith*', that is *Abraham's*.[59] This is in line with his 'spiritual' reading of 'seed of Abraham' discussed above, however this solution fixes one-sidedly on the martyrological aspect of Jesus' death, ignoring the 'flesh and blood' theme of which the passage makes much, and it can claim credence only if it is established elsewhere, which, as we have seen, it is not.

The conclusion reached above, in exploring the concept of 'son of Abraham', that it has wide associations with other terms –

[54] Moffatt, *Hebrews*, p. 32. Attridge, *Hebrews*, p. 89, sees a deliberate ambiguity, evoking a range of meanings to emphasise that 'the scope of the sonship is natural and *universal*'.

[55] Riggenbach, Seeberg, cited in Käsemann, *Wandering People*, p. 145.

[56] Snell, *New and Living Way*, p. 65; Nairne, *Priesthood*, pp. 45, 53.

[57] Buchanan, *To the Hebrews*, p. 32. The argument which follows will hope to show that Käsemann's dismissal of this option on the grounds that 'Abraham ... is not mentioned at all' is based on a narrow definition of the context.

[58] In fact, its attack on the rule of Torah is even more radical than Paul's. See Manson, *Hebrews*, ch. 2.

[59] Swetnam, *Jesus*, pp. 133ff.

including 'son of Adam', 'son of Man' and 'son of God', all of which are also possible readings of this verse – suggests that the alternatives posed may be false ones. Jesus' unity with humanity is mediated through Abraham, but in the comprehensive sense described above: he helps the 'offspring of Abraham' rather than angels (v. 16), but Abraham's children are in need of help, not because of their ancestry (A) but because of their weakness in the face of death and of 'him who has the power of death' (vv. 14f) (B), their participation in the universal human condition of mortality.

The meaning of this basic unity becomes clearer when the manner of their sharing is spelt out in verse 14:

> 'Επεὶ οὖν τὰ παιδία κεκοινώνηκεν αἵματος καὶ σαρκός
> καὶ αὐτὸς παραπλησίως μετέσχεν τῶν αὐτῶν.

This distinguishes two kinds of sharing, and two stages of Christ's relations: the 'children' ontologically 'share in blood and flesh' as their common inheritance; Jesus 'likewise partook of these' and, with them, human mortality. Whatever is meant by being ἐξ ἑνὸς πάντες (v. 11) gives Christ grounds for calling people 'brothers' but does not itself establish that brotherhood in fleshly form. If Jesus and the children are one, therefore, in being of the 'seed of Abraham', they necessarily fit this description in different sense: they in any of senses A–C (as Jews, as mortal, perhaps as rising to true faith), he in sense D, the eternally prepared bringer of salvation. What is therefore 'fitting' is that the 'Seed' should bring salvation to the 'seed' by entering into their condition in every sense, their flesh and blood, their need for faith, even to the extent of re-enacting and making actual the sacrificial 'death' (and 'resurrection') which Isaac did not in fact undergo (or underwent only figuratively, ἐν παραβολῇ).

The 'children' are in verse 16 clearly identified as 'seed of Abraham', but Jesus has already been named 'Son of God' (1:2–9). How, then, does a son of Abraham become a son of God? – by being 'truly' a son of Abraham, as we saw above, not by birth only but by trusting God and his covenant-faithfulness (his promise to Abraham) even through death itself. And, conversely, how does the son of God become a son of Abraham? – not by being born a Jew, merely, but by being born 'in the likeness of sinful flesh' (Rom. 8:3), entering into their state and undergoing the act of faith *in extremis* by which they become 'truly' sons of Abraham, and sons of God too.[60] As Abraham was tested (πειραζόμενος 11:17; cf. Gen. 22:1) and proved faithful, as his sons are constantly tested (πειραζομένοις 2:18), so he, by being tested and proved true (πειρασθείς 2:18, πεπειρασμένον 4:15), 'tested in every way as we are, but without sin', is able to establish his unity with them, and theirs with him.

The contention offered here, then, is that what Jesus and those he saves share is an existence capable of being described, in different conditions, as that of 'sons of Adam', 'sons of Abraham', 'sons of God'. The relational terms which abound in this passage ('all from one', many sons, brothers, children, seed of Abraham) appear vague only because their meaning is establishing itself in the course of the events being narrated. Isaac and his 'binding' are present, not as a specific remembered event, but as a mythic pattern, the ground of God's covenant-relation by which 'sons of men' become in all possible senses 'sons of Abraham' and so finally 'sons of God' too; he who effects this last stage is the ideal Son, who is called 'Son of Man' (2:6), brother of the 'seed of Abraham' and 'Son of God' (1:2), whose role is compounded of those of Abraham and Isaac, as well as those of the messianic king (1:8) and the ideal priest.

Salvation through death

The 'seed of Abraham' pattern necessarily gives crucial importance to the encounter with death, understood as a test of faith, and perhaps as a sacrificial offering. Confirmation of its role will be found by examining the understanding of death and salvation in verses 14b−16, and the word ἐπιλαμβάνεται in particular:

> verses 14b−15: ἵνα διὰ τοῦ θανάτου καταργήσῃ τὸν τὸ κράτος ἔχοντα τοῦ θανάτου, τοῦτ' ἔστιν τὸν διάβολον, καὶ ἀπαλλάξῃ τούτους ὅσοι φόβῳ θανάτου διὰ παντὸς τοῦ ζῆν ἔνοχοι ἦσαν δουλείας.

---

[60] Commenting on Gal. 3−4, Betz finds a fusion of two separate Christologies: (1) by being 'under the law' Christ redeems those who are 'under the Law' (4:4f); (2) by becoming subject to the 'curse of the law' Christ redeems those who suffer under its curse (3:13) (H. D. Betz, *Galatians* (Philadelphia, 1979), p. 144, n. 57). The double link through law and through Christ, however, indicates that this is not Paul's coinage for the occasion, and that identification with fleshly existence and subjection to the power of evil are closely connected ideas, as we find here, and as we find in the idea of Christ becoming 'sin' in 2 Cor. 5:21. On the uniting of the Son of God with the curse, see further n. 22 to ch. 8 below.

verse 16: οὐ γὰρ δήπου ἀγγέλων ἐπιλαμβάνεται ἀλλὰ
σπέρματος 'Αβραὰμ ἐπιλαμβάνεται.

This book does not use the Pauline language of 'slavery to sin',
but here and in two other places it makes significant reference
to those who are bound. In 10:34, having compassion on prisoners
is seen as a sign of willingness to accept similar persecution in
faith; in 13:3, remembering those imprisoned and ill-treated is
enjoined on the grounds that 'you also are in the body': these are
not only ethical examples, but symbols of a faith-response (C)
to a shared human need (B), which have behind them the bondage/son
of Abraham motif, where lifelong enslavement to the Devil resulting
from fear of death is a condition immediately associated with
that of the 'seed of Abraham'. The imagery is of battle (compare
'your struggle against sin' 12:4), perhaps depicting the son entering
the abode of the Angel of death and there defeating him (as in
John 16:11; 1 Cor. 15:26; Col. 2:15; 2 Tim. 1:10, Rev. 12:9). This
is more than a commendation or example of faith, though, for
what is defeated is not 'the fear of death' but death itself, and it
is accomplished, not 'by his death' (as JB) as a closed event (almost
as an incident in an eternal life) but *'through death'*, Jesus' entry
into the condition of death being the ground and condition (by
what means is not yet explained) of human release.[61]

Also in mind here, perhaps, is the meditation on the fate of
God's righteous one found in the Wisdom of Solomon (2:12–3:10).
There the δίκαιος, who calls himself a παῖς κυρίου (2:13), is to
be tested (πειράσωμεν 2:17, ἐτάσωμεν, δοκιμάσωμεν 2:19) and
condemned to a 'shameful death' to see if God will 'help' and
'deliver' him (ἀντιλήψεται, ῥύσεται, 2:18) and so prove him to
be his 'son' (υἱὸς θεοῦ, 2:18). Despite the machinations of their
enemies, 'the souls of the righteous are in the hand of God' (3:1)
and death, being the creation not of God but of the devil (2:24),
has no effect on them, God's faithful ones (3:9), who have been
'disciplined' and 'tested' (παιδευθέντες, ἐπείρασεν 3:5) and accepted
'like a sacrificial burnt-offering' (3:6). Here we find not only the
martyrology, the testing and the sacrificial metaphor, but also the
question of the relation of God to death. Note the ambiguity of
the phrase used in Hebrews 2:14, 'he who has the power of death'
(τὸν τὸ κράτος ἔχοντα τοῦ θανάτου), which refers to the devil

---

[61] Westcott, *Hebrews*, p. 53.

but could as well mean *God*: the appositional comment ('that is, the devil') is really necessary.

There is here a fundamental ambiguity which is opened up by the approach to the mystery of death, for it is death which throws God's covenant-faithfulness into doubt, and his distance from it, and opposition to it, has to be established. Like the author of the Wisdom of Solomon, the author of Hebrews offers a double answer, making a dualistic distinction between God and the devil (compare the dualistic versions of Passover and Akedah[62]) but also claiming that the trials suffered at the hands of evil are from God, part of the divine discipline, the testing of faith (Heb. 5:8f, 12:3–11).

Entry into death is, however, necessary – for 'it is not with angels that he is concerned but the descendants of Abraham'. The crucial verb ἐπιλαμβάνομαι has been variously understood. Its basic sense, 'take hold of', has yielded readings such as 'assume' or 'seize', readings which give insights into the way the letter as a whole is being interpreted, though inadmissible in exegesis of this passage.[63] Today it is generally understood in the sense of 'aid' or 'lead to safety',[64] a sense supported by the verses following, which reassert the idea of helping (βοηθῆσαι, v. 18) and go on to supply the means of Jesus' helping (as 'high priest'). A number of scriptural passages lie in the background here. Isaiah 41:8f (LXX) addresses Israel as παῖς μου and σπέρμα ᾿Αβραάμ ὃν ἠγάπησα οὗ ἀντελαβόμεν ἀπ᾿ ἄκρων τῆς γῆς. The two compounds of λαμβάνειν have virtually the same sense, though the idea of helping in this passage is made explicit in Luke's use of it in the Magnificat: ἀντελάβετο ᾿Ισραὴλ παιδὸς αὐτοῦ (Luke 1:54) as well as in the exhortation to 'help the weak' according to Jesus' example (δεῖ ἀντιλαμβάνεσθαι τῶν ἀσθενούντων, Acts 20:35); see also Wisdom of Solomon 2:18, in the passage quoted above, 'if the righteous man is God's son he will help him' (ἀντιλήψεται). Several further echoes of Isaiah 41:10 (LXX) are to be found in Hebrews, too: Israel is urged not to fear (μὴ φοβοῦ, cf. Heb. 2:15), nor to go astray (μὴ πλανῶ, cf. Heb. 3:10) 'because I

---

[62] See nn. 23f above.

[63] See Westcott, *Hebrews*, pp. 54f; Moffatt, *Hebrews*, pp. 36f.

[64] Montefiore, *Hebrews*, p. 66; Westcott, *Hebrews*, pp. 54f; Moffatt, *Hebrews*, pp. 36f; Bruce, *Hebrews*, p. 51. Buchanan, *To the Hebrews*, pp. 35f, offers a variant of this reading, to 'take' in the sense of 'choose' or 'prefer', which he supports by means of Isa. 41:8f (LXX); other uses of the term with a claim to lie in the background of its use here are not considered, however.

have helped you' (ἐβοήθησά σοι cf. Heb. 2:18), the help coming τῇ δεξιᾷ τῇ δικαίᾳ μου, a term which might well have a Christological sense for the author of Hebrews (cf. 1:3, 13); the passage also contains the divine promise οὐκ ἐγκατέλιπόν σε (41:9, cf. Heb. 13:5) and a reference to the earth (γῆ) as the place from which salvation is needed (41:9). This last unites it with Jeremiah 38:32 (LXX = 31:32 MT), quoted in Hebrews 8:9, in which the Exodus is described as: ἐν ἡμέρᾳ ἐπιλαβομένου μου τῆς χειρὸς αὐτῶν ἐξαγαγεῖν αὐτοὺς ἐκ γῆς Αἰγύπτου, where γῆ = the place of bondage out of which God leads his people. A third passage is also worth quoting: 'Wisdom exalts her sons, and gives help to those who seek her' (ἡ σοφία υἱούς ἑαυτῇ ἀνύψωσε καὶ ἐπιλαμβάνεται τῶν ζητούντων αὐτήν, Sir. 4:11), a verse which has much in common with the letter's thought about exaltation, sonship and 'drawing near' to God through Christ (4:16, 7:25).

Jesus 'takes to himself' those who fall under the power of evil through entering into their condition wholly: the incarnation is completed and characterised by his entry into death, death undertaken for these others, by which he becomes qualified to be representative of humanity before God and of God before humanity in need of help (2:17f).

A martyr's death

The same theme is presented briefly and vividly, in the context of Jesus' appointment as high-priest, in chapter 5, verses 7–10 where all that has been said about incarnation as solidarity with human weakness is recalled by the phrase 'in the days of his flesh', and in the confrontation with death which provokes 'prayer and supplication' and even 'loud cries and tears'. The detail of the loud crying may be compared to the cry of the psalmist uttered by Jesus on the cross (Ps. 22:1; Matt. 27:46), or to the desperate pleas of the saints in the Maccabean writings (2 Macc. 11:6; 3 Macc. 1:16, 6:14[65]) but the general situation is more clearly reminiscent of the trial of Jesus in Gethsemane, where he warned his disciples, 'Watch and pray that you may not enter into temptation (εἰς πειρασμόν)' (Matt. 26:41), and begged God, 'Father, let this cup pass from me' (Matt 26:39).[66] Though his words in Gethsemane are completed

[65] See Spicq, *Hébreux*, vol. II, p. 113.
[66] Michel, *Der Brief*, pp. 133f; Moffatt, *Hebrews*, p. 66; Spicq, *Hébreux*, vol. II, p. 113; Westcott, *Hebrews*, p. 126; R. E. Omark, 'The saving of the Saviour (Heb. 5:7–10)', *Interpretation*, 12 (1958), 39–51.

by, 'nevertheless, not as I will, but as thou wilt', Jesus is described in Hebrews 5 as praying in the most natural human way for escape from death, whether in hope of a continued earthly life or of a painless assumption into heaven.[67]

In what sense can it be said that Jesus was 'saved'? The anguish of his prayer is such undeniable testimony to his full participation in the 'flesh and blood' that is subject to 'fear of death' (2:14f), that some have argued that the salvation he received was deliverance from this *state of fear*.[68] This enables us to reconcile the author's statement that he 'was heard' with the fact that he nonetheless died (and in dying a noble death, like the Maccabean martyrs, became a good example to others in similar plight and a suitable spokesman (high priest) for them in heaven). This reading is only plausible, though, if εὐλάβεια is understood as 'terror' despite the evidence of its use in 11:7 and 12:28 where it certainly means 'reverence', and if the idea of deliverance is implanted into the phrase εἰσακουσθεὶς ἀπὸ τῆς εὐλαβείας.

But in what other way can these tears shed for his own safety qualify Jesus to be high priest of the faithful?[69] A better model is provided by Psalm 22, quoted at 2:12 and again here, understood (as by the Synoptics) as an utterance of faith. When God is described as 'he who was able to save him from death' the preposition used is not ἀπὸ θανάτου but ἐκ θανάτου, not salvation 'from' but salvation 'out of' death: granting, with Bruce and Westcott,[70] that the ideas are not wholly exclusive of each other, σώζειν αὐτὸν ἐκ θανάτου conveys the idea that Jesus prays for deliverance *in the midst* of death, from death's power. Like the psalmist, he experiences it already ('you have laid me in the dust of death' Ps. 22:15), yet is delivered 'out of death' on the third day: he was '*heard*' as the speaker in Psalm 22:24 was 'heard' (Ps. 21:25 LXX, in explicit reversal of v.3: οὐκ εἰσακούσῃ), and having been exalted (one sense of τελειωθείς[71]), is able to represent in heaven those who are or will be under death's power.

[67] Montefiore, *Hebrews*, p.98; see Héring, *Hebrews*, p.40n.

[68] Montefiore, *Hebrews*, p.99, Héring, *Hebrews*, pp.39f.

[69] See H.W. Attridge, ' "Heard because of his reverence", Heb. 5:7–10', *JBL*, 98 (1979), 90–3; J. Jeremias, 'Heb. 5:7–10', *ZNW*, 44 (1952–3), 107–11; Attridge, *Hebrews*, p.150.

[70] Bruce, *Hebrews*, p.100; Westcott, *Hebrews*, p.126.

[71] See below, pp.203ff. Michel, *Der Brief*, p.137, and Jeremias, 'Heb. 5:7–11', link the three aorists in 5:7–10 (εἰσακουσθείς, τελειωθείς, προσαγορευθείς) as functionally equivalent: being heard = being perfected = being exalted.

Jesus' representative status cannot be introduced as an afterthought, and nor is it, since it is implicit, for this letter, in his *choosing* to share in fleshly existence, so that his prayers and supplications are a priestly intercession, a sacrificial offering (προσενέγκας) made for and on behalf of his 'brethren'. Through this event (and the idea of resurrection or exaltation is, in the New Testament, essentially an anticipation of general salvation), he is said to become a 'source of salvation' (αἴτιος σωτηρίας). This term can have either a personal or an impersonal sense (Philo uses it to refer to Aaron's bronze serpent and the Red Sea, and also to Noah and God).[72] Jesus is both 'means' and 'author' of the salvation achieved through his fully personal identification with the suffering of the descendants of Abraham, and communicated to them through personal obedience in imitation of his.

The image of Jesus as martyr, faith-witness for the sake of others, through his voluntary death, appears again in chapter 12, verses 1–3: here Jesus is the greatest of the 'cloud of witnesses' described in chapter 11, who despite having set aside all hindrances have not received the promise (11:13, 39, *pace* 6:15). Jesus also has to set aside sin and 'run the race' (ἀγῶνα, cf. 4 Macc. 17:10–22) to become τελειωτὴς τῆς πίστεως, perfecting faith in himself for the sake of others, through the 'shame' of the cross and exaltation to God's right hand as victor and priest. The one puzzle here is the phrase: ἀντὶ τῆς προκειμένης αὐτῷ χαρᾶς ('for the joy that was set before him' RSV). Ἀντί may mean 'in place of': as Montefiore argues, who sees Jesus surrendering his pre-incarnate bliss, an idea he finds in Philippians 2:5–11.[73] So Buchanan argues, too, seeing Jesus surrendering his material wealth and security, as in 2 Corinthians 8:9 (literally) 'becoming poor'.[74] Paradoxically, it may also mean 'in order to secure'. This causes Nairne to picture Jesus seeking 'the joy of battle',[75] but Moffatt, Bruce and Attridge, more plausibly, see Jesus seeking the 'reward' (cf. 11:26) of heavenly bliss.[76] They are careful to add that this cannot be understood in any selfish sense: intrinsic to all these passages is a chosen identification, leading to death, so what he seeks cannot be 'something for himself alone, but something to be shared with those for whom he died as a sacrifice

[72] Cited by Bruce, *Hebrews*, p. 105.
[73] Montefiore, *Hebrews*, p. 215.
[74] Buchanan, *To the Hebrews*, pp. 208f.
[75] Nairne, *Hebrews*, p. 97.
[76] Moffatt, *Hebrews*, pp. 196f; Bruce, *Hebrews*, p. 353; Attridge, *Hebrews*, p. 357.

and lives as high priest'.[77] The joy of Christ is the eternal redemption
of those who are, or may become, 'descendants of Abraham'.

The perfecting of the high priest

The Son of Man

This writer's concept of human being is governed by the symbol
'flesh and blood', with its implications of life limited by and over-
shadowed by death, and therefore subject to fear and faithlessness.
Against this background, and overlapping each other, we have
found three patterns and three images of Christ. There is first the
martyrological image: the perfecting of the ἀρχηγὸς τῆς σωτηρίας
through the concrete experience of death, 'tasting' it for all. There
is second, the *mythological* image of the defeat of death: when
the ἀρχηγός accepts and undergoes death he defeats it and the
power of fear by which it enslaves. There is therefore, finally,
the *priestly* image: in this event Jesus sanctifies through the offering
of 'blood and flesh', the fruit of obedience (see 10:5–10) offered
'for everyone' (2:9). To this last we now turn.

The earliest and most comprehensive exploration of this perfection-
through-suffering theme, which identifies Jesus as representative
of humanity in his *death* above all, lies in the prologue to the
passage we started with. In chapter 2, verses 5–9, the author quotes
Psalm 8:4–6: 'What is man that thou art mindful of him, or the
son of man that thou carest for him?' There is no doubt that 'man'
and 'son of man' are equivalents in the Hebrew, and that the
Septuagint's wording, ἠλάττωσας αὐτὸν βραχύ τι παρ' ἀγγέλους,
means the same as the Hebrew phrase it translates: 'you have made
humanity to be only a little lower than angels (gods)'. In the early
church, the understanding of 'Son of Man' as a title for Christ,
combined with the substitution of a temporal sense of βραχύ τι
('for a little while'), offered a possible Christological reading for
both the psalm and this citation of it.[78] Exegetically this has much
to commend it, as 2:5–9 is then a continuation of the comparison
of Jesus with angels begun in 1:5–14 and interrupted by 2:1–4.
Such a Christological sense is certainly given by Paul to Psalm 8:7b
('putting everything in subjection under his feet', quoted in 2:8)
when he conflates it with Psalm 110:1b ('sit at my right hand

---

[77] Bruce, *Hebrews*, p. 353.
[78] See B. S. Childs, 'Psalm 8 in the context of the Christian canon', *Interpretation*,
23 (1969), 20–31.

until I make your enemies a stool for your feet', quoted in 1:13).[79] On the other hand 'Son of Man' is not a title used elsewhere in Hebrews,[80] and, if 'Son of Man' is being used as a known title, the argument of 2:8b–9 puts some distance between this figure and Jesus, primarily *contrasting* the vision of 'the Son of Man' in control of all things with the fact of the crucified and risen Christ.

Alternatively, we may understand 'son of man' to mean 'humanity', created lower than the angels but promised control of all things, a promise not yet fulfilled (2:8b) but in some way *anticipated* in Jesus, whose subordination to angels is manifested in his death but whose 'glory and honour' is shown in his exaltation to heaven and in his bearing 'a more excellent name' than theirs. 'Son of man', which begins by referring to humanity in general, comes to refer specifically to Jesus, not as an already-existing title but in and through the argument of these verses: Jesus *becomes* 'son of man' by establishing himself as representative of the 'children of men'. This accords with the way in which the meanings of crucial terms in 2:10–18 (brethren, seed of Abraham) are worked out through the functions they serve in that context; it accords also with the probability that Jesus' own use of the term 'Son of Man' was highly allusive and context-dependent.[81] It receives oblique confirmation from the Midrash on Psalms, which relates Psalm 8:5(4) to the Akedah, understanding the 'man' for whom God cares as Abraham, and therefore the 'son of the man' as Isaac:[82] although there is no evidence of such an association in the first century, the reference must be noted since it coincides with the son-of-Abraham pattern explored elsewhere in Hebrews, by which the son, entering into 'flesh' and 'death', becomes first a man, then representative man and finally 'source of salvation' for humanity as heavenly high priest. It is the presence of this pattern which explains why his death is 'fitting' (2:10).

As representative of humanity, Jesus fills the role assigned by Paul to 'the Last Adam', the one who, being made in the image of God, is able to restore humanity, made in God's image but spoiled from the beginning. Adam himself is not named in Hebrews,

---

[79] Compare 1 Cor. 15:25–7 and possibly Eph. 1:20–3, 1 Pet. 3:22; and see Swetnam, *Jesus*, pp. 146–9.

[80] Swetnam, *Jesus*, pp. 153–7, attempts unconvincingly to base a Son of Man Christology on (among others) an analysis of Heb. 1:2f.

[81] See Dunn, *Christology*, pp. 84–7.

[82] Midr. Teh. on Ps. 8:4, cited in Swetnam, *Jesus*, p. 160.

though the motif of *primal rebellion* is reflected through several traditions: Cain and Abel, Esau, Korah, the Wilderness provocation. For Hebrews, as for Paul, the originary act of 'disobedience' and 'disbelief' requires a corresponding 'obedience' and 'faith' to set it right. Paul does not attribute faith to Christ, though it is the primary characteristic of those who are 'in Christ', and Hebrews, too, shows a certain reserve in this respect, though it calls him 'faithful' (πιστόν 3:2). But through the theme of temptation (2:18, 4:15) and learned obedience (5:8) it becomes clear that the 'faith' which he 'perfects' for others is first his own.

These passages cohere with Philippians 2:5–11 and 1 Corinthians 15 in placing the decisive identification of Christ as Last Adam in a context of death.[83] Salvation is described as the subjugation of τὰ πάντα (2:8f), and chief among 'all things' to be subjected must be death (1 Cor. 15:25–7); similarly, when Jesus is said to be 'like his brethren in all things (κατὰ πάντα)' (2:17) and 'tempted like them in every way (κατὰ πάντα)' (4:15) it is chiefly the sharing of death that is in mind, encompassing all other similarities.[84] However, there is no idea of resurrection as transformation; rather, death is the moment of supreme moral testing, leading either to defeat or to exaltation. Death, which is the human race's punishment for Adam's sin, provides its opportunity for rising above Adamic status: those who will be 'like gods' must first be faithful to God 'in every way' appropriate to humanity.

Perfecting and consecration

The idea of 'perfection' in Hebrews is extremely complex and has lately been made the subject of a full-length study by D. Peterson. Opposing particularly one-sided 'moral' and 'cultic' interpretations of the term, Peterson argues for a 'vocational' sense of perfecting,[85] which takes account of the special character of Jesus as Son but gives real value to the 'learning obedience': suffering is the process by which Jesus comes to know and fulfil his vocation as Son of God; it 'qualifies' him to be heavenly high priest and representative of humanity before God. The concept of 'perfecting' which emerges from our study of these martyrological passages is also 'vocational' in that it gives central importance to the completion of a pattern,

---

[83] For the interpretation of Phil. 2:5ff in terms of Adam, see Dunn, *Christology*, pp. 114–21; for comments on 1 Cor. 15:45ff, see *ibid.*, pp. 107f, 123f, 127.

[84] Swetnam, *Jesus*, pp. 152f.

[85] Peterson, *Hebrews and Perfection*, pp. 66–73.

being 'son of Abraham' uniquely in every sense. This naturally has a moral side, in Jesus' obedience and faithfulness to God, in the concentration of his will on the sharing of 'blood and flesh', and therefore death, and in the fruit of this, the experiential identification with the 'seed of Abraham' which enables him to 'sympathise' and therefore to help.

How does this relate to his role as 'high priest'? The element of psychological or spiritual development which a moral understanding of perfection introduces into Christology has been welcomed and thoroughly exploited by many writers; perhaps in reaction against the dogmatic implications of this, other writers have interpreted 'perfection' in a cultic and therefore formal sense, a metaphor in which Jesus' cross and exaltation are the fulfilment of a predetermined pattern laid down in the incarnation.[86] Though Jesus' establishment in the office of sacrificing priest is fundamental to the argument of the book, his life is not presented under the guise of a cultic preparation for consecration, nor (with one significant exception) does the term consecration or any other element from the Old Testament ordination-rites appear in relation to Jesus and his appointment as high priest.[87] However, the language of the institutional cultus is sometimes employed, as when we are told that ('Today') Jesus, having been 'appointed' (5:1, 7:28), 'chosen' (5:1), 'called' (5:4) and 'designated by God' (5:10) like the sons of Aaron, 'becomes' high priest (6:20, 7:20), is 'glorified' (5:5), 'obtains this ministry' (8:6) and 'appears' in God's presence to exercise it (9:11, 26).

The exception just mentioned is this important verb τελειοῦν.[88] In the Septuagint, τελειοῦν can have the sense of 'consecrate' (Lev. 8:22, 21:10), at least in places where the context indicates that it is an abbreviation of τελειοῦν τὰς χεῖρας (Lev. 8:33), more literally rendered in other verses by πληροῦν τὰς χεῖρας (Num. 7:88): to 'fill the hands' of the priest (perhaps by providing him with meat for his first wave-offering), and thus to 'consecrate'.[89] It is clear that it is only the cultic context which gives the verb this particular technical sense: but this is precisely the subject of Hebrews

---

[86] See *ibid.*, pp. 96ff, 188ff.
[87] On the ordination-rites, see de Vaux, *AI*, pp. 346–8. However, it was argued above (ch. 4) that the idea of priestly consecration does appear in relation to Christians in the invitation to 'draw near'.
[88] See Peterson, *Perfection*, pp. 26–30.
[89] See de Vaux, *AI*, p. 346.

7:28, where Jesus, in being compared to other high priests, is said to have been 'made perfect for ever' (εἰς τὸν αἰῶνα τετελειωμένον) – or, therefore, 'consecrated for ever'. The same connection is found also in two of the passages discussed above (2:10, 5:9), in which 'perfecting' through suffering is the process by which Jesus becomes 'the source of eternal salvation' as high priest.

This is another example of the way sacrificial terminology is, in Hebrews, dangerous but indispensable. In 10:14, referring to ordinary believers, τελειοῦν is used as a synonym for ἁγιάζειν, and elsewhere 'perfecting' is used in parallel with 'purifying' (compare 9:9, 14). The 'perfecting' bestowed by Jesus can be presented as the fruit of either cultic action ('perfected by a single offering' 10:14) or moral effort (11:40): this coincides with the distinction between perfecting as a past, completed action (as in 10:14), and as a continuing process (as when the readers are urged to become τέλειος, mature, 5:14), but it also points to the fact that Christ's offering was not literally a cultic observance but, in human terms, an heroic act of faith and the completion of human self-offering foreshadowed in the myth of Isaac. To treat this as if really referring to cultic action in a technical sense would be to reduce the unique to the routine and the real to 'types and shadows'. Yet it is impossible to deny the secondary presence of consecratory ideas, as redefined by application to this event we have called the 'Testing', the 'tragic' encounter of Jesus with death which believers are called to imitate (if necessary) and to acknowledge as their situation (face to face with the power of God which is the power of death) and their redemptive sacrifice.

In other words, the concept of 'consecration' is to be found in the letter, but only in an ironic sense which tests very sharply whatever motives might lead readers to wish to conform Jesus to the pattern of the Aaronic priesthood. A measure of this is the reading of the last clause of 2:9, given in the great majority of MSS. as ὅπως χάριτι θεοῦ ὑπὲρ παντὸς γεύσεται θανάτου, but in a few MSS. and many of the Fathers as ὅπως χωρὶς θεοῦ ὑπὲρ παντὸς γεύσεται θανάτου.[90] As Bruce says, 'the reading χωρὶς θεοῦ ("apart from God") ... is so obviously *lectio ardua* as to call for consideration',[91] and it has been preferred by a number of modern

---

[90] Westcott, *Hebrews*, pp. 60–2.

[91] Bruce, *Hebrews*, p. 32. Many of those who opt for this reading take it to be a pedantic gloss, excluding God either from the process of redemption (Christ died for all, except God), or from being subjected to Jesus' power (all things are put in subjection under him, except God: cf. 1 Cor. 15:27b).

commentators. Harnack argued that the Nestorian reading of χωρὶς θεοῦ as 'apart from his divinity' accounts for its emendation on doctrinal grounds.[92] Even if textual evidence, taken alone, should incline us to the majority reading, the question is whether adopting what Moffatt calls, before rejecting it, 'an apt, but daring, sense', better explains the function of this verse in the context of the whole letter. Χωρίς is one of this author's key words: he uses it thirteen times, almost always with the sense of structural (quasi-spatial) separation.[93] The idea that Jesus died 'separated from God' is found also in 5:7ff where, it was argued earlier, he is rescued 'out of death', death understood in the Old Testament sense as the state of separation from Yahweh, being 'cut off out of the land of the living', death defined neither biologically nor psychologically, but relationally, as a state of hopelessness which can be entered while alive.[94] It is the state also into which the sacrificial victim enters when 'set apart' and conveyed into the Temple, and the gospel passion narratives similarly depict Jesus as 'among the dead' from the time of his arrest (or his anointing) up to the cry of dereliction on the cross (this is another 'synoptic' feature of Heb. 5:7ff). In contrast to the security enjoyed by the agent of institutional mediation, Jesus is high priest because he is willing to be cut off from God for the sake of his people (Isa. 53:8); in so doing he makes himself, or is made, a victim, a sin-offering (Isa. 53:10) on their behalf.

This ironic form of consecration may be compared with the hints of a regal initiation or *enthronement ceremony* discernible in Hebrews 1. Spicq describes this as a threefold action: appointment to royal office (v. 5), presentation to the subject angels (vv. 6f), enthronement at God's right hand (vv. 8–13)).[95] Outside chapter 1, the imagery of enthronement is not a strong theme in the letter, which prefers to speak of 'Jesus' than to use the quasi-kingly 'Christos'. However, it does make use of this title at certain points (3:6, 14, 5:5, 6:1, 9:11,

[92] Bruce, *Hebrews*, p. 32; Moffatt, *Hebrews*, pp. 26f. This is the most convincing reconstruction of the history of this phrase, providing a likely 'original sense' can be found for it. Though inadmissible as exegesis, the Antiochene reading was in its own terms a fine representation of the letter's thought.

[93] See further, pp. 235f below.

[94] See above, p. 94 and n. 94 to ch. 3. Cf. Swetnam, *Jesus*, pp. 140f. It is understood in this way by Montefiore, *Hebrews*, p. 59, though he gives it an unnaturally subjective emphasis ('Jesus suffered in desolation, without the comfort and consolation of his heavenly Father'), and also by Michel, *Der Brief*, pp. 72–4, who speaks, more theologically, and more objectively, of Jesus' 'Godforsakenness'.

[95] Spicq, *Hébreux*, vol. II, p. 23; Michel, *Der Brief*, p. 54; Swetnam, *Jesus*, pp. 142–5.

14, 24, 28, 10:10, 13:8, 21 and perhaps 11:26); it places psalms (explicitly ascribed to David, 4:7) on the lips of this Son (2:12f, 10:5−7), and elsewhere applies them to him and his work; and it repeatedly calls Jesus 'priest for ever after the order of Melchizedek', a description which raises the question whether it is as *priest-king* that Christ resembles Melchizedek (a possibility found particularly in 3:6, where ὁ Χριστός is faithful 'over God's house' (= Temple, dynasty, nation?) 'as a Son'). Yet these verses say almost nothing about kingship as possession of glory or power: even the divine judgement revealed at the Parousia is associated with God, not with his Christ (9:28, 12:28). In chapter 1, on the other hand, Jesus is acknowledged as first-born (1:6, compare Isaac), as Son (1:5) and heir (1:2), in words redolent of Davidic kingship, drawn from Psalm 2:7, 2 Samuel 7:14 and framed by reference to his session at God's right hand in words from Psalm 110:1 (1:3, 13).

What is remarkable is that the bringing of Christ into the world, which is elsewhere associated with abasement (1 Cor. 8:6, Rom. 15:1−3, John 13, Phil. 2:5−11), even though an abasement leading ultimately to a greater glory, is here presented as an *exaltation*: 'When he brings the first-born into the world he says 'Let all God's angels worship him' (1:6).[96] In 1:8f, in words drawn from a royal psalm (Ps. 45:6f), he is ascribed a throne, a sceptre (ῥάβδος),[97] and anointing 'beyond thy fellows (παρὰ τοὺς μετόχους σου)', a phrase which both recognises the theme of sharing (2:14) and differentiates Jesus from it. The point is simply being reversed when, in 2:9, in an after-echo of this motif, he who is 'crowned with glory and honour' is he who has cut himself off from God and 'tasted death for all'.

The aim of this chapter has been to explore a range of seminal ideas, by identifying two structural patterns found widely in Biblical literature, the myth of the testing and the seed of Abraham, and by showing how these are worked out in detail in relation to the person and work of Christ in certain key passages of Hebrews. The perception of the ambivalence of God encapsulated in the symbol of the Akedah (the God of the Binding of Isaac, both merciful and merciless), and likewise the experience of being human (Abraham's seed) in face of that deity, present the central theological issue

[96] This refers to the incarnation (cf. Bruce, *Hebrews*, p. 15; Spicq, *Hébreux*, vol. II, p. 17; Moffatt, *Hebrews*, pp. 10f), not to the parousia, as Westcott (*Hebrews*, pp. 22f) and Michel (*Der Brief*, p. 51) argue (linking πάλιν to εἰσάγαγῃ).

[97] See pp. 162f above.

of the work. Jesus, in fulfilling the role of the Son of Abraham, entering into death, offers a way towards resolving the tension which these symbols express. What, then, is the new order, the new covenant which opens up beyond that saving event?

7

THE NECESSITY OF BLOOD

In Genesis 15, God's promise to Abraham, that he will have descendants 'as many as the stars of heaven', is sealed by the bisection of a heifer, a she-goat and a ram, and in the holy space 'between the pieces', at sunset, while Abraham is in a 'deep sleep', the covenant is made and a vision of his children's future shown. Many later writers generalise this as a vision of salvation or the end of the times,[1] or specify a revelation of the heavenly Jerusalem.[2] The previous chapters have tried to show that Hebrews presents itself implicitly as such a vision 'between the pieces', in the place of sacrificial death, in which past and future are summed up in the present, and in which the barrier separating earthly and heavenly realities is cast down.

It goes without saying that any such vision is, in the Biblical perspective, a revealing of the deepest truth; however, such a fusion is hard to achieve or to sustain, and it is not surprising that interpretation falls back from it into questions about whether Hebrews is really concerned with past or future, old covenant or new, sacrifice or faith, salvation in history or in the realm of Platonic Ideas. Discussion of Jewish and Christian eschatology has been vitiated by a false disjunction between 'vertical' and 'horizontal' dimensions, supposed to represent 'Greek' and 'Hebrew' thought, 'two worlds' versus 'two ages', despite the historical confluence of the two perspectives (for example, the fact that αἰών can be used in both spatial and temporal senses[3]), and despite the concern of apocalyptic writers with heavenly figures and objects (Elijah, the New Jerusalem, the 'ten things made between the suns') both as ideal and as awaiting

[1] PRE 28 (Friedlander, *PRE*, pp. 197ff); Ps.-Philo, *Bib. ant.*, 23:6 (Bowker, *Targums*, p. 312); 2 Esdras 3:14f; FT (PV) on Gen. 15:12, 17 (Klein, *Fragment Targums*, pp. 13, 99). (In PRE 28 (Friedlander, p. 198) we are told the event occurred at Passover.)
[2] 2 Bar. 4:4: this vision is shown also to Adam and to Moses on Mount Sinai.
[3] See Lincoln, *Paradise*, pp. 171f.

manifestation in the fullness of time.[4] In the New Testament we discover not only a 'realised eschatology' but also a 'realised heaven-liness' (Eph. 2:6, Col. 3:1),[5] and instances of 'metaphysical dualism' can be accommodated within a Jewish cosmology. So also in Hebrews we find both the presence of the end (6:4f) and the presence of heaven (11:16, 12:22), but crossing such boundaries into the unseen is the function, not of 'philosophy' but of *faith* (11:1): though deeply concerned with timeless realities, its debt to Philo and the Platonic tradition he represents is at best indirect.[6] The divergence is rather between realised and futurist types of Jewish eschatology, juxtaposed here with particular sharpness. Hughes has shown that this duality is directly related to that between the book's theological and paraenetic strands ('We have such a High Priest ... therefore let us run with perseverance the race that is set before us', 8:1, 12:1), and that tension in turn, between salvation already and not yet, governs the dual treatment of the Old Testament and the covenant it mediates, as being on the one hand surpassed and nullified by Christ, and on the other remaining the 'word of God' to those who are on the way.[7]

The question of the continuity of the new covenant with the old is raised in an acute form by the symbolic procedures being studied here. The sacrificial symbolism of Hebrews insists on its own necessity. It cannot be consigned to an isolated role as a superstructural phenomenon, or as an illustration, in terms of Old Testament sym-bolism, of an essentially non-symbolic argument, even though it can be shown sometimes to be restating in cultic terms things expressed elsewhere in the letter in symbols of a different sort. For example, the reason for Jesus' death is given both in terms of a blood-sacrifice, and in the 'myth' of the Testing; in structuralist terms, both the myth and the sacrifice are elements in the *langue* of Israel's religion, which in Hebrews finds comprehensive expression through varied means. Yet if this symbolism is conceived in the essentially synchronic category of *langue*, the 'new covenant' is implicitly contained within the form of the old, as one *parole* among others: one of the uses of Hebrews in the Christian church has been to justify and buttress

---

[4] For the contents of Heaven, see Rowland, *The Open Heaven*, pp. 78ff. Rowland argues earlier (pp. 23–48) that the importance of eschatology in apocalyptic thought has been greatly exaggerated, and that its central impulse is the speculative interest in the ideal.

[5] Lincoln, *Paradise*, p. 173.

[6] For discussion of this issue, see Spicq, *Hébreux*, vol. I, pp. 39–91, and the riposte by Williamson, *Philo and the Epistle to the Hebrews*.

[7] Hughes, *Hebrews and Hermeneutics*, pp. 66–73.

a concept of a Christian separative priesthood and an interpretation of the eucharist as a Christian expiatory sacrifice.[8] The liturgical presentation of Hebrews, given here, may even seem to invite such misunderstanding. Since every renewal of the covenant presents itself liturgically, not as a renewal, but as the covenant's *fulfilment* – the translation of life into the new mode in which what liturgy foresees and foreshadows is actualised – how is the covenant's fulfilment in Christ to be distinguished from another, merely liturgical, renewal?

The new and better covenant

This author declines to promote the new order by denigrating or setting aside the old. When Hebrews casts doubt on the efficacy of the old covenant, calling it weak, its sacrifices incapable of removing sins (10:1, 11) and appropriate only to external matters (9:9f), its criticism does not amount to a dismissal, for the ancient rites are also said to suffice and sanctify, at least at that external level (9:13). A tactic more representative of the book, though, is to praise the new covenant and its agents, expressing moderated criticism of the old through the use of comparative formulae. Of these the most frequent is the word κρείττων: Christ is 'superior' to angels (1:4) and Melchizedek to Abraham (7:7); the salvation which God offers humanity is a 'better' country (11:16), a 'better' life (ἵνα κρείττονος ἀναστάσεως τύχωσιν 11:35). Above all, the new covenant is 'better' than the old (7:22, 8:6), enacted on 'better promises' (8:6), offering a 'better hope' (7:19), through 'better sacrifices' (9:23). The same point is made in other words, too: Christ's is 'a more excellent name' than that of the angels, and his ministry 'more excellent' than Aaron's (διαφορώτερον, 1:4, –ας, 8:6); the heavenly Tent is 'greater (μείζων) and more perfect' than the earthly (9:11), just as abuse suffered for Christ is 'greater wealth' than all Egypt's treasures (11:26).

In some of these instances the comparison is between the conditions of earthly life and the hope of salvation, in others between the old means of salvation and the new. In effect these comparisons are

[8] The process is already at work in 1 Clem. 40ff (see N. Lash and J. Rhymer, *The Christian Priesthood* (London, 1970), pp. 31ff), although the conceptual distinction of the eucharist as thank-offering and the priest as representative rather than mediator was retained until the fourth century, when both were reinterpreted as vehicles of the atonement flowing from Christ's death. See Young, *SI*, pp. 269ff, 278ff; J.N.D. Kelly, *Early Christian Doctrines* (London, 1958), pp. 449ff.

the same, for in this book's perspective the old covenant yielded only earthly satisfactions, and though it could point to the 'better hope' it could not bring it about. In chapters 10 and 11, the new covenant is compared with human life regarded as unfulfilled and painful for all (10:34, 11:16, 26, 35, 40), especially for those who have surrendered such earthly goods as they possess in the hope of receiving heavenly security; elsewhere earthly goods as such (including the salvation available under the old covenant) are compared with the grace of Christ. However, the striking point is that these, too, are presented as *goods*: only provisionally good, no doubt, but still things good in themselves.[9]

Yet despite its affirming of the old covenant, this book asserts that Christ is to be distinguished from Moses and Aaron, and his salvation from theirs, in kind rather than in degree. Often the context indicates that the comparative terminology is really an understated form of superlative: however 'excellent' angels are (1:4), they cannot approach the unique status ('name') of the Son, so the extravagant praise of angels succeeds in elevating the Son still higher by comparison; likewise the extent to which the heavenly 'Tent' is 'greater' than the tabernacle of Israel (9:11), is made clear when it is described as the original of which the earthly Tent is only a 'copy and shadow' (8:5).[10] More generally, the constant repetition of this relative praise, always favouring the new over the old, accumulates into an impression of a total and qualitative superiority.

There might be simpler and more direct ways of making this point, of course, but what this stylistic restraint conveys is the sense that such simpler ways would be untrue to the workings of God, and that any understanding or appreciation of the new covenant must begin from a recognition of the goodness of the world as created by God and the graciousness and power of the old covenant made with Israel. The author's criticism of the old is that it did not sufficiently show the goodness of God and the possibilities of praising him.

---

[9] Westcott, commenting on the use of διαφορωτέρας in 8:6, says that it 'recognises an exceptional excellence in that which is surpassed' (*Hebrews*, p. 218), a point which is true also, at a lower level, of the use of κρείττων and the *a fortiori* formula 'how much more' (9:14, 10:25, 29, 12:9, 25).

[10] Hurst, 'How "Platonic" are Heb. 8:5 and 9:23f?', *JTS*, 34 (1983), 156–68, argues for a non-Platonic, eschatological reading of these terms: an 'anticipatory glimpse'. The comparative force remains the same.

The symbolism of blood

It still remains a question, though, whether asserting the superiority of the new covenant is sufficient to give it control over the materials it draws from the old. Insofar as Hebrews attempts a Christian rational reordering of Israel's symbol-system, this is extremely unlikely to succeed. We saw in chapter 3 the struggle of the Priestly code to define acceptable uses and understandings of the power of blood and to outlaw others, in particular, any idea that blood possesses a divine power in itself;[11] we saw also that despite this intention the Day of Atonement appears to ascribe to blood just such an intrinsic power to purify the Temple in its state of defilement.[12]

The blood of Jesus is better than that of the old covenant in being human blood, voluntarily offered, and therefore embracing a moral as well as a ritual dimension;[13] it alone may truly be said to have intrinsic power as the body and blood of the one sent by God, a purifying and hallowing force coming into the defiled system from outside; as such, it can be claimed to be different in kind, and therefore final and unique, leaving no need of repetition.[14] That provides an answer to the problem of the Old Testament, but it leaves the framework untouched. We have seen that in the Old Testament 'purification' means separation from wrath. To describe the effect of Christ's self-offering as a perfect and final defence of humanity against God's wrath is to make it the fulfilment of the old covenant, but not properly a new one – certainly not the new covenant envisaged, from within the old, by Jeremiah and Ezekiel, and quoted here (8:8–12).

[11] See above, pp. 100–3, 105f.　　　[12] See above, pp. 99f.
[13] On moral conceptions of sacrifice, and their background, see Young, *SI*, pp. 57–66, 102–11.
[14] In what does the sin-offering of Christ consist? It is not necessary here to enter into the debate (largely conducted on confessional grounds) as to whether the sacrifice consists in Jesus' death on Calvary, equivalent to the sacrificial immolation of the victims and their offering on the altar (see Bruce, *Hebrews*, pp. 231ff; W. Stott, 'The conception of "offering" in the Epistle to the Hebrews', *NTS*, 9 (1962–3), 62–7), or with the presentation of the 'blood', signifying death, in the heavenly sanctuary (see W. E. Brooks, 'The perpetuity of Christ's sacrifice in the Epistle to the Hebrews', *JBL*, 89 (1970), 205–14; J. Swetnam, 'On the imagery and significance of Heb. 9:9–10', *CBQ*, 28 (1966), 155–73). But expiatory sacrifice has to be considered as a total action (see above, pp. 93–6) in which the death of the victim and the bringing of the symbols of death, including blood, into contact with the symbols of deity are all essential elements. Death without offering is guilty death (Lev. 17:3ff); offering without blood is not atoning (Lev. 17:11). This is the logic of Hebrews' 'double soteriology' (Käsemann, *Wandering People*, pp. 217ff): Christ is both the pioneer and conqueror of death, sharing flesh and blood' to the utmost, and the victim and high priest, the means of expiation.

Even the terms which the author chooses for affirming that this covenant transcends the old, when comparing the sacrifices appropriate to the instruments of the old covenant with Christ's sacrifice, plunge us back into the old. The dangers inherent in the language of expiatory 'blood' re-emerge in full force when Christ's one true sacrifice is described as the 'purifying of the heavenly things' (9:23). Perhaps the idea of 'purifying' the heavenly sanctuary and its instruments is a mere analogy, describing the *inauguration* of the new covenant in the same terms as Moses' inauguration of the old in the previous verses;[15] at another level, though, the suggestion that evil has entered the dwelling of God has to be taken seriously. There can be no question of assigning the 'heavenly sanctuary' to some intermediary zone, 'in the heavens', where a mythological defeat of demons can be imagined without strain.[16] That is ruled out by the argument that Christ himself is not to be given an intermediary status, as one of the angels, but identified at once with God, as the ἀπαύγασμα τῆς δόξης αὐτοῦ (1:3), and with the sons of Abraham: similarly, his sacrifice takes place in his suffering 'outside the gate' (13:12) and in heaven itself, before God, and nowhere in between. The idea that God himself has to be defended against the encroaching power of evil − and by the ritual manipulation of blood − was, it was argued, the unthinkable but inescapable message of the rite for the Day of Atonement.[17] In Israel's religion, as recast in this disjunctive mould, the sense of evil seems to operate at a deeper level than the conviction of divine mercy (Hag. 2:11−14), and the use of

[15] Buchanan, *To the Hebrews*, p. 153. Spicq's attempt (*Hébreux*, vol. II, p. 267) to substitute the 'inauguration' of the heavenly sanctuary for its 'cleansing' fails on the grammatical grounds in which it is presented (cf. Westcott, *Hebrews*, p. 270), but conceptually he is right: 'purifying a sanctuary' and 'inaugurating a covenant' are two ways of describing the same event (that is, the event depicted in 9:18−22). Earlier in the same passage (9:18), the 'purification' of the instruments of the cultus (9:22) was called 'inauguration' (ἡ πρώτη [διαθήκη] χωρὶς αἵματος ἐγκεκαίνισται), and the same word is used later to describe the establishing of the 'new and living way into the sanctuary' (10:20). Bruce, *Hebrews*, p. 219, and Montefiore, *Hebrews*, p. 160, avoid the issue by adopting a spiritualised reading: the purification of consciences.

[16] See Héring, *Hebrews*, p. 82, 'the purification of the lower reaches of heaven'; Michel, *Der Brief*, pp. 213f.

[17] See above, pp. 97ff. Nairne adopts this reading of Heb. 9:23: 'There is no place, however near to God, where his will is not working against opposition' (*Hebrews*, p. 71); as do Westcott (*Hebrews*, pp. 270f) and Johnsson, 'Defilement and Purgation', pp. 235−38. It is dismissed by Spicq (*Hébreux*, vol. II, pp. 266f), and by Moffatt (*Hebrews*, p. 132), who rather confusingly calls it both 'almost fantastic' and 'a passing lapse into the prosaic'. However, we have found that the theme of God's proximity to evil is by no means restricted to this verse.

purificatory language appears to introduce the same tension into the 'new' covenant.

However, we have been told that Christians 'have been sanctified through the offering of the body of Jesus Christ once for all' (10:10), and we are not justified in finding here a separative ethos such as would lead to a reconstructed expiatory system. Hebrews points to obviously separative features of the old covenant in order to distance itself from them: 'Into the second [Tent] only the High Priest goes…' (9:7); 'the way into the sanctuary is not yet opened' (9:8); ' "If even a beast touches the mountain it shall be stoned" ' (12:20). The author shows a deep sense of the awesomeness of God, the terror of meeting him face to face (4:12f, 10:30f, 12:28f), and is aware of the human motivation behind the separation, able, like the Aaronic priest, to 'deal gently (μετριοπαθεῖν) with the ignorant and wayward' (5:2); yet although it is taken for granted that the instruments of Israel's worship are laid down by God ('the covenant I made with their fathers', 8:9; 'the Holy Spirit indicates', 6:8), the book nowhere opens itself to the view that such a separation is a gracious gift inspired by divine compassion (as Jesus in Mark 10:5 (= Matt. 19:8) says divorce was permitted 'for your hardness of heart'). On the contrary, it is Jesus' ability to 'sympathise (συμπαθῆσαι) with our weaknesses' that distinguishes him from the Aaronic priests and furnishes encouragement to 'draw near' (4:15f), while the failure of the old system is characterised by pointless repetition (9:6, 10:11), by merely outward efficacy (9:9f, 13, 10:2–4), by having 'only a shadow of the good things to come' (10:1) and implicitly by the name of an idolatrous system, 'made with hands' (9:11) and leading away from God.

That remission of sin means, in Hebrews, not separation, but *access* to God (8:10–12, 10:19–22) is made plain by its selective treatment of the Day of Atonement, omitting the radically disjunctive symbol of the scapegoat altogether and presenting separation as an example of *limited access*, so that, on this view, the central feature of the rite is the High Priest's entry into the shrine, rather than the manipulation of the blood while there; the offering made there, though it 'purifies your conscience' (9:14), is as frequently considered from a different angle, as a *gift-offering* (8:3, 10:5–10) and therefore implicitly conjunctive.[18] Regarded as a system-affirming event, the uniqueness of the access afforded by the Day of Atonement and its occurrence only in the context of the deepest penitence emphasise the normativeness of separation in the old covenant; under the new

[18] See below, pp. 242–4.

covenant, the same entry, with a greater claim to uniqueness, serves to establish access which is unrestricted and joyful. To argue, on the basis of word-order, that in 10:20 Jesus is being described as a 'veil' between humanity and God, is to plunge Christian salvation back into the separative state of the old order: on the contrary, his flesh is the 'new and living way' *through* the veil into God's presence.[19]

The place of encounter

Those who live under the new covenant are described, at one moment, as entering God's presence; at another, with implicit echoes of the scapegoat rite, as outcasts, 'strangers and exiles' (11:13), those who have gone into the place of symbolic death, in imminent danger (4:13) and identified with those mysterious figures who, though departed from life, never die (11:5), and who, though dead, still speak (11:4) and bear or beget children (11:12, 18f). The idea of marginality can be developed in either direction: is a martyr's death a sacrifice, or is it waste? This aspect of the book is close to 1 Peter, with its collocation of the 'fiery ordeal' and 'aliens and exiles' (4:12, 2:11) with 'a chosen race, a royal priesthood, a holy nation' (2:9); but in Hebrews, although the language of access to the sanctuary (10:19ff) implies a privilege belonging specially to priests, the Christians are never explicitly addressed in these terms. Partly, this is because for this group the author needs still to emphasise the continuing pilgrimage with its demands of endurance and commitment; but more especially it is because the argument is to be taken one stage further to show that what has changed, with the transition into the new covenant, is not the Christians' position in the structure of divine–human relations, but the entire structure itself. The whole of the New Testament asserts that a new marginal phenomenon has appeared ('life in Christ', 'eternal life') and that, though ordinary life goes on, it is 'passing away', while this and this alone is the sphere of salvation. Hebrews' particular manner of screwing up the eschatological tension is the complete abolition of any sense of the 'normal' continuing alongside the redeemed (for example, by means of the selective account of Israel's history[20]), together with a

[19] This reading is supported by Buchanan (*To the Hebrews*, p. 168), Héring (*Hebrews*, p. 91), Nairne (*Hebrews*, p. 78), Spicq (*Hébreux*, vol. II, p. 316), Westcott (*Hebrews*, pp. 319–21), contradicting Bruce (*Hebrews*, pp. 247–9), Michel (*Der Brief*, pp. 229f), Moffatt (*Hebrews*, p. 143), Johnsson ('Defilement and Purgation', pp. 333–5).

[20] See above, p. 143.

presentation of the remaining 'marginal' zone as highly charged and unstable. In place of the old order, in which one could be more or less sinful, more or less good (and for which a mediating priesthood was needed) there is now only the pilgrimage which dares to draw near to the throne of grace (4:16, 6:19f, 10:19ff), or else the falling away into 'consuming fire' (12:29, 10:26−31). The contrast is presented most succinctly in 10:36−11:1, in the choice between the ὑπόστασις offered by faith and the ὑποστολή which leads to destruction.

Standing both on earth and in heaven, then, or in some intermediate zone which participates at once in the reality of both, the inescapable ambivalence of the sacred causes joyful dependency on the Holy Spirit to be accompanied by profound insecurity in the fearful possibility of falling away. That feature, though it casts a shadow over the hopefulness of the book, is true to the perception of divine power on which the whole argument rests. The same could be said of the use of imagery from the Day of Atonement, and the purification of the sanctuary, already discussed. So too, the death of Jesus is presented as a self-offering, which is both a defeat of death (and of 'him who has the power of death', 2:14), and an act of submission to death's power (2:9, 5:7−10, 12:1f). In the 'shame' of the cross and the 'suffering of death' evil triumphs − even if only temporarily or apparently. The reality of evil in the world is not to be bypassed nor overcome without cost; the union of God and humanity cannot occur, it seems, without God putting himself into the presence and power of evil (whether in heaven or in 'flesh and blood') and there overcoming both evil and the separation it has begotten in creation. When the Christians enter into the presence of God and find him both gracious and terrifying,[21] they are passing through the trial and temptation of Jesus, and meeting in themselves the risk of the event of salvation: nor is there security about its outcome (for Jesus or for them) but only fear and promise.

One vehicle of this cultic eschatology of identification and separation is the author's distinctive use of the quasi-spatial preposition χωρίς ('without', 'apart from'). It appears twelve or thirteen times,[22] and the verb χωρίζειν appears also together with related negative concepts (7:26): in only one of these instances is it used casually,[23] and in all the rest (with the possible exception of 10:28) it refers

---

[21] See the analysis of 12:18−28, pp. 144−6 above.
[22] 2:9 (a disputed case), 4:5, 7:7, 20 (twice), 9:7, 18, 22, 28, 10:28, 11:6, 12:8, 14.
[23] 7:7, probably echoing the use of ἀντιλογία in 6:16.

precisely to *structural separation*. Thus in 9:7, 18, 22 there is no
priestly offering or forgiveness 'without blood' (χωρὶς αἵματος;
χωρὶς αἱματεκχυσίας); equally, human beings cannot please God
'without faith' (11:6), nor see him 'without holiness' (12:14), nor,
by extension, be called 'sons of God' 'without discipline' (12:8).
All these are essential qualifications for occupying the same intermediate place, between human sinfulness and the holiness of God,
variously under the old and the new dispensations. This is the place
of salvation from which, it could be argued, the transgressor in
10:28, who dies 'without mercy', is being expelled, placed beyond
the reach of God's mercy. Certainly God's plan is that the patriarchs
should not inherit the promises 'apart from us' (11:40), that is,
without the creation through Christ of a people 'apart from sin' as
he is himself (χωρὶς ἁμαρτίας, 9:28), despite having been tempted
in every way (4:15).[24] For Christ's priesthood transcends that of
Aaron by being conferred 'not without an oath' (the other being
specifically 'without an oath' (7:20);[25] he is therefore the unique,
eternal priest who can remove sin completely, and return a second
time to a situation which is now 'without sin' (9:28) to bring final
salvation. If, therefore, we read at 2:9 that for our sake Jesus
tasted death 'apart from God' (χωρὶς θεοῦ),[26] this not only fits but
precisely complements the conclusion in 9:28. Unlike the earthly priest
who stands between Israel and God and who, though he partakes of
both the human and the divine, becomes less like one the more he
resembles the other (4:15, 5:2), Jesus is the priest who is fully identified with both (2:14ff, 1:2ff) yet who also shares the knowledge
of that separation, and is able to stand, with God, 'apart from sin',
and to endure a human death 'apart from God'.

It is in this middle ground of separation, thus negatively defined,
that Jesus has carved out an enclave of salvation (characterised, as
we have seen, by all those things one must be 'not without': faith,
holiness, discipline, and the blood, mercy and oath of God's grace),
where humans who are already cut off from God are called to be
cut off from sin too, and then to go forwards in faith to complete
the positive identification that Jesus has pioneered (2:10, 12:2), and,
though still vulnerably human, to stand in God's presence. From this

---

[24] See also 7:26: κεχωρισμένος ἀπὸ τῶν ἁμαρτωλῶν; ἄκακος ἀμίαντος; and
9:14: ἄμωμον. Compare the negatives in the description of Melchizedek, 7:3.
[25] That is, Jesus' priesthood, unlike that derived from Aaron, is located in the
place of sacred speaking. See ch. 8 below.
[26] See the discussion in ch. 6 above, pp. 223–5.

place of salvation and danger, as from Noah's Ark (11:7), though they can fall out they cannot go back (11:15). The author is thus not finally interested in cultic matters – the readers as 'priests', sin as ritual defilement – but in a state of eschatological peril and hope. However, the language of sacrifice is more than an extended simile: it provides a coherent and nuanced vocabulary for setting out the work's cosmology, encompassing creation, evil and the nature of humanity within the framework of a doctrine of salvation. In this cosmology, sin and sanctification, though they take in the lives of individuals and nations the form of moral qualities, are ways of perceiving the power which transcends all human life, the power which bestows both life and death, over against which all human being is set, and about which terms like 'good' and 'evil' have only relative validity.

An expiatory cultus is an instrument for the control of power. Its function is to separate the sphere of the normal from that of the divine power of the 'holy', diverting it into the fire on the altar and the priests' sphere of operation. In effect, the process either characterises the divine power as evil, destructive, to be avoided, except that God's goodwill is shown in giving the means of separation – for 'humankind cannot bear very much reality' – or else it posits a division of power between the God who gives life and health and the Devil who gives death and destruction. Jesus, according to this letter, exposes himself to the flesh's weakness, to temptation, even to death, as if they were *channels of grace*, and in so doing demonstrates (as Abraham and Moses had done, though imperfectly) that that is what they are. He is 'pioneer of faith', demonstrating that even in the experience of 'evil' God is gracious and personal, while the knowledge of God as evil and impersonal (a devouring fire) remains in the end only for those who cannot greet him as he is. However, what is determined by the human response is not God, but only our experience of him, whether we find God to be loving or wrathful, and not his being in himself. This is indicated in Hebrews by the exposition of Jesus' coming into the world, his death and exaltation, as a divine initiative, God's participation in worldly reality: the effective action which opens, within the temporal and the disorderly, a 'new and living way' into God's presence.

If the argument for this act of atonement is to carry conviction, the reality of life 'within the veil', the peculiar quality of living 'Today', in constant rededication to God, cannot be allowed to remain as something merely theoretical, or less impressive than the ease and consequences of its loss. In fact the celebration of this possibility runs all through the work, as the final chapter in this part will seek to show.

8

WORSHIP IN THE NEW COVENANT

The argument running through this book has been that the cultic elements in Hebrews are if anything more extensive and more integral to the work than is usually claimed, but that their type and meaning have been misunderstood when viewed selectively in the light of an expiatory ideology. As in early Judaism, the main impulse appears to be towards systematising, synthesising the sacral types so that each composite symbol or rite expresses the whole of the sacral system; and Hebrews continues also the tendency to move away from the expiatory centre which characterises Leviticus and towards an inclusive covenant-symbolism. This means that in the typology set out in chapter 3 (figure 3),[1] type I, personal-conjunctive, becomes the organising centre on which the rest, and especially its opposite, type IV, impersonal-disjunctive, are united. The expiatory is still of course present in Hebrews, with the sense that there remains an appropriate fear of God, but in a subordinate place corresponding to the book's argument that it has been wholly subsumed under Christ's once-for-all sacrifice. It is necessary now to examine the positive presentation of a personal-conjunctive perspective, and to show that this is a fully sacral understanding of God and his working, a different form of sacrality and not a non-sacral alternative.

Communion with God

The New Testament as a whole proclaims the message that humanity and God have now entered into a new relationship through Jesus. Without looking at the arguments it offers for how this relationship has been established, Christians are conceived as coming close to God in at least six ways:

[1] See above, pp. 77–9.

(1) by the presence of the Holy Spirit (John 14, Acts 2, Rom. 8)
(2) by becoming 'sons of God' (Rom. 8, Gal. 4, the Lord's Prayer)
(3) by being sanctified as a 'royal priesthood' (1 Pet. 2)
(4) by sharing the eucharistic anamnesis (John 6, 1 Cor. 10–11)
(5) by incorporation in 'the body of Christ' (Rom. 6, 1 Cor. 12, John 15)
(6) by offering 'spiritual sacrifices' (Rom. 12, Rev. 4f, John 4)

(1) The presence of God in the human sphere through his Holy Spirit is seen in 10:29 ('the spirit of grace') and again in 6:4 ('become partakers of the Holy Spirit'), both passages notable for the substantiality of their imagery. The 'law written on the heart' (8:10) implies this idea, though not made explicit in Jeremiah 31:31ff (but compare Ezek. 11:19).

(2) The idea of sonship is found especially in 12:3–17, but more generally in the description of the readers as 'sons of Abraham' (2:16), as 'heirs' of God's promises (6:17, 11:7) and as 'first-born' (11:17, 12:23). It is also at the root of the developed concept of 'God's household' (3:6, 10:21).[2]

(3) Though we have seen that the phrase 'royal priesthood' does not appear, no doubt advisedly, the concept governs the major theme of 'drawing near' (10:19–23, 12:18–29).

(4) The absence of any direct treatment of the eucharist is notorious:[3] against the omission, in Hebrews 7, of any mention of the bread and wine offered to Abraham in Genesis 14 by Melchizedek the type of Christ, and the polemic against 'foods which have not benefited their adherents' (13:9, cf. 9:9f), suggesting actual or potential hostility to the eucharist, it is possible to set only the argument that when the author writes 'we have an altar from which those who serve the tent have no right to eat' (13:10), the implication is that Christians do, in fact, 'eat from an altar', and in a literal sense. R. Williamson has shown how little substance there is in claims to detect a eucharistic interest in the book. It may be that

[2] See above, pp. 32–7.
[3] For a recent treatment of the literature, see R. Williamson, 'The eucharist and the Epistle to the Hebrews', *NTS*, 21 (1974–5), 300–12, who rules out a eucharistic reading, though this has been given a vigorous, if tendentious, defence in numerous recent articles by Roman Catholic writers: see, for example, two articles on Heb. 9:11: A. Vanhoye, '"Par la tente plus grande et plus parfaite..." (Héb. 9:11)', *Biblica*, 46 (1965), 1–28; J. Swetnam, 'The greater and more perfect Tent: a contribution to the discussion of Heb. 9:11', *Biblica*, 47 (1966), 91–106.

this church had no knowledge of the eucharist. Perhaps, though it had such a knowledge, the author chose not to refer to it, either because it seemed to add no sacrificial significance to what had already been said, or possibly, and conversely, because it appeared to be a dangerous, quasi-theophagous act. The theophagous understanding of the eucharist as eating and drinking Christ himself reflects a later influence from the pagan mysteries on the church's understanding of its central rite, and is not found in the New Testament itself.[4] Hebrews flatly denies the power of material sacrifices, including 'food and drink', to convey salvation to *persons* (9:9f, 10:4), and 13:9 makes clear that this does not apply only to such sacrifices made under the old covenant. Any value attaching to an 'agape' or eucharist would rest either in its being a gift-offering, or in its being a fellowship-meal, the 'meeting together' (10:25) of God's people, or, through these, in its being a kind of *zebah*-type communion by which the 'household of God' enters into his personal presence: however, that is by definition not something Christians might do, but something they *are*.

(5) The Pauline concept of incorporation ἐν Χριστῷ does not appear in Hebrews at all, though chapter 6 has shown that we do find the incarnational–Adamic Christology on which it is based.

(6) In 13:15 the readers are urged to offer up through Christ a 'sacrifice of praise' which is 'the fruit of lips that acknowledge his name'. The 'sacrifice' cannot be separated from one of two outward expressions: either the confession of the name of Christ, and holding fast to that through all difficulties (3:1, 4:14, 10:23, 11:13), or else the act of 'going out' into the unknown in faith, which includes identifying with those who suffer for God's sake (10:32–9, 11:24–6) and therefore identifying with Christ himself (12:1–3, 13:11–16). These, and not any narrow or merely verbal style of 'worship', must be what is meant by the concluding exhortation: 'let us offer to God acceptable worship, with reverence and awe' (12:28).

If Hebrews contains no reference to the eucharist it is not because the author is not interested in the relationship to God which, for later writers, it mediated, but because 'foods' could not mediate sufficiently closely or powerfully the relationship perceived here, which is strong, direct and irreducibly *personal*. The book speaks

---

[4] See Young, *SI*, pp. 243–8.

of *tasting* the heavenly gift and the powers of the age to come, on
earth and in this age, to convey the reality and substantiality of
this knowledge of God such that, for anyone who has known it
and rejected it, there is no doubt that it is *God* who is being rejected,
and not merely symbols of God, which is why no 'sacrifice for
sins' or other symbol (10:26) has any relevance. It is in connection
with such rejection that the hard impersonal images of God as
fire and storm and sword occur (6:8, 12:18, 4:12), to remind us
that 'drawing near' to the personal God to offer him a 'sacrifice
of praise', when it does not mean only a 'worship-service' but
lives cast adrift from their security, is a profoundly dangerous
activity, and one which involves risk not only to some (the priests)
at certain times (the hours of sacrifice), but places the whole community permanently in the liminal zone.

Gift exchange

Another angle from which the personal-conjunctive ideology of
Hebrews can be viewed is as the construction of an economy of
gift-exchange. For our purposes, differences between types of
gift in Greek or Hebrew sacrificial regulations (as between thank-
offerings and votive (dedicatory) offerings) are not specially relevant.
More important is the work of modern anthropologists, such as
Mauss and van Baal,[5] in demonstrating the potentiality of the
gift as a primary means of social relations which can obtain also,
by analogy and with necessary alterations, between humanity and
God. The mainspring of a gift-economy is the *obligation* of each
individual to give and to receive tokens of value, according to
known rules. These are, of course, highly variable across cultures,
but as regards sacrificial systems an essential distinction has to be
made between gift and trade. Van Baal points to these polarities,
among others (table 3).[6]

---

[5] The classic study is M. Mauss, *Essai sur le don* (Paris, 1925); this section relies
more particularly on van Baal, 'Offering, sacrifice and gift'. For gift-exchange in ancient
society, see S. C. Mott, 'Reciprocity in Hellenistic benevolence', in G. Hawthorne (ed.),
Current Issues in Biblical and Patristic Interpretation (Grand Rapids, MI, 1975),
pp. 60–72, especially pp. 64–7 where the use of gifts in relations with the gods is
discussed, and the inherent dangers of the development of reciprocity into 'trade'; see
also S. C. Mott, *Biblical Ethics and Social Change* (Oxford, 1982), p. 57, for the tension
between Hellenistic reciprocity and the Christian concept of benevolence.
[6] Van Baal, 'Offering, sacrifice and gift', p. 166.

Table 3. Economies of trade and gift

Trade	Gift exchange
Traders functionally each-others' equals	Participants not necessarily equals
Social relations weak: exhausted by completed exchange	Social relations strong: strengthened by completed exchange
Aims at the other's goods	Aims at the other's person
Goods exchanged often of low value	Goods exchanged often of high value
Strictly balanced reciprocation	Reciprocation not necessarily balanced
No obligation to trade or to accept offer	Obligation to give and to accept offer

Van Baal argues that the concept of gift employed by Tylor is essentially a *trade*, because he misinterpreted token sacrificial offerings as a corrupt trading practice, seeking big returns on a minimal investment, whereas it is a regular feature of gift-systems that non-reciprocal gifts may be exchanged between persons at different social levels. For this reason, the sacrificial code in Leviticus prescribes different offerings for poor and rich, but none of the offerings are reckoned to be commensurate with the gifts bestowed by God, in relation to which they are sometimes responses (for example, the first-fruits offering, Lev. 3) and sometimes pleas (for example, the sin-offering, Lev. 4). The tendency towards multiplication of gifts (holocausts) was criticised in chapter 3 for its propitiatory character;[7] it is also an indication of a tendency to quantification which should pertain more to trade than to the exchange of gifts. In this respect, the post-exilic dominance of the sin-offering represents a healthy return to a controlled and non-quantified concept of offering for specific needs, while the daily *tamid* remained as a prescribed thanksgiving for the creation and election of Israel.

Part of the critique of Judaism given in the New Testament consists in seeing it as a trade-system of 'works' or 'law-observance', in contrast to the Christian gift-exchange based on 'faith' and 'forgiveness' (Matt. 23; Luke 10:38–11:13, 18:9–14; Rom. 3). Hebrews too notes the sheer amount of routine exchange under the old covenant, the daily offering of 'gifts and sacrifices for sins' (5:1, 7:27, 10:11) as 'the priests go continually into the outer tent performing their ritual

[7] See above, pp. 92f.

duties' (9:6), but maintains that since 'it is impossible that the blood of bulls and goats should take away sins' (10:4, 11), it is not only a trade, but a highly inefficient one. What is received in return for all this restless giving? No perfection (7:11, 9:9), no forgiveness (10:11), no rest (3:18), no fulfilment of the promise (11:39), and no right now to eat from the 'altar' of the Christians. Though Israel has received the 'good news' (4:2), the promise (6:13), and the covenant (9:18ff), these are portrayed as either flawed (8:5) or disobeyed (2:2): it is fitting that such a system should be represented by the grim and awestruck encounter at Sinai (12:18ff) which does not hint at the graciousness which some writers perceived in the law-giving (Pss. 19, 119 for example). Such productive exchanges as there are in relation to the old covenant are pointing towards Christ and the life of 'faith': Abel's 'acceptable sacrifice' (11:4) and those of Noah and Abraham (11:7, 17–19); the blessing of Melchizedek, in return for which Abraham gave him 'a tenth of everything' (and turned Levi, a gift-receiver under the law, into a gift-giver (7:9f)).

The new covenant is characterised, by contrast, as a gift-system, in which total and spontaneous giving is abundantly rewarded. The centre of it is Jesus' once-for-all sacrifice of his own 'blood' (8:3, 9:11–14), a pure unblemished offering of the whole self which alone can 'purify your conscience' (9:14) because not a material sacrifice at all but a voluntary obedience to the will of God (10:5–7). Other acts of obedience are therefore part of that one great sacrifice: those of Abel, Abraham and Moses because done, though during the time of the old covenant, 'by faith'; and those of the readers for the same reason, 'going out' in faith, and in return receiving the abundant 'reward' (10:35, 11:26, 12:2): the 'gifts of the Holy Spirit' (2:4), the 'heavenly gift' (6:4), the 'good things that have come' (or perhaps 'are to come') (9:11),[8] the blessing and the birthright (12:17, 23), grace (4:16, 13:9) and finally 'a kingdom that cannot be shaken' (12:28) – in return for all of which 'a sacrifice of praise' is surely due (13:15).

---

[8] The division of critical opinion between these two readings is a significant index of the dynamic co-presence of future and realised eschatologies here. See Bruce, *Hebrews*, p. 198.

Sacred speech

Speech as event

A special type of gift-system, and a special mode of communion, is found in the power of sacred speech. Among goods exchanged we find divine blessing, and human praise and confession, but these are only examples from a wider field, an *economy of verbal exchange* which is the medium through which the divine–human relationship in the new covenant is largely conveyed. In form as well as content this expresses the direct and intimate communion which it inaugurates, and the *personal* nature of its 'cultus'. That which is spoken or written – and, despite the self-consciously literary character of this work, it is usually spoken[9] – and which can be understood and affirmed, replaces the brute 'burnt-offerings' as the form of obedient action:

> When [Christ] came into the world he said:
> 'Sacrifices and offerings you have not desired,
> but a body you have prepared for me ...
> Then I said, "See, I have come to do your will, O God,"
> as it is written of me in the scroll of the book.'   (10:5)

The importance of words is made clear from the start: 'God spoke of old to our fathers through the prophets but at the end of these days he has spoken to us by a Son' (1:1f), and the rest of the first chapter hangs its argument for the superiority of Christ over angels on the different things God has said, to him and to them. The declaration:

> 'You are my son,
> today I have begotten you'   (1:5)

is the first of a long series of performative or *illocutionary acts*,[10] words which *do* what they refer to, not merely describe it, so that

---

[9] M. Barth, 'The Old Testament in Hebrews: an essay in biblical hermeneutics', in W. Klassen and G. F. Snyder (eds.), *Current Issues in New Testament Interpretation*, Essays in honour of Otto Piper (London, 1962), pp. 53–78, stresses the living and authoritative quality of the divine voice, as testimony demanding response (see especially pp. 58–61). On the background and theological implications of this use of the voice, see J. H. Charlesworth, 'The Jewish roots of Christology: the discovery of the hypostatized voice', *SJT*, 39 (1986), 19–44.

[10] The concept is derived from J. L. Austin, *How to do Things with Words* (New York, 1965). See especially pp. 98ff.

here (as normally in Hebrews) the perfect tense has to be given its full stative force, describing the new state of affairs which this proclamation has brought about;[11] and similarly, in the second part of the same verse, 'he shall be to me a son' is not a prediction but a commitment. Earlier we were told that Christ is 'upholding the universe by the word (ῥῆμα) of his power' (1:3), and we can observe a repeated stylistic pattern in this letter, to supplement the use of words in what might seem a merely descriptive fashion by actions which 'witness' to their truth (2:3f). Words are acts, and actions speak.

The most convenient way of surveying this material will be to adopt the fivefold classification of illocutionary acts used by Austin, despite their admittedly 'rebarbative' names: verdictives, exercitives, commissives, behabitives, expositives:[12]

(1) *Verdictives*, for example, the giving of a verdict, judgement or estimate ('I acquit', 'I reckon'). Divine judgements should be the chief example here, though they are more discussed than given, as in 13:4: 'God will judge the immoral and adulterous' (cf. 10:26–30). On the other hand Noah, by his *action*, 'condemned the world' (11:7), and the 'word of God' is a word of discernment and judgement (4:12f).

(2) *Exercitives*, that is, the exercise of authority or influence, for example to appoint, order, warn or plead. In this group must be included Christ's 'word of power' (1:3), and the ubiquitous language of ordination and appointment, especially in relation to Christ (1:2, 5, 3:2, 5:5f, 7:21, 28, 9:27), and conversely the rejection of Esau (12:17). The pronouncements of the Torah are of this type: 'in connection with [the tribe of Judah] Moses said nothing about priests' (7:14); 'Moses ... was instructed by God, saying: See that you make everything according to the pattern that was shown you on the mountain' (8:5). The words of scripture have always this character of authoritative utterance, which automatically takes effect: ' "The Lord has sworn ..." ' – this makes Jesus the surety of a better covenant' (7:21f); the 'message declared by angels' (ὁ δι'ἀγγέλων λαληθεὶς λόγος) and the 'salvation declared (λαλεῖσθαι) at first by the Lord' (2:2f). In 9:18–20, 'when every commandment had been declared by Moses' the covenant was ratified (ἐγκεκαίνισται) with blood and the words: τοῦτο τὸ αἷμα τῆς διαθήκης: here we have

[11] See Westcott, *Hebrews*, p. 177.
[12] Austin, *How to do Things with Words*, pp. 150ff.

a performative utterance by which this substance *becomes* the 'blood of the covenant' (when spoken by one with due authority, as by Jesus at his Last Supper, of which these words may be a reminiscence).[13] In this class also we should include the authoritative non-verbal *witnessing* of God to Christ expressed in 'signs and wonders' (2:4); to Abel in accepting his sacrifice (11:4); to Enoch in his being taken up into heaven (11:5) and perhaps to the heroes of Israel 'through their faith' (μαρτυρηθέντες διὰ τῆς πίστεως 11:39). Then there are *warnings*: 'As the Holy Spirit says, "Today ... when you hear his voice, do not harden your hearts"' (3:7); 6:4f, 10:26ff and 12:25ff are solemn warnings made by the writer, distinguished from any mere private opinion by the adoption of a self-consciously authoritative tone. There are also *exhortations*, which carry some authority too, but without compelling force. Examples are very numerous (such as 12:12 ('therefore lift your drooping hands') and 13:1 ('Let brotherly love continue')); indeed the author calls the entire work a '*word of exhortation*' (13:22), a speech-act designed but, in the nature of things, not bound, to secure the readers' salvation. In 3:13 there is an example of exhortation between equals, seeking to create authority, or anyway influence for good (compare 10:24f). A *prayer* or *plea* is different only in stemming from an acknowledged position of weakness: examples include the 'prayers and supplications' of Jesus (5:7) and Esau (12:17), the requested prayers of 13:18, and a special category which changes the nature of all prayers, the *authoritative* high-priestly intercession of Christ in heaven (6:20, 7:25, 9:24, 12:24).

(3) *Commissives*, that is promises and other words which commit the speaker to certain actions. These acts by which both God and humans bind themselves in obligations to each other are the dynamic force of the 'system' under discussion. God makes his *promise* to Abraham (6:14, 11:11, 18), and promises to 'us' a new *covenant* 'written on the heart' (8:6ff, 10:15), as also he promised (to Joshua (Jos. 1:5) and to the present generation (13:5)) 'I will never fail you nor forsake you'.[14] In response there are the promises of the Christ in 2:12f ('I will proclaim thy name ...', 'I will put my

---

[13] This is particularly suggested by the change from ἰδοὺ τὸ αἷμα (Exod. 24:8) to τοῦτο τὸ αἷμα (cf. Mark 14:24). But commentators are agreed that it is no more than a reminiscence: see Héring (*Hebrews*, p. 80), Spicq (*Hébreux*, vol. II, p. 264), Westcott (*Hebrews*, p. 268), Montefiore (*Hebrews*, pp. 157f).

[14] The major theme of the *oath* with which God's promise is affirmed will be treated separately below, pp. 249–51.

trust in him') and 10:5–7 ('I have come to do thy will'), and the recurrent mention of the readers' 'confession' which is their (precarious) orientation on God, expressed in a public statement of commitment.

(4) *Behabitives*, that is, acts expressing attitudes and related to social behaviour. These are admittedly 'very miscellaneous' and most of the examples in Hebrews can more usefully be classified elsewhere; however it would include praising and thanking God (12:28, 13:15) or alternatively 'spurning the Son of God' (10:29 – but see the full treatment of the curse below[15]), greeting each other (13:24), showing hospitality (13:2), encouraging each other (10:25) or alternatively offering abuse (10:33, 11:26).

(5) *Expositives*, finally, which are reflexive first-person statements about the discourse itself, such as 'I contend that . . .' or 'I deny . . .' There are two pure examples, both direct statements of the author (6:9: 'though I speak thus . . .'; 13:19: 'I urge you . . . to do this'), though neither is especially significant. More interesting examples emerge in some scriptural quotations, if the tenses are allowed to be effectively present rather than future or past, and therefore expressing a performance rather than a description. These include the words attributed to Jesus: 'I will proclaim thy name . . .' (2:12); compare the commissive 'I will put my trust in him', 2:13), and 'then I said, "Lo, I have come . . ."' (10:7); they could include also the divine oath-making ('I swore in my wrath' (3:11)) since the content gives this aorist effectively a stative quality, continuing into the present, and the same argument applies to the author's assertion 'I have written (= am now writing) to you briefly' (13:22).

The aim of this survey has been to illustrate the variety and pervasiveness of a performative concept of speech as event, amounting to an alternative system of liminal events capable of replacing, at least in the literary context of this letter but implicitly also in the life of the Christian congregation, the physical offering of gifts and sacrifices under the old covenant. Many of these items are not in themselves 'sacred' or liminal, but acquire this character by functioning in a system directed towards God, and dominated by two types of speech-event not yet dealt with: oaths, and blessings and curses.

---

[15] See below, pp. 251–6.

Oaths and the covenant

An oath is distinguished from a promise by being uttered 'solemnly', taken out of the normal into the marginal zone. To be an oath-taker is to put oneself at risk by calling on 'the powers that be', whether those of the state, or public opinion, or the divinity, to be witnesses to a promise in order to ensure that it is kept, and presumably to correct and where necessary punish any infringement. In an oath, speech is publicly and explicitly raised to the level of event (whatever physical or verbal actions this may be signalled by), and an event with existential implications: where there are no recognised 'powers', and therefore no certainty of risk, oath-taking lapses into common promising. The form of oaths is of course culturally relative, but in both Greek and Hebrew they often take the form of a *conditional self-curse*,[16] the swearer invoking upon his or her own head penalties to follow any breach of the undertaking: these penalties may be stated, as when the king swears, 'may God do so to me, and more also, if the head of Elisha the son of Shaphat remains on his shoulders today' (2 Kgs. 6:31; see also 1 Sam. 20:13, 2 Sam. 3:35, 1 Kgs. 2:23, 20:10), or unstated, as in Ruth's oath, 'May the Lord do so to me and more also, if even death parts me from you' (Ruth 1:17, see also 2 Sam. 19:13); but even where the context is non-legal and the vagueness of the penalty shows the formula on the way to becoming a figure of speech, in every case the invocation of death is the guarantee of sincerity, placing the whole person behind the promise made.

Oaths and the finality they confer are deeply important in Hebrews, especially the unique status and revolutionary consequence of *divine* oaths. There is the reported oath drawn from Psalm 110:4:

> The Lord has sworn and will not repent:
> Thou art a king for ever after the order of Melchizedek,

quoted first at 5:6 and later cited as evidence that, in contrast to the Levitical rites of ordination, which contained no such oath and conferred only temporary priesthood, the priesthood conferred on Christ is indeed eternal. In 13:5 God's promise of faithfulness: οὐ μή σε ἀνῶ οὐδ᾽ οὐ μή σε ἐγκαταλίπω is confirmed by emphatic double-negatives. Two other oaths are given verbatim, and in these the form

[16] See de Vaux, *AI*, pp. 157f, 465f. In addition to the examples quoted below, see Job 31, the whole of which is a composite conditional self-cursing.

of the oath as a conditional self-curse is clear. First, there is God's rejection of the wilderness generation: εἰ εἰσελεύσονται εἰς τὴν κατάπαυσίν μου (3:11, quoting Ps. 94:11 LXX), usually translated 'they shall not enter my rest' but literally an uncompleted conditional clause: 'if they should enter my rest...' Second, there is God's oath to Abraham from Genesis 22:17 quoted in 6:14: εἰ μὴν εὐλογῶν εὐλογήσω σε καὶ πληθύνων πληθυνῶ σε (τὸ σπέρμα σου LXX), usually translated 'surely I will bless you and multiply you', though literally: 'if I do not bless you with blessing and multiply you with multiplying...'

How far are we justified in taking this 'self-cursing' literally, rather than as another stylistic device for emphasis? The answer is given by the very literal way the author deals with the issue of God's oath in 6:12–18, placing it on a similar footing to a human oath. Human promises being so unreliable, people need, on occasion, to make solemn oaths, and the power of oaths to settle disputes (ἀντιλογία) rests in their calling on 'one greater than themselves' as guarantor; when God also finds himself needing 'to show more convincingly to the heirs of the promise the unchangeable character of his purpose', he also resorts to an oath, and therefore needs to find a guarantor of unimpeachable integrity and irresistible power. Since he alone is qualified to be that guarantor, the situation is absurd, but if we treat this oath as literally as the author does, speaking of God's oath and his intrinsic faithfulness as 'two unchangeable things' guaranteeing the Abrahamic covenant, then we have to conclude that the penalty for non-delivery is the collapse of that authority, the dethronement of God. God's very being is at stake in this promise of blessing, without that separation which under the old covenant protected God from defilement by human impurity as surely as it kept people safe from the power of God: like Shakespeare's Antonio he has signed his bond and must, if necessary, forfeit the penalty. In confirmation of this, the passage goes on to describe God's oath as a 'hope' which enters, like Jesus, 'into the inner shrine behind the curtain' (εἰς τὸ ἐσώτερον τοῦ καταπετάσματος 6:19), bringing humanity and God dangerously face to face.

Perhaps this helps to shed further light on the sense in which death is 'necessary' for the enactment of a covenant (9:15–18). Among the many references to covenants, new and old, the word-play on διαθήκη which compares them to a secular will seems strangely banal, and the argument that Jesus' death was necessary because 'where there is a will the death of the testator must be established' (9:16) simply irrelevant to the theology of the new covenant. The passage retains its dignity only if the author is giving priority to the symbolic rather than the functional necessity of death in establishing both a private will (9:16f) and a sacred national covenant (9:18–22). It is not because while a testator lives he may change his mind, or may have need of his goods, but because a will, like an oath, has no force without the existential commitment of the swearer, the symbolically represented *standing in the place of death*: just as, in Israel's covenant, 'without the shedding of blood there is no remission of sins' (9:22). Perhaps the 'will' is introduced in verse 16, at the risk of bathos, to remind us, if we were disposed to think it, that such death might be 'merely' symbolic, for there *is* a death in relation to the new covenant (9:15) which − if anyone should be tempted to banish God to the realm of mere symbolic appearances − places the whole discussion at the existential level. God invokes a curse on himself; his son, sharing flesh and blood, offers himself wholly to God to ratify the new covenant which places humanity and God together, knowing each other, in the place of death which is also the place of life.

Blessing and curse

There are no human oaths in the letter. Those who respond to the unbreakable oaths and covenant of God do so by showing their trust: either 'going out' into the place of risk, 'in faith' that the God who has invoked the curse on himself is with them there; or by 'drawing near', believing that, if Christ is his high priest, his is a 'throne of grace' (4:16). The latter account, though cultic in its terminology, is not essentially expiatory, but presupposes an economy of prayers and benedictions, a pattern of divine–human relations expressed as blessing and curse, which must be set out here. By 'blessing' will be meant any kind of conjunctive sacral speech; by 'cursing' will be meant any kind of disjunctive sacral speech; either may be personal or impersonal. This gives us some fundamental types, which can be oriented from humanity to God (a), or from God to humanity, the latter being either direct (b), or indirect (c).

Type I, *Personal-conjunctive* blessing can be:

(a) Human praise of God − for his goodness, benefits etc.
(b) God declaring his goodwill towards human individuals or groups

(c) God's goodwill channelled indirectly:
  (i)   declared authoritatively through prophet or priest
  (ii) invoked as by the prayers of equals
  (iii) authoritatively invoked, as by a leader's prayers.

All these must be distinguished sharply from blessing Type II, *Impersonal-conjunctive*, which is the transfer of divine life-power to a person or a thing, whether this be:

(b) directly from God, as in a mechanically conceived 'providence'
(c) indirectly, by authoritative ('sacerdotal') act.

There can be no category (a) corresponding to that above, since humans cannot impart power to God, though they may claim to; nor the indirect categories (c-ii) and (c-iii) since these rely on *personal* volition for their channel.

Similarly, cursing can be Type III, *Personal-disjunctive*:

(a) Human rejection of God
(b) God's declaration of ill-will towards individuals or groups
(c) God's displeasure channelled indirectly:
  (i)   declared authoritatively by priest, shaman or other
  (ii) invoked by equals
  (iii) authoritatively invoked by those with influence.

It may also be Type IV, *Impersonal-disjunctive*, transfer of destructive power of death (limited to two categories for the same reasons as Type II above):

(b) directly from God − as in Fate, or 'the plague'
(c) indirectly, by authoritative ('sacerdotal') act.

Westcott, in a very useful review of the Biblical conception of blessing,[17] shows that though etymologically the Hebrew term *beraka* should mean 'prostration', human adoration of the greatness of God, in fact its use comes closer to the etymology of the Greek term εὐλογεῖν, 'to pronounce good towards', often synonymous with 'thank'. This turns on the fundamental distinction between worship of God as impersonal power and worship of God as personal creator: only in this personal sense can a person 'bless God' as Israel is repeatedly urged to do (Pss. 16:7, 26:12, 103:1). The blessing of persons in the Old Testament is the authoritative pronouncing of

[17] Westcott, *Hebrews*, pp. 203–10.

God's goodwill for an individual, as by the patriarchs (Gen. 27:33, 48:14ff) and later by the priests (2 Sam. 6:18, Lev. 9:22, Num. 6:22ff); and equals may invoke on each other a blessing from God which they cannot 'pronounce' (Ps. 122:6–8). Most important, when objects are blessed it is as vehicles of God's goodwill towards his human creation (Exod. 23:25, Ps. 132:15). There is only one example in the Old Testament of 'blessing a sacrifice' (1 Sam. 9:13) which is actually (as Mishnah Berakoth 6:1ff makes plain) a way of giving thanks.[18] Though the dramatic pathos of a scene such as Isaac's blessing of Jacob depends on his blessing carrying overtones of automatic efficacy which would make it unretractable, prophetic blessings are effective not through the transfer of impersonal power but because they are articulating God's goodwill: the Balak–Balaam cycle (Num. 22–4) refutes any notion of an automatic power of blessing or curse vested in humanity.[19] With curses as with blessings, there is a consistent policy of assimilating texts of non-Yahwistic origin, some of which include the idea of magical efficacy, into the cult of Yahweh, by recasting them as instruments of divine judgement.[20]

In the New Testament, the Lucan texts are particularly full of examples of blessings. These include blessing God for his salvific gifts (Luke 1:64, 68, 2:28, 24:53; also Eph. 1:3a; Jas. 3:9), and the pronouncing of God's blessing on individuals by those to whom he gives authority, Jesus (Luke 24:50, Acts 3:26), Simeon (Luke 2:34), Jesus' disciples (Luke 6:28, cf. Rom. 12:14). Εὐλογεῖν is used in the sense of εὐχαριστεῖν in relation to the Feeding of the 5,000 and the Last Supper.[21] New Testament curses are characteristically pronouncements of doom, as in the Matthaean woes (Matt. 23), and as in the disciples' command to shake from their feet the dust of those towns which reject them (Luke 10:11 par.), regardless of whether that action is interpreted as a pronouncement addressed to the townsfolk or as an 'authoritative invocation' addressed to God (see also Luke 6:28, 9:52–5). The uses of κατάρα and ἀνάθεμα, which are with two exceptions hypothetical, stand squarely within the personal conception (Matt. 25:41; Rom. 9:3).[22]

[18] *Ibid.*, p.205; Danby, *The Mishnah*, p.6.
[19] See A. C. Thiselton, 'The supposed power of words in the biblical writings', *JTS*, 25 (1974), 293–6.
[20] See Num. 5:11–28, 21:3, Deut. 7:26, 27–8, Josh. 6:17, 26, 2 Kgs. 2:24. See Ringgren, *Israelite Religion*, pp.209f.
[21] Compare Mark 14:22 with Luke 22:19; also Mark 8:6–7.
[22] The exceptions are 2 Pet. 2:14 and, more significantly, Gal. 3:10, 13: 'Christ became a curse (κατάρα) for us, who were under the Law's curse.' See n.60 to ch.6

The incidence of both motifs in Hebrews is within the mainstream of biblical usage. There is no concept of impersonal blessing of objects, nor of a priest's blessing pronounced on people, except as an expression of God's will for them. There is an element of impersonal cursing (type IVb) in the representation of God's judgement in physical terms as 'a consuming fire' (6:7f, 10:26ff, 12:29), however, what is being presented in this fashion is the personal judgement of the 'living God', and all other phenomena of cursing are thoroughly personal. They include:

(IIIa) the solemn rejection of God by humans (6:6, 10:29; both hypothetical);
  (b) God's solemn curse on Esau (12:17) and the (hypothetical) apostates (6:8, 10:30f), and on himself (3:13, 6:14);[23]
(c-i) authoritative pronouncements of God's curse, as when Noah 'condemned' the world (11:7) and Moses warned Israel 'if even a beast touches the mountain it shall be stoned' (12:20: it would have become 'ἀνάθεμα');
(c-ii) an invoked curse, in Abel's cry to God for vengeance on Cain and his kind (Gen. 4:10) if this is what is meant in Hebrews (11:4, 12:24);[24] and other invoked curses, ultimately ineffective, in the 'abuse' or 'reproach' suffered by Christ and his followers, including Moses (10:33, 11:26).

Similarly, and conversely, the concepts associated with blessing play a most important part in the book's depiction of life before God; and whereas the element of cursing is nearly always hypothetical, an irreducible negative possibility, blessing is presented as an experienced and tangible reality giving substance to the hope of further blessings, and to the fear of judgement. The blessings include:

(Ia) the praise of God by Christ and his disciples with hymns (2:12), reverence and awe (5:7, 12:28), a 'sacrifice of praise' (13:15), and their sustained 'confession' (3:1, 4:14, 10:23, 11:13);

above, and the discussion of incarnation and identification with flesh and blood in pp. 209–19. From a trinitarian perspective, in the light of the concept of 'oath' set out in the present chapter, the incarnation may be described as an unfulfilled conditional divine self-curse: 'If to live in flesh is to be accursed, may I be so also.' The resurrection is the sign that the condition is unfulfilled, and that this self-curse too is for us an unshakeable promise.
[23] On self-cursing, see above.
[24] See above, pp. 149–52.

(b) God's blessing of those who please him (6:7, 14, 11:4−6), which takes two forms: first, the concrete bestowal of heavenly gifts, namely progeny (6:14, 11:11f), defence against the Destroyer (11:28−31), the honour of sonship (12:5−11), the Holy Spirit (6:4), the 'good things that have come' (9:11: or should these be in the second group, below as being yet 'to come'?), knowledge of the truth (10:26) and of the Lord (8:6−12); second, the granting of the further but conditional promise (10:36) of entering God's rest (4:1), receiving 'a kingdom that cannot be shaken' (12:28), enrolment in the heavenly assembly of the first-born (12:23);

(c-i) blessings pronounced by authoritative intermediaries: the priest Melchizedek's blessing of Abraham his 'inferior' (7:1, 6f); the blessing of their children by the patriarchs Isaac and Jacob (11:20f), and Joseph's vision of the Exodus which, though different in form, is a similar pronouncement of divine covenanted blessings on his descendants (11:22); the 'gentle treatment' given to the 'ignorant and wayward' by the Aaronite priests (5:1f) (though their authority is now seen to be strictly limited in scope (9:9), and they should therefore more properly be counted under (c-iii); finally, the 'grace' and 'help' provided for these same human needs and temptations by Christ the High Priest (2:18, 4:16), and his final bringing of 'salvation' (9:28, cf. 5:9) to those who wait;

(c-ii) blessings invoked by equals, perhaps implied in the mutual encouragement of the Christian congregation (10:24f) and their concern for prisoners and strangers (10:34, 13:2f); this would include the intercession of the sons of Aaron, if their weakness and sinfulness (5:2f, 7:27f) were reckoned to be such as to remove from them all effective authority as intermediaries of salvation (though this is not stated) − see further below; it is Jesus' equality with the seed of Abraham that provides the ground of his ability to bless;

(c-iii) blessings invoked by those with responsibility for others: the 'speaking' of Abel the righteous (11:4, 12:24 − if this is not in fact a curse (see above)); the concluding benediction and grace given to the readers by the author (13:20f, 25);
the intercession of the Levitical priests, understood as

part of, or the purpose of, their action 'on the Godward side'[25] on behalf of humanity (5:1: perhaps, as suggested above, resulting in blessings pronounced (c-i), or perhaps even reduced by sinfulness to the invocation of equals (c-ii)) (see above);

most important of all, this includes the intercession of Christ, the eternal, unstained high priest 'seated at the right hand of the Majesty in heaven' (7:25, 8:1, 9:24), which brings 'salvation' (5:9, 7:25) − except that his will is so closely identified with that of God that his intercession (c-iii) is not in fact distinguishable from his pronouncement of blessing in imparting grace (c-i), or indeed from the saving action of God himself (b) (1:2).[26]

Although, as discussed in the last chapter, the old covenant is accorded relative and provisional value, we see here that the distinctions which it deems essential to the functioning of the Aaronid priesthood have been undermined: sharing the common sinfulness of humanity, their authority as priests is merely earthly, as of responsible equals (compare the Christian 'leaders', 13:7, 17). This abolition of distinctions is paradoxically the source of Christ's authority as high priest, his ultimate identification with the needs of flesh and blood, on the one hand, and, on the other, with the image and purpose of God.

The new priesthood

'When there is a change in the priesthood there is necessarily a change in the law' (7:12). What we find depicted in Hebrews is a major change in the law, the fulfilment and abolition at one stroke of the expiatory cultus which existed to maintain and to mediate the separation between humanity and God; and in the same action the inauguration of a new cultus based in communion, expressing the direct relationship between humanity and God, experienced now symbolically through the mediation of the one person who has passed into God's presence, but about to issue, for those who acknowledge his priesthood, in an unmediated communion with God himself. 'Today' is therefore not only the 'Day of Atonement' when the expiatory system becomes obsolete;

[25] Nairne, *Hebrews*, pp. 23, lxv–lxvii.
[26] See Bruce, *Hebrews*, pp. 154f.

and the day of the Renewal of the Covenant, in which the age-old covenantal traditions, symbols, paraeneses and promises are transformed into realities of the new age; it is also the day of the new priesthood of meeting 'face to face', a priesthood 'after the order of Melchizedek'.

The media of the operation of this priesthood are the various forms of direct communion, supplication, intercession, promise and blessing described above. Though the unity of these different types of verbal exchange is not systematically set out in the letter, this chapter has tried to show that there is nonetheless a pattern, both distinct and coherent, and that this is fitly named after that priest who, owing no allegiance to Aaron, makes his amply heralded entry in 7:1, with the act of blessing Abraham. This figure does not offer a complete blueprint, however, and to decide what it means to call Jesus 'a priest ... after the order of Melchizedek' the whole pattern has to be looked at. Though its most characteristic actions are blessing and intercession, Melchizedek does not intercede, and Jesus is never explicitly said to 'bless' (εὐλογεῖν), though he is clearly presented as a receiver of supplications who communicates in return 'grace to help in time of need' (4:16) and 'salvation to all who obey him' without need of further offerings (5:9). A chain of associations is established (figure 6).

Figure 6   A new priesthood

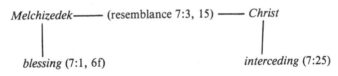

Melchizedek——— (resemblance 7:3, 15) ——— Christ

blessing (7:1, 6f)   interceding (7:25)

Here blessing and intercession are set in parallel but not explicitly linked, but we may note a further set of associations, in the preceding passage (6:14–7:1), where a symbolic equation is made between God's blessing of Abraham (6:13–15) and Jesus' entry into the inner shrine (6:19f), as interchangeable (transformational) covenant-sacrifices assuring us of hope (figure 7). In any case, the action here focussed through the rather artificial figure of Melchizedek has many more natural occurrences in the early history of Israel, in the non-institutional priestly role of the patriarchs and clan-chiefs, the prophets and charismatic judges, as well as in the less formal and more localised priesthood of a cultus based on communion-sacrifices

Figure 7   A new covenant

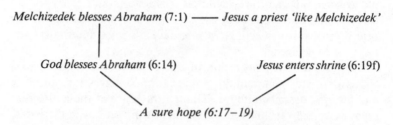

Melchizedek blesses Abraham (7:1) ——— *Jesus a priest 'like Melchizedek'*

God blesses Abraham (6:14)   *Jesus enters shrine* (6:19f)

A sure hope (6:17–19)

and the sacred oracle.[27] This style is represented here overtly by Moses (3:2–5) and the patriarchs (11:20–2), and by the Christian 'leaders' (13:17) including the book's own author, deeply concerned for the readers' needs (5:11ff, 13:20f). It is essentially the priesthood of the household-chief, preserved in the Passover, but elsewhere devolved on to sacral specialists (at first individuals, later the Aaronic institution), a priesthood in which sacral responsiblity is inseparable from personal knowledge of the suppliants and their situation, and cultic action is interwoven with the secular authority of the judge.

A hint of this style of priesthood is given even in describing the sons of Aaron in their work 'on behalf of humanity' (ὑπὲρ ἀνθρώπων) and their ability to 'deal gently' (μετριοπαθεῖν) with sinners (5:1–3). In the same passage they are said to be 'chosen', 'appointed' and 'called' (5:1, 4). This favourable depiction, which seems to give away too much to the other side of the argument, provides an initial general definition of the function and essential personal qualities of a priest, introducing Jesus' priesthood in closely similar terms (2:17f, 4:14–5:5); later the contrast between Jesus' perfect priesthood and its imperfect counterpart is articulated at length (7:11–10:18), when the latter is confined to a set of sacrifices associated with subhuman material elements which 'can never take away sins' (10:4). As we saw above,[28] the actions mentioned in 5:1–4 are hard to classify precisely, because what is presented initially as compassionate and purposeful action is later dismissed as futile and therefore deceptive. The image of a priesthood mediating between God and the 'ignorant and wayward' remains, but the task of fulfilling it falls to Jesus.[29]

---

[27] See above, pp. 38, 104f.   [28] See above, pp. 255f.

[29] On the background to this presentation of the Jewish priesthood, see W. Horbury, 'The Aaronic priesthood in the Epistle to the Hebrews', *JSNT*, 19 (1983), 43–71.

The cultic imagery causes us inevitably to think of the Christian readers, dwelling in the sacred margin, as if they were priests, but they are not called priests here (compare 1 Pet. 2:5, 9), and probably for two reasons. First, the precariousness of their position, which gives this work its occasion, would make it quite improper to suggest in any way that these readers enjoy some sacerdotal privilege or right to divine favour, or that their status was independent of God's continuing grace. Second, there is nowhere in the letter any conception of a sacrificing function for these Christians, individually or collectively. All mediation is now exercised by Jesus Christ, through whom alone they draw near. They are 'ignorant and wayward' like the rest, except that in them the divine message has met with faith (4:2). The salvation of those who have 'spurned the Son of God' is declared impossible; and there is no consideration of a third category, a group, with missionary implications, consisting of those who do not believe because they have never heard the gospel. In view of the urgency of their own danger, and the imminence of the Parousia, preserving the hope of the Christian community is the letter's overriding aim; if salvation is to be cast more widely, that is God's business, but not theirs.[30]

For the same reason, it is more plausible to argue that the eucharist plays no part at all in the author's thinking, or that it is consciously excluded, than to find in the cultic imagery grounds for detecting here a fully institutionalised sacramental practice. The 'heavenly gift' which Christians have 'tasted' (6:4) may include, and even be, for them, represented by the eucharist, but, in the context of the work's eschatological and theocentric vision, to define the 'heavenly gift' by, or restrict it to, a liturgical celebration of the Lord's Supper, is to revert to 'shadows and copies'. Sacrificial symbols are in Hebrews far more than 'mere signs' to be dispensed with; they are a fundamental part of the created order and pointers to the nature of God:[31] that is why it is possible to find in strands of the Old Testament and outside terms in which to describe the new covenant's 'cultus'. But in the new age these symbols are wholly transparent to the personal relations they mediate. This is the situation hinted at in 11:4, where the sacrifice of Abel is syntactically inseparable from and interchangeable with his 'faith'. The same is true of Noah's 'faith' and his action in 11:7, and the similarity

---

[30] There is no equivalent to the Pauline theology of history in Rom. 9–11.

[31] On the role of creation, see T. Radcliffe, 'Christ in Hebrews: cultic irony', *New Blackfriars*, 68 (1987), 494–504.

between the pattern of these verses indicates that Noah's constructing an ark for the saving of his household is effectively a sacrifice.[32] If these readers are called to 'address' the world, it is by means of such an action, in imitation of Noah and of Jesus, an action which confers the authority of those who surrender their authority and the salvation of those who dwell 'outside the Camp'.

[32] Compare pp. 179–81 above.

CONCLUSION

Whatever its outer genre may be – letter, sermon or tract – and however it was composed and delivered, Hebrews claims for itself the image of a *liturgy*, a symbolic action in the sacred sphere: more particularly, a *covenant-renewal rite*, of which the book's words comprise a long prophetic exhortation. This is its inner genre, its fictive character, and this is the medium of its proclamation of a new and better covenant. In its presentation of holiness as deeply ambivalent power, in its reworking of Israel's sacred history through the interlocking marginal roles of Priest and Stranger, in the interwoven images of the readers' situation in the sacred margin, apparently random signs are organised around an ideal image of life before God (an image very different from that of the 'Camp' which dominates the Priestly document), with a cumulative force and a shape which is far from arbitrary. It is this, rather than the argument, which provides the work with its controlling principle and its theological centre. For what in fact does the complex argument of Hebrews amount to, except another variant, or transformation into cultic language, of the common Christian kerygma of Jesus as the Christ? Such a claim – that Jesus the Christ is the high priest – has only as much force as the symbols it employs, and it is to giving force to the necessary network of symbols that the book is directed – a reinterpretation of the symbolism of the old covenant, through reapplication of its symbols in the light of Christ.

What results is a liturgical understanding of the present moment, expressing a theology of the actual presence of God. If Christians have found here warrant for a Christian expiatory cultus and a Christian separative priesthood it has been in contravention of the argument – for it insists that 'there is no longer any offering for sin' (10:18) and that Christ alone is the priestly mediator – and equally in contravention of the pattern of symbolism taken as a whole. This has been illustrated by the book's vision of worship as face-to-face relationship between humanity and God expressed in a pattern of *speech-acts* – oaths, promises, blessings, curses and praise – a whole economy of verbal exchange which is tacitly offered here in place of the subpersonal mediation of 'goats and calves', an interchange of gifts replacing the trade in blood, and which fills in the sense of what is really meant by the metaphor of 'drawing near to the throne of grace'.

In terms of the typology of sacrifice, then, Hebrews both argues for and vividly presents a theology of *communion*, but in doing so it makes two concessions which have seriously impaired its reception. First, it accepts entirely the Levitical conviction of the need for expiation, except that it argues that that need has now been met, and second it contains a small number of verses in which the fearsomeness of God is vividly and unforgettably depicted: 'our God is a consuming fire' (12:28), 'it is a fearful thing to fall into the hands of the living God' (10:31), and 'it is impossible to restore again to repentance those who have once been enlightened … if they then commit apostasy' (6:4ff), and for those who 'deliberately persist in sin' there remains only a 'fury of fire' (10:26f). A realistic account of entry into divine presence demands realism about the ambivalence of God, who is creator of death as well as life, and whom, we are told, even Moses (favourably represented in this book, on the whole) trembled to meet face to face (12:21). Problems have arisen from the interpretation of this symbolic utterance in a legal sense, but that does not mean that it can be dispensed with or that God, for Hebrews, is not a God of judgement: on the contrary, the point is that God *is* to be feared as well as loved, and that turning away from his fearfulness provides no escape. The element of risk, of pain, which Hebrews calls filial discipline (12:7), is essential both for the readers (including us) and for Jesus.

Whether we like it or not, this darkness is not an incidental feature of the book, and failure to account for its obsession with death is a major weakness of the Platonic type of reading. Death is the subject of blood-sacrifice of all sorts (including the communion-sacrifice), arising, as the anthropological evidence suggests, from a deep human need to recognise death at the boundary of human life, and so in some way to control it and remove its fear. When Jesus' death is described as an expiatory offering, a final atonement, it is proclaimed as doing exactly that; but there is also in Hebrews another, complementary account of Jesus' death, narrative in form, which has been called the 'Myth of the Testing', the 'cult-myth' of the sacrifice of covenant-renewal: 'Jesus, who for a little while was made lower than the angels, is now crowned with glory and honour because of the suffering of death, so that by the grace of God [or apart from God] he might taste death for everyone.' The story is not unique to Hebrews, but should be seen as part of a wider mythological pattern. The ambivalence of God, who appears as both destroyer and preserver, is a feature of the chief covenantal texts in the Old Testament: for example, Genesis 9:14, the bow set in the clouds as a sign of peace; circumcision as the ritual death which guarantees life; in the Passover narrative, the 'Destroyer' who is at one moment God, at another his enemy; in Genesis 22, the Lord who both gives a son and takes him away. The very existence of these texts shows that the destructive aspect of God is not cancelled out by the covenant, but held in tension through symbolic means. It has been shown that a similar tension runs through Hebrews 11, and that the sacrifice of Isaac (vv. 17f) and the Passover (vv. 28–31) provide the central moments of its narrative: 'for it is not angels that Christ is concerned with but the *sons of Abraham*'. What is sometimes called the 'low' Christology of the book is an incarnational narrative of Jesus as the eternal Son who, by sharing flesh and blood as a 'son of Abraham', enters into the place of ambivalence, death, where he is, we are told, 'tested in every way as we are, only without sin' (4:15). Is it possible, the text asks, to retain faith, to affirm the goodness of God, even in death? Jesus, by doing so, reorders ambivalence into a dualism, showing that 'he who has the power of death' is in fact the devil (2:14), and so becomes 'pioneer and perfecter of faith' (12:2), mediator of God's aid for the children of Abraham. And yet our God is still 'a consuming fire' (12:28).

These, then, are some of the lines which are opened up by reading Hebrews through the social and cosmological functions of religious symbolism.

The Letter to the Hebrews positively rejoices in whatever is anomalous or strange: it is a rich meditation on the glorious oddness of God's dealings with humanity. The chief recommendation of structuralism as an interpretative tool is its aliveness to the importance of anomaly, its ability to treat it seriously by showing that that which 'makes no sense' on its own does have meaning within a wider pattern, and is in fact frequently a guide through superficial layers of what makes obvious sense to deeper, more opaque structures of meaning. Far from obliterating particularity, a structural reading is often able to affirm the value of the irreducibly particular by placing it within a system, providing a context in which the 'harder reading' may be not only more 'authentic' but preferable. We have seen this to be true at several levels – in questions of text (2:9, 11:11) and of translation (9:16f, 23), in the interpretation of symbolic figures (7:1, 12:24) and of statements (2:10, 6:4): what we cannot understand, and what may not have been understood by the author either, may yet be a clue to a deeper meaning. It is in fact conventional historical criticism, with its pursuit of the one original sense, which tends to reduce the unusual and the ambiguous to uniformity.

One of the odder features of God's dealing with humanity is his choosing to do so through a ceaseless commerce in the 'blood of bulls and goats' and all the other paraphernalia of the Temple. The author has some critical comments to make about this, but cannot simply dismiss it as of no account, nor question that as a system of divine–human relations it is established by God and (within limits) mediates divine power. In imitating both the form and the content of the Pentateuch (the repetitive and allusive style, the axiomatic pronouncements, the dwelling on whatever is mysterious and 'fraught with background'[1]) Hebrews is confessing that it is not only interpreting scripture, but also being interpreted by it.[2] Whatever the newness of the gospel and the authority of the Christ-event which it proclaims, it must be subject to the shape and power of the old covenant, be a 'transformation' of it, spring from the same root in God. Such a two-way process of interpretation is the dynamic behind the book's sustained meditation on death, on whether death should be construed as waste or as sacrifice, on whether God is to be found in the place of death, and whether the world's evil constitutes a denial of God's covenant-faithfulness. Like much of the Old Testament, too, Hebrews is literature for a crisis, a crisis of faith which it confronts by redescription in terms of entering the gracious–dangerous presence of God.

As a book, it is anonymous for the same reason that Deuteronomy is anonymous – even assuming that its first readers knew who

---

[1] E. Auerbach, *Mimesis*, p. 12, referring to Gen. 22.

[2] See Hughes, *Hebrews and Hermeneutics*, pp. 124–30, for a discussion of the interaction of the writer's creative 'freedom' with his submission to the conceptual 'frames' of the Old Testament and the limits they set to 'permitted' interpretation.

wrote it — because it derives its authority not from its writer, even its writer as servant or apostle of God, but from conforming itself to the address of God himself, as expressed in scripture, in his Son, and in the pattern of obedient action and worship which Jesus lays down. In addressing its readers in frankly fictitious terms ('You have come to Mount Zion'), but also realistically ('Recall the former days, when you endured a hard struggle with suffering'), it depicts a world of the religious imagination, a 'possible world', in Ricoeur's phrase,[3] and asserts that it is continuous with the real world. Though it contains both argument and exhortation, the ground of that assertion is primarily symbolic, the isomorphic or mimetic relation which it establishes between itself and the scriptural tradition that it interprets, while also retaining a critical distance.

The method used in this book necessarily also attempts to establish a partial isomorphism between itself and its subject, in seeking not only to name but to reflect and realise the power of particular symbolic structures, even though it does so by borrowing from secular disciplines tools devised to provide explanations of religious behaviour, without need of religious premises. That attempt is necessary because, whatever the value of critical distance, it is not possible to perceive the meaning of symbol-systems without entering into them as our meanings, at least in imagination, and therefore being open to the question of their truth. The 'truth' of Hebrews is not the truth of its argument — as we saw in chapter 2 it is inconsistent with structural method to give that or any other single element interpretative priority, and in any case the argument that Jesus is the true high priest has meaning only in a very particular context of sacrificial symbolism — but the truth of the 'possible world' which the book, taken as a whole, opens up.

To speak of 'truth' is not to turn away from questions towards answers. There are no definitive statements to be made (any more than Hebrews has said the last word about Leviticus). But we can look for 'an objective process of interpretation which would be the act *of* the text', as Ricoeur does, in the interaction of our questions:

> to *explain* is to bring out the structure, that is, the internal relations of dependence which constitute the statics of the

[3] Ricoeur, *Hermeneutics*, p. 177.

text; to *interpret* is to follow the path of thought opened up by the text, to place oneself *en route* towards the *orient* of the text.[4]

To 'follow the path' opened up by Hebrews truthfully depends on confronting contemporary explanations (even potentially destructive explanations) of symbolism, but also, and in the light of this, taking seriously the 'possible world' which the text offers: life as worship, life as rejoicing in the dangerous—gracious presence of God. As a step towards this, the reading contained here has tried to show that *worship* is the context of the creation, and the creative appropriation, of scripture (and of Hebrews in particular) — though only worship that is able to co-exist with its own doubts and fears.

[4] *Ibid.*, pp. 161f.

BIBLIOGRAPHY

Abrahams, R.G. 'Spirit, twins and ashes in Labwor, N. Uganda', in
   J.S. La Fontaine (ed.), *The Interpretation of Ritual*, London, 1972,
   pp. 115–31
Adams, J.C. 'The Exegesis of Hebrews 6.1f', *NTS*, 13 (1966–7), 378–85
Albanese, C.L. 'The multi-dimensional mandala', *Numen*, 24 (1977),
   1–25
Alexander, T.D. 'Genesis 22 and the covenant of circumcision', *JSOT*,
   25 (1983), 17–22
Attridge, H.W. *The Epistle to the Hebrews*, Philadelphia, 1989
   ' "Heard because of his reverence", Heb. 5:7–10', *JBL*, 98 (1979), 90–3
Auerbach, E. *Mimesis*, Princeton, 1953
Austin, J.L. *How to do Things with Words*, New York, 1965
Baal, J. van. 'Offering, sacrifice and gift', *Numen*, 23 (1975), 161–78
Baaren, T.P. van. 'Theoretical speculations on sacrifice', *Numen*, 11
   (1964), 1–12
Barr, J. *Explorations in Theology 7*, London, 1980
   Holy Scripture, Oxford, 1983
Barrett, C.K. 'The eschatology of the Epistle to the Hebrews', in W.D.
   Davies and D. Daube (eds.), *The Background of the New Testament
   and its Eschatology*, Studies in honour of C.H. Dodd, Cambridge,
   1956, pp. 363–93
Barth, K. *Church Dogmatics*, 4 vols., ET Edinburgh 1936–62
Barth, M. 'The Old Testament in Hebrews: an essay in biblical hermeneutics',
   in W. Klassen and G.F. Snyder (eds.), *Current Issues in New Testament
   Interpretation*, Essays in honour of Otto Piper, London, 1962, pp. 53–78
Barthes, R. *Image-Music-Text*, ET Glasgow, 1977
   with F. Bovon, *Structural Analysis and Biblical Exegesis*, Pittsburgh
   Theological Monograph Series 3, Pittsburgh, 1974
Beattie, J.H.M. 'On understanding sacrifice', in M.F.C. Bourdillon and
   M. Forter (eds.), *Sacrifice*, London, 1980
Beck, B.E. ' "Imitatio Christi" and the Lucan passion narrative,' in
   W. Horbury and B. McNeal (eds.), *Suffering and Martyrdom in the
   New Testament*, Cambridge, 1981, pp. 28–47
Berger, P.L. *The Social Reality of Religion*, London, 1969
Betz, H.D. *Galatians*, Philadelphia, 1979
Black, M. *The Scrolls and Christian Origins*, London, 1961
Bleicher, J. *Contemporary Hermeneutics*, London, 1980

Bott, E. 'Psychoanalysis and ceremony', in J.S. La Fontaine (ed.), *The Interpretation of Ritual*, London, 1972

Bourdillon, M.F.C. and M. Fortes (eds.) *Sacrifice*, London, 1980

Bovon, F. and G. Rouiller (eds.), *Exegesis*, Pittsburgh, 1978

Bowker, J. *The Targums and Rabbinic Literature*, Cambridge, 1969
  The Sense of God, Oxford, 1973

Brooks, W.E. 'The perpetuity of Christ's sacrifice in the Epistle to the Hebrews', *JBL*, 89 (1970), 205–14

Brown, R.E. *'Rachab* in Matt. 1:5 probably is Rahab of Jericho', *Biblica*, 63 (1982), 79f

Bruce, F.F. *The Epistle to the Hebrews*, Edinburgh, 1964
  ' "To the Hebrews" or "To the Essenes"?', *NTS*, 9 (1963), 217–32

Buchanan, G.W. *To the Hebrews*, New York, 1972

Budd, P.J. *Numbers*, Waco, TX, 1984

Calloud, J. *Structural Analysis of Narrative*, Philadelphia, 1976

Charlesworth, J.H. (ed.). *The Old Testament Pseudepigrapha*, 2 vols., London, 1983–5
  'The Jewish roots of Christology: the discovery of the hypostatized voice', *SJT*, 39 (1986), 19–44

Childs, B.S. *Introduction to the Old Testament as Scripture*, London, 1979
  The New Testament as Canon: An Introduction, London, 1984
  'Psalm 8 in the context of the Christian canon', *Interpretation*, 23 (1969), 20–31

Chilton, B.D. 'Isaac and the second night', *Biblica*, 61 (1980), 78–88

Coats, G.W. 'Abraham's sacrifice of faith (a form-critical study of Gen. 22)', *Interpretation*, 27 (1973), 389–400

Cody, A. *Heavenly Sanctuary and Liturgy in the Epistle to the Hebrews*, St Meinrad, IN, 1960

Cohn, R. and J. Middleton (eds.), *Comparative Political Systems*, New York, 1967

Coleridge, S.T. *Biographia Literaria* (ed. G. Watson), London, 1956

Collins, T. 'Decoding the Psalms – a structural approach to the Psalter', *JSOT*, 37 (1987), 41–60

Crenshaw, J.L. (ed.) *Theodicy in the Old Testament*, London, 1983
  'Journey into oblivion: a structural analysis of Gen. 22', *Soundings*, 58 (1975), 243–56

Culler, J. *Saussure*, Glasgow, 1976

Culley, R.C. 'Some comments on structural analysis and biblical studies', *VT*, supplementary vol. 22 (1972), 129–42

Cullmann, O. *Early Christian Worship*, London, 1953
  The Christology of the New Testament, London, 1959

Dahl, N.A. 'The Atonement – an adequate reward for the Akedah (Rom. 8:32)?', in E.E. Ellis and M. Wilcox (ed.), *Neotestamentica et Semitica*, Studies in honour of M. Black, Edinburgh, 1969, pp. 15–29
  'The story of Abraham and Luke-Acts', in N.A. Dahl, *Jesus in the Memory of the Early Church*, Minneapolis, 1976, pp. 66–86

Daly, R.J. *The Origins of the Christian Doctrine of Sacrifice*, London, 1978
  'The soteriological significance of the sacrifice of Isaac', *CBQ*, 39 (1977), 45–75

Danby, H. (ed. and trans.). *The Mishnah*, Oxford, 1933

D'Angelo, M.R. *Moses in the Letter to the Hebrews*, SBL Dissertation Series 42, Missoula, 1979

Davies, D. 'An interpretation of sacrifice in Leviticus', *ZAW*, 89 (1977), 387–99

Davies, P.R. and B. Chilton 'The Aqedah: a revised tradition-history', *CBQ*, 40 (1978), 514–46

Davies, W.D. 'The Dead Sea Scrolls and Christian origins', in W.D. Davies, *Christian Origins and Judaism*, London, 1962, pp.97–117

Deaut, R. le. *La Nuit pascale* Analecta Biblica, Rome, 1963

Derrida, J. *Of Grammatology*, ET Baltimore, 1976
Writing and Difference, ET London, 1978

Dewar, L. 'The biblical use of the term "Blood"', *JTS*, 4 (1953), 204–8

Dey, L.K.K. *The Intermediary World and Patterns of Perfection in Philo and Hebrews*, SBL Dissertation Series 25, Missoula, 1975

Diez Macho, A. (ed. and trans.). *Neophyti I*, 2 vols., Madrid, 1970–1

Doty, W.G. 'Linguistics and biblical criticism', *JAAR*, 41 (1973), 114–21

Douglas, M. *Purity and Danger*, London, 1966
Natural Symbols, 2nd edn, London, 1973

Downing, J. 'Jesus and martyrdom', *JTS*, 14 (1963), 29–93

Dozeman, T.B. 'Sperma Abraam in John 8 and related literature – cosmology and judgement', *CBQ*, 42 (1980), 342–58

Dunn, J.D.G. *Christology in the Making*, London, 1980

Dyson-Hudson, N. 'Structure and infrastructure in primitive society', in R. Macksey and E. Donato (ed.), *The Structuralist Controversy*, Baltimore, 1972, pp.218–46

Eichrodt, W. *Theology of the Old Testament*, ET London, 1961–7

Eliade, M. *Patterns in Comparative Religion*, London, 1958
The Myth of the Eternal Return, London, 1989

Elliott, J.H. *A Home for the Homeless*, London, 1982

Encyclopedia Judaica, Jerusalem, 1972

Fernandez, J. 'The mission of metaphor in expressive culture', *Current Anthropology*, 15 (1974), 119–47

Filson, F.V. *'Yesterday': A Study of Hebrews in the Light of Ch.13*, Studies in Biblical Theology 4, London, 1967
'The significance of the early house churches', *JBL*, 58 (1939), 105–12

Finley, M.I. *The Ancient Economy*, London, 1973

Fitzmyer, J.A. *Essays on the Semitic Background of the New Testament*, London, 1971

Flusser, D. 'The Dead Sea sect and pre-Pauline Christianity', *Scripta Hierosolymitana*, 4 (1958), 215–66

Ford, J.M. 'Was Montanism a Jewish-Christian heresy?', *JEH*, 17 (1966), 145–58

Freedman, H. (ed. and trans.). *Genesis Rabbah*, London, 1939

Frend, W.H.C. 'The ecology of the early Christianities', in G. Irvine (ed.), *Christianity in its Social Context*, London, 1967, pp.15–28
'Town and countryside in early Christianity', in D. Baker (ed.), *Studies in Church History*, vol.XVI, Oxford, 1979, pp.27–42
'The winning of the countryside', *JRH*, 18 (1967), 1–14

Friedlander, G. (ed. and trans.). *Pirke de Rabbi Eliezer*, New York, 1965
Fuller, R. H. *The Foundations of New Testament Christology*, Glasgow, 1965
Gadamer, H.-G. *Truth and Method*, 2nd edn, ET London, 1979
Gager, J. G. *Kingdom and Community*, Englewood Cliffs, 1975
Gardner, H. *The Quest for Mind*, London, 1976
Geertz, C. *The Interpretation of Cultures*, New York, 1973
Girard, R. 'Differentiation and reciprocity in Lévi-Strauss and contemporary theory', in R. Girard, *'To Double Business Bound'*, London, 1978
Gluckman, M. 'Rituals of rebellion in S. E. Africa', in M. Gluckman, *Order and Rebellion in Tribal Africa*, London, 1963, pp. 110–36
Greenwood, D. *Structuralism and the Biblical Text*, Berlin, 1985
Grintz, J. M. ' "Do not eat of the blood" ', *Annual of the Swedish Theological Institute*, 8 (1972), 78–105
Habermas, J. 'The hermeneutic claim to universality', ET in J. Bleicher, *Contemporary Hermeneutics*, London, 1980, pp. 181–211
Hanson, A. T. 'Rahab the harlot in early Christian tradition', *JSNT*, 1 (1978), 53–60
Hardy, D. W. and D. F. Ford *Jubilate*, London, 1984
Hays, R. B. ' "Have we found Abraham to be our forefather according to the flesh?" – Rom 4:1', *NovT*, 27 (1985), 76–98
Hayward, R. 'The present state of research into the targumic account of the sacrifice of Isaac', *JJS*, 32 (1981), 127–50
'The sacrifice of Isaac and the Jewish polemic against Christianity', *CBQ*, 52 (1990), 286–306
Heider, G. C. *The Cult of Molek*, Sheffield, 1985
Hengel, M. *Judaism and Hellenism*, 2 vols., ET London, 1974
Héring, J. *The Epistle to the Hebrews*, ET London, 1970
Higgins, A. J. B. 'The priestly Messiah', *NTS*, 13 (1966–7), 211–39
Hirsch, E. D. *Validity in Interpretation*, London, 1967
Hofius, O. 'Στόματα μαχαίρης (Heb. 11:34)', *ZNW*, 62 (1971), 129f
Horbury, W. 'The Aaronic priesthood in the Epistle to the Hebrews', *JSNT*, 19 (1983), 43–71
Horton, F. L. *The Melchizedek Tradition*, SNTS Monograph Series 30, Cambridge, 1976
Howlett, D. *The Essenes and Christianity*, New York, 1957
Hubert, H. and M. Mauss. *Sacrifice – Its Nature and Function*, ET London, 1964
Hughes, G. *Hebrews and Hermeneutics*, SNTS Monograph Series 36, Cambridge, 1979
Hurst, L. D. *The Epistle to the Hebrews: Its Background of Thought*, SNTS Monograph Series 65, Cambridge, 1990
'How "Platonic" are Heb. 8:5 and 9:23?', *JTS*, 34 (1983), 156–68
Israelstam, J. and J. J. Slotki (ed. and trans.). *Leviticus Rabbah*, London, 1939
Jacobson, R. 'The structuralists and the Bible', *Interpretation*, 28 (1974), 146–64
James, E. O. *The Nature and Function of Priesthood*, London, 1955
Sacrifice and Sacrament, London, 1962

Jeremias, J. 'Heb. 5:7–10', *ZNW*, 44 (1952–3), 107–11

'Heb 10:20: τοῦτ' ἔστιν τῆς σαρκὸς αὐτοῦ', *ZNW*, 62 (1971), 131

Johnson, A. M. (ed.). *The New Testament and Structuralism*, Pittsburgh Theological Monograph Series 11, Pittsburgh, 1976

(ed.) *Structuralism and Biblical Hermeneutics*, Pittsburgh, 1979

Johnson, S. E. 'Unsolved questions about early Christianity in Anatolia', *Supplement to NovT*, 33 (1972), 181–93

Johnsson, W. G. 'Defilement and purgation in the Book of Hebrews', unpublished Ph.D. thesis, Vanderbilt University, 1973

'The cultus of Hebrews in twentieth-century scholarship', *ExpT*, 89 (1978), 104–8

'The pilgrimage motif in the Book of Hebrews', *JBL*, 97 (1978), 239–51

Josephus *Works*, Loeb Classical Library, London, 1930

Judge, E. A. *The Social Pattern of Christian Groups in the First Century*, London, 1960

'The early Christians as a scholastic community', *JRH*, 1 (1960), 4–15, 125–37

'The social identity of the first Christians', *JRH*, 11 (1980), 201–17

Käsemann, E. *The Wandering People of God*, ET Minneapolis, 1984

Kaufman, S. A. 'On methodology in the study of the targums and their chronology', *JSNT*, 23 (1985), 117–24

Kee, H. C. *The Community of the New Age*, London, 1977

Christian Origins in Sociological Perspective, London, 1980

Kelly, J. N. D. *Early Christian Doctrines*, London, 1958

The Epistles of Peter and Jude, London, 1969

Kermode, F. *The Genesis of Secrecy*, Cambridge, 1979

Kierkegaard, S. *Fear and Trembling*, ET New York, 1954

Kiuchi, N. *Purification Offering in the Priestly Literature*, Sheffield, 1987

Klein, M. *The Fragment Targums of the Pentateuch*, Analecta Biblica, Rome, 1980

Kümmel, W. G. *Introduction to the New Testament*, London, 1966

The Theology of the New Testament, London, 1974

Lack, R. 'Le Sacrifice d'Isaac – Analyse structurale de la couche élohiste dans Gen. 22', *Biblica*, 56 (1975), 1–12

Lash, N. and J. Rhymer (eds.), *The Christian Priesthood*, London, 1970

Laughlin, J. C. H. 'The "strange fire" of Nadab and Abihu', *JBL*, 95 (1976), 559–65

Leach, E. R. (ed.). *The Structural Study of Myth and Totemism*, ASA Monograph Series, London, 1967

Lévi-Strauss, rev. ed., Glasgow, 1974

Culture and Communication, Cambridge, 1976

'Ritual', in *International Encyclopedia of the Social Sciences*, vol. XIII, pp. 520–6

Leach, E. R. and D. A. Aycock *Structural Interpretations of Biblical Myth*, Cambridge, 1983

Lehrmann, S. M. (ed. and trans.). *Exodus Rabbah*, London, 1939

Leon, H. J. *The Jews of Ancient Rome*, Philadelphia, 1960

Lévi-Strauss, C. *Tristes tropique*. Paris, 1955

Structural Anthropology, ET Harmondsworth, 1968

Structural Anthropology II, ET Harmondsworth, 1978

The Raw and the Cooked, ET Harmondsworth, 1986

Lewy, J. 'The origin and significance of the biblical term "Hebrew"',
HUCA, 28 (1957), 1–13

Lienhardt, R. G., *Divinity and Experience*, Oxford, 1961

Lincoln, A. T. *Paradise Now and Not Yet*, SNTS Monograph Series 43,
Cambridge, 1981

Lindbeck, G. A. *The Nature of Doctrine*, London, 1984

McCarthy, D. J. *The Old Testament Covenant*, Oxford, 1972

MacMullen, R. *Roman Social Relations*, New Haven, 1974

MacRae, G. W. 'Heavenly temple and eschatology in the Letter to the
Hebrews', *Semeia*, 12 (1978), 179–200

Magie, D. *Roman Rule in Asia Minor*, Princeton, 1950

Malherbe, A. *Social Aspects of Early Christianity*, Philadelphia, 1983

Malina, B. J. 'The social sciences and biblical interpretation', *Interpretation*,
36 (1982), 229–42

Mann, T. W. 'Theological reflections on the denial of Moses', *JBL*, 98
(1979), 481–94

Manson, W. *The Epistle to the Hebrews*, London, 1951

Mauss, M. *Essai sur le don*, Paris, 1925

Meeks, W. A. *The First Urban Christians*, London, 1983

'The Man from Heaven in Johannine sectarianism', *JBL*, 91 (1972), 44–72

Mendenhall, G. E. 'Covenant forms in Israelite tradition', *Biblical Archaeologist*, 17 (1954), 50–76

Michel, O. *Der Brief an die Hebräer*, Göttingen, 1949

Milgrom, J. 'Sin-offering or purification-offering?', *VT*, 21 (1971), 237–9

Milner, M. 'The role of illusion in symbol-formation', in M. Klein (ed.),
New Directions in Psychoanalysis, London, 1955

Moffatt, J. *The Epistle to the Hebrews*, Edinburgh, 1924

Mol, H. *Identity and the Sacred*, Oxford, 1976

Montefiore, H. W. *The Epistle to the Hebrews*, London, 1964

Morgan, R. with J. Barton. *Biblical Interpretation*, Oxford, 1988

Morris, B. *Anthropological Studies of Religion*, Cambridge, 1987

Morris, L. 'The biblical use of the term "blood"', *JTS*, 3 (1952), 216–27

'The biblical use of the term "blood"', *JTS*, 6 (1955), 77–82

Mott, S. C. *Biblical Ethics and Social Change*, Oxford, 1982

'Reciprocity in Hellenistic benevolence', in G. Hawthorne (ed.) *Current
Issues in Biblical and Patristic Interpretation*, Grand Rapids, 1975,
pp. 60–72

Moule, C. F. D. 'Sanctuary and sacrifice in the church of the New Testament',
JTS, 1 (1950), 29–41

Muilenburg, J. 'The form and structure of the covenantal formulations',
VT, 9 (1959), 247–65

Nairne, A. *The Epistle of Priesthood*, Edinburgh, 1913

The Epistle to the Hebrews, Cambridge, 1921

Needham, R. *Symbolic Classification*, Santa Monica, 1979

Nicholson, E. W. *Deuteronomy and Tradition*, Oxford, 1967

Nickelsburg, G. W. E. *Jewish Literature between the Bible and the Mishnah*,
London, 1981

Noth, M. *Leviticus*, London, 1965
Numbers, London, 1968
Omark, R. E. 'The saving of the Saviour (Heb. 5:7–10)', *Interpretation*, 12 (1958), 39–51
Otto, R. *The Idea of the Holy*, 2nd edn, Oxford, 1950
Pannenberg, W. *Jesus, God and Man*, London, 1968
Patte, D. *What is Structural Exegesis?*, Philadelphia, 1976
Perrin, N. *The New Testament: An Introduction*, New York, 1974
Peterson, D. *Hebrews and Perfection*, SNTS Monograph Series 47, Cambridge, 1982
Peterson, N. R. *Rediscovering Paul*, Philadelphia, 1985
Petuchowski, J. J. 'The controversial figure of Melchizedek', *HUCA*, 28 (1957), 127–36
Philo *Works*, Loeb Classical Library, London, 1929
Piaget, J. *Structuralism*, ET New York, 1970
Pickthall, M. M. (trans.). *The Meaning of the Glorious Koran*, New York, n.d.
Pocock, D. F. 'North and south in the Book of Genesis', in J. H. M. Beattie and R. G. Lienhardt (eds.) *Studies in Social Anthropology*, Oxford, 1975, pp. 273–84
Polanyi, M. *Personal Knowledge*, London, 1962
Polzin, R. M. *Biblical Structuralism – Method and Subjectivity in the Study of Ancient Texts*, Philadelphia, 1977
Quinn, J. D. 'Is 'Ραχαβ in Matt. 1:5 Rahab of Jericho?', *Biblica*, 62 (1981), 225–8
Rad, G. von. *Old Testament Theology*, 2 vols., ET London, 1960/1965
Deuteronomy, London, 1966
The Form-Critical Problem of the Hexateuch, ET London, 1966
Radcliffe, T. 'Christ in Hebrews: cultic irony', *New Blackfriars*, 68 (1987), 494–504
Ray, B. 'Sacred space and royal shrines in Buganda', *History of Religions*, 16 (1977), 363–73
Richter, P. J. 'Recent sociological approaches to the study of the New Testament', *Religion*, 14 (1984), 77–90
Ricoeur, P. *The Conflict of Interpretations*, Evanston, 1974
Essays on Biblical Interpretation, London, 1981
Hermeneutics and the Human Sciences, ET Cambridge, 1981
Ringgren, H. *Israelite Religion*, London, 1966
Robertson Smith, W. *The Religion of the Semites*, rev. edn, London, 1889
Robey, D. (ed.). *Structuralism: an introduction*, Oxford, 1973
Robinson, J. A. T. *Twelve New Testament Studies*, Studies in Biblical Theology 34, London, 1962
Rodwell, J. M. (trans). *The Koran*, London, 1909
Rogerson, J. W. *Myth in Old Testament Interpretation*, ZAW Supplementary vol. 134, Berlin, 1974
Anthropology and the Old Testament, Oxford, 1978
'Sacrifice in the Old Testament', in M. F. C. Bourdillon and M. Fortes (eds), *Sacrifice*, London, 1980
Rosenberg, R. A. 'Jesus, Isaac and the "suffering servant"', *JBL*, 84 (1965), 381–8

Rowland, C. *The Open Heaven*, London, 1982
Rowley, H. H. 'The meaning of sacrifice in the Old Testament', in H. H.
    Rowley, *From Moses to Qumran*, London, 1963
Safrai, S. and M. Stern (eds.). *The Jewish People in the First Century*,
    (= *Compendium Rerum Iudaicorum ad Novum Testamentum*), 2 vols.
    Assen, 1974/76
Ste Croix, G. E. M. de. 'Early Christian attitudes to property and slavery',
    in D. Baker (ed.), *Church, Society and Politics*, Ecclesiastical History
    Society Studies in Church History 12, Oxford, 1975
Sanders, E. P. *Paul and Palestinian Judaism*, London 1977
    Paul, the Law and the Jewish People, Philadelphia, 1983
Sandmel, S. *Judaism and Christian Beginnings*, New York, 1978
Saussure, F. de. *Course in General Linguistics*, ET Glasgow, 1974
Schaefer, J. R. 'The relationship between priestly and servant Messianism
    in the Epistle to the Hebrews', *CBQ*, 30 (1968), 359–85
Schillebeeckx, E. *Christ: The Christian Experience in the Modern World*,
    ET London, 1980
Scott, E. F. *The Epistle to the Hebrews*, Edinburgh, 1922
Scroggs, R. 'The earliest Christian communities as a sectarian movement',
    in J. Neusner (ed.), *Christianity, Judiasm and other Greco-Roman
    Cults*, Leiden, 1975, vol. II, pp. 1–23
    'Sociological interpretation of the New Testament – the present state
    of research', *NTS*, 26 (1980), 164–79
Searle, J. R. *Speech Acts*, Cambridge, 1969
Seters, J. van. *Abraham in History and Tradition*, London, 1975
Seung, T. K. *Structuralism and Hermeneutics*, New York, 1982
Simon, M. *Jewish Sects at the Time of Jesus*, Philadelphia, 1967
Skinner, Q. (ed.), *The Return of Grand Theory in the Social Sciences*,
    Cambridge, 1985
Smith, J. Z. 'The social description of early Christianity', *Religious
    Studies Review*, 1 (1975) 19–25
Snaith, N. H. 'Sin-offering and guilt-offering', *VT*, 15 (1965), 73–80
Snell, A. *A New and Living Way*, London, 1959
Sperber, D. *Rethinking Symbolism*, Cambridge, 1975
    'Is symbolic thought prerational?', in M. L. Foster and S. H. Brandes
    (eds.), *Symbol as Sense*, New York, 1980
Spicq, C. *L'Epître aux Hébreux*, 2 vols., Paris, 1952–3
Spiegel, S. *The Last Trial*, New York, 1967
Spivey, R. A. 'Structuralism and biblical studies – the uninvited guest',
    Interpretation, 28 (1974), 133–45
Steiner, G. *Language and Silence*, Harmondsworth, 1969
Starobinski, J. 'The Gerasene Demoniae', in R. Barthes, with F. Bovon,
    Structural Analysis and Biblical Exegesis, Pittsburgh Theological
    Monograph Series 3, Pittsburgh, 1974
Stott, W. 'The conception of "offering" in the Epistle to the Hebrews',
    NTS, 9 (1962–3), 62–7
Sturrock, J. (ed.) *Structuralism and Since*, Oxford, 1979
Swetnam, J. *Jesus and Isaac: A study of the Epistle to the Hebrews in
    the light of the Aqedah*, Analecta Biblica, Rome, 1981

' "The greater and more perfect Tent": a contribution to the discussion of Heb. 9:11', *Biblica*, 47 (1966), 91–106

'On the imagery and significance of Heb. 9:9–10', *CBQ*, 28 (1966), 155–73

'Jesus as Λόγος in Heb. 4:12f', *Biblica*, 62 (1981), 214–24

Tambiah, S. J. 'The form and meaning of magical acts: a point of view', in R. Horton and R. Finnegan (eds.) *Modes of Thought*, London, 1973

Theissen, G. *The First Followers of Jesus*, ET London, 1978

The Social Setting of Pauline Christianity, ET Edinburgh, 1982

Thiselton, A. C. *The Two Horizons*, Exeter, 1980

'The supposed power of words in the biblical writings', *JTS*, 25 (1974), 283–99

'Structuralism and biblical studies: method or ideology?', *ExpT*, 89 (1977–8), 329–35

Thomas, D. *Collected Poems*, London, 1953

Thompson, J. W. 'The midrash in Heb. 7', *NovT*, 19 (1977), 209–23

Thompson, R. J. *Penitence and Sacrifice in Early Israel outside the Levitical Law*, Leiden, 1963

Thornton, T. C. G. 'The meaning of αἱματεκχυσία in Heb. 9:22', *JTS*, 15 (1964), 63–5

Tidball, D. *Introduction to the Sociology of the New Testament*, Exeter, 1983

Tödt, H. *The Son of Man in the Synoptic Tradition*, London, 1965

Turner, V. W. *The Forest of Symbols*, New York, 1967

The Ritual Process, Chicago, 1969

'Sacrifice as quintessential process – prophylaxis or abandonment?', *History of Religions*, 16 (1976–7), 189–215

Vanhoye, A. *La Structure littéraire de l'Epître aux Hébreux*, Analecta Biblica, Rome, 1963

' "Par la tente plus grande et plus parfaite ..." (Héb. 9:11)', *Biblica*, 46 (1965), 1–28

'Longe marche, ou accès tout proche? – La contexte biblique de Héb. 3:7–4:11', *Biblica*, 49 (1968), 9–26

Vaux, R. de. *Studies in Old Testament Sacrifice*, Cardiff, 1964

Ancient Israel, Its Life and Institutions, 2nd edn, London, 1965

Vermes, G. *The Dead Sea Scrolls in English*, 2nd edn, Harmondsworth, 1975

Scripture and Tradition in Judaism, Leiden, 1961

Post-Biblical Jewish Studies, Leiden, 1975

'He is the Bread – Tg. Neofiti Ex. 16.15', in E. E. Ellis and M. Wilcox, *Neotestamentica et Semitica*, Studies in honour of M. Black, Edinburgh, 1969

Via, D. O. 'A structuralist approach to Paul's Old Testament hermeneutic', *Interpretation*, 28 (1974), 201–20

Weber, M. *The Sociology of Religion*, ET London, 1963

Weinfeld, M. *Deuteronomy and the Deuteronomic School*, Oxford, 1972

Wellhausen, J. *Prolegomena to the History of Ancient Israel*, ET Cleveland, 1965

Wensinck, A. J. *The Ideas of the Western Semites concerning the Navel of the Earth*, Amsterdam, 1916

Westcott, B.F. *The Epistle to the Hebrews*, 2nd edn, London, 1892

Westermann, C. *Genesis 12–36*, ET London, 1986

White, H.C. 'The initiation legend of Isaac', *ZAW*, 91 (1979), 1–30

Wilcox, M. 'The promise of the "seed" in New Testament and the targumim', *JSNT*, 5 (1979), 2–20

Williamson, R. *Philo and the Epistle to the Hebrews*, Leiden, 1970

'The eucharist and the Epistle to the Hebrews', *NTS*, 21 (1974–5), 300–12

Wilson, B.R. 'An analysis of sect development', in B.R. Wilson (ed.), *Patterns of Sectarianism*, London, 1967, pp. 22–45

'A typology of sects', in R. Robertson (ed.), *Sociology of Religion* Harmondsworth, 1969, pp. 361–81

Wilson, R.McL. *Hebrews*, Basingstoke, 1987

Wittig, S. 'The historical development of structuralism', *Soundings*, 58 (1975), 145–66

Wolff, H.W. *Anthropology of the Old Testament*, London, 1974

Wood, J.E. 'Isaac typology in the New Testament', *NTS*, 14 (1967–8), 583–9

Yadin, Y. 'The Dead Sea Scrolls and the Epistle to the Hebrews', *Scripta Hierosolymitana*, 4 (1958), 36–55

York, A.D. 'The dating of targumic literature', *JSJ*, 5 (1974), 49–62

Young, F.M. *The Use of Sacrificial Ideas in Greek Christian Writers from the New Testament to John Chrysostom*, Patristic Monograph Series 5, Philadelphia, 1979

Young, N.H. 'τουτ' ἔστιν τῆς σαρκὸς αὐτοῦ in Heb. 10.20', *NTS*, 20 (1974), 100–4

'αἱματεκχυσία: a comment', *ExpT*, 90 (1978–9), 180

INDEX OF PASSAGES QUOTED

INDEX OF MODERN AUTHORS

SUBJECT INDEX

Aaron, 88–90, 95, 99, 147f, 160–4, 182, 218, 230
  sons of, 88–90, 147f
Aaron's rod, 89, 138f, 160–4
Abel, 36, 124f, 135, 149–53, 157, 167, 181, 183f, 187, 255, 259
Abraham, 19f, 35–9, 104f, 123f, 143, 154, 164f, 167, 172–87, 188–206 *passim*, 227, 229, 250
  descendants (seed) of, 108, 183–6, 194, 197f, 203–16, 219–26 *passim*, 263
Adam, 125, 211–13
Akedah (Binding of Isaac), 108, 110, 123f, 138, 140, 177–206
  and ambivalence of God, 177, 191–203, 213–19
  and Christology, 175f, 192, 198–203
  and martyrdom, 181–3, 196f
  and Passover, 108, 174–7, 194–8, 202
  and descendants (seed) of Abraham, 183–6, 194, 197f, 203–26 *passim*
  as covenant-sacrifice, 108, 173–83
  as pattern (myth) of testing, 190–226
  in Hebrews, 177–81, 203–26
  in New Testament, 177f, 198–203
  tradition-history, 174–7
altars, 92, 97–100, 125, 128
angels, 139, 210–12, 215, 219f, 225, 229f, 232
anthropology, social, 47, 51–6, 64–6, 69–79
apotropaic rites, 54, 79, 85, 93–101, 106–8, 124, 160–4, 195, 198
Ark of the covenant, 87
ashes, 80f, 108, 175
Asia Minor, 16, 23f
associations, voluntary, 26–8
atonement, 87f, 93–106

Atonement, day of, 95, 99f, 125–7, 136f, 139–41, 157, 161f, 165, 231–3, 235, 256
aversion, *see* apotropaic rites

Biblical Theology movement, 68
binary opposition, 51–3, 69–75
blessing, 36, 105, 167, 251–6
blood, 6f, 78, 91–103, 105–10, 117f, 121, 126–8, 145–7, 175, 177f, 231–4, 244, 251
burnt-offerings (holocausts), 81, 92f, 101, 176–8

Cain, 36, 124f, 138f, 149–53, 157f
Camp, the, 85–90, 97–9, 109, 260f
canon of scripture, 1, 43–5, 68f
canonical criticism, 43f, 88f
child-sacrifice, 176f, 197f
circumcision, 107f, 123, 131, 172, 177, 195
citizens, 26f, 30–2
classification systems, 69–75, 82–90
communion, as mode of relation, 75, 78, 239–42, 261f
  communion-sacrifices, 91f, 101
consecration, 75–7, 100f, 222–4
covenant, as mode of relation, 78, 103–11, 123–34, 179–81, 186f, 191–203, 227–30, 237–9
  covenant, new, 32–9, 111, 115, 122f, 126–48, 152f, 163f, 167f, 183, 228–60
  covenant-renewal rites, 106f, 128–48 *passim*, 171f, 181f, 227–38, 261–3
  covenant-sacrifices, 106–9, 126–8, 173, 176f, 179–203, 213–19, 227–3, 246f, 249–51
curse, 105, 251–6